A C BILBREW

R016.305488
96

Bullwinkle, Davis.

African women, a general bibliography, 1976-1985.

$45.00

DATE			

FOR LIBRARY USE ONLY

Ref.
BRC

53010

© THE BAKER & TAYLOR CO.

AFRICAN WOMEN

Recent Titles in
African Special Bibliographic Series

American-Southern African Relations: Bibliographic Essays
Mohamed A. El-Khawas and Francis A. Kornegay, Jr.

A Short Guide to the Study of Ethiopia: A General Bibliography
Alula Hidaru and Dessalegn Rahmato

Afro-Americans and Africa: Black Nationalism at the Crossroads
William B. Helmreich

Somalia: A Bibliographical Survey
Mohamed Khalief Salad

Ethiopian Perspectives: A Bibliographical Guide to the History of Ethiopia
Clifton F. Brown

A Bibliography of African Ecology: A Geographically and Topically Classified List of Books and Articles
Dilwyn J. Rogers, compiler

Demography, Urbanization, and Spatial Planning in Kenya: A Bibliographical Survey
Robert A. Obudho

Population, Urbanization, and Rural Settlement in Ghana: A Bibliographic Survey
Joseph A. Sarfoh, compiler

AFRICAN WOMEN

A General Bibliography, 1976–1985

Compiled by
Davis A. Bullwinkle

African Special Bibliographic Series, Number 9

Greenwood Press
New York • Westport, Connecticut • London

53010

Library of Congress Cataloging-in-Publication Data

Bullwinkle, Davis.
African women, a general bibliography, 1976-1985 / compiled by Davis A. Bullwinkle.
p. cm. — (African special bibliographic series, ISSN 0749-2308 ; no. 9)
Bibliography: p.
Includes index.
ISBN 0-313-26607-7 (lib. bdg. : alk. paper)
1. Women—Africa—Bibliography. I. Title. II. Series.
Z7964.A3B84 1989
[HQ1787]
016.3054'096—dc19 88-37379

British Library Cataloguing in Publication Data is available.

Copyright © 1989 by Davis A. Bullwinkle

All rights reserved. No portion of this book may be reproduced, by any process or technique, without the express written consent of the publisher.

Library of Congress Catalog Card Number: 88-37379
ISBN: 0-313-26607-7
ISSN: 0749-2308

First published in 1989

Greenwood Press, Inc.
88 Post Road West, Westport, Connecticut 06881

Printed in the United States of America

The paper used in this book complies with the Permanent Paper Standard issued by the National Information Standards Organization (Z39.48-1984).

10 9 8 7 6 5 4 3 2 1

For Judy

Who in my middle years I have
found to share my life
And who brings joy and love,
support, kindness and meaning
to my life

And for Carol

Who showed me the true value of loving
another human being and whose
lifetime of love
I shall cherish for all my years

I dedicate this work

Contents

CONTENTS

Foreword

This work is the outgrowth of a paper I wrote a number of years ago that was published by the African Bibliographic Center in Washington, D.C. That paper, a bibliography on women in Africa during the 1970's stimulated my interest in creating a work that would bring together all the English language publications written about women in Africa during the United Nations Decade for Women from 1976-1985.

The work could never have been completed without the tremendous help of two people. During the research phase of this work, I discussed the computer needs of the work with a friend named Vicki Tynan. Over the next five months, Vicki wrote a complete computer program for this project. Due to the size and complexity of a project like this, the program was extremely time consuming to produce. Few works of this scope have ever been attempted and we were soon to learn we were on the fringe of computer technology as it applies to manipulating a large amount amount of data.

Vicki's son Dylan, already a computer whiz at sixteen, helped get me through my first major computer project and, orientation with my computer and the integrated software.

Their help during every conceivable hour of the day made this project a much easier and manageable one. I am very grateful to them both for their time and patience.

Preface

"African Women: A General Bibliography, 1976-1985" is the first of a three volume African Special Bibliographic Series to be published by Greenwood Press. This initial volume includes those citations not identified by a region or nation in Africa.

The first volume also establishes the subject headings to be used in that volume as well as subsequent volumes. Although thirty-four subject headings will be utilized over the entire three volume set, only thirty-two headings are employed in this first volume. While coding the original references, I found that all available citations on divorce fell into national categories only. For that reason the subject heading of divorce will not be used in the general bibliography. The subject heading of apartheid and race relations, while not unique to South Africa, will only be used in the South African national bibliography. The volume of information concerning this significant social issue necessitated a separate heading under South Africa. While material on this subject did appear in other national divisions, the small number of citations and the few countries in which they appeared did not justify the subject heading being widely used.

The second and third volumes of the series will be called respectively, "Women of Northern, Western and Central Africa: A Bibliography, 1976-1985" and "Women in Eastern and Southern Africa: A Bibliography, 1976-1985." The research in these volumes will be divided by six geographical regions and fifty-three countries. National divisions will be divided by those subject headings for which there is data. Countries with fewer than thirty citations will not be divided by subject headings. Instead, that material will be alphabetized by author.

The complete three volume work incorporates over forty-one hundred original English language research works on women in Africa. The original citations are cross-referenced into as many subject headings as possible for best coverage.

The scope of this project encompasses all aspects of women's lives, not just traditional topics such as "development" or the "status of women" as have been addressed in more recent bibliographic research. I have made a conscientious effort to cover African women in all facets of their world including such diverse subject areas as sexual mutilation, nutrition, abortion, and literature.

While the first volume of this work is over three hundred pages in length, the two future volumes will number from five to seven hundred pages each. A follow-up volume to this work is already being researched. It will cover the years from 1986-1990 and hopefully will be published in 1993.

Introduction

Over forty years ago, the nations of the world met in San Francisco to sign the charter of a new international organization to be known as the United Nations. Among its stated goals were the "attainment of world peace, the reaffirmation of faith in human rights, the dignity of worth of the human person as well as the equal rights of men and women of all nations."

Since 1945, the United Nations has encountered a greater degree of difficulty than anticipated in achieving the goals of its original charter. Nations are constantly warring with each other and the number of repressive governments has increased through the years. Hundreds of thousands of people have been oppressed by their own governments for their actions of speaking out against government policies to quash the goals of human dignity and freedom.

Thousands of women, children and men have died of starvation and disease because governments have neither taken the steps needed to prevent the problems nor the steps needed to have the international community involved in the solutions.

Due to the conditions that created these problems, as well as the traditional, social and economic roles played by women in the developing world, the United Nations became alarmed that the goals of equality among the sexes were not being achieved by its members. Two years after the United Nations charter was signed, the organization created its Commission on the Status of Women.

In 1972, twenty-four years after the creation of the U.N., a group of non-governmental organizations (NGOs) sent a request to the United Nations Commission on the Status of Women to look into the possibility of having the U.N. choose a one year period to focus attention on the problems faced by women in the world. Egypt, Finland, France, Hungry, Romania and the Phillipines introduced a resolution to the

U.N. General Assembly which had been previously adopted by the Commission. 1975 was declared the International Women's Year. The goals of this one year period were stated as being, "to intensify action to promote equality between women and men and to increase women's contribution to national and international development." The U.N. delegates agreed, while approving the Commission's declaration, to add peace and equality to the already stated goals for the year.

Specific objectives for each of the individual goals stated in the declaration were established. Among them were: "to achieve full equality before the law in all fields where it did not already exist; to meet the health needs of girls and women equally with those of boys and men; to promote equality of economic rights; to improve the quality of rural life; and to eliminate illiteracy and ensure equality of educational opportunities." Emphasis was placed on "realizing the principle of the rights of people to self determination; combating racism and racial discrimination wherever it manifests itself; and lending support to the victims of racism, apartheid and colonialism as well as supporting women and children in armed struggle."

In May of 1974, the United Nations Economic and Social Council requested a United Nations conference to scrutinize U.N. agencies as to how they had carried out the recommendations for the elimination of discrimination against women made by the Commission on the Status of Women. In November of that year, the United Nations chose Mexico as the site of what would be the first of three world conferences on the plight of women throughout the world.

In June of 1975, the World Conference of the International Women's Year convened in Mexico City. United Nations members from one hundred and thirty-three nations attended. The African continent was represented by thirty-nine delegates. Other than United Nations delegates, representatives from one hundred and fourteen non-governmental organizations also attended. Specific African NGO's attending were the African National Congress (ANC), the African National Council, and four national liberation groups.

During the two weeks of meetings, the delegates labored to create a World Plan of Action that could be used to implement the stated objectives of the International Women's Year. The plan was divided into actions that could be taken by national governments and actions that could be undertaken by NGO's and other inter-national organizations. Those actions included social, economic, legal, administrative and educational proposals. To governments it was suggested that a 'national machinery' be established to manage and promote efforts in-country to advance the status of women. To international and regional organizations, particularly the United Nations and its agencies, it was proposed that they extend assistance to individual governments and non-governmental organizations to support their efforts in achieving the recommendations.

The conference stressed the objective of achieving a partial number of the goals from the Plan of Action by 1980. Among the goals for that five year period were a decrease in the illiteracy rate; a concerted effort to create more employment opportunities; the acknowledgement of the economic value of women's work in the home, in food production and in marketing; and the commitment to the development of modern rural technology. Another important objective of this five year period was that individual governments undertake the responsibility to guarantee women equality in the execution of their civil, social and political rights, especially those associated with economic, marital and civil matters.

Once the Plan of Action was complete, thirty-five resolutions attached to the plan were approved by the conference. These resolutions dealt with such diverse issues as the integration of women in development; the establishment of research and training centers for women in Africa; the status of women under apartheid; the condition of women in rural areas, and the health needs of the Third World women.

From this two week conference came the recommendation that the United Nations proclaim the decade from 1976-1985 as the United Nations Decade for Women and Development. The delegates believed that this proclamation would guarantee that national and international activity on the equality of women would maintain its momentum and continue, and that agencies of the United Nations would take steps to enact the Plan of Action and evaluate their previous achievements to advance the status of women. Support from international and regional intergovernmental organizations outside the United Nations would result in the development of programs to carry out the Plan of Action and achieve the objectives of the United Nations International Women's Year as well as the United Nations Decade for Women.

At the end of 1975, the U.N. General Assembly voted to support the report of the World Plan of Action and its resolutions. The assembly proclaimed the years, 1976-1985 as "The United Nations Decade for Women, Equality, Development and Peace." They declared this ten year period to be one in which a concerted effort would be made by national, regional, and international organizations to implement the Plan of Action and related resolutions. Nations were called upon to act quickly and establish short, medium and long term goals, including by 1980 the implementation of a minimum number of the plan's objectives.

As a final action on this issue, the United Nations announced that a second world conference would be held, to convene in 1980, to evaluate and appraise the accomplishments made by member nations in achieving the partial goals and objectives of the International Women's Year and Decade. Held in Copenhagen, Denmark in mid-July of 1980, the conference attracted delegates from one hundred forty-five nations. This almost ten per cent increase in participation by member nations once again emphasized the growing importance of women's issues on the international scene. Among the African NGOs who attended were representatives from the African National Congress (ANC), the South West Africa People's Organization (SWAPO), and the Pan African Congress. Along with the reevaluation of the previous five years work and the realization of the objectives drawn in Mexico City, the important issues of health, education and employment were added as additional themes of this conference.

The program of the conference included four important topics. Among these were the effects of apartheid on women in Southern Africa and special measures to assist them; a mid-decade review and evaluation of the successes and obstacles to achieving the objectives of the decade; the effects of the Israeli occupation on Palestinian women; and the study and creation of proposals for advancing the status of women and reinforcing established strategies to displace hurdles to full and equal participation in development.

A second Plan of Action for the concluding five years of the decade (1980-1985) was discussed and promulgated. This Plan of Action emphasized the achievement of equality, development and peace with special emphasis on health, education and employment. The forty-eight resolutions adopted by the conference were aimed at attaining the goals of the next five year period and the decade overall.

On December 11, 1980, the United Nations General Assembly adopted a resolution supporting the conference's Plan of Action for the second half of the decade. Also set in motion was the planning for the end of the decade world conference to be held in Nairobi, Kenya, in mid 1985.

The last of the three world conferences convened in Nairobi, July 25, 1985. Representatives from one hundred forty nations attended. Eighteen thousand women, nearly three times as many as had attended the first world conference in Mexico City, arrived in Nairobi. The conference's theme was the review and appraisal of the achievements and the failures of the decade. Almost twelve hundred NGO workshops were conducted in overcrowded classrooms and outdoor spaces. Oriented around the main themes of development, equality and peace, the workshops also dealt with the issues of health, education, and employment.

The results of the three world conferences and the United Nations Decade for Women highlighted the wretched conditions faced by the women of Africa and the Third World. As a continent, Africa has the highest per cent of illiterate women in the world. It is estimated that under twenty per cent of all African women can read and write and that may be a liberal figure. Children are brought into this world by the fewest number of trained maternity personnel and suffer from the lowest birthrates in the developing world. It is believed that African infant mortality rates in excess of ninety-five per one thousand live births while being the highest in the world, are also responsible for the low expectation of life in Africa. Female children attend primary schools in smaller numbers then males. Secondary education, while limited to both sexes, is still undertaken by three times as many boys as girls. African women marry at younger ages than their peers throughout the world, usually between fifteen and seventeen years of age. They also produce more children than any group of women on earth averaging six and a half children for every childbearing woman in Africa. It is no wonder that African women have the lowest life expectancy on earth. That tragic age is just 48.6 years.

Historically, the women of Africa have been the principle contributors for labor needed to produce Africa's food crops. They have suffered from unequal access to extension services and training and have been discriminated against in their efforts to gain credit. It is estimated that African women deliver eighty per cent of the labor and organization needed in the production of Africa's food. Women often spend from nine to ten hours a day laboring in the fields, then a sizeable number of hours performing other tasks such as gathering firewood, preserving food, caring for their children and elderly relatives, putting food in storage, making meals and retrieving water. They may also be involved in some form of work that produces saleable commodities such as soap, vegetables and handicrafts that can be traded for necessities such as food and household items.

In the not too distant past, Africa as a continent fulfilled her needs by producing all of the food her people required. By 1980, Africa was forced to import almost fifteen per cent of her total food essentials. Africa's inability to produce enough food to feed her people is due to a number of factors, not the least of which were colonial policies and the introduction of cash crop economies by those governments. As a result of these governmental policies, women have found themselves overburdened in their roles as primary food producers. Over the last twenty-five to thirty years, large numbers of African men have left their native land holdings and migrated to Africa's cities looking for work. While African men historically have never had a great penchant for working the land, the loss of their labor seriously affected Africa's women. The amount of work expected or required of women increased dramatically.

In Sub-Saharan Africa the rights to land have generally traditionally belonged to women. Colonial governments, ignoring historic cultural patterns, allocated land ownership to men. These policies displaced subsistance agriculture with cash crop commodities such as coffee and cotton. Development projects instigated by new national governments also discriminated against women by recognizing men as the owners of projects. Men have been encouraged to grow cash crops for the economic rewards available to them while women have still been responsible for a large part of the labor required to grow these crops. The rewards of independence and supposedly egalitarian governments have not been kind to Africa's women. The benefits still elude them.

Another of the major problems faced by women throughout the Third World has been the failure of governments and development agencies to acknowledge women as a factor in development projects and in the decision making. While women make up over fifty per cent of the world's population, only a small percentage of them hold administrative careers in Third World governments. As a result of this, women are not involved in the decision making processes and their opinions are often ignored. A crisis of self image has also hurt African and Third World women. They themselves do not value their own labor in food production by the same criteria as men's labor in agriculture. The same views are prevalent among agricultural economists and development planners who also do not take into consideration the time women spend planting, weeding, harvesting and the other daily chores previously mentioned. Acceptance of the facts concerning the role of women in food production is still slow in coming. Many research studies support the efforts of women to execute and oversee agricultural projects successfully. Still, agricultural development planning continues to ignore their position of importance or their capabilities. The role of women as food producers must be recognized before the problems of food shortages can be eliminated.

If conditions for women in Africa and the Third World are to be improved, governments must provide their female citizens the same opportunities they afford their male citizens. Equal opportunities in the areas of education and training, the elimination of illiteracy, and the equal access to credit sources would provide some solutions to the problems women face in Third World development. Women must have equal access to agricultural extension services to help provide them with the information and technological data they need to compete and increase crop yields. The employment of more female agricultural extension professionals might also be of great help. Between 1977 and 1984 less than one-fifth of all those sent overseas for professional training programs were women. The introduction of modern rural technology is a necessity women must have for them to gain advancements in mechanization, improved water systems, better methods of food production and preservation, and greater access to fuel resources.

INTRODUCTION

A special emphasis by African governments is also quickly needed in the field of women's health. Programs begun by the World Health Organization (WHO) in 1980 in a number of African nations have been very successful. Women's volunteer organizations are being trained at the WHO Regional Training Center in Mauritius. There they are instructed in maternal health care, family planning and child health. Promising results have been achieved in West Africa. The vaccination of children against childhood diseases such as tetanus, measles, poliomyelitis, tuberculosis and diphtheria have commenced. Governments throughout the Third World must move quickly and have relative success in dealing with the problems of their female citizens. The health of their nations sit in the balance. Development of any kind cannot succeed without a population free of the worries of catastrophic diseases that plague the African continent and other Third World nations. In Africa, 48.6 years of age certainly cannot be accepted as a fulfilled lifetime.

While the achievements of the United Nations Decade for Women, or the lack of them, will be discussed and debated for years, it is promising to know that the decade forced many governments to take a more objective look at the position women hold and the problems they face in their countries. The world conference and the media forced them to recognize the reality they refused to face. Two-thirds of all illiterates are women and most refugees are women and children. It is they who are facing major health problems that could dramatically alter the history of nations.

Technology, while helping to develop nations and making labor less difficult for men, and therefore more profitable, has actually failed to help women and in many cases has made their lives more demanding. Technology must be shared amongst all people in rural developing countries.

While achievements during the decade were exemplified by dramatic increases in women and girls' participation in educational programs and small gains in employment opportunities, they have been minimal to say the least. Access to credit through new organizations such as the Women's Bank will be helpful if they continue to receive support from the international financial institutions.

This bibliographic research project was initiated in the anticipation of it becoming a major contribution in the Social Sciences and the field of African Studies. Comprehensive research was conducted over a three year period at the University of Arkansas at Little Rock, Memphis State University, the University of Texas and the University of Nebraska. The citations that follow were arranged into five specific groups. They included articles appearing in edited books and journals, as well as Masters theses, Ph.D dissertations, conference papers and individual books on women in Africa and the Third World.

INTRODUCTION

Unlike the two previous world conferences in Mexico City and Copenhagen, a complete bibliography of papers presented at the conference has not and probably will not be published by the NGO committee. Research on this project was delayed for a period of time in the hope that such a list would be forthcoming. A final document for the Nairobi conference was published by the NGO (see page 265 under NGO Planning Committee). This document lists titles of some papers by the themes which they were presented. Access to these papers may be possible through the Economic Commission for Africa's African Training and Research Center for Women in Addis Ababa, Ethiopia, the International Women's Tribunal Center in New York City, or the International Center for Research on Women in Washington, D.C. Addresses for these organizations can be found in Appendix A of this document.

It is unfortunate to say the least, that a document as comprehensive as this one is not able to contain a list of the papers from the last world conference and the NGO workshops. Their inclusion would have made this a more complete document.

In publishing this comprehensive work on previously written research on African women, I hope that those of you using this document and contemplating further research on African and Third World women will use it to analyze where future research might best take place. This work is unique. No other book, periodical or database has in the past brought together the amount of information on African women that this project has. This work is only the beginning of an ongoing project that will disseminate accummulated data on women in Africa. A five year update of the research covering the post decade period will be forthcoming in a few years.

The gains of the decade have been disappointing. That a decade had to be chosen to underscore the injustices and widespread inequalities of women throughout the world is a tragedy in itself. I hope the decade and its poor results will demonstrate to all who care in this world that so much more needs to be done to guarantee that all peoples of this planet have the chance to live fulfilling lives. And, I hope it will inspire further research to help solve the problems of the oppressed and underprivileged.

AFRICAN WOMEN

Abortion

Chi, C. and Miller, E.R. and Fortney, J.A. and Bernard, Roger P.
"A Study of Abortion in Countries Where Abortions are Legally Restricted." Journal of Reproductive Medicine. Volume 18 #1 January, 1977. pp. 15-26.

Cook, Rebecca J. and Dickens, Bernard N.
"Abortion Law in African Commonwealth Countries." Journal of African Law. Volume 25 #2 1981. pp. 60-79.

Cook, Rebecca J. and Dickens, Bernard M.
"A Decade of International Change in Abortion Law: 1967-1977." American Journal of Public Health. Volume 68 #7 July, 1978. pp. 637-644.

Liskin, L.S.
"Complications of Abortion in Developing Countries." Population Reports. #F-7 July, 1980. pp. 107-155.

Mati, J.K.
Abortion in Africa. (In) International Planned Parenthood Federation (IPPF). Proceedings of the IPPF Africa Regional Conference. London: IPPF. 1977. pp. 74-79.

Monreal, T. and Nasah, B.T.
"Illegal Abortion in Selected African Capital Cities, 1976." (In) Sai, Fred T. (ed.). A Strategy for Abortion Management: A Report of the IPPF Africa Regional Workshop, March 20-23, 1978. London: International Planned Parenthood Federation. Nairobi, Kenya. 1978. pp. 48-91.

Sai, Fred T.
"Report of the Conference on the Medical and Social Aspects of Abortion in Africa." (In) Sai, F.T. (ed.). A Strategy for Abortion Management. London: International Planned Parenthood Federation. 1978. pp 6-22.

Schick, Barbara
"Women: An Untapped Resource in a Hungry World." Agenda. Volume 1 #6 June, 1978. pp. 1-4.

Agriculture

Abbott, Susan
"In the End You Will Carry Me in Your Car--Sexual Politics in the Field." Women's Studies. Volume 10 #2 1983. pp. 161-178.

Abbott, Susan
"Full-Time Farmers and Week-End Wives, an Analysis of Altering Conjugal Roles." Journal of Marriage and the Family. Volume 38 #1 February, 1976. pp. 165-174.

Agarwal, Bina
"Women and Technological Change in Agriculture: The Asian and African Experience." (In) Ahmed, Iftikhar (ed.). Technology and Rural Women: Conceptual and Empirical Issues. Boston: George Allen and Unwin. 1985. pp. 67-114.

Agarwal, Bina
"Women and Technological Change in Agricultural Change: The Asian and African Experience." (In) Ahmed, I. (ed.). Technology and Rural Development: Conceptual and Empirical Issues. London: Allen and Unwin. 1985. pp. 67-114.

Ahmed, Iftikhar
"Technologies for Rural Women." Women at Work. #3 1977.

Ahmed, Iftikhar
"Technology and Rural Women in the Third World." International Labour Review. Volume 122 #4 July-August, 1983. pp. 493-505.

Ahmed, Iftikhar (ed.)
Technology and Rural Women: Conceptual and Empirical Issues. Boston: George Allen and Unwin. 1985. 383p.

Allison, C.
"Women, Land, Labour and Survival: Getting Some Basic Facts Straight." IDS Bulletin. Volume 16 #3 1985. pp. 24-30.

Anonymous
"The Contribution of Women to the Development of the Pan

African World." (In) Resolutions and Selected Speeches From the Sixth Pan African Congress. Dar-es-Salaam, Tanzania: Tanzania Publishing House. 1976. pp. 190-194.

Anonymous
"The Position of Women in Africa." Rural Progress. Volume 1 #3 1979. pp. 20-23.

Anonymous
"Women, Food and Nutrition in Africa: Economic Change and the Outlook for Nutrition." Food and Nutrition. Volume 10 #1 1984. pp. 71-79.

Anonymous
"Women in Africa." Agenda. Volume 1 #2 February, 1978. pp. 1-7.

Anonymous
Women in Rural Development: Critical Issues. Geneva: International Labour Organization. 1980. 51p.

Anonymous
"Women in Rural Development: Recommendations and Realities." Ceres. May-June, 1980. pp. 15-42.

Anonymous
"Workshop on Better Quality of Life for Rural Women Leaders." Rural Progress. Volume 2 #2 January, 1982. pp. 12-13.

Asare, Janet
"Making Life Easier for Africa's Rural Women." UNICEF News. #90 1976. pp. 20-23.

Ashworth, Georgina and May, Nicky (eds.)
Of Conjuring and Caring: Women in Development. London: Change. 1982. 28p.

Blumberg, Rae
"Rural Women in Development: Veil of Invisibility, World of Work." International Journal of Intercultural Relations. Volume 3 #4 1979. pp. 447-472.

Blumberg, Rae
"Rural Women in Development." (In) Black, Naomi and Cottrell, Ann B. (eds.). Women and World Change: Equity Issues in Development. Beverly Hills, California: Sage Publications. 1981. pp. 32-56.

Boulding, Elise
Women Peripheries and Food Production. (In) University of Arizona. "Proceedings and Papers of the International Conference on Women and Food: Consortium for International Development. Tucson, Arizona: University of Arizona. 1978. pp. 22-44.

Brabin, Loretta
"Polygyny: An Indicator of Nutritional Stress in African Agricultural Societies." Africa. Volume 54 #1 1984. pp. 31-45.

Broch-Due, Vigdis and Garfield, Patti
"Women and Pastoral Development: Some Research Priorities for the Social Sciences." (In) Galaty, John G. and Aronson, Dan and Salzman, Philip C. (eds.). The Future of Pastoral Peoples. Ottawa, Canada: International Development Research Centre. 1981. pp. 251-257.

AGRICULTURE

Bujra, Janet M.
"Production, Property, Prostitution--Sexual Politics in Atu." Cahiers d'Etudes Africaines. Volume 17 #1 1977. pp. 13-40.

Bukh, Jette
"Women in Food Production, Food Handling and Nutrition." Paper Presented to the Association of African Women for Research and Development (AAWORD) Workshop. Dakar, Senegal: AAWORD. December, 1977.

Burfisher, Mary E. and Horenstein, Nadine R.
"Incorporating Women Into Agricultural Development Planning: A Methodology." Paper Presented at the Annual Meeting of the African Studies Association. Paper #15. Washington, D.C. November 4-7, 1982.

Buvinic, Mayra
Women and World Development: An Annotated Bibliography. Washington D.C.: Overseas Development Council. 1976. 162p.

Callear, D.
Women and Coarse Grain Production in Africa. Expert Consultation on Women in Food Production. Rome: United Nations Food and Agriculture Organization. December 7, 1983. 13p.

Carew, Joy
"A Note on Women and Agricultural Technology in the Third World." Labour and Society. Volume 6 #3 July-September, 1981. pp. 279-285.

Carr, Marilyn
"Appropriate Technology for Rural African Women." Development Digest. Volume 20 #1 January, 1982. pp. 87-98.

Carr, Marilyn
Appropriate Technology for African Women. Addis Ababa, Ethiopia: United Nations Economic Commission for Africa. African Training and Research Center for Women. 1978. 105p.

Carr, Marilyn
"Technologies for Rural Women: Impact and Dissemination." (In) Ahmed, Iftikhar (ed.). Technology and Rural Women: Conceptual and Empirical Issues. Boston: George Allen and Unwin. 1985. pp. 115-153.

Carr, Marilyn
Technology and Rural Women in Africa. Addis Ababa, Ethiopia: United Nations Economic Commission for Africa. African Training and Research Center for Women. Joint Project With the International Labour Organization. ILO World Employment Programme Research Working Paper #61. 1980.

Carr, Marilyn
"Appropriate Technology for Women." Appropriate Technology. Volume 1 1979.

Castillo, Gelia T.
The Changing Role of Women in Rural Societies: A Summary

of Trends and Issues. New York: Agricultural Development Council Inc. RTN Seminar Reports 12. February, 1977. 11p.

Caton, Douglas D.
Elements of the Food Production-Distribution System: An Overview on How Women Can Contribute. Proceedings and Papers of the International Conference on Women and Food Consortium for International Development. Tucson, Arizona: University of Arizona. 1978. pp. 45-61.

Caughman, Susan H.
Women at Work in Mali: The Case of the Markala Cooperative. Boston: Boston University. African Studies Center. Working Papers in African Studies #50. 1981. 72p.

Chan, S.
"Young Women and Development in Africa--Some Generally Unconsidered Considerations." Community Development Journal. Volume 18 #3 1983. pp. 257-262.

Chaney, Elsa M. and Simmons, Emmy and Staudt, Kathleen
Women in Development. Washington, D.C.: U.S. Department of State. U.S. Agency for International Development. Background Papers for the U.S. Delegation Attending the World Conference on Agrarian Reform and Rural Development. July, 1979. 40p.

Chaney, Elsa M. and Lewis, Martha W.
Women, Migration and the Decline of Smallholder Agriculture. Washington, D.C.: U.S. Department of State. U.S. Agency for International Development. Office of Women in Development. October, 1980.

Charlton, Sue E.
Women in Third World Development. Boulder, Colorado: Westview Press. 1984. 240p.

Claffey, Joan M. and Pigozzi, Mary J. and Axinn, Nancy W.
"Women in Development: A Selected Annotated Bibliography." International Journal of Intercultural Relations. Volume 3 1979.

Clark, Garcia
Fighting the African Food Crisis: Women Food Farmers and Food Workers. New York: United Nations Development Fund for Women. 1985.

Cloud, Kathleen
"Sex Roles in Food Production and Distribution Systems in the Sahel." (In) Cowen, Ann B. (ed.). Proceedings and Papers of the International Conference on Women and Food: Consortium for International Development. Tucson, Arizona: University of Arizona. 1978. pp. 62-89.

Cloud, Kathleen
Sex Roles in Food Production and Food Distribution Systems in the Sahel. Washington, D.C.: U.S. Department of State. U.S. Agency for International Development. Office of Women in Development. 1977. 20p.

Cohen, Ronald and Knipp, Maggie
"Women and Change in West Africa: A Synthesis." Paper

Presented at the Annual Meeting of the African Studies Association. Paper #16. Philadelphia, Pennsylvania. 1980.

Cohn, Steven and Wood, Robert and Haig, Richard
"U.S. Aid and Third World Women: The Impact of Peace Corps Programs." Economic Development and Cultural Change. Volume 29 #4 July, 1981. pp. 795-811.

Creative Associates, Inc.
Participation of Women in the Economic Development Process: A Suggested Strategy for the African Bureau. Washington, D.C.: Creative Associates, Inc. 1980. 20p.

Cutrufelli, Maria R.
Women of Africa: Roots of Oppression. Totowa, New Jersey: Zed Press. 1983. 186p.

D'onofrio-Flores, Pamela M. and Pfafflin, Sheila M. (eds.)
Scientific-Technological Change and the Role of Women in Development. Boulder, Colorado: Westview Press. Published for the United Nations Institute for Training and Research. 1982. 206p.

Danforth, Sandra C.
Women and National Development. Monticello, Illinois: Vance Bibliographies. #P-916. February, 1982. 35p.

Date-Bah, Eugenia
"Rural Development and the Status of Women." Paper Presented at a Seminar on the Role of Population Factor in the Rural Development Strategy." Monrovia, Liberia. 1980.

Dauber, Roslyn and Cain, Melinda (eds.)
Women and Technological Change in Developing Countries. Boulder, Colorado: Westview Press. AAAS Selected Symposium #53. 1980. 266p.

Dawit, T.
"Mass Media and Rural Women in Africa." Assignment Children. Volume 38 #2 April-June, 1977. pp. 119-120.

De Sardan, Jean-Pierre O.
"The Songhay-Zarma Female Slave: Relations of Production and Ideological Status." (In) Robertson, Claire C. and Klein, Martin A. (eds.). Women and Slavery in Africa. Madison, Wisconsin: University of Wisconsin Press. 1983. pp. 130-143.

Deheusch, L.
"The Good Usage of Wives and Cattle-Transformation of Marriage in Southern Africa." L'Homme. Volume 23 #4 1983.

Dey, Jennie M.
Women in Food Production and Food Security in Africa. Rome: United Nations Food and Agriculture Organization. Women in Agriculture Series #3. 1984. 101p.

Dey, Jennie M.
"Women in African Rice Farming Systems." International Rice Commission Newsletter. Volume 32 #2 December, 1983. pp. 1-4.

Dey, Jennie M.
Women in Rice Farming Systems, Focus: Subsaharan Africa.

Rome: United Nations Food and Agriculture Organization. Women in Agriculture Series #2. 1984. 106p.
Dey, Jennie M.
"Women in African Rice Farming Systems." (In) International Rice Research Institute. 'Women in Rice Farming': Proceedings of a Conference on Women in Rice Farming Systems. September 26-30, 1983. Brookfield, Vermont: Gower Publishing Co. 1985. pp. 419-444.
Dhamija, Jasleen
"Income-Generating Activities for Rural Women in Africa: Some Successes and Failures." (In) International Labour Organization (ILO). Rural Development and Women in Africa. Geneva: ILO. 1984. pp. 75-78.
Dirasse, Laketch
The Critical Needs of African Women and Appropriate Strategies in the Framework of the Gisenyi and Lusaka MULPOCS. Addis Ababa, Ethiopia: United Nations Economic Commission for Africa. African Training and Research Centre for Women. 1981. 35p.
Dixon, Ruth B.
"Women in Agriculture: Counting the Labor Force in Developing Countries." Population and Development Review. Volume 8 #3 September, 1982. pp. 539-566.
Dixon, Ruth B.
"Land, Labour and the Sex Composition of the Agricultural Labour Force: An International Comparison." Development and Change. Volume 14 #3 July, 1983. pp. 347-372.
Dixon, Ruth B.
"Jobs for Women in Rural Industry and Services." Paper Presented at the Conference on Agrarian Reform and Rural Development. Rome: United Nations Food and Agriculture Organization. Washington, D.C.: U.S. Department of State. U.S. Agency for International Development. Office of Women in Development. July, 1979.
Dixon, Ruth B.
"Seeing the Invisible Women Farmers in Africa: Improving Research and Data Collection Methods." (In) Monson, J. and Kalb, M. (eds.). Women as Food Producers in Developing Countries. Los Angeles: University of California-Los Angeles. African Studies Center and OEF International. 1985. pp. 19-35.
Dixon-Mueller, Ruth
Women's Work in the Third World Agriculture: Concepts and Indicators. Geneva: ILO. Women, Work and Development Series. Volume 9. 1985. 151p.
Dulansey, Maryanne L.
Can Technology Help Women Feed Their Families? Post Harvest Storage, Processing and Cooking: Some Observations. Washington, D.C.: Consultants in Development. 1979. 9p.
Dulansey, Maryanne L.
Women in Development Program Concerns in Francophone Sahel: Report of a Workshop. Washington, D.C.: U.S.

Department of State. U.S. Agency for International Development. Bobo-Dioulasso, Upper Volta. June 5-7, 1979. 11p.

Eide, Wenche B. and Skjonsberg, Else and Pala, Achola O. and Bathily, Abjoulaye
"Women in Food Production, Food Handling and Nutrition With Special Emphasis on Africa." PAG Bulletin. Volume 7 #3/4 Sept.-Dec., 1977. pp. 40-49.

Eide, Wenche B. and Steady, Filomina C.
"Individual and Social Energy Flows: Bridging Nutritional and Anthropological Thinking About Women's Work in Rural Africa: Some Theoretical Considerations." (In) Jerome, Norge W. and Kandel, Randy F. and Pelto, Gretel H. (eds.). Nutritional Anthropology: Contemporary Approach to Diet and Culture. New York: Redgrave Publishing. 1980. pp. 61-84.

Eide, Wenche B. and Skjonsberg, Else and Bathily, Abjoulaye and Pala, Achola O. and Krystall, Abigail and Millwood, D.
Women in Food Production, Food Handling and Nutrition With Special Emphasis on Africa. Final Report. New York: United Nations. Protein-Calorie Advisory Group of the U.N. System. FAO Food and Nutrition Paper #8. June, 1977. 224p.

Ember, C.R.
"Relative Decline in Women's Contribution to Agriculture With Intensification." American Anthropologist. Volume 85 #2 June, 1983. pp. 285-304.

Engberg, L.E.
"Emphasis on Economics--A Way to Strengthen the Relationship of Home Economics With Agriculture." Paper Presented at the Workshop on the Role of Women and Home Economics in Rural Development in Africa. Rome: United Nations Food and Agriculture Organization. Alexandria, Egypt. October 17, 1983. 10p.

Fapohunda, Eleanor R.
"Female and Male Work Profiles." (In) Oppong, Christine (ed.). Female and Male in West Africa. London: George Allen and Unwin. 1983. pp. 32-53.

Fortmann, Louise P.
Tillers of the Soil and Keepers of the Hearth: A Bibliographic Guide to Women and Rural Development. Ithaca, New York: Cornell University. Center for International Studies. Rural Development Committee. Bibliography Series #2. 1979. 53p.

Fortmann, Louise P.
"The Plight of the Invisible Farmer: The Effect of National Agricultural Policy on Women in Africa." (In) Dauber, Roslyn and Cain, Melinda L. Women and Technological Change in Developing Countries. Boulder, Colorado: Westview Press. 1981. pp. 205-214.

Fortmann, Louise P.
"A Role for Women in Agroforestry Projects." (In) United Nations Food and Agriculture Organization (FAO). 1983

Training for Agriculture and Rural Development. Rome: FAO. Economic and Social Development Series #31. 1984. pp. 21-26.

Fraser, Arvonne
Women in Development. Washington, D.C.: U.S. Department of State. U.S. Agency for International Development. Office of Women in Development. 1977. 12p.

Germain, Adrienne
"Poor Rural Women: A Policy Perspective." Journal of International Affairs. Volume 3 #2 Fall-Winter, 1976. 20p.

Germain. Adrienne
"Research on Women in Agricultural Production in Eastern and Southern Africa." Paper Presented at a Workshop on Women in Agricultural Production in Eastern and Southern Africa. Nairobi, Kenya. April 9-11, 1980.

Gilligan, John J.
"Importance of Third World Women." Rivista di Studi Politici Internazionali. Volume 45 #3 July-September, 1978.

Gladwin, Christina and Staudt, Kathleen A. and McMillan, Della
Reaffirming the Agricultural Role of Women: One Solution to the Food Crisis. (In) Association of Facilities of Agriculture in Africa. Proceedings of the Fifth General Conference on Food Security. Manzini, Swaziland. April, 1984.

Guenther, Mathias G.
"Bushman Hunters as Farm Labourers." Canadian Journal of African Studies. Volume 11 #2 1977.

Guyer, Jane I.
The Raw, the Cooked and the Half-Baked: A Note on the Division of Labor by Sex. Brookline, Massachusetts: Boston University. African Studies Center. Working Papers in African Studies #48. 1981. 12p.

Guyer, Jane I.
Women's Work in the Food Economy of the Cocoa Belt: A Comparison. Brookline, Massachusetts: Boston University. African Studies Center. Working Paper #7. 1978. 34p.

Hagan, A.L.
"The Role of Women in Rural Development: Some Critical Issues." (In) Mondjanagni, A.C. La Participation Populaire an Developpement en Afrique Noire. Paris: Karthala; Doula, Institut Pan Africain Pour Le Developpement. 1984. pp. 75-87.

Haile, Tsehaye
"Community Participation in Rural Water Supply Development." (In) International Development Research Centre (IDRC). 'Rural Water Supply in Developing Countries' Workshop on Training, Zomba, Malawi, August 5-12, 1980. Ottawa, Canada: IDRC. 1981. pp. 89-95.

Halperin, Rhoda
Ecology and Mode of Production: Seasonal Variation and the Division of Labor by Sex Among Hunter-Gatherers.

Cincinnati, Ohio: University of Cincinnati. Department of Anthropology. 1979.
Henn, Jeanne K.
"Feeding the Cities and Feeding the Peasants: What Role for Africa's Women Farmers." World Development. Volume 11 #12 1983.
Henn, Jeanne K.
"Women in the Rural Economy: Past, Present and Future." (In) Hay, Margaret J. and Stichter, Sharon (eds.). African Women South of the Sahara. New York: Longman. 1984. pp. 1-18.
Huggard, Marianne
"The Rural Woman as a Food Producer: An Assessment of the Resolution on Women and Food From the World Food Conference in Rome, 1974." Paper Presented at the International Conference on Women and Food: Consortium for International Development. Tucson, Arizona. 1978. 10p.
International Center for Research on Women
The Productivity of Women in Developing Countries: Measurement Issues and Recommendtions. Washington, D.C.: U.S. Department of State. U.S. Agency for International Development. Office on Women in Development. 1980. 46p.
International Development Research Centre (IDRC)
Rural Water Supply in Developing Countries: Proccedings of a Workshop on Training. Ottawa, Canada: IDRC. Zomba, Malawi. August 5-12, 1981. 144p.
International Institute for Labour Studies (IILS) and Organization of African Unity (OAU)
Food Self-Sufficiency, Technological Autonomy, and Social Progress in Africa: A Research Guide. Geneva: IILS/Addis Ababa, Ethiopia: OAU. 1984. 144p.
International Labour Office (ILO)
Improved Village Technology for Women's Activities: A Manual for West Africa. London: ILO. 1985.
International Labour Organization (ILO)
Rural Development and Women in Africa: Papers of the ILO Tripartite African Regional Seminar on Rural Development and Women, June 15-19, 1981. Geneva: ILO. Dakar, Senegal. 1984. 157p.
International Labour Organization (ILO)
Women, Technology and the Development Process. Paper Presented to the African Regional Meeting of UNCSTD. Geneva: ILO. Cairo, Egypt. July 24-29, 1978.
International Maize and Wheat Improvement Center (CIMMYT)
"CIMMYT's Experience With the User's Perspective in Technology Development." (In) Rockefeller Foundation (eds.). Women and Agricultural Technology: Relevance for Research. Volume 2-Experiences in International and National Research. New York: Rockefeller Foundation. 1985. pp. 13-26.
Javillonar, Gloria W.
Rural Development, Women's Roles and Fertility in Developing Countries: Review of the Literature. Chapel

Hill, North Carolina: Research Triangle Institute. 1979. pp. 32-75.
Jewsiewicki, B.
"Lineage Mode of Production: Social Inequalities in Equatorial Central Africa." (In) Crummey, Donald and Steward, C.C. (eds.). Modes of Production in Africa: The Precolonial Era. Beverly Hills, California: Sage Publications. 1981. pp. 93-114.
Jorgensen, Kirsten
"Water Supply Projects in Africa: The Need to Involve the Main Users--Women." Ideas and Action Bulletin. #150 1983. pp. 14-18.
Kamba, Kate
"Fuel Wood and Energy Development for African Women." Paper Presented at the Workshop on Women in Agricultural Development. Addis Ababa, Ethiopia: United Nations Economic Commission for Africa. Awassa, Ethiopia. June 26, 1983. 13p.
King-Akerele, O.
Traditional Palm Oil Processing, Women's Role and the Application of Appropriate Technology. Addis Ababa, Ethiopia: United Nations Economic Commission for Africa. Research Series. 1983.
Kizerbo, Joseph
"Women and the Energy Crisis in the Sahel Africa. From the Seminar on Fuel and Energy Development for African Women in Rural Areas, Bamako, Mali, December, 1980." Unasylva. Volume 33 #133 1981. pp. 5-10.
Kocher, James E.
"Socioeconomic Development and Fertility Change in Rural Africa." Paper Presented at the Annual Meeting of the African Studies Association. Paper #44. Boston, Massachusetts. 1976. 22p.
Kocher, James E.
"Supply-Demand Disequilibria and Fertility Change in Africa--Toward a More Appropriate Economic Approach." Social Biology. Volume 30 #1 1983. pp. 41-58.
Lancaster, Chet S.
"Women, Horticulture and Society in Sub-Saharan Africa." American Anthropologist. Volume 78 #3 September, 1976. pp. 539-564.
Lewis, Barbara C. (ed.)
The Invisible Farmer: Women and the Crisis in Agriculture. Washington, D.C.: U.S. Department of State. U.S. Agency for International Development. Office of Women in Development. 1982. 456p.
Lewis, Shelby
"African Women and National Development." (In) Lindsay, Beverly (ed.). Comparative Perspectives of Third World Women: The Impact of Race, Sex and Class. New York: Praeger Publishers. 1980. pp. 36-54.
Lindsay, Beverly
"Women and National Development in Africa." Western Journal of Black Studies. Volume 1 #1 March, 1977. pp. 53-58.

Loutfi, Martha F.
Rural Women: Unequal Partners in Development. Geneva: International Labour Organization. 1982. 80p.
Mair, Lucille
"Adult Learning. Women and Development." Prospects 7. #2 1977. pp. 238-443.
Matsepe, Ivy F.
"Underdevelopment and African Women." Journal of Southern African Affairs. Volume 2 #2 April, 1977. pp. 135-143.
Matsepe-Casaburri, Ivy F.
"Underdevelopment and African Women." Paper Presented at the Conference of the Southern Africa Research Group. College Park, Maryland: Southern Africa Research Group. September, 1976.
Max-Forson, Margaret
"The Role of Women and Youth in Development." Rural Progress. Volume 1 #3 1979. pp. 28-30.
Max-Forson, Margaret
Progress and Obstacles in Achieving the Minimum Objectives of the World and Africa Plans of Action: A Critical Review. Report Presented to the Second Regional Conference on the Integration of Women in Development. Addis Ababa, Ethiopia: United Nations Economic Commission for Africa. Lusaka, Zambia. December 3-7, 1979. 56p.
McDowell, James and Hazzard, Virginia
"Village Technology and Women's Work in Eastern Africa." Assignment Children. Volume 36 Oct.-Dec., 1976. pp. 53-65.
McGrath, Mary J.
"What Private Institutions, Particularly Cooperative, Can do to Facilitate Full Participation of Women in Meeting Food and Nutrition Needs." (In) University of Arizona. Proceedings and Papers of the International Conference on Women and Food: Consortium for International Development. Tucson, Arizona: University of Arizona. 1978. pp. 145-153.
McSweeney, Brenda G.
"Collection and Analysis of Rural Women's Time Use." Studies in Family Planning. Volume 10 #11/12 Nov.-Dec., 1979. pp. 379+.
Mies, M.
"Consequences of Capitalist Penetration for Women's Subsistence Reproduction." Paper Presented at the Seminar on Underdevelopment and Subsistence Production in South East Africa. April, 1978.
Mitchnik, David A.
Improving Ways of Skill Acquisition of Women for Rural Employment in Some African Countries. Geneva: International Labour Organization. World Employment Programme Research. Education and Employment Research Project. Working Papers. February, 1977. 78p.
Monson, Jamie and Kalb, Marion
Women as Food Producers in Developing Countries. Los Angeles: University of California-Los Angeles. African

Studies Center. African Studies Association. OEF International. 1985. 118p.
Moris, J.R.
Reforming Agricultural Extension and Research Services in Africa. London: Overseas Development Institute. Discussion Paper #11. 1983.
Moss, G. and Dunn, M. and Nsarko, J.D.
"Home Economics in Rural Development in Africa: The Village Woman's Day." Paper Presented at the Workshop on the Role of Women and Home Economics in Rural Development in Africa. Rome: United Nations Food and Agricultural Organization. 1983. 7p.
Murray, Colin G.
"Migrant Labour and Changing Family Structure in the Rural Periphery of Southern Africa." Journal of Southern African Studies. Volume 6 #2 1980. pp. 139-156.
Ndongko, T.
"Tradition and the Role of Women in Africa." Presence Africaine. Volume 99/100 1976. pp. 143-152.
Nelson, Nici (ed.)
African Women in the Development Process. Totowa, New Jersey: F. Cass. 1981. 136p.
Newman, Katherine S.
"Women and Law: Land Tenure in Africa." (In) Black, Naomi and Cottrell, Ann B. Women and World Change: Equity Issues in Development. Beverly Hills, California: Sage Publications. 1981. pp. 120-138.
Norem, R.H.
"The Integration of a Family Systems Perspective Into Farming Systems Projects." (In) Caldwell, John and Rojas, Mary (eds.). Family Systems and Farming Systems: A Second Annual Conference in the World of Women in Development Series. Blacksburg, Virginia: Virgnia Polytechnic Institute and State University. 1983.
North, Jeanne
"Women Participants in the Food Marketing System in West Africa." (In) University of Arizona. Proceedings and Papers of the International Conference on Women and Food: Consortium for International Development. Tucson, Arizona: University of Arizona. 1978. pp. 103-111.
O'Kelly, Elizabeth
Rural Women: Their Integration in Development Programmes and How Simple Intermediate Technologies Can Help Them. Available From the Author: 3 Cumberland Gardens, Lloyd Square, London, England WC1X 9AF. $4.00. 1978. 84p.
Okali, Christine
"The Changing Economic Position of Women in Rural Communities in West Africa." Africana Marburgensia. Volume 12 #1/2 1979. pp. 59-93.
Okeyo, Achola P.
"African Women in Changing Rural Economies." Courier. Volume 57 Sept.-Oct., 1979. pp. 63-65.
Okeyo, Achola P.
The Role of Women in Changing Traditional Farming Systems. Paper Presented at the Workshop on Policies and

Programmes for Increased Food and Agricultural Production in Traditional Subsistence Farms in Africa. Rome: United Nations Food and Agriculture Organization. Arusha, Tanzania. December 10, 1984. 27p.

Oomen-Myim, Marie A.
"Involvement of Rural Women in Decision-Making Within Smallscale Agricultural Projects." Paper Presented at the Workshop on Women's Studies and Development. Dar-es-Salaam, Tanzania: University of Dar-es-Salaam. Bureau of Resource Assessment and Land Use Planning. Paper #44. September 24-29, 1979. 7p.

Overholt, C. and Anderson, M. and Cloud, K. and Austin, J.
Gender Roles in Development Projects: A Casebook. West Hartford: Connecticut: Kumarian Press. Kumarian Press Case Studies Series. 1985. 326p.

Pala, Achola O.
African Women in Rural Development: Research Trends and Priorities. Washington, D.C.: American Council on Education. Overseas Liaison Committee. OLC Paper #12. December, 1976. 35p.

Palmer, Ingrid
"Rural Women and the Basic Needs Approach." International Labour Review. Volume 115 #1 January-February, 1977. pp. 97-98.

Palmer, Ingrid
"Women in Rural Development." International Development Review. Volume 22 #2/3 1980. pp. 39-45.

Palmer, Ingrid
"The Role of Women in Agrarian Reform and Rural Development." (In) United Nations. Land Reform. Rome: United Nations Food and Agriculture Organization. 1979. pp. 57-70.

Palmer, Ingrid
'The Nemow Case', Case Studies of the Impact of Large Scale Development Projects on Women: A Series for Planners. New York: Population Council. International Programs Working Paper #7. September, 1979. 92p.

Palmer, Ingrid
"Seasonality of Women's Work: Patterns and Trends." (In) University of Sussex. Papers From the Conference on Seasonal Dimensions to Rural Poverty. Brighton, England: Sussex University. Institute of Development Studies. July 3-6, 1978. 8p.

Palmer, Ingrid
The Impact of Male Out-Migration on Women in Farming. West Hartford, Connecticut: Kumarian Press. 1985. 78p.

Papanek, Hanna
"Development Planning for Women." (In) Wellesley Editorial Committee. Women and National Development: The Complexities of Change. Chicago: University of Chicago Press. 1977. pp. 14-21.

Phillips, Beverly
Women in Rural Development: A Bibliography. Madison,

Wisconsin: University of Wisconsin-Madison. Land Tenure Center Library. Training and Methods Series #29. 1979. 45p.
Phillott-Almeida, Ralphina
"Women and Water Resources Management for Socio-Economic Development in Africa: Health, Sanitation and Environmental Aspects." (In) United Nations Economic Commission for Africa (UNECA) (eds.). Regional Meeting on Socio-Economic and Policy Aspects of Water Management in Africa. Addis Ababa, Ethiopia: UNECA. June, 1986.
Ritchie, Jean A.
"Training Women for Development in Africa." (In) United Nations Food and Agriculture Organization (FAO). Training for Agriculture and Rural Development, 1977. Rome: United Nations. FAO. Economic and Development Series #7. 1977. pp. 19-26.
Ritchie, Jean A.
"Impact of Changing Food Production. Processing and Marketing Systems on the Role of Women." (In) Proceedings of the World Conference. Ames, Iowa: Iowa State University Press. 1977. pp. 129-144.
Ritchie, Jean A.
General Conclusions on the Integration of Women in Agrarian Reform and Rural Development in Africa. Rome: United Nations Food and Agriculture Organization. 1978.
Ritchie, Jean A.
The Integration of Women in Agrarian Reform and Rural Development in English Speaking Countries of the African Region. Rome: United Nations Food and Agriculture Organization. March, 1978. 95p.
Roark, Paula
Successful Rural Water Supply Projects and the Concerns of Women. Washington, D.C.: U.S. Department of State. U.S. Agency for International Development. Office of Women in Development. September, 1980. 66p.
Roboff, Farron V. and Renwick, Hilary L.
"The Changing Role of Women in the Development of the Sahel." Paper Presented to the Annual Meeting of the African Studies Association. Paper #92. Boston, Massachusetts. 1976. 12p.
Rogers, Barbara
"What do Women Want?" Appropriate Technology. Volume 4 1979.
Rogers, Barbara
"Women's Projects: New Segregation?" Africa Report. Volume 23 #3 May-June, 1978. pp. 48-50.
Rogers, Barbara
The Domestication of Women: Discrimination in Developing Societies. New York: St. Martin's Press. 1980. 200p.
Rogombe, Rose F.
"Equal Partners in Development." Africa Report. Volume 30 #2 March-April, 1985. pp. 17-20.
Rugh, Andrea B.
Women, Agriculture and Rural Development. Report Presented to the U.S. Agency for International

Development Mission in Cairo, Egypt. Washington, D.C.: U.S. Department of State. U.S. Agency for International Development. 1979.
Sachak, N.
"Agricultural Research: Priorities for Women." (In) Bengtsson, Bo and Tedla, Getachew. Strengthening National Agricultural Research: Report From a SAREC Workshop, September 10-17, 1979. Stockholm, Sweden: Swedish Agency for Research Cooperation in Developing Countries. 1980. pp. 62-69.
Sachs, Carolyn E.
Invisible Farmers: Women in Agricultural Production. Totowa, New Jersey: Rowman and Allen Held. 1983. 153p.
Sacks, Karen
Sisters and Wives: The Past and Future of Sexual Equality. Westport, Connecticut: Greenwood Press. Contributions in Women's Studies #10. 1979. 274p.
Safilios-Rothschild, Constantina
The State of Statistics on Women in Agriculture in the Third World. New York: United Nations. 1983.
Safilios-Rothschild, Constantina
The Role of Women in Modernizing Agricultural Systems. Washington, D.C.: U.S. Department of State. U.S. Agency for International Development. Office of Women in Development. May, 1981. 31p.
Safilios-Rothschild, Constantina
Can Agriculture in the Third World Modernize With Traditional Female Agricultural Labor? State College, Pennsylvania: Pennsylvania State University. Department of Sociology. 1981.
Savane, M.A.
"Women and Rural Development in Africa." (In) International Labour Organization (ILO). Women in Rural Development: Critical Issues. Geneva: ILO. 1980. pp. 26-32.
Scandinavian Institute of African Studies
Women in Africa and Development Assistance. Report From a Seminar. Uppsala, Sweden: Scandinavian Institute of African Studies. 1978. 55p.
Schutjer, Wayne A. and Stokes, C. Shannon
"Agricultural Policies and Human Fertility: Some Emerging Connections." Population Research and Policy Review. Volume 1 October, 1982. pp. 225-244.
Schutjer, Wayne A. and Stokes, C. Shannon
The Human Fertility Implications of Food and Agricultural Policies in Less-Developed Countries. University Park, Pennsylvania: Pennsylvania State University. College of Agriculture. Agriculture Experiment Station Bulletin #835. January, 1982. 14p.
Schutjer, Wayne A. and Stokes, C. Shannon (eds.)
Rural Development and Human Fertility. New York: MacMillan. 1984. 380p.
Sen, G.
"Women Workers and the Green Revolution." (In) Beneria, Lourdes (ed.). Women and Development: The Sexual

Division of Labor in Rural Societies. New York: Praeger Publishers. 1985.

Skjonsberg, Else
Women and Food and the Social Sciences: Perspectives on African Food Production and Food Handling. Oslo, Norway: Mimeo. Available From the International Center for Research on Women, Washington, D.C. 1977.

Spencer, Dunstan S.C.
Women in a Developing Economy: A West African Case Study. East Lansing, Michigan: Michigan State University. 1979. 134p.

Staudt, Kathleen A.
"The Umoja Federation: Women's Cooptation Into a Local Power Structure." Western Political Quarterly. Volume 33 #2 June, 1980. pp. 278-290.

Staudt, Kathleen A.
Women's Organizations in Rural Development. Washington, D.C.: U.S. Department of State. U.S. Agency for International Development. Office of Women in Development. February, 1980. 71p.

Staudt, Kathleen A.
"Women Farmers and Inequalities in Agricultural Services." Rural Africana. Volume 29 Winter, 1976. pp. 81-94.

Staudt, Kathleen A.
"Women in Development--Policy Strategies at the End of the Decade." Africa Report. Volume 30 #2 March-April, 1985. pp. 71-74.

Staudt, Kathleen A.
"Class and Sex in the Politics of Women Farmers." Journal of Politics. Volume 41 #2 May, 1979. pp. 492-512.

Staudt, Kathleen A.
Women and Participation in Rural Development: A Framework for Project Design and Policy-Oriented Research. Ithaca, New York: Cornell University. Center for International Studies. Rural Development Monograph #4. 1979. 78p.

Staudt, Kathleen A.
"Women Farmers and Inequities in Agricultural Services." (In) Bay, Edna G. (ed.). Women and Work in Africa. Boulder, Colorado: Westview Press. Westview Special Studies in Africa. 1982. pp. 207-224.

Staudt, Kathleen A.
"Organizing Rural Women in the Third World." Paper Presented at the Annual Meeting of the Western Political Science Association. March 27-29, 1980.

Staudt, Kathleen A.
"Agricultural Productivity Gaps: A Case Study of Male Preference in Government Policy Implementation." Development and Change. Volume 9 #3 July, 1978. pp. 439-458.

Staudt, Kathleen A.
"Tracing Sex Differences in Donor Agricultural Programs." Paper Presented at the American Political Science Association Annual Meeting. Washington, D.C. 1979.

Steckle, Jean M.
"Improving Food Utilization in Developing Countries." Canadian Home Economics Journal. Volume 27 #4 October, 1977. pp. 34-39.
Tadesse, Zenebeworke
"African Women in Rural Development: A New Group of African Women Researchers." Ideas and Action. #127 1979. pp. 7-10.
Tadesse, Zenebeworke
"Studies on Rural Women in Africa: An Overview." (In) International Labour Organization (ILO). Rural Development and Women in Africa. Geneva: ILO. 1984. pp. 65-73.
Tadesse, Zenebeworke
Women and Technological Development in Agriculture: An Overview of the Problems in Developing Countries. New York: United Nations Institute for Training and Research. Science and Technology Working Paper Series #9. 1979.
Tau, Mildred M.
"Women: Critical to African Development." Africa Report. Volume 26 #2 March-April, 1981. pp. 4-6.
Tinker, Irene
New Technologies for Food Chain Activities: The Imperative of Equity for Women. Washington, D.C.: U.S. Department of State. U.S. Agency for International Development. Office of Women in Development. 1979. 43p.
Tinker, Irene
"New Technologies for Food Related Activities: An Equity Strategy." (In) Dauber, Roslyn and Cain, Melinda L. (eds.). Women and Technological Change in Developing Countries. Boulder, Colorado: Westview Press. 1981. pp. 51-88.
U.S. Agency for International Development (U.S. AID)
Training Women in the Sahel. Washington, D.C.: U.S. Department of State. U.S. AID. Office of Women in Development. 1978. 47p.
U.S. Agency for International Development (U.S. AID)
The Productivity of Women in Developing Countries: Measurement Issues and Recommendations. Washington, D.C.: U.S. Department of State. U.S. AID. International Center for Research on Women. Office of Women in Development. 1980. 46p.
U.S. Agency for International Development (U.S. AID)
Examples of Women in Development Programs in Sahel Francophone West Africa. Washington, D.C.: U.S. Department of State. U.S. AID. Office of Sahel and Francophone West Africa, Bureau for Africa. 1979. 27p.
United Nations Ctr. for Social Dev. and Humanitarian Affairs
Water, Women and Development. New York: United Nations. February 19, 1977.
United Nations Economic Commission for Africa (UNECA)
"Women as Clientele of Non-Formal Education." Paper Presented to the Regional Symposium on Non-Formal

Education for Rural Development. Addis Ababa, Ethiopia: UNECA. Aug. 28-Sept. 8, 1978. 12p.

United Nations Economic Commission for Africa (UNECA) "Technical Co-Operation Among Developing Countries and Human Resource Development: The Experience of the African Training and Research Centre for Women of the Economic Commission for Africa." Paper Presented at the United Nations Conference on Technical Co-Operation Among Developing Countries. Addis Ababa, Ethiopia: UNECA. Buenos Aires, Argentina. 1978. 16p.

United Nations Economic Commission for Africa (UNECA) "The Role of Women in the Utilization of Science and Technology for Development: An ECA Contribution to the African Regional Meeting of the United Nations Conference on Science and Technology for Development (UNCSTD)." Addis Ababa, Ethiopia: UNECA. African Training and Research Centre for Women. Cairo, Egypt. July 24-29, 1978. 62p.

United Nations Economic Commission for Africa (UNECA) Women Population and Rural Development in Africa. Addis Ababa, Ethiopia: UNECA/FAO Women's Development Programme Unit. 1976.

United Nations Economic Commission for Africa (UNECA) "Women in Development: Moving Away From Tradition." U.N. Chronicle. Volume 19 #11 December, 1982. pp. 105-106.

United Nations Economic Commission for Africa (UNECA) Summary of On-Going and Planned Projects of the United Nations Agencies and Organizations for the Integration of Women in Development in the African Region. Addis Ababa, Ethiopia: UNECA. 1980. 72p.

United Nations Economic Commission for Africa (UNECA) "Women in African Development." Paper Presented at the ACOSCA Bilingual Regional Seminar on Increasing Women's Access to Credit Unions in West Africa. Dakar, Senegal, March. 1981. Addis Ababa, Ethiopia: UNECA. 1981.

United Nations Economic Commission for Africa (UNECA) Report: ECA/FAO Subregional Seminar on Fuelwood and Energy Development for African Women, April 18, 1983. Addis Ababa, Ethiopia: UNECA. Lusaka, Zambia. November, 1984. 25p.

United Nations Economic Commission for Africa (UNECA) The Critical Needs of African Women and Appropriate Strategies in the Framework of the Gisenyi and Lusaka MULPOCS. Addis Ababa, Ethiopia: UNECA. 1981.

United Nations Economic Commission for Africa (UNECA) "The Role of Women in the Solution of the Food Crisis in Africa (Implementation of the Lagos Plan of Action)." Paper Presented at the Regional Intergovernmental Preparatory Meeting for the World Conference to Review and Appraise the Achievements of the United Nations Decade for Women: Equality, Development and Peace/Third Regional Conference on the Integration ofWomen in Development. Arusha, Tanzania. October 8-12, 1984. Addis, Ababa, Ethiopia: UNECA. 1984.

United Nations Educational, Scientific and Cultural Organ.
Description of Projects Relevant to the Integration of Women in Development: Africa. Paris: UNESCO. May 16, 1979. 10p.

United Nations Food and Agriculture Organization (FAO)
The State of Food and Agriculture; 1983: World Review: The Situation in Sub-Saharan Africa; Women in Developing Agriculture. New York: FAO. FAO Agriculture Series #16. 1984. 221p.

United Nations Food and Agriculture Organization (FAO)
Food Aid and the Role of Women in Development. Rome: FAO. 1976. 43p.

United Nations Food and Agriculture Organization (FAO)
The Role of Women in Population Dynamics Related to Food and Agriculture and Rural Development in Africa. Rome: FAO. United Nations Economic Commission for Africa. Women's Program Unit. Joint Agriculture Division. 1976.

Von Blanckenberg, P.
Agricultural Extension Systems in Some African Countries. Rome: United Nations Food and Agriculture Organization (FAO). FAO Economic and Social Development Paper. 1984.

Weekes-Vagliani, Winifred and Grossat, Bernard
Women in Development: At the Right Time for the Right Reason. Paris: Organization for Economic Cooperation and Development. 1980. 330p.

Weekes-Vagliani, Winifred
"Women, Food and Rural Development." (In) Rose, T. (ed.). Crisis and Recovery in Subsaharan Africa. Paris: OECD Development Center. 1985. pp. 104-110.

Whalen, Irene T.
Women and Livestock: The Impact of Technological Innovations on Women. Addis Ababa, Ethiopia: International Livestock Center, Africa. P/O Box 5689. 1984.

White, Douglas R. and Bruton, Michael L. and Dow, Malcolm M.
"Sexual Division of Labor in African Agriculture: A Network Autocorrelation Analysis." American Anthropologist. Volume 83 #4 December, 1981. pp. 824-849.

Wipper, Audrey
"Women's Voluntary Associations." (In) Hay, Margaret J. and Stichter, Sharon (eds.). African Women South of the Sahara. New York: Longman. 1984. pp. 69-86.

World Bank
Rural Development Projects: A Retrospective View of Bank Experience in Sub-Saharan Africa. Washington, D.C.: World Bank. Report #2242. October 13, 1978.

World Bank
Recognizing the 'Invisible' Woman in Development: The World Banks Experience. Washington, D.C.: World Bank. October, 1979. 33p.

World Health Organization (WHO)
Improving Ways of Skill Acquisition of Women for Rural Development in Some African Countries. Geneva: World

Health Organization. World Employment Programme Research Working Papers. WEP 2-18/WP 15. 1977. 76p.

Wright, Marcia
"Technology and Women's Control Over Production: Three Case Studies From East-Central Africa and Their Implications for Esther Boserup's Thesis About the Displacement of Women." Paper Presented at the Rockefeller Foundation Workshop on Women, Household and Human Capital Development in Low Income Countries. New York: Rockefeller Foundation. July, 1982.

Youssef, Nadia H.
Women and Work in Developing Societies. Westport, Connecticut: Greenwood Press. 1976. 137p.

Youssef, Nadia H.
"Women and Agricultural Production in Muslim Societies." Studies in Comparative International Development. Volume 12 #1 Spring, 1977. pp. 41-58.

Arts

African American Institute (AAI)
African Women/African Art: An Exhibition of African Art Illustrating the Different Roles of Women in African Society. New York: AAI. 1976. 62p.

Aronson, Lisa
"Women in the Arts." (In) Hay, Margaret J. and Stichter, Sharon (eds.). African Women South of the Sahara. New York: Longman. 1984. pp. 119-138.

Burton, M. and Kirk, L.
"Sex Differences in Maasai Cognition of Personality and Social Identity." American Anthropologist. Volume 81 #4 December, 1979. pp. 841-901.

Hanna, J.L.
"Dance and the Women's War." Dance Research Journal. Volume 14 #1/2 1981. pp. 25-28.

High-Wasikhongo, Freda
Traditional African Art: A Female Focus. Madison, Wisconsin: University of Wisconsin-Madison. Elvehjem Museum of Art. 1981.

Hinckley, Priscilla
"The Sowo Mask: Symbol of Sisterhood." Boston: Boston University. African Studies Center. Working Papers in African Studies #40. 1980.

Jeffries, Rosalind
"The Image of Women in African Cave Art." Journal of African Civilizations. Volume 6 #1 1984. pp. 98-122.

McCall, Daniel
"Rank, Gender, Cult Affiliation Proclaimed in the Arts of Apparel: Reflections on Esie Sculpture." Paper Presented at the Annual Meeting of the African Studies Association. Paper #34. Bloomimgton, Indiana. 1981.

Nicolls, Andrea
"Women in African Art." M.A. Thesis: City College of New York. Department of Art. New York, New York. 1977. 91p.

Teilhetfisk, J.
"Djuka Women and Mens Art." African Arts. Volume 17 #2 1984. pp. 63+.

Thea, Carolee
"Masks, Power and Sisterhood in an African Society." Heresies. Volume 12 #1 1982. pp. 106-111.

Tonkin, Elizabeth
"Women Excluded? Masking and Masquerading in West Africa." (In) Holden, P. (ed.). Women's Religious Experience. Totowa, New Jersey: Barnes and Noble. 1983. pp. 163-174.

United Nations Educational, Scientific and Cultural Organ.
Final Report: Regional Workshop on Women's Crafts in Developing Countries. Paris: UNESCO. CREA #14. Katiola, Ivory Coast. 22p. 1983.

Wass, Betty M.
"The 'Kaba Sloht': Women's Dress and Ethnic Consciousness in Krio Society." Paper Presented at the Annual Meeting of the African Studies Association. Paper #92. Houston, Texas. 1977. 19p.

Bibliographies

Abdel Kader, Soha
"Research on the Status of Women, Development and Population Trends in Arab States: An Annotated Bibliography." (In) UNESCO. Bibliographic Guide to Studies on the Status of Women: Development and Population. Paris: United Nations Educational, Scientific and Cultural Organization. 1983. pp. 67-81.

Al-Qazza, Ayad
Women in the Middle East and North Africa: An Annotated Bibliography. Austin, Texas: University of Texas Press. Center for Middle Eastern Studies. Middle East Monograph #2. 1977. 179p.

Anonymous
"Women in Southern Africa: Bibliography." Africa Report. Volume 28 #2 March-April, 1983. pp. 54-55.

Anonymous
Women and Family in Rural Development: An Annotated Bibliography. Rome: United Nations Food and Agriculture Organization. Documentation Centre and Population Documentation Centre. 1977. 66p.

Berrian, Brenda F.
"Bibliographies of Nine Female African Writers." Research in African Literatures. Volume 12 #2 Summer, 1981. pp. 214-236.

Berrian, Brenda F.
Bibliography of African Women Writers and Journalists (Ancient Egypt-1984). Washington, D.C.: Three Continents Press. 1985. 279p.

Bullwinkle, Davis A.
"Women and Their Role in African Society: The Literature of the 70's." Current Bibliography on African Affairs. Volume 15 #4 1982. pp. 69-98.

Buvinic, Mayra
Women and World Development: An Annotated Bibliography. Washington D.C.: Overseas Development Council. 1976. 162p.

BIBLIOGRAPHIES

Claffey, Joan M. and Pigozzi, Mary J. and Axinn, Nancy W.
"Women in Development: A Selected Annotated Bibliography." International Journal of Intercultural Relations. Volume 3 1979.

Danforth, Sandra C.
Women and National Development. Monticello, Illinois: Vance Bibliographies. #P-916. February, 1982. 35p.

Durban Women's Bibliography Group
Women in Southern Africa: A Bibliography. Durban, South Africa: The Group. 1985. 107p.

Epskamp, C.
Inequality in Female Access to Education in Developing Countries: A Bibliography. Hague, Netherlands: Centre for the Study of Education in Developing Countries. 1979. 42p.

Fikry, M.
Traditional Maternal and Child Health Care and Related Problems in the Sahel: A Bibliographic Study. Washington, D.C.: U.S. Department of State. U.S. Agency for International Development. Sahel Development Project. 1977. 123p.

Fortmann, Louise P.
Tillers of the Soil and Keepers of the Hearth: A Bibliographic Guide to Women and Rural Development. Ithaca, New York: Cornell University. Center for International Studies. Rural Development Committee. Bibliography Series #2. 1979. 53p.

Geletkanycz, Christine and Egan, Susan
Literature Review: The Practice of Female Circumcision. Washington, D.C.: U.S. Department of Health, Education and Welfare. Office of International Health. Mimeo. 1979.

Hafkin, Nancy J.
Women and Development in Africa: An Annotated Bibliography. Addis Ababa, Ethiopia: United Nations Economic Commisssion for Africa. African Training and Research Centre for Women. Bibliographic Series #1. 1977. 177p.

Harder, Gudrun M.
"Problems of Women in Developing Countries: A Selected Bibliography." Verfassung unp Recht in Ubersee. #10 1977. pp. 133-160.

Kelly, David H. and Kelly, Gail P.
"Women and Schooling in the Third World: A Bibliography." (In) Kelly, Gail P. and Elliott, Carolyn M. (eds.). Women's Education in the Third World: Comparative Perspectives. Albany, New York: State University of New York Press. 1982. pp. 345-397.

Kelly, Gail P. and Lulat, Younus
"Women and Schooling in the Third World: A Bibliography." Comparative Education Review. Volume 24 #2 June, 1980. pp. S224-S263.

Kharas, Purveen
Women in Development--Africa: An Annotated Bibliography.

Rome: United Nations Food and Agriculture Organization. 1978. 12p.
Kisekka, Mere N.
"The Status of Women, Development and Population Trends in Africa: An Annotated Bibliography." Paper Presented at the Meeting of Experts on Research on the Status of Women, Development and Population Trends: Evaluation and Prospects. Paris: United Nations Educational, Scientific and Cultural Organization. 1980. 66p.
Kisekka, Mere N.
"Research on the Status of Women, Development and Population Trends in Africa: An Annotated Bibliography." (In) United Nations Educational, Scientific and Cultural Organization. Bibliographic Guide to Studies on the Status of Women: Development and Population. Paris: UNESCO. 1983. pp. 41-66.
McFalls, Joseph A. and McFalls, Marguerite H.
Disease and Fertility. Orlando, Florida: Academic Press Inc. 1984. 593p.
Meghdessian, S.R.
The Status of Arab Women: A Select Bibliography. Westport, Connecticut: Greenwood Press. 1980. 176p.
Moody, Elizabeth J.
Women and Development: A Select Bibliography. Pretoria, South Africa: Africa Institute of South Africa. Occasional Papers #43. 1979. 28p.
Nwanosike, Eugene O.
Women and Development: A Select Bibliography: A Select and Partially Annotated Bibliography. Buea, Cameroon: Regional Pan-African Institute for Development/West Africa. Bibliographic Series #10. 1980. 63p.
O'Kelly, Elizabeth
Rural Women: Their Integration in Development Programmes and How Simple Intermediate Technologies Can Help Them. Available From the Author: 3 Cumberland Gardens, Lloyd Square, London, England WC1X 9AF. $4.00. 1978. 84p.
Phillips, Beverly
Women in Rural Development: A Bibliography. Madison, Wisconsin: University of Wisconsin-Madison. Land Tenure Center Library. Training and Methods Series #29. 1979. 45p.
Raccagni, Michelle
The Modern Arab Women: A Bibliography. Metuchen, New Jersey: Scarecrow Press. 1978. 262p.
Rihani, May
Development as if Women Mattered: An Annotated Bibliography With a Third World Focus. Washington, D.C.: Overseas Development Council. Occasional Paper #10. 1978. 137p.
Ritchie, Maureen
Women's Studies: A Checklist of Bibliographies. London: Mansell. 1980. 107p.
Saulniers, Suzanne S. and Rakowski, Cathy A.
Women in the Development Process: A Select Bibliography on Women in Sub-Saharan Africa and Latin America.

Austin, Texas: University of Texas Press. Institute of Latin American Studies. 1977. 287p.

Secretariat for Women in Development
Women in Development: A Resource List. Washington, D.C.: Secretariat for Women in Development. A Transcentury Publication. 1979. 86p.

United Nations Educational, Scientific, and Cultural Organ.
Bibliographic Guide to Studies on the Status of Women: Development and Population Trends. Paris: UNESCO. Epping, England: Bowker. 1983. 284p.

Vavrus, Linda G.
Women in Development: A Selected Annotated Bibliography and Resource Guide. East Lansing, Michigan: Michigan State University. Institute for International Studies in Education. Non-Formal Education Information Center. 1980. 69p.

Wadsworth, Gail M.
Women in Development: A Bibliography of Materials Available in the Library and Documentation Centre, Eastern and Southern African Management Institute. Arusha, Tanzania: Eastern and Southern African Management Institute. Library and Documentation Centre. February, 1982. 106p.

Cultural Roles

Abbott, Susan
"In the End You Will Carry Me in Your Car--Sexual Politics in the Field." Women's Studies. Volume 10 #2 1983. pp. 161-178.

Abbott, Susan
"Full-Time Farmers and Week-End Wives, an Analysis of Altering Conjugal Roles." Journal of Marriage and the Family. Volume 38 #1 February, 1976. pp. 165-174.

Aborampah, Osei-Mensah
"Family Structure in African Fertility Studies: Some Conceptual and Methodological Issues." Current Bibliography on African Affairs. Volume 18 #4 1986. pp. 319-335.

Accad, Evelyne
"The Theme of Sexual Oppression in the North African Novel." (In) Beck, Lois and Keddie, Nikki R. (eds.). Women in the Muslim World. Cambridge, Massachusetts: Harvard University Press. 1978. pp. 617-628.

Accad, Evelyne
"Complex Inter-Relation of Women's Liberation and Arab Nationalism in North African Novels Written by Women." Paper Presented at the Annual Meeting of the African Studies Association. Paper #1. Boston, Massachusetts. 1976. 16p.

Accad, Evelyne
"The Prostitute in Arab and North African Fiction." (In) Horn, Pierre L. and Pringle, Mary B. (eds.). The Image of the Prostitute in Modern Literature. New York: Ungar. 1984. pp. 63-75.

Accad, Evelyne
Veil of Shame: The Role of Women in the Contemporary Fiction of North Africa and the Arab World. Sherbrooke, Canada: Editions Naaman. 1978. 182p.

Acsadi, George T.
"Effect of Economic Development on Fertility Trends in Africa." (In) Cairo Demographic Centre (CDC). Aspects

of Population Change and Development in Some African and Asian Countries. Cairo, Egypt: CDC. CDC Research Monograph Series #9. 1984. pp. 57-105.

Adamson, Kay
"Approaches to the Study of Women in North Africa: As Reflected in Research of Various Scholars." Maghreb Review. Volume 3 #7-8 May-August, 1978. pp. 22-31.

Adedeji, John A.
"Social Change and Women in African Sport." International Social Science Journal. Volume 34 #2 1982. pp. 210-218.

Adepoju, Aderanti
"Patterns of Migration by Sex." (In) Oppong, Christine (ed.). Female and Male in West Africa. London: George Allen and Unwin. 1983. pp. 54-66.

Adler, A.
"Avunculate and Matrilateral Marriage in Africa." L'Homme. Volume 16 October-December, 1976. pp. 7-28.

African American Institute (AAI)
African Women/African Art: An Exhibition of African Art Illustrating the Different Roles of Women in African Society. New York: AAI. 1976. 62p.

Agarwal, Bina
"Women and Technological Change in Agriculture: The Asian and African Experience." (In) Ahmed, Iftikhar (ed.). Technology and Rural Women: Conceptual and Empirical Issues. Boston: George Allen and Unwin. 1985. pp. 67-114.

Agarwal, Bina
"Women and Technological Change in Agricultural Change: The Asian and African Experience." (In) Ahmed, I. (ed.). Technology and Rural Development: Conceptual and Empirical Issues. London: Allen and Unwin. 1985. pp. 67-114.

Aguta, M.O. and Exedij, F.O. (eds.)
Changing Status of Women in Africa. Addis Ababa, Ethiopia: United Nations Economic Commission for Africa. African Training and Research Centre for Women. 1978.

Ahmed, Iftikhar
"Technologies for Rural Women." Women at Work. #3 1977.

Ahmed, Iftikhar
"Technology and Rural Women in the Third World." International Labour Review. Volume 122 #4 July-August, 1983. pp. 493-505.

Ahmed, Iftikhar (ed.)
Technology and Rural Women: Conceptual and Empirical Issues. Boston: George Allen and Unwin. 1985. 383p.

Aidoo, Christina A.
"Images of Women." Paper Presented at the Women and Work in Africa Symposium #6. Urbana, Illinois: University of Ilinois. April 29, 1979.

Aidoo, Christina A.A.
"Images of Women." (In) University of Illinois (ed.). Women and Work in Africa, April 29-May 1, 1979,

University of Illinois, Urbana-Champaign: A Project of the Africn Studies Association. Urbana, Illinois: University of Illinois. 1979.

Al-Qazza, Ayad
"Current Status of Research on Women in the Arab World." Middle Eastern Studies. Volume 14 #3 October, 1978. pp. 372-384.

Al-Qazza, Ayad
Women in the Middle East and North Africa: An Annotated Bibliography. Austin, Texas: University of Texas Press. Center for Middle Eastern Studies. Middle East Monograph #2. 1977. 179p.

Alausa, O. and Osoba, A.O.
"The Role of Sexually Transmitted Diseases in Male Infertility in Tropical Africa." Nigerian Medical Journal. Volume 8 #3 May, 1978. pp. 225-229.

Allison, C.
"Women, Land, Labour and Survival: Getting Some Basic Facts Straight." IDS Bulletin. Volume 16 #3 1985. pp. 24-30.

Allman, James
"Family Patterns, Women's Status and Fertility in Middle-East and North-Africa." International Journal of Sociology of the Family. Volume 8 #1 1978. pp. 19-35.

Allman, James
"Family Life, Women's Status, and Fertility: Middle East and North African Perspectives." (In) Allman, James (ed.). Women's Studies and Fertility in the Muslim World. New York: Praeger Publishers. Praeger Special Studies. 1978. pp. 24-47.

Allman, James
"The Demographic Transition in the Middle East and North Africa." International Journal of Middle East Studies. Volume 12 #3 November, 1980. pp. 277-301.

Allman, James (ed.)
Women's Status and Fertility in the Muslim World. New York: Praeger Publishers. Praeger Special Studies. 1978. 378p.

Alpers, Edward
"The Story of Swema: Female Vulnerability in Nineteenth-Century East Africa." (In) Robertson, Claire C. and Klein, Martin A. (eds.). Women and Slavery in Africa. Madison, Wisconsin: University of Wisconsin Press. 1983. pp. 185-219.

Amon-Nikoi, Gloria
"Women and Work in Africa." (In) Damachi, Ukandi G. and Diejomaoh, Victor P. Human Resources and African Development. New York: Praeger Publishers. 1978. pp. 188-219.

Anker, Richard and Buvinic, Mayra and Youssef, Nadia H. (eds.)
Women's Roles and Population Trends in the Third World. London: Croon Helm Ltd. 1982. 288p.

Anonymous
"International Conference on the Role of Women in

Liberation Struggles and Women in Development." IDOC Bulletin. #50/51 December-January, 1976. pp. 4-21.
Anonymous
"Mothers, Babies and Health." Agenda. Volume 1 #2 February, 1978. pp. 8-14.
Anonymous
"The Position of Women in Africa." Rural Progress. Volume 1 #3 1979. pp. 20-23.
Anonymous
"Southern African Women Speak Out." Africa Report. Volume 28 #2 March-April, 1983. pp. 15-19.
Anonymous
"Two Views of Liberation." Agenda. Volume 1 #2 February, 1978. pp. 19-22.
Anonymous
"Women Against Mutilation." Off Our Backs. Volume 9 December, 1979. pp. 7.
Anonymous
"Women in Africa." Agenda. Volume 1 #2 February, 1978. pp. 1-7.
Anyaoku, Emeka
"Changing Attitudes: A Cooperative Effort." Africa Report. Volume 30 #2 March, 1985. pp. 21-25.
Appelbaum, P.C. and Ross, S.M. and Dhupelia, I. and Naeye, R.L.
"The Effect of Diet Supplementation and Addition of Zinc in Vitro on the Growth Supporting Property of Amniotic Fluid in African Women." American Journal of Obstetrics and Gynacology. Volume 135 #1 September, 1979. pp. 82-84.
Appiah-Kubi, Kofi
"Monogamy: Is it Really So Christian?" African Women. #5 July-August, 1976. pp. 46-48.
Arens, W. and Arens, Diana A.
"Kinship and Marriage in a Polyethnic Community." Africa. Volume 48 1978. pp. 149-160.
Aronson, Lisa
"Women in the Arts." (In) Hay, Margaret J. and Stichter, Sharon (eds.). African Women South of the Sahara. New York: Longman. 1984. pp. 119-138.
Ashworth, Georgina and May, Nicky (eds.)
Of Conjuring and Caring: Women in Development. London: Change. 1982. 28p.
Attah, E.B.
Family Nucleation and Fertility Change in Tropical Africa: Background to the Demographic Transition. Atlanta, Georgia: Atlanta University. Department of Sociology. 1985.
Axinn, Nancy W.
Female Emancipation Versus Female Welfare. East Lansing, Michigan: Michigan State University. Institute for International Studies in Education. College of Education. Non-Formal Education Information Center. 1979. 5p.

Badran, Margot F.
"Middle East and North Africa: Women." Trends in History. Volume 1 #1 1979. pp. 123-129.
Baffoun, Alya
"Women and Social Change in the Muslim Arab World." Women's Studies International Forum. Volume 5 #2 1982.
Balakrishnan, Revathi and Firebaugh, Francille M.
Roles of Women in Third World Economic Development From a Systems Perspective of Family Resource Management. Columbus, Ohio: Ohio State University. Department of Home Management and Housing. School of Home Economics. Working Papers #81-01. 1981. 39p.
Baldwin, Lewis V.
"Black Women and African Union Methodism, 1813-1983." Methodist History. Volume 21 July, 1983. pp. 225-237.
Barber, Elinor G.
"Some International Perspectives on Sex Differences in Education." Signs. Volume 4 #3 Spring, 1979. pp. 584-592.
Bates, C.J. and Whitehead, Roger G.
"The Effect of Vitamin C Supplementation on Lactating Women in Keneba, a West African Rural Community." International Journal of Vitamin Nutrition Research. Volume 53 #1 1982. pp. 68-76.
Bates, C.J. and Prentice, Andrew M. and Prentice, Ann and Whitehead, Roger G.
"Vitamin C Supplementation of Lactating Women in Keneba: A West African Rural Community." Proceedings of the Nutrition Society. Volume 41 #3 1982. pp. 124A.
Bay, Edna G. and Hafkin, Nancy J. (eds.)
"Women in Africa: Studies in Social and Economic Change." Stanford, California: Stanford University Press. 1976. 306p.
Bay, Edna G.
Women and Work in Africa. Boulder, Colorado: Westview Press. Westview Special Studies on Africa. 1982. 310p.
Beddada, Belletech
"Traditional Practices in Relation to Pregnancy and Childbirth." Paper Presented at the Seminar on Traditional Practices Affecting the Health of Women and Children. World Conference of the United Nations Decade for Women. New York: United Nations. Copenhagen, Denmark. July 14-30, 1980.
Bell, Roseann C.
"Absence of the African Women Writer." CLA Journal. Volume 21 June, 1978. pp. 491-498.
Beneria, Lourdes
Women and Development: The Sexual Division of Labor in Rural Societies: A Study. New York: Praeger Publishers. Praeger Special Studies. 1982. 257p.
Bennett, T.W. and Peart. Nicola S.
"The Dualism of Marriage Laws in Africa." ACTA Juridica. 1983. pp. 145-169.
Berger, Iris
"Rebels or Status Seekers? Women as Spirit Mediums in

East Africa." (In) Hafkin, N.J. and Bay, Edna (eds.). Women in Africa: Studies in Social and Economic Change. Stanford, California: Stanford University Press. 1976. pp. 157-181.

Berger, Iris
"Women, Religion and Social Change: East and Central African Perspectives." Paper Presented at the Conference on Women and Development. Wellesley, Massachusetts: Wellesley College. Wellesley College Center for Research on Women. June 2-6, 1976. 25p.

Bingham, Marjorie W. and Gross, Susan H.
Women in Africa of the Sub-Sahara. Hudson, Wisconsin: Gem Publishers. Volume One: Ancient Times to the Twentieth Century. Volume Two: The Twentieth Century. 1982. 260p.

Birdsall, Nancy and McGreevey, William P.
"The Second Sex in the Third World: Is Female Poverty a Development Issue?" Paper Prepared for the International Center for Research on Women Policy Roundtable. Washington, D.C. June 21, 1978.

Bisilliat, Jeanne
"The Feminine Sphere in the Institutions of Songhay-Zarma." (In) Oppong, Christine (ed.). Female and Male in West Africa. London: George Allen and Unwin. 1983. pp. 99-106.

Bongaarts, John and Frank, Odile and Lesthaeghe, Ron J.
"The Proximate Determinants of Fertility in Sub-Saharan Africa." Population and Developement Review. Volume 10 #3 September, 1984. pp. 511-538+.

Bongaarts, John
"The Impact on Fertility of Traditional and Changing Child-Spacing Practices." (In) Page, Hilary J. and Lesthaeghe, Ron (eds.). Child-Spacing in Tropical Africa. New York: Academic Press. 1981. pp. 111-129.

Boserup, Ester
"Economic and Demographic Interrelationships in Sub-Saharan Africa." Population and Development Review. Volume 11 #3 September, 1985. pp. 383-397+.

Boserup, Ester (ed.)
Traditional Division of Work Between the Sexes, A Source of Inequality: Research Symposium on Women and Decision Making: A Social Policy Priority. Geneva: International Institute for Labour Studies. Research Series #21. 1976. 32p.

Boulding, Elise
"Productivity and Poverty of Third World Women: Problems in Measurement." (In) Buvinic, Mayra and Lycette, Margaret C. and McGreevey, William P. (eds.). Women and Poverty in the Third World. Baltimore, Maryland: Johns Hopkins University. 1983.

Bourguignon, Erika
A World of Women: Anthropological Studies of Women in the Societies of the World. New York: Praeger Publishers. Praeger Special Studies. 1980. 364p.

Bowman, Mary J. and Anderson, C. Arnold
"The Participation of Women in Education in the Third World." Comparative Education Review. Volume 24 #2 Pt. 2 June, 1980. pp. S13-S32.
Bowman, Mary J. and Anderson, C. Arnold
"The Participation of Women in Education in the Third World." (In) Kelly, Gail P. and Elliott, Carolyn M. (eds.). Women's Education in the Third World. Albany, New York: State University of New York Press. 1982. pp. 11-30.
Bowman, Mary J. and Anderson, C. Arnold
The Participation of Women in Education in the Third World. New York: Ford Foundation. 1978. 278p.
Brabin, Loretta
"Polygyny: An Indicator of Nutritional Stress in African Agricultural Societies." Africa. Volume 54 #1 1984. pp. 31-45.
Brandel, Syrier M.
"The Role of Women in African Independent Churches (Manyanos)." Missionalia. Volume 12 #1 April, 1984. pp. 13-18.
Broch-Due, Vigdis and Garfield, Patti
"Women and Pastoral Development: Some Research Priorities for the Social Sciences." (In) Galaty, John G. and Aronson, Dan and Salzman, Philip C. (eds.). The Future of Pastoral Peoples. Ottawa, Canada: International Development Research Centre. 1981. pp. 251-257.
Brown, Judith E.
"Polygyny and Family Planning in Sub-Saharan Africa." Studies in Family Planning. Volume 12 #8-9 August-September, 1981. pp. 322-326.
Bruner, Charlotte H.
"Been-To or Has-Been: A Dilemma for Today's African Women." Paper Presented at the African Literature Association Conference. 1976. 15p.
Bruner, Charoltte H.
"Been-To or Has-Been: A Dilemma for Today's African Women." Ba Shiru. Volume 8 #2 1977. pp. 23-31.
Bryant, Coralie
"Women Migrants, Urbanization and Social Change: An African Case." Paper Presented at the American Political Science Association Annual Meeting. Washington, D.C. September, 1977.
Bujra, Janet M.
"Production, Property, Prostitution--Sexual Politics in Atu." Cahiers d'Etudes Africaines. Volume 17 #1 1977. pp. 13-40.
Bujra, Janet M.
"Female Solidarity and the Sexual Division of Labour." (In) Caplan, P. and Bujra, J. (eds.). Women United, Women Divided: Cross-Cultural Perspectives on Female Solidarity. London: Tavistock. 1978. pp. 13-45.
Bujra, Janet M.
"Prostitution, Class and the State." (In) Sumner, Colin (ed.). Crime, Justice, and Underdevelopment. London:

Heineman. Cambridge Studies in Criminology. #46. 1982. pp. 145-161.
Bukh, Jette
"Women in Food Production, Food Handling and Nutrition." Paper Presented to the Association of African Women for Research and Development (AAWORD) Workshop. Dakar, Senegal: AAWORD. December, 1977.
Bulatao, R.A.
"Transitions in the Value of Children and the Fertility Transition." Paper Presented at the Seminar on Determinants of Fertility Trends: Major Themes and New Directions for Research. International Union for the Scientific Study of Population. Bad Homburg, Germany. 1980.
Burton Claire
"Woman Marriage in Africa: A Critical Study For Sex-Role Theory?" Australian and New Zealand Journal of Sociology. Volume 15 #2 July, 1979. pp. 65-71.
Burton, M. and Kirk, L.
"Sex Differences in Maasai Cognition of Personality and Social Identity." American Anthropologist. Volume 81 #4 December, 1979. pp. 841-901.
Buvinic, Mayra and Youssef, Nadia H. and Schumacher, Ilsa
Women-Headed Households: The Ignored Factor in Development Planning. Washington D.C.: U.S. Department of State. U.S. Agency for International Development. International Center for Research on Women. Women in Development Office. March, 1978. 113p.
Buvinic, Mayra and Lycette, Margaret A. and McGreevey, William P.
Women and Poverty in the Third World. Baltimore, Maryland: Johns Hopkins University. Johns Hopkins Studies in Development. 1983. 329p.
Cairo Demographic Center (CDC)
Determinants of Fertility in Some African And Asian Countries. Cairo, Egypt: CDC. CDC Research Monograph Series #10. 1982. 698p.
Cairo Demographic Centre (CDC)
Family and Marriage in Some African and Asian Countries. Cairo, Egypt: CDC. CDC Research Monograph Series #6. 1976.
Caldwell, John C. and Caldwell, Pat
"The Achieved Small Family: Early Fertility Transition in an African City." Studies in Family Planning. Volume 9 #1 January, 1978. pp. 2-18.
Caldwell, John C.
"Towards a Restatement of Demographic Transition Theory: An Investigation of Conditions Before and at the Onset of Fertility Declining Employing Primarily African Experience and Data." Population and Development Review. Volume 2 #3 1976. pp. 321-366.
Caldwell, John C. and Caldwell, Pat
Cultural Forces Tending to Sustain High Fertility in Tropical Africa. Canberra, Australia: Australian National University. 1984.

Caldwell, John C. and Caldwell, Pat
"Demographic and Contraceptive Innovators: A Study of Transitional African Society." Journal of Biosocial Science. Volume 8 #4 October, 1976. pp. 347-366.

Caldwell, John C.
"Measuring Wealth Flows and the Rationality of Fertility: Thoughts and Plans Based in the First Place on African Work." (In) Ruzicka, Lado T. (ed.). The Economic and Social Supports for High Fertility: Proceedings of the Conference. Canberra, Australia: Australian National University. Development Studies Center. November 16-18, 1977. pp. 439-454.

Caldwell, Pat
"Issues of Marriage and Marital Change: Tropical Africa and the Middle East." (In) Huzayyin, S.A. and Acsadi, G.T. (eds.). Family and Marriage in Some African and Asiatic Countries. Cairo, Egypt: Cairo Demographic Centre. Research Monograph Series #6. 1976. pp. 325-335.

Caldwell, Pat and Caldwell, John C.
"The Function of Child-Spacing in Traditional Societies and the Direction of Change." (In) Page, Hilary J. and Lesthaeghe, Ron (eds.). Child-Spacing in Tropical Africa: Traditions and Change. New York: Academic Press. 1981. pp. 73-92.

Callear, D.
Women and Coarse Grain Production in Africa. Expert Consultation on Women in Food Production. Rome: United Nations Food and Agriculture Organization. December 7, 1983. 13p.

Campbell, Penelope
"Presbyterian West African Missions: Women as Converts and Agents of Social Change." Journal of Presbyterian History. Volume 56 #2 Summer, 1978. pp. 121-132.

Canady, Hortense
"Women in Development: The African Diaspora." Africa Report. Volume 30 #2 March-April, 1985. pp. 75.

Cantrelle, Pierre and Ferry, Benoit and Mondot, J.
"Relationships Between Fertility and Mortality in Tropical Africa." (In) Preston, Samuel H. (ed.). The Effects of Infant and Child Mortality on Fertility. New York: Academic Press. 1978. pp. 181-205.

Caplan, Patricia and Bujra, Janet M. (eds.)
Women United Women Divided: Comparative Studies of Ten Contemporary Cultures. Bloomington, Indiana: Indiana University Press. 1979. 288p.

Caplan, Patricia
"Cognatic Descent, Islamic Law, and Women's Property on the East African Coast." (In) Hirschon, Renbee (ed.). Women and Property--Women as Property. New York: St. Martin's Press. 1983.

Carroll, Theodora F.
Women, Religion and Development in the Third World. New York: Praeger Publishers. 1983. 292p.

Carter, Ann L.
"African Women and Career Counseling: A Model." Journal of Non-White Concerns in Personnel and Guidance. Volume 9 #1 October, 1980. pp. 23-33.
Casajus, Dominique
"The Wedding Ritual Among the Kel Ferwan Tuaregs." Journal of the Anthropological Society of Oxford. Volume 14 #2 1983. pp. 227-257.
Case, Frederick
"Workers Movements: Revolution and Women's Consciousness in God's Bits of Wood." Canadian Journal of African Studies. Volume 15 #2 1981. pp. 272-292.
Casteinuovo, Shirley
"The Impact of Urbanization on the Family in Light of Recent Changes in African Family Law." Paper Presented at the Annual Meeting of the African Studies Association. Paper #11. Houston, Texas. 1977.
Castillo, Gelia T.
The Changing Role of Women in Rural Societies: A Summary of Trends and Issues. New York: Agricultural Development Council Inc. RTN Seminar Reports 12. February, 1977. 11p.
Catchpole, David R.
"The Fearful Silence of the Women at the Tomb: A Study in Markan Theology." Journal of Theology for Southern Africa. #18 March, 1977. pp. 3-10.
Chamie, Joseph and Weller, Robert H.
Levels, Trends and Differentials in Nuptiality in the Middle East and North Africa. Tallahassee, Florida: Florida State University. Center for the Study of Population. College of Social Sciences. Working Paper #83-02. 1983. 12p.
Chamie, Joseph and Weller, Robert H.
"Levels, Trends and Differentials in Nuptiality in the Middle East and North Africa." Genus. Volume 39 #1-4 January-December, 1983. pp. 213-231.
Chamie, Joseph
Polygamy Among Arabs. New York: United Nations. U.N. Population Division. 1985.
Chaney, Elsa M. and Simmons, Emmy and Staudt, Kathleen
Women in Development. Washington, D.C.: U.S. Department of State. U.S. Agency for International Development. Background Papers for the U.S. Delegation Attending the World Conference on Agrarian Reform and Rural Development. July, 1979. 40p.
Chaney, Elsa M.
Women in International Migration: Issues in Development Planning. Washington, D.C.: U.S. Department of State. U.S. Agency for International Development. Office of Women in Development. June, 1980.
Chaney, Elsa M. and Lewis, Martha W.
Women, Migration and the Decline of Smallholder Agriculture. Washington, D.C.: U.S. Department of State. U.S. Agency for International Development. Office of Women in Development. October, 1980.

Chi, C. and Miller, E.R. and Fortney, J.A. and Bernard, Roger P.
"A Study of Abortion in Countries Where Abortions are Legally Restricted." Journal of Reproductive Medicine. Volume 18 #1 January, 1977. pp. 15-26.
Chojnacka, Helena
"Polygyny and the Rate of Population Growth." Human Resources Research Bulletin. #78/05 1978. 34p.
Chojnacka, Helena
"Polygyny and the Rate of Population Growth." Population Studies. Volume 34 #1 March, 1980. pp. 91-107.
Clark, Garcia
Fighting the African Food Crisis: Women Food Farmers and Food Workers. New York: United Nations Development Fund for Women. 1985.
Cleveland, David
"Fertility and the Value of Children in Subsistence Agriculture: Savanna West Africa." Paper Presented at the Annual Meeting of the American Anthropological Association. Cincinnati, Ohio. November, 1979.
Clignet, Remi and Sween, Joyce A.
"Ethnicity and Fertility: Implications for Population Programs in Africa." Africa. Volume 48 #1 1978. pp. 47-65.
Cloud, Kathleen
"Sex Roles in Food Production and Distribution Systems in the Sahel." (In) Cowen, Ann B. (ed.). Proceedings and Papers of the International Conference on Women and Food: Consortium for International Development. Tucson, Arizona: University of Arizona. 1978. pp. 62-89.
Cloud, Kathleen
Sex Roles in Food Production and Food Distribution Systems in the Sahel. Washington, D.C.: U.S. Department of State. U.S. Agency for International Development. Office of Women in Development. 1977. 20p.
Cook, Rebecca J.
"A Law on Family Welfare and Development in Africa." (In) International Planned Parenthood Federation (IPPF). Proceedings of the IPPF Africa Regional Conference. London: IPPF. 1977. pp. 241-246.
Cook, Rebecca J. and Dickens, Bernard N.
"Abortion Law in African Commonwealth Countries." Journal of African Law. Volume 25 #2 1981. pp. 60-79.
Cosminsky, Sheila
"The Role and Training of Traditional Midwives: Policy Implications for Maternal and Child Health Care." Paper Presented at the Annual Meeting of the African Studies Association. Paper #17. Houston, Texas. 1977. 25p.
Cutrufelli, Maria R.
Women of Africa: Roots of Oppression. Totowa, New Jersey: Zed Press. 1983. 186p.
D'onofrio-Flores, Pamela M. and Pfafflin, Sheila M. (eds.)
Scientific-Technological Change and the Role of Women in Development. Boulder, Colorado: Westview Press.

Published for the United Nations Institute for Training and Research. 1982. 206p.
Dahlberg, Frances (ed.)
Woman the Gatherer. New Haven, Connecticut: Yale University Press. 1981. 250p.
Davis, W.T.
"Rome and the Ordination of Women." West African Religion. Volume 17 #2 1978. pp. 3-8.
Dawit, T.
"Mass Media and Rural Women in Africa." Assignment Children. Volume 38 #2 April-June, 1977. pp. 119-120.
De Graft-John, K.E.
"Issues in Family Welfare and Development in Africa." (In) International Planned Parenthood Federation (IPPF). Proceedings of the IPPF Africa Regional Conference. London: IPPF. 1977. pp. 33-45.
De Sardan, Jean-Pierre O.
"The Songhay-Zarma Female Slave: Relations of Production and Ideological Status." (In) Robertson, Claire C. and Klein, Martin A. (eds.). Women and Slavery in Africa. Madison, Wisconsin: University of Wisconsin Press. 1983. pp. 130-143.
Deheusch, L.
"The Good Usage of Wives and Cattle-Transformation of Marriage in Southern Africa." L'Homme. Volume 23 #4 1983.
Dhamija, Jasleen
"Income-Generating Activities for Rural Women in Africa: Some Successes and Failures." (In) International Labour Organization (ILO). Rural Development and Women in Africa. Geneva: ILO. 1984. pp. 75-78.
Dhamija, Jasleen
"Technology as a Target to the Development of Women's Skills in Africa." Ceres. # 84 November, 1981. pp. 24-27.
Di Domenico, Catherine M. and Asuni, Judy and Scott, Jacqueline
"Family Welfare and Development in Africa." (In) International Planned Parenthood Federation (IPPF). Proceedings of the IPPF Africa Regional Conference, University of Ibadan. London: IPPF. 1976. pp. 283-284.
Dirasse, Laketch
The Critical Needs of African Women and Appropriate Strategies in the Framework of the Gisenyi and Lusaka MULPOCS. Addis Ababa, Ethiopia: United Nations Economic Commission for Africa. African Training and Research Centre for Women. 1981. 35p.
Dixon, Ruth B.
"Women in Agriculture: Counting the Labor Force in Developing Countries." Population and Development Review. Volume 8 #3 September, 1982. pp. 539-566.
Dixon, Ruth B.
Assessing the Impact of Development Projects on Women. Washington, D.C.: U.S. Department of State. U.S. Agency for International Development. Office of Women in

Development. AID Program Evaluation Discussion Paper #8. 1980. 105p.

Dixon-Mueller, Ruth
Women's Work in the Third World Agriculture: Concepts and Indicators. Geneva: ILO. Women, Work and Development Series. Volume 9. 1985. 151p.

Donhoff, Christoph G.
"The Women of Africa." Africa Insight (Pretoria). Volume 12 #1 1982. pp. 25-26.

Due, Jean M. and Summary, Rebecca
"Constraints to Women and Development in Africa." Journal of Modern African Studies. Volume 20 #1 March, 1982. pp. 155-166.

Due, Jean M. and Summary, Rebecca
"Constraints to Women and Development in Africa." Paper Presented at the Annual Meeting of the African Studies Association. Paper #35. Los Angeles, California. 1979. 23p.

Due, Jean M. and Summary, Rebecca
Constraints to Women and Development in Africa. Urbana, Illinois: University of Illinois-Urbana-Champaign. Department of Agricultural Economics. Staff Paper Series E. Agricultural Economics 79-E-83. May, 1979. 27p.

Dulansey, Maryanne L.
Can Technology Help Women Feed Their Families? Post Harvest Storage, Processing and Cooking: Some Observations. Washington, D.C.: Consultants in Development. 1979. 9p.

Dulansey, Maryanne L.
Women in Development Program Concerns in Francophone Sahel: Report of a Workshop. Washington, D.C.: U.S. Department of State. U.S. Agency for International Development. Bobo-Dioulasso, Upper Volta. June 5-7, 1979. 11p.

Dunbar, Roberta
"Legislative Reform and Muslim Family Law: Effects Upon Women's Rights in Africa South of the Sahara." Paper Presented at the Annual Meeting of the African Studies Association. Paper #25. Philadelphia, Pennsylvania. October 15-18, 1980.

Duza, M. Badrud and Sivamurthy, M.
"Household Structure in Selected Urban Areas of Four Arab and African Cities." (In) Huzayyin, S.A. and Acsadi, G.T. (eds.). Family and Marriage in Some African and Asiatic Countries. Cairo, Egypt: Cairo Demographic Centre. Research Monograph Series #6. 1976. pp. 267-284.

Duza, M. Badrud and Seetharam, K.S. and Sivamurthy, M.
"Patterns of Family Cycles in Selected Areas of Four Arab and African Cities: Some Demographic Implications." (In) Huzayyin, S.A. and Acsadi, G.T. (eds.). Family and Marriage in Some African and Asiatic Countries. Cairo, Egypt: Cairo Demographic Centre. CDC Research Monograph Series #6. 1976. pp. 245-265.

Dwyer, Daisy H.
"Outside the Courts: Extra-Legal Strategies for the Subordination of Women." (In) Hay, Margaret J. and Wright, Marcia (eds.). African Women and the Law: Historical Perspectives. Boston: Boston University. African Studies Center. Boston University Papers on Africa. Volume Seven. 1982. pp. 90-109.

Edwards, Felicity
"The Doctrine of God and the Feminine Principle." Journal of Theology for Southern Africa. #37 December, 1981. pp. 23-37.

Eide, Wenche B. and Skjonsberg, Else and Pala, Achola O. and Bathily, Abjoulaye
"Women in Food Production, Food Handling and Nutrition With Special Emphasis on Africa." PAG Bulletin. Volume 7 #3/4 Sept.-Dec., 1977. pp. 40-49.

Eide, Wenche B. and Steady, Filomina C.
"Individual and Social Energy Flows: Bridging Nutritional and Anthropological Thinking About Women's Work in Rural Africa: Some Theoretical Considerations." (In) Jerome, Norge W. and Kandel, Randy F. and Pelto, Gretel H. (eds.). Nutritional Anthropology: Contemporary Approach to Diet and Culture. New York: Redgrave Publishing. 1980. pp. 61-84.

Eide, Wenche B. and Skjonsberg, Else and Bathily, Abjoulaye and Pala, Achola O. and Krystall, Abigail and Millwood, D.
Women in Food Production, Food Handling and Nutrition With Special Emphasis on Africa. Final Report. New York: United Nations. Protein-Calorie Advisory Group of the U.N. System. FAO Food and Nutrition Paper #8. June, 1977. 224p.

Ekechi, Felix K.
"African Polygamy and Western Christian Ethnocentrism." Journal of African Studies. Volume 3 #3 August, 1976. pp. 329-349.

El Bushra, Judy and Bekele, Abebech and Hammour, Fawzia
"Socio-Economic Development and Women Changing Status." Paper Presented to the Conference on Women and the Environment. Khartoum, Sudan: University of Khartoum. Institute of Environmental Studies. April 4-7, 1981.

El Sadaawi, Nawal
The Hidden Face of Eve: Women in the Arab World. Boston: Beacon Press. 1982. 212p.

El-Badry, M.A.
"Determinants of Fertility in African and Asian Countries: An Introductory Overview." (In) Cairo Demographic Centre (CDC). Determinants of Fertility in Some African and Asian Countries." Cairo, Egypt: CDC. CDC Monograph Series #10. 1982. pp. 3-11.

El-Khorazaty, Mohamed Nabil E.
"Regional Differences in Attitudes Toward Family Norms and Planning, 1979/80." Population Studies. Volume 12 #72 January-March, 1985. pp. 3-28.

Elwert, Georg
"Conflicts Inside and Outside the Household: A West

African Case Study." (In) Smith, Joan (ed.). Households and the World Economy. Beverly Hills, California: Sage. 1984. pp. 272-296.
Ember, C.R.
"Relative Decline in Women's Contribution to Agriculture With Intensification." American Anthropologist. Volume 85 #2 June, 1983. pp. 285-304.
Emecheta, Buchi
"Building on Tradition: Can the Past Provide Direction for the Future." Paper Presented at the 'Women and Work Symposium #6'. Urbana, Illinois: University of Illinois. 1979.
Emecheta, Buchi
"Building on Tradition: Can the Past Provide for the Future?" (In) University of Illinois (eds.). Women and Work in Africa, April 29-May 1, 1979, University of Illinois, Urbana-Champaign: A Project of the African Studies Association. Urbana, Illinois: University of Illinois. 1979.
Ensor, Linda and Cooper, Carole
The African Women's Handbook on the Law. Johannesburg: South African Institute of Race Relations. 1980. 41p.
Epskamp, C.
Inequality in Female Access to Education in Developing Countries: A Bibliography. Hague, Netherlands: Centre for the Study of Education in Developing Countries. 1979. 42p.
Epstein, Trude S.
Place of Social Anthropology in a Multidisciplinary Approach to the Study of Women's Roles and Status in Less Developed Countries. Geneva: International Labour Organization. 1978.
Esposito, John L.
Women in Muslim Family Law. Syracuse, New York: Syracuse University Press. Contemporary Issues in the Middle East Series. 1982. 172p.
Faulkner, Constance
"Women's Studies in the Muslim Middle East." Journal of Ethnic Studies. Volume 8 #3 Fall, 1980. pp. 67-76.
Fernea, Elizabeth W.
Women and the Family in the Middle East: New Voices of Change. Austin, Texas: University of Texas Press. 1984. 368p.
Fields, Karen E.
"Political Contingencies of Witchcraft in Colonial Central Africa." Canadian Journal of African Studies. Volume 16 #3 1982. pp. 567-593.
Fikry, M.
Traditional Maternal and Child Health Care and Related Problems in the Sahel: A Bibliographic Study. Washington, D.C.: U.S. Department of State. U.S. Agency for International Development. Sahel Development Project. 1977. 123p.
Fortes, Meyer
"Parenthood, Marriage and Fertility in West Africa."

Journal of Development Studies. Volume 14 #4 July, 1978. pp. 121-149.
Fortes, Meyer
"Family, Marriage and Fertility in West Africa." (In) Oppong, C. and Adaba, G. and Bekombo-Priso, M. and Mogey, J. (eds.). Marriage, Fertility and Parenthood in West Africa. Canberra, Australia: Australian National University Press. 1978. pp. 17-54.
Fortmann, Louise P.
Tillers of the Soil and Keepers of the Hearth: A Bibliographic Guide to Women and Rural Development. Ithaca, New York: Cornell University. Center for International Studies. Rural Development Committee. Bibliography Series #2. 1979. 53p.
Fortmann, Louise P.
"The Plight of the Invisible Farmer: The Effect of National Agricultural Policy on Women in Africa." (In) Dauber, Roslyn and Cain, Melinda L. Women and Technological Change in Developing Countries. Boulder, Colorado: Westview Press. 1981. pp. 205-214.
Fraker, Anne and Harrell-Bond, Barbara
"Feminine Influence." West Africa. December 17, 1979. pp. 2182-2186.
Frank, Odile
The Demand for Fertility Control in Sub-Saharan Africa. New York: Population Council. Center for Policy Studies. Working Paper #117. November, 1985. 50p.
Frank, Odile
Child Fostering in Sub-Saharan Africa. New York: Population Council. Center for Policy Studies. 1984.
Fraser, Arvonne
Women in Development. Washington, D.C.: U.S. Department of State. U.S. Agency for International Development. Office of Women in Development. 1977. 12p.
Gadalla, Saad M.
Population Policy and Family Planning Communication Strategies in the Arab States Region. Paris: UNESCO. Volume One: Summaries of Pertinent Literature and Research Studies. 1978.
Galaty, J.G. and Aronson, D. and Salzman, P.C. and Chouinard, A.
The Future of Pastoral Peoples. Paper Presented at the Conference on the Future of Pastoral Peoples. Ottawa, Canada: International Development Research Center. Nairobi, Kenya. August 4-8, 1981. 396p.
Gebre-Selassie, Alasebu
"The Situation of Women in Africa: A Review." Nairobi: UNICEF. Eastern Africa Regional Office. 1979. 65p.
Geletkanycz, Christine and Egan, Susan
Literature Review: The Practice of Female Circumcision. Washington, D.C.: U.S. Department of Health, Education and Welfare. Office of International Health. Mimeo. 1979.
Germain, Adrienne
"Poor Rural Women: A Policy Perspective." Journal of

International Affairs. Volume 3 #2 Fall-Winter, 1976. 20p.

Germain. Adrienne
"Research on Women in Agricultural Production in Eastern and Southern Africa." Paper Presented at a Workshop on Women in Agricultural Production in Eastern and Southern Africa. Nairobi, Kenya. April 9-11, 1980.

Ghulam, L.J.
"Early Teenage Childbirth, Consequences of This for Child and Mother." Paper Presented at the Seminar on Traditional Practices Affecting the Health of Women and Children. World Conference of the United Nations Decade for Women. Copenhagen, Denmark. July 14-30, 1980.

Gilligan, John J.
"Importance of Third World Women." Rivista di Studi Politici Internazionali. Volume 45 #3 July-September, 1978.

Ginat, Joseph (ed.)
Women in Muslim Rural Society: Status and Role in Family Community. New Brunswick, New Jersey: Transition Books. 1981. 268p.

Goody, Esther N.
"Some Theoretical and Empirical Aspects of Parenthood in West Africa." (In) Oppong, C. and Adaba, G. and Bekombo-Priso, M. and Mogey, J. (eds.). Marriage, Fertility and Parenthood in West Africa. Canberra, Australia: Australian National University. Department of Demography. Volume One. 1978. pp. 227-272.

Goody, Esther N.
"Parental Strategies: Calculation or Sentiment: Fostering Practices Among West Africans." (In) Medick, Hans and Sabean, David W. (eds.). Interest and Emotion: Essays on the Study of Family and Kinship. Cambridge, New York: Cambridge University Press. 1984. pp. 266-277.

Goody, Jack
Production and Reproduction: A Comparative Study of the Domestic Domain. Cambridge, New York: Cambridge University Press. Cambridge Studies in Social Anthropology #17. 1976. 157p.

Grandmaison, C. LeCour
"Economic Contracts Between Married People in the West African Area." L'Homme. Volume 19 #3/4 July-December, 1979. pp. 159-170.

Gray, R.H.
"Birth Intervals, Postpartum Sexual Abstinence and Child Health." (In) Page, Hilary J. and Lesthaeghe, Ron (eds.). Child-Spacing in Tropical Africa: Traditions and Change. New York: Academic Press. 1981. pp. 93-109.

Green, Ronald M.
"Religion and Mortality in the African Traditional Setting." Journal of Religion in Africa. Volume 14 #1 1983. pp. 1-23.

Guenther, Mathias G.
"Bushman Hunters as Farm Labourers." Canadian Journal of African Studies. Volume 11 #2 1977.

Gugler, Josef
"The Second Sex in Town." (In) Steady, Filomina C. (ed.). The Black Woman Cross-Culturally. Cambridge, Massachusetts: Schenkman Publishing. 1981. pp. 169-184.
Guyer, Jane I.
The Raw, the Cooked and the Half-Baked: A Note on the Division of Labor by Sex. Brookline, Massachusetts: Boston University. African Studies Center. Working Papers in African Studies #48. 1981. 12p.
Guyer, Jane I.
Women's Work in the Food Economy of the Cocoa Belt: A Comparison. Brookline, Massachusetts: Boston University. African Studies Center. Working Paper #7. 1978. 34p.
Guyer, Jane I.
"Household and Community in African Studies." African Studies Review. Volume 24 #213 June-September, 1981. pp. 87-137.
Guyot, Jean
Migrant Women Speak: Interviews. London: Search Press Ltd. for the Churches Committee on Migrant Workers. 1978. 164p.
Gyepi-Garbrah, Benjamin and Nichols, Douglas J. and Kpedekpo, Gottlieb M.
Adolescent Fertility in Sub-Saharan Africa: An Overview. Boston: Pathfinder Fund. 1985. 51p.
Hadri, Gasim
"Opinions About Female Circumcision." Paper Presented at the Seminar on Traditional Practices Affecting the Health of Women and Children. World Conference of the United Nations Decade for Women. Copenhagen, Denmark. July 14-30, 1980.
Hafkin, Nancy J. and Bay, Edna G. (eds.)
Women in Africa: Studies in Social and Economic Change. Stanford, California: Stanford University Press. 1976. 306p.
Halperin, Rhoda
Ecology and Mode of Production: Seasonal Variation and the Division of Labor by Sex Among Hunter-Gatherers. Cincinnati, Ohio: University of Cincinnati. Department of Anthropology. 1979.
Hanna, J.L.
"Dance and the Women's War." Dance Research Journal. Volume 14 #1/2 1981. pp. 25-28.
Hanson, F. and Miller, F.
"The Wife's Brother's Wife and the Marriage Contract: A Structural Analysis." Bijdragen Tot de Taal-, Land-en Volkenkunde. Volume 133 #1 1977. pp. 11-22.
Haq, Khadija (ed.)
Equality of Opportunity Within and Among Nations. New York: Praeger Publishers. Praeger Special Studies in International Economics and Development. 1977. 223p.
Hawthorn, Geoffrey (ed.)
Population and Development: High and Low Fertility in Poorer Countries. London: Frank Cass. 1978. 210p.

Hay, Margaret J. and Stichter, Sharon B. (eds.)
African Women South of the Sahara. New York: Longman. 1984.

Hay, Margaret J. and Wright, Marcia (eds.)
African Women and the Law: Historical Perspectives. Boston, Masachusetts: Boston University. African Studies Center. Boston University Papers on Africa. Volume 7. 1982. 173p.

Hayani, Ibrahim
"The Changing Role of Arab Women." Convergence. Volume 13 #1 1980. pp. 136-142.

Henin, Roushdi A.
"Fertility, Infertility and Sub-Fertility in Eastern Africa." (In) International Union for the Scientic Study of Population (IUSSP). International Population Conference: Solicited Papers. Liege, Netherland: IUSSP. Volume Three. 1981. pp. 667-697.

Henn, Jeanne K.
"Feeding the Cities and Feeding the Peasants: What Role for Africa's Women Farmers." World Development. Volume 11 #12 1983.

Henn, Jeanne K.
"Women in the Rural Economy: Past, Present and Future." (In) Hay, Margaret J. and Stichter, Sharon (eds.). African Women South of the Sahara. New York: Longman. 1984. pp. 1-18.

High-Wasikhongo, Freda
Traditional African Art: A Female Focus. Madison, Wisconsin: University of Wisconsin-Madison. Elvehjem Museum of Art. 1981.

Hinckley, Priscilla
"The Sowo Mask: Symbol of Sisterhood." Boston: Boston University. African Studies Center. Working Papers in African Studies #40. 1980.

Hoch-Smith, Judith and Spring, Anita (eds.)
Women in Ritual and Symbolic Roles. New York: Plenum Press. 1978. 289p.

Hosken, Fran P.
"A Crucial New Direction for International Family Planning." Humanist. Volume 44 #1 January-February, 1984.

Hosken, Fran P.
"Women and Health: Genital And Sexual Mutilation of Females." International Journal of Women's Studies. Volume 3 #3 May-June, 1980. pp. 300-316.

Hosken, Fran P.
"The Violence of Power: The Genital Mutilation of Females." Heresies. Volume 6 #2 Summer, 1978. pp. 28-36.

Hosken, Fran P.
"Female Circumcision in Africa." Victimology. Volume 2 #3/4 1977. pp. 487-498.

Hosken, Fran P.
"Genital Mutilation of Women in Africa." Munger Africana Library Notes. #36 October, 1976. 21p.

Hosken, Fran P.
"Towards an Epidemiology of Genital Mutilation of Females in Africa." Paper Presented at the Annual Meeting of the African Studies Association. Paper #43. Baltimore, Maryland. 1978. 20p.

Hosken, Fran P.
The Hosken Report: Genital and Sexual Mutilation of Females. Lexington, Massachusetts: Women's International Network News. 1982. 327p.

Hosken, Fran P.
Female Sexual Mutilations: The Facts and Proposals for Action. Lexington, Massachusetts: Women's International Network News. 1980. 102p.

Hosken, Fran P.
"Female Genital Mutilation in the World Today: A Global Review." International Journal of Health Services. Volume 11 #3 1981. pp. 415-430.

Hosken, Fran P.
"Female Circumcision and Fertility in Africa." Women and Health. Volume 1 #6 Nov.-Dec., 1976. pp. 3-11.

Hosken, Fran P.
"The Epidemiology of Female Genital Mutilation." Tropical Doctor. July, 1978. pp. 150-156.

Hosken, Fran P.
"Women and Health in East and West Africa: Family Planning and Female Cicumcision." Paper Presented at the Seminar on Traditional Practices Affecting the Health of Women and Children. World Conference of the United Nations Decade for Women. New York: United Nations. Copenhagen, Denmark. July 14-30, 1980.

Hosken, Fran P.
"Women and Health in East and West Africa: Family Planning and Female Circumcision." Paper Presented at the Seminar on Traditional Practices Affecting the Health of Women and Children: Female Circumcision, Childhood Marriage, Nutritional Taboos, etc. Alexandria, Egypt: World Health Organization. Eastern Mediterranean Regional Office. Khartoum, Sudan. February 10-15, 1979.

Hosken, Fran P.
"Female Circumcision in the World of Today: A Global Review." Paper Presented at the Seminar on Traditional Practices Affecting the Health of Women and Children. World Conference of the United Nations Decade for Women. New York: United Nations. Copenhagen, Denmark. July 14-30, 1980.

Hosken, Fran P.
"Female Circumcision in the World of Today: A Global View." Paper Presented at the Seminar on Traditional Practices Affecting the Health of Women and Children: Female Circumcision, Childhood Marriage, Nutritional Taboos, etc. Alexandria, Egypt: World Health Organization. Eastern Mediterranean Regional Office. Khartoum, Sudan. February 10-15, 1979.

Howard, R.
"Women's Rights in English-Speaking Sub-Saharan Africa."

(In) Welch, Claude E. and Meltzer, Ronald I. (eds.). Human Rights and Development in Africa. Albany, New York: State University of New York Press. 1984.

Howard, Rhoda E.
"Women and the Crisis in Commonwealth Africa." International Political Science Review. Volume 6 #3 1985. pp. 287-296.

Huelsman, Ben R.
"An Anthropological View of Clitoral and Other Female Genital Mutilations." (In) Lowery, T.P. and Lowery, T.S. (eds.). The Clitoris. St. Louis, Missouri: Warren H. Green. 1976. pp. 111-161.

Hussain, Freda (ed.)
Muslim Women. New York: St. Martin's Press. 1983. 240p.

Huston, Perdita
"To Be Born a Woman is a Sin." Populi. Volume 4 #3 1977. pp. 27-36.

Huzayyin, S.A. and Acsadi, George T. (eds.)
Family and Marriage in Some African and Asiatic Countries. Cairo, Egypt: Cairo Demographic Center. CDC Research Monograph Series #6. 1976. 570p.

Huzayyin, S.A.
"Marriage and Remarriage in Islam." (In) Dupaquier, J. and Helin, E. and Laslett, P. and Livi-Bacci, M. (eds.). Marriage and Remarriage in Populations of the Past. New York: Academic Press. Population and Social Structure: Advances in Historical Demography Series. 1981. pp. 95-109.

Igbinovia, Patrick E.
"Prostitution in Black Africa." International Journal of Women's Studies. Volume 7 #5 Nov.-Dec., 1984. pp. 430-449.

Imam, Ayesha M.
"The Presentation of African Women Through History." Paper Presented at the Meeting of Experts on Theoretical Frameworks and Methodological Approaches to Studies on the Role of Women in History as Actors in Economic, Social, Political and Ideological Processes. Paris: United Nations Educational, Scientific and Cultural Organization. 1984. 28p.

International Center for Research on Women
Women in Migration: A Third World Focus. Washington, D.C.: U.S. Department of State. U.S. Agency for International Development. Office of Women in Development. 1979.

International Center for Research on Women
The Productivity of Women in Developing Countries: Measurement Issues and Recommendtions. Washington, D.C.: U.S. Department of State. U.S. Agency for International Development. Office on Women in Development. 1980. 46p.

International Development Research Centre (IDRC)
Rural Water Supply in Developing Countries: Proccedings

of a Workshop on Training. Ottawa, Canada: IDRC. Zomba, Malawi. August 5-12, 1981. 144p.

International Development Research Centre (IDRC)
Nutritional Status of the Rural Population of the Sahel: Report of a Working Group, Paris, France, April 28-29, 1980. Ottawa, Canada: IDRC. 1981. 92p.

International Institute for Labour Studies (IILS) and Organization of African Unity (OAU)
Food Self-Sufficiency, Technological Autonomy, and Social Progress in Africa: A Research Guide. Geneva: IILS/Addis Ababa, Ethiopia: OAU. 1984. 144p.

International Labour Organization (ILO)
Female Power, Autonomy and Demographic Change in the Third World. Geneva: ILO. The Role of Women and Demographic Change Research Programme. 1980.

International Planned Parenthood Federation (IPPF)
Family Welfare and Development in Africa: Proceedings of the IPPF Africa Regional Conference, University of Ibadan. August 29-September 3, 1976. London: IPPF. 1977. 327p.

Isley, R.
Medical, Socio-Cultural, Economic and Psychological Correlates of Childlessness in Africa. Research Triangle Park, North Carolina: Research Triangle Institute. RTI Concept Paper #24-CP-80-01. 1980.

Jeffries, Rosalind
"The Image of Women in African Cave Art." Journal of African Civilizations. Volume 6 #1 1984. pp. 98-122.

Jett, Joyce
The Role of Traditional Midwives in the Modern Health Sector in West and Central Africa. Washington, D.C.: U.S. Department of State. U.S. Agency for International Development. January, 1977. 150p.

Jett, Joyce
The Role of Traditional Midwives in the Modern Health Sector in West and Central Africa. Washington, D.C.: U.S. Department of State. U.S. Agency for International Development. January, 1977. 150p.

Jewsiewicki, B.
"Lineage Mode of Production: Social Inequalities in Equatorial Central Africa." (In) Crummey, Donald and Steward, C.C. (eds.). Modes of Production in Africa: The Precolonial Era. Beverly Hills, California: Sage Publications. 1981. pp. 93-114.

Johnson, B.C.
"Traditional Practices Affecting the Health of Women." Paper Presented at the Seminar on Traditional Practices Affecting the Health of Women and Children. World Conference of the United Nations Decade for Women. New York: United Nations. Copenhagen, Denmark. July 14-30, 1980.

Johnson, B.C.
"Traditional Practices Affecting the Health of Women." Paper Presented at the Seminar on Traditional Practices Affecting the Health of Women and Children. World

Conference of the United Nations Decade for Women. New York: United Nations. Copenhagen, Denmark. July 14-30, 1980.

Jorgensen, Kirsten
"Water Supply Projects in Africa: The Need to Involve the Main Users--Women." Ideas and Action Bulletin. #150 1983. pp. 14-18.

Joseph, Roger
"Sexual Dialectics and Strategy in Berber Marriage." Journal of Comparative Family Studies. Volume 7 #3 Autumn, 1976. pp. 471-481.

Joseph, Terri B.
"Poetry as a Strategy of Power: The Case of Riffian Berber Women." Signs. Volume 5 #3 Spring, 1980. pp. 418-434.

Jules-Rosette, Bennetta
"Changing Aspects of Women's Initiation in Southern Africa: An Exploratory Study." Canadian Journal of African Studies. Volume 13 #3 1980. pp. 389-406.

Jules-Rosette, Bennetta
"Sources of Women's Leadership in an Indigenous African Church." Sociological Symposium. #17 Fall, 1976. pp. 69-89.

Kabagambe, John C.
"Family Planning Concepts: Myths and Realities." (In) International Planned Parenthood Federation (IPPF). Proceedings of the IPPF Africa Regional Conference. London: IPPF. 1977. pp. 55+.

Kalugila, Leonidas
"Women in the Ministry of Priesthood in the Early Church: An Inquiry." Africa Theological Journal. Volume 14 #1 1985. pp. 35-45.

Kamanga, Kawaye
"The Dilemma of High Fertility in Sub-Saharan Africa." Ph.D Dissertation: University of Pittsburgh. Pittsburgh, Pennsylvania. 1985. 140p.

Kamba, Kate
"Fuel Wood and Energy Development for African Women." Paper Presented at the Workshop on Women in Agricultural Development. Addis Ababa, Ethiopia: United Nations Economic Commission for Africa. Awassa, Ethiopia. June 26, 1983. 13p.

Kapalo, Ancilla
"African Sisters' Congregations: Realities of the Present Situation." (In) Fashole-Luke, Edward. Christianity in Independent Africa. London: R. Collings. 1978. pp. 122-135.

Karanja, Wambui Wa
"Women and Work: A Study of Female and Male Attitudes in the Modern Sector of an African Metropolis." (In) Ware, Helen (ed.). Women, Education and Modernization of the Family in West Africa. Canberra, Australia: Australian National University. Department of Demography. Changing African Family Project Series. Monograph #7. 1978.

Karoun, Haddad O.
"Adolescent Pregnancy and Childbirth." Paper Presented at the Seminar on Traditional Practices Affecting the Health and Children. World Conference of the United Nations Decade for Women. New York: United Nations. Copenhagen, Denmark. July 14-30, 1980.

Kayongo-Male, Diane
The Sociology of the African Family. New York: Longman. 1984. 124p.

Kazeze, Z.W.
"Review of Some Determinants of Fertility in Africa." (In) Cairo Demographic Centre (CDC). Determinants of Fertility in Some African and Asian Countries. Cairo, Egypt: CDC. CDC Research Monograph Series #10. 1982. pp. 391-414.

Keenan, Jeremy
"Power and Wealth Are Cousins: Descent, Class and Marital Strategies Among the Kel Ahaggar." Africa. Volume 47 #3 1977. pp. 242-252.

Keenan, Jeremy
"The Tuareg Veil." Middle East Studies. Volume 13 #1 January, 1977. pp. 3-13.

Keim, Curtis A.
"Women in Slavery Among the Mangbetu, c. 1800-1910." (In) Robertson, Claire C. and Klein, Martin A. (eds.). Women and Slavery in Africa. Madison, Wisconsin: University of Wisconsin Press. 1983. pp. 144-159.

Keller, Bonnie B
"Marriage by Elopment." African Social Research. #27 June, 1979. pp. 565-585.

Keller, Bonnie B.
"Marriage and Medicine: Women's Search for Love and Luck." African Social Research. #26 December, 1978. pp. 489-505.

Kelly, Gail P. and Elliott, Carolyn M. (eds.)
Women's Education in the Third World: Comparative Perspectives. Albany, New York: State University of New York Press. 1982. 406p.

Kenton, J.
"Health of Women and Children in Africa." Midwives Chronicle. Volume 98 #1165 February, 1985. pp. 44-45.

Kerri, James
"Understanding the African Family: Persistence, Continuity and Change." Western Journal of Black Studies. Volume 3 #1 Spring, 1979. pp. 14-17.

Kilson, Marion
"Women and African Literature." Journal of African Studies. Volume 4 #2 Summer, 1977. pp. 161-166.

Kilson, Marion
"Women in African Traditional Religions." Journal of Religion in Africa. Volume 8 #2 1976. pp. 133-143.

King-Akerele, O.
Traditional Palm Oil Processing, Women's Role and the Application of Appropriate Technology. Addis Ababa,

Ethiopia: United Nations Economic Commission for Africa. Research Series. 1983.
Kisekka, Mere N.
"Polygyny and the Status of African Women." African Urban Notes. Volume 2 #3 Fall/Winter, 1976. pp. 21-42.
Kitching, Gavin
"Proto-Industrialization and Demographic Change: A Thesis and Some Possible African Implications." Journal of African History. Volume 24 #2 1983. pp. 221-240.
Kizerbo, Joseph
"Women and the Energy Crisis in the Sahel Africa. From the Seminar on Fuel and Energy Development for African Women in Rural Areas, Bamako, Mali, December, 1980." Unasylva. Volume 33 #133 1981. pp. 5-10.
Kocher, James E.
"Socioeconomic Development and Fertility Change in Rural Africa." Paper Presented at the Annual Meeting of the African Studies Association. Paper #44. Boston, Massachusetts. 1976. 22p.
Kocher, James E.
"Supply-Demand Disequilibria and Fertility Change in Africa--Toward a More Appropriate Economic Approach." Social Biology. Volume 30 #1 1983. pp. 41-58.
Konie, Gwendoline
"Women in Southern Africa: Gaining Political Power." Africa Report. Volume 28 #2 March-April, 1983. pp. 11-14.
Koning, Karen L.
"Revolutionary Potential Among Arab Women Today." Mawazo. Volume 4 #4 1976. pp. 48-57.
Kouba, Leonard J. and Muasher, Judith
"Female Circumcision in Africa: An Overview." African Studies Review. Volume 28 #1 1985. pp. 95-110.
Kpedekpo, Gottlieb M.
"Age Patterns of Fertility in Selected African Countries." Jimlar Mutane. Volume 1 #1 February, 1976. pp. 9-26.
Kuper, Adam
"Symbolic Dimensions of the Southern Bantu Homestead." Africa. Volume 50 #1 1980. pp. 8-23.
Kuper, Adam
"Cousin Marriage Among the Thembu?" African Affairs. Volume 40 #1 1981. pp. 41-42.
Kurian, George and Ratna, Ghosh (eds.)
Women in the Family and the Economy: An International Comparative Survey. Westport, Connecticut: Greenwood Press. Contributions in Family Studies #5. 1981. 451p.
Kurian, George and Ratna, Ghosh (eds.)
Women in the Family and the Economy: An International Comparative Survey. Westport, Connecticut: Greenwood Press. Contributions in Family Studies #5. 1981. 451p.
Kusin, Jane A. and Thiuri, B. and Lakhani, S.A. and Tmannetje, J.W.
"Anthropometric Changes During Pregnancy in Rural African

Women." Tropical and Geographic Medicine. Volume 36 #1 1984. pp. 91-97.
Kuteyi, P.V.
"Nutritional Needs of the Child Especially in the First Year." Paper Presented at the Seminar on Traditional Practices Affecting the Health of Women and Children. World Conference of the United Nations Decade for Women. New York: United Nations. Copenhagen, Denmark. July 14-30, 1980.
Kwawu, J.
"The Role of Home Economics in Rural Development: A Focus on Family Planning." Paper Presented at the Workshop on the Role of Women and Home Economics in Rural Development in Africa. Rome: United Nations Food and Agricultural Organization. Alexandria, Egypt. October 17, 1983. 20p.
Ladner, Joyce A.
"Racism and Tradition: Black Womanhood in Historical Perspective." (In) Carroll, Berenice A. (ed.). Liberating Women's History. Chicago: University of Chicago Press. 1976. pp. 179-193.
Lancaster, Chet S.
"Women, Horticulture and Society in Sub-Saharan Africa." American Anthropologist. Volume 78 #3 September, 1976. pp. 539-564.
LeVine, Robert A. and Richman, Amy and Welles, Barbara and O'Rourke, Shelagh and Caron, James W.
Women's Education and Maternal Behavior in the Third World: A Report to the Ford Foundation. New York: Ford Foundation. 1978. 52p.
LeVine, Robert A.
"Influences of Women's Schooling on Maternal Behavior in the Third World." Comparative Education Review. Volume 24 #2 Part Two June, 1980. pp. S78-S105.
LeVine, Robert A. and Dixon, Suzanne and LeVine, Sarah
"High Fertility in Africa: A Consideration of Causes and Consequences." Paper Presented at the Annual Meeting of the African Studies Association. Paper #48. Boston, Massachusetts. 1976. 18p.
LeVine, Sarah
"Crime or Afflictions: Rape in an African Community." Culture, Medicine and Psychiatry. Volume 4 #2 1980.
Lee, S.
"The Image of the Woman in the African Folktale From the Sub-Saharan Francophone Area." Yale French Studies. #53 1976. pp. 19-28.
Leis, Nancy B.
"West African Women and the Colonial Experience." Western Canadian Journal of Anthropology. Volume 6 #3 1976. pp. 123-132.
Leke, R. and Nash, B.
"Biological and Socio-Cultural Aspects of Infertility and Subfertility in Africa." (In) United Nations Economic

Commission for Africa (UNECA). Population Dynamics: Fertility and Mortality in Africa. Addis Ababa, Ethiopia: UNECA. May, 1981. pp. 488-498.

Lesthaeghe, Ron J.
"Fertility and its Proximate Determinants in Sub-Saharan Africa: The Record of the 1960's and 70's." Brussels, Belgium: Vrije Universiteit Brussel. Interuniversity Programme in Demography. IPD Working Paper #1984-2. 1984. 117p.

Lesthaeghe, Ron J. and Ohadike, Patrick O. and Kocher, James E. and Page, Hilary J.
"Child-Spacing and Fertility in Sub-Saharan Africa: An Overview of Issues." (In) Page, Hilary J. and Lesthaeghe, Ron (eds.). Child-Spacing in Tropical Africa: Traditions and Change. New York: Academic Press. 1981. pp. 3-23.

Levine, Nancy E.
"Nyinba Polyandry and the Allocation of Paternity." Journal of Comparative Family Studies. Volume 11 #3 Special Iss. August, 1980. pp. 283-298.

Levine, Nancy E. and Sangree, Walter H.
"Asian and African Systems of Polyandry." Journal of Comparative Family Studies. Volume 11 #3 Special Iss. August, 1980. pp. 385-410.

Levine, Nancy E. and Sangree, Walter H.
"Women With Many Husbands--Polyandrous Alliance and Marital Flexibility in Africa and Asia." Journal of Comparative Family Studies. Volume 11 #3 Special Iss. August, 1980.

Levine, Nancy E.
"Belief and Explanation in Nyinba Women's Witchcraft." Man. Volume 17 #2 1982.

Lewis, Barbara C.
"State/Society; Public/Private and Women: A Political Scientist's View." Paper Presented at the Annual Meeting of the African Studies Association. Paper #75. Bloomington, Indiana. October 21-24, 1981.

Lewis, Barbara C.
"Fertility and Employment: An Assessment of Role Incompatibility Among African Urban Women." (In) Bay, Edna G. Women and Work in Africa. Boulder, Colorado: Westview Press. Westview Special Studies. 1982. pp. 249-276.

Lewis, Barbara C. (ed.)
The Invisible Farmer: Women and the Crisis in Agriculture. Washington, D.C.: U.S. Department of State. U.S. Agency for International Development. Office of Women in Development. 1982. 456p.

Lewis, Shelby
"African Women and National Development." (In) Lindsay, Beverly (ed.). Comparative Perspectives of Third World Women: The Impact of Race, Sex and Class. New York: Praeger Publishers. 1980. pp. 36-54.

Lindsay, Beverly
"Women and National Development in Africa." Western

Journal of Black Studies. Volume 1 #1 March, 1977. pp. 53-58.
Lindsay, Beverly (ed.)
Comparative Perspectives of Third World Women: The Impact of Race, Sex and Class. New York: Praeger Publishers. Praeger Special Studies. 1980. 318p.
Liskin, L.S.
"Complications of Abortion in Developing Countries." Population Reports. #F-7 July, 1980. pp. 107-155.
Little, Kenneth L.
"Women's Strategies in Modern Marriage in Anglophone West Africa: An Ideological and Sociological Appraisal." Journal of Comparative Family Studies. Volume 8 #3 Autumn, 1977. pp. 341-356.
Little, Kenneth L.
"Women's Strategies in Modern Marriage in Anglophone West Africa: An Ideological and Sociological Appraisal." (In) Kurian, George (ed.). Cross-Cultural Perspectives of Mate Selection and Marriage. Westport, Connecticut: Greenwood Press. Contributions in Family Studies #3. 1979. pp. 202-217.
Loutfi, Martha F.
Rural Women: Unequal Partners in Development. Geneva: International Labour Organization. 1982. 80p.
Lukutati, Bwembya
"The Concept of Parenthood in African Societies." (In) International Planned Parenthood Federation (IPPF). Proceedings of the IPPF Africa Regional Conference. London: IPPF. 1977. pp. 145-152.
M'bow, Amadou-Mahtar
"The United Nations Decade for Women: Towards a New Order With Regard to the Status of Women." Cultures. Volume 8 #4 1982.
Mabogunje, A.L.
"The Policy Implications of Changes in Child-Spacing Practices in Tropical Africa." (In) Page, Hilary J. and Lesthaeghe, Ron (eds.). Child-Spacing in Tropical Africa: Traditions and Changes. New York: Academic Press. 1981. pp. 303-316.
MacCormack, Carol P.
"Biological Events and Cultural Control." Signs. Volume 3 #1 Autumn, 1977. pp. 93-100.
MacGaffey, Wyatt
"Lineage Structure, Marriage and the Family Amongst the Central Bantu." Journal of African History. Volume 24 #2 1983. pp. 173-187.
Mahran, M.
"Medical Dangers of Female Circumcision." International Planned Parenthood Federation (IPPF) Medical Bulletin. Volume 15 #2 April, 1981.
Makundi, K. and Warioba, Evelyn
"Psychological Relationship Between Men and Women." Paper Presented at the Workshop on Women's Studies and Development. Dar-es-Salaam, Tanzania: University of

Dar-es-Salaam. Bureau of Resource Assessment and Land Use Planning. Paper #27. September 24-29, 1979. 5p.
Marks, Shula and Rathbone, Richard
"The History of the Family in Africa: Introduction." Journal of African History. Volume 24 #2 1983. pp. 145-161.
Martin-Cisse, Jeanne
"Family Problems in Africa." National Law Guild Practitioner. Volume 37 Winter, 1980. pp. 23-26.
Mati, J.K.
Abortion in Africa. (In) International Planned Parenthood Federation (IPPF). Proceedings of the IPPF Africa Regional Conference. London: IPPF. 1977. pp. 74-79.
Matsepe-Casaburri, Ivy F.
"Women in Southern Africa: Legacy of Exclusion." Africa Report. Volume 28 #2 March-April, 1983. pp. 7-10.
Matsepe-Casaburri, Ivy F.
"Underdevelopment and African Women." Paper Presented at the Conference of the Southern Africa Research Group. College Park, Maryland: Southern Africa Research Group. September, 1976.
Mazrui, Ali A.
"Military Technology and the Masculinity of War: An African Perspective." Impact of Science on Society. Volume 26 #1/2 January-April, 1976. pp. 71-75.
Mbevi, Grace and Njoki, Margaret
"Traditional Practices in Relation to Child Health." Paper Presented at the Seminar on Traditional Practices Affecting the Health of Women and Children. World Conference of the United Nations Decade for Women. New York: United Nations. Copenhagen, Denmark. July 14-30, 1980.
Mbilinyi, Marjorie J.
"Women as Labor in Underdevelopment." Paper Presented at the Wellesley Conference on Women and Development. Wellesley, Massachusetts: Wellesley College. Wellesley Center for Research on Women. June, 1976.
Mbilinyi, Marjorie J.
"Patriarch Relations in the Peasant Household." Paper Presented at the Workshop on Women's Studies and Development. Dar-es-Salaam, Tanzania: University of Dar-es-Salaam. Bureau of Resource Assessment and Land Use Planning. Paper #20. September 24-29, 1979. 12p.
McCall, Daniel
"Rank, Gender, Cult Affiliation Proclaimed in the Arts of Apparel: Reflections on Esie Sculpture." Paper Presented at the Annual Meeting of the African Studies Association. Paper #34. Bloomimgton, Indiana. 1981.
McDowell, James and Hazzard, Virginia
"Village Technology and Women's Work in Eastern Africa." Assignment Children. Volume 36 Oct.-Dec., 1976. pp. 53-65.
McFadden, Patricia
"Women Workers in Southern Africa." Journal of African

Marxists. #4 September, 1983. pp. 54-62.
McFalls, Joseph A. and McFalls, Marguerite H.
Disease and Fertility. Orlando, Florida: Academic Press Inc. 1984. 593p.
McLean, Scilla
"Female Genital Mutilation." ISIS Women's International Bulletin. #25 1982. pp. 26-32.
McLean, Scilla and Graham, Stella E.
Female Circumcision, Excision and Infibulation: The Fact and Proposals for Change. London: Minority Rights Group. Report #47. Second Revised Edition. 1985. 21p.
McSweeney, Brenda G.
"Collection and Analysis of Rural Women's Time Use." Studies in Family Planning. Volume 10 #11/12 Nov.-Dec., 1979. pp. 379+.
Meer, Fatima (ed.)
The African Woman at Home and in Gainful Employment. Collection of Unpublished Papers. 1980.
Meillassoux, Claude
"Female Slavery." (In) Robertson, Claire C. and Klein, Martin A. (eds.). Women and Slavery in Africa. Madison, Wisconsin: University of Wisconsin Press. 1983. pp. 49-66.
Meillassoux, Claude
Maidens, Meal and Money: Capitalism and the Domestic Community. Cambridge, New York: Cambridge University Press. 1981. 196p.
Mernissi, Fatima
"Women, Saints and Sanctuaries." Signs. Volume 3 #1 Autumn, 1977. pp. 101-112.
Mernissi, Fatima
"Women, Saints and Sanctuaries." (In) Wellesley Editorial Committee. Women and National Development: The Complexities of Change. Chicago: University of Chicago Press. 1977. pp. 101-112.
Mgone, C.S.
"Reproductive Behavior and Attitudes of African Mothers Following Birth of a Downs Syndrome Child." East African Medical Journal. Volume 59 #8 1982. pp. 555-559.
Mikhail, Mona
Images of Arab Women: Fact and Fiction. Washington, D.C.: Three Continents Press. 1979. 137p.
Minces, Juliette
The House of Obedience: Women in Arab Society. London: Zed Press. Westport, Connecticut: Lawrence Hill. 1982. 114p.
Moen, Elizabeth W.
Genital Mutilation: Everywoman's Problem. East Lansing, Michigan: Michigan State University. Office of Women in International Development. Working Paper #22. April, 1983.
Moots, Patricia A. and Zak, Michele (eds.)
Women and the Politics of Culture: Studies in the Sexual Economy. New York: Longman. 1983. 452p.

Morris, H.F.
"The Development of Statutory Marriage Law in 20th Century British Colonial Africa." Journal of African Law. Volume 23 #1 1979. pp. 37-64.

Moss, G. and Dunn, M. and Nsarko, J.D.
"Home Economics in Rural Development in Africa: The Village Woman's Day." Paper Presented at the Workshop on the Role of Women and Home Economics in Rural Development in Africa. Rome: United Nations Food and Agricultural Organization. Alexandria, Egypt. 1983. 7p.

Mott, Frank L. and Mott, Susan H.
"Household Fertility Decision-Making in a West African Setting: Do Male and Female Surveys Lead to Similar Interpretations?" Worthington, Ohio: Ohio State University. Center for Human Resource Research. 1984.

Muchena, Olivia N.
"Women in Southern Africa: Are Women Integrated Into Development?" Africa Report. Volume 28 #2 March-April, 1983. pp. 4-6.

Mukhtar, Behiza
"A Question of Our Children's Bodies: The Medical Injury Caused to a Girl by Circumcision." Paper Presented at the Conference on Islam and Family Planning. Sponsored by the International Planned Parenthood Federation. Banjul, Gambia. October 21-24, 1979. 7p.

Murray, Colin G.
"Migrant Labour and Changing Family Structure in the Rural Periphery of Southern Africa." Journal of Southern African Studies. Volume 6 #2 1980. pp. 139-156.

Musallam, B.
Sex and Society in Islam: Birth Control Before the 19th Century. Cambridge, New York: Cambridge University Press. Cambridge Studies in Islamic Civilization. 1983. 176p.

Mushanga, Tibamanya M.
"Wife Victimization in East and Central Africa." Victimology. Volume 2 #3/4 1977. pp. 479-486.

Nagi, Mostafa H. and Stockwell, Edward G.
"Muslim Fertility: Recent Trends and Future Outlook." Journal of South Asian and Middle Eastern Studies. Volume 6 #2 Winter, 1982. pp. 48-70.

Nagi, Mostafa H.
"Trends and Differentials in Moslem Fertility." Journal of Biosocial Science. Volume 16 #2 April, 1984. pp. 189-204.

Ndeti, K.
"Concept of Parenthood in Africa: An Exploratory Study of Complexity." (In) International Planned Parenthood Federation (IPPF). Proceedings of the IPPF Africa Regional Conference. London: IPPF. 1977. pp. 119-144.

Ndongko, T.
"Tradition and the Role of Women in Africa." Presence Africaine. Volume 99/100 1976. pp. 143-152.

Ndulo, Muna
"Liability of a Paramour in Damages for Adultery in

Customary Law." African Social Research. #28 December, 1979. pp. 655-666.
Netting, Robert M. and Wilk, Richard R. and Arnold, Eric J, (eds.).
Households: Comparative and Historical Studies of the Domestic Group. Berkeley, California: University of California Press. 1984. 480p.
Newman, Jeanne S.
Women of the World: Sub-Saharan Africa. Washington, D.C.: U.S. Department of Commerce. U.S. Agency for International Development. Office of Women in Development. August, 1984. 200p.
Newman, Katherine S.
"Women and Law: Land Tenure in Africa." (In) Black, Naomi and Cottrell, Ann B. Women and World Change: Equity Issues in Development. Beverly Hills, California: Sage Publications. 1981. pp. 120-138.
Nicolls, Andrea
"Women in African Art." M.A. Thesis: City College of New York. Department of Art. New York, New York. 1977. 91p.
Njoku, John E.
The World of the African Woman. Metuchen, New Jersey: Scarecrow Press. 1980. 132p.
Norem, R.H.
"The Integration of a Family Systems Perspective Into Farming Systems Projects." (In) Caldwell, John and Rojas, Mary (eds.). Family Systems and Farming Systems: A Second Annual Conference in the World of Women in Development Series. Blacksburg, Virginia: Virgnia Polytechnic Institute and State University. 1983.
Ntiri, Daphne W. (ed.)
One is Not a Woman--One Becomes....The African Woman in a Transitional Society. Troy, Michigan: Bedford Publishers. 1982. 137p.
Nurse, G.T.
"Meity Endogamy and Anthropometric Variation Among the Maravi." Man. Volume 12 #3/4 December, 1977. pp. 397-404.
Nwagwu, Nicholas A.
"Equalization of Educational Opportunities in African Countries." Journal of Educational Administration. Volume 14 #2 October, 1976. pp. 270-278.
O'Barr, Jean F.
"Pare Women: A Case of Political Involvement." Rural Africana. Volume 2 1976. pp. 121-134.
O'Barr, Jean F.
Third World Women: Factors in Their Changing Status. Durham, North Carolina: Duke University. Center for International Studies. Occasional Paper #2. 1976. 94p.
O'Barr, Jean F.
African Women in Politics. (In) Hay, Margaret J. and Stichter, Sharon (eds.). African Women South of the Sahara. New York: Longman. 1984. pp. 140-155.

O'Barr, Jean F. (ed.)
Perspectives on Power: Women in Africa, Asia and Latin America. Durham, North Carolina: Duke University. Center for International Studies. Occasional Paper #13. 1982. 120p.

O'Brien, Denise
"Female Husbands in Southern Bantu." (In) Schlegal, A. (ed.). Sexual Stratification: A Cross-Cultural View. New York: Columbia University Press. 1977. pp. 109-126.

O'Shaughnessey, T.J.
"Growth of Educational Opportunity for Muslim Women, 1950-1973." Anthropos. Volume 73 #5/6 1978. pp. 887-901.

Obbo, Christine S. and Nelson, Nici
African Women: Their Struggle for Economic Independence. Westport, Connecticut: Lawrence Hill. 1980. 176p.

Obbo, Christine S.
"Town Migration is Not for Women." Ph.D. Dissertation: University of Wisconsin-Madison. Madison, Wisconsin. 1977. 329p.

Obbo, Christine S.
"Dominant Male Ideology and Female Options: Three East African Case Studies." Africa. Volume 46 #4 1976. pp. 371-389.

Oduyoye, Mercy Amba
"Feminism: A Pre-Condition for a Christian Anthropology." Africa Theological Journal. Volume 11 #3 1982. pp. 193-208.

Ogbu, John U.
"African Bridewealth and Women's Status." American Ethnologist. Volume 5 #2 May, 1978. pp. 241-262.

Ogundipe-Leslie, Molara
"African Women, Culture and Another Development." Journal of African Marxists. #5 February, 1984. pp. 77-92.

Okali, Christine
"The Changing Economic Position of Women in Rural Communities in West Africa." Africana Marburgensia. Volume 12 #1/2 1979. pp. 59-93.

Okanlawon, Tunde
Deterioration of Collective Identity: The Case of Women. Papers of the International Congress of African Studies. 1978. 8p.

Okediji, Frances Olu
"The Limitations of Family Planning Programmes in the Developing Nations." (In) Oppong, C. and Adaba, G. and Bekombo-Priso, M. and Mogey, J. (eds.). Marriage, Fertility and Parenthood in West Africa. Canberra, Australia: Australian National University. Department of Demography. Volume Two. 1978. pp. 617-639.

Okediji, Peter A.
"The Status of African Women in Family Planning." (In) Oppong, C. and Adaba, G. and Bekombo-Priso, M. and Mogey, J. (eds.). Marriage, Fertility and Parenthood in West Africa. Canberra, Australia: Australian National

University. Department of Demography. Volume Two. 1978. pp. 673-676.
Okeyo, Achola P.
"Women in the Household Economy: Managing Multiple Roles." Studies in Family Planning. Volume 10 #11/12 Nov.-Dec., 1979. pp. 337-343.
Okeyo, Achola P.
The Role of Women in Changing Traditional Farming Systems. Paper Presented at the Workshop on Policies and Programmes for Increased Food and Agricultural Production in Traditional Subsistence Farms in Africa. Rome: United Nations Food and Agriculture Organization. Arusha, Tanzania. December 10, 1984. 27p.
Okeyo, Acholo P.
"Women and Africa: Reflections on Development Myths." Africa Report. Volume 26 #2 March-April, 1981. pp. 7-10.
Okonjo, Kemene
"Women in Contemporary Africa." (In) Mojekwu, Christopher C. and Uchendu, Victor C. and Hoey, Leo F. (eds.). African Society, Culture and Politics: An Introduction to African Studies. Washington, D.C.: University Press of America. 1978. pp. 201-214.
Oloko, Olatunde
Modernization and Social Problems in Africa. Lagos, Nigeria: University of Lagos. United Nations Economic Commission for Africa. 1979.
Omran, Abdel R. and Johnston, Alan G.
Family Planning for Health in Africa. Chapel Hill, North Carolina: University of North Carolina. Carolina Population Center. 1984. 190p.
Onyango, Philista P.M.
"The Working Mother and the Housemaid as a Substitute: Its Complications on the Children." Journal of Eastern African Research and Development. Volume 13 1983. pp. 24-31.
Oomen-Myim, Marie A.
"Involvement of Rural Women in Decision-Making Within Smallscale Agricultural Projects." Paper Presented at the Workshop on Women's Studies and Development. Dar-es-Salaam, Tanzania: University of Dar-es-Salaam. Bureau of Resource Assessment and Land Use Planning. Paper #44. September 24-29, 1979. 7p.
Oppong, Christine
Family Structure and Women's Reproductive and Productive Roles: Some Conceptual and Methodological Issues. Geneva: International Labour Office. The Role of Women and Demographic Change Research Program. 1980.
Oppong, Christine
A Synopsis of Seven Roles and Status of Women: An Outline of a Conceptual and Methodological Approach. Geneva: International Labour Organization. World Employment Programme. Research Working Paper. Mimeo. (Restricted) 1980.

Oppong, Christine
"Some Aspects of Anthropological Contributions to the Study of Fertility." (In) Farooq, G.M. and Simmons, G.B. (eds.). Fertility in Developing Countries: An Economic Perspective on Research and Policy Issues. New York: St. Martin's Press. 1985.

Oppong, Christine
"Family Structure and Women's Reproductive and Productive Roles: Some Conceptual and Methodological Issues." (In) Anker, Richard and Buvinic, Mayra and Youssef, N. (eds.). Women's Roles and Population Trends in the Third World. London: Croom Helm. 1982.

Oppong, Christine and Adaba, Gemma and Bekomba-Priso, Manga and Mogey, J. (eds.)
Marriage, Fertility and Parenthood in West Africa. Canberra, Australia: Australian National University. Department of Demography. Changing African Family Project. Monograph #4. Two Volumes. 1978. 848p.

Oppong, Christine (ed.)
Female and Male in West Africa. Boston: George Allen and Unwin. 1983. 402p.

Oucho, John O.
"Socio-Economic Perspectives of Fertility Regulation in Traditional and Modern African Societies." (In) University of Nairobi. Papers of the Seminar on Oral Traditions: Past Growth and Future Development in East Africa. Nairobi: University of Nairobi. UNESCO Institute of African Affairs. Kisumu, Kenya. April 18-22, 1979. 18p.

Overholt, C. and Anderson, M. and Cloud, K. and Austin, J.
Gender Roles in Development Projects: A Casebook. West Hartford: Connecticut: Kumarian Press. Kumarian Press Case Studies Series. 1985. 326p.

Page, Hilary J. and Lesthaeghe, Ron J. (eds.)
Child-Spacing in Tropical Africa: Traditions and Change. New York: Academic Press. Studies in Population Series. 1981. 332p.

Pagezy, Helen
"Some Aspects of Daily Work of Women Oto and Twa Living in Equatorial Forest Middle." L'Anthropolgie. Volume 80 #3 1976. pp. 465-906.

Pala, Achola O.
African Women in Rural Development: Research Trends and Priorities. Washington, D.C.: American Council on Education. Overseas Liaison Committee. OLC Paper #12. December, 1976. 35p.

Pala, Achola O. and Seidman, Ann
"A Proposed Model of the Status of Women in Africa." Paper Presented at the Conference on Women and Development. Wellesley, Massachusetts: Wellesley College. June, 1976.

Palmer, Ingrid
"Rural Women and the Basic Needs Approach." International Labour Review. Volume 115 #1 January-February, 1977. pp. 97-98.

Palmer, Ingrid
"Women in Rural Development." International Development Review. Volume 22 #2/3 1980. pp. 39-45.

Palmer, Ingrid
"The Role of Women in Agrarian Reform and Rural Development." (In) United Nations. Land Reform. Rome: United Nations Food and Agriculture Organization. 1979. pp. 57-70.

Palmer, Ingrid
'The Nemow Case', Case Studies of the Impact of Large Scale Development Projects on Women: A Series for Planners. New York: Population Council. International Programs Working Paper #7. September, 1979. 92p.

Palmer, Ingrid
"Seasonality of Women's Work: Patterns and Trends." (In) University of Sussex. Papers From the Conference on Seasonal Dimensions to Rural Poverty. Brighton, England: Sussex University. Institute of Development Studies. July 3-6, 1978. 8p.

Palmer, Ingrid
The Impact of Male Out-Migration on Women in Farming. West Hartford, Connecticut: Kumarian Press. 1985. 78p.

Paraiso, Maitre A.
"Family Planning Legislation in the Francophone Countries of Africa." (In) International Planned Parenthood Federation (IPPF). Proceedings of the IPPF Africa Regional Conference. London: IPPF. 1977. pp. 247-255.

Paulme, Denise
"The Devouring Mother: Essay on the Morphology of African Tales." Journal of African Studies. Volume 4 Winter, 1977. pp. 480+.

Pauwels, Johan M.
"Nullity of Marriage and Divorce: Relevance of a Western Distinction to Modern African Law." (In) Roberts, Simon (ed.). Law and the Family in Africa. Hague, Netherlands: Mouton. 1977. pp. 225-239.

Peart, Nicola S.
"Civil or Christian Marriage and Customary Unions: The Legal Position of the 'Discarded' Spouse and Children." Comparative and International Law Journal of Southern Africa. Volume 16 #1 1983. pp. 39-64.

Peel, J.D.Y.
"The Changing Family in Modern Ijesha History." Paper Presented at the Conference on the History of the Family in Africa. London: Cambridge University. School of Oriental and African Studies. September, 1981.

Peil, Margaret
African Urban Life: Components of Satisfaction. Birmingham, England: Birmingham University. Centre for West African Studies. 1982.

Peil, Margaret
"Urban Women in the Labor Force." Sociology of Work and Occupations. Volume 6 #4 November, 1979. pp. 482-501.

Pernet, Henry
"Masks and Women: Toward a Reappraisal." History of

Religions. Volume 22 #1 August, 1982. pp. 45-59.
Peters, Emrys L.
"The Status of Women in Four Middle East Communities." (In) Beck, Lois and Keddie, Nikki R. (eds.). Women in the Muslim World. Cambridge, Massachusetts: Harvard University Press. 1978. pp. 311-350.
Petty, Irene M.
The Role of African Women in Identifying Needs for Labor Saving Devices. Prepared for the AAAS Workshop on Women and Development for UNCSTD. New York: United Nations. 1979.
Pieters, Guy and Lowenfels, A.
"Infibulation in the Horn of Africa." New York State Journal of Medicine. Volume 77 April, 1977. pp. 729-731.
Porter, J.R. and Albert, A.A.
"Subculture or Assimilation? A Cross-Cultural Analysis of Religion and Women's Role." Journal of the Scientific Study of Religion. Volume 16 #4 December, 1977. pp. 345-359.
Pratt, Edward O.
"Current Status of Family Planning in Africa." (In) International Planned Parenthood Federation (IPPF). Proceedings of the IPPF Africa Regional Conference. London: IPPF. 1977. pp. 61-65.
Prentice, Andrew M. and Prentice, Ann and Lamb, W.H. and Lunn, P.G. and Austin, S.
"Metabolic Consequences of Fasting During Ramadan in Pregnant and Lactating Women." Human Nutrition. Clinical Nutrition. Volume 37 #4 July, 1983. pp. 283-294.
Rainey, Mary C.
"Non-Formal Education and Third World Women." Paper Presented at the International Conference on Human Lactation. New York: New York Academy of Science. March, 1977. 12p.
Ravenhill, Phillip L.
"The Interpretation of Symbolism in Wan Female Initiation." Africa. Volume 48 #1 1978. pp. 66-78.
Reyna, Stephen P.
"Economics and Fertility: Waiting for the Demographic Transition in the Dry Zone of Francophone West Africa." (In) Caldwell, John C. (ed.). The Persistence of High Fertility: Population Prospects in the Third World." Canberra, Australia: Australian National University. Department of Demography. Volume One. 1977. pp. 393-426.
Richardson, Barbara D. and Pieters, Linda
"Menarche and Growth." American Journal of Clinical Nutrition. Volume 30 #12 December, 1977. pp. 2088-2091.
Riesman, Paul
"Opulence and Pride in a Rite of Passage: A Comparison of the Weddings of Nobles and of Commoners in Fulani Society." Paper Presented at the Annual Meeting of the

African Studies Association. Paper #102. Bloomington, Indiana. 1981.
Ritchie, Jean A.
General Conclusions on the Integration of Women in Agrarian Reform and Rural Development in Africa. Rome: United Nations Food and Agriculture Organization. 1978.
Ritchie, Jean A.
The Integration of Women in Agrarian Reform and Rural Development in English Speaking Countries of the African Region. Rome: United Nations Food and Agriculture Organization. March, 1978. 95p.
Roberts, Pepe
"The Sexual Politics of Labor and the Household in Africa." (In) Guyer, Jane I. and Peters, Pauline E. (eds.). Conceptualizing the Household: Issues of Theory, Method and Application. Charlottesville, Virginia: Teleprint. Papers From a Workshop Held at Harvard University, November 2-4, 1984. 1984.
Roberts, Simon (ed.)
Law and the Family in Africa. Hague, Netherlands: Mouton. 1977. 267p.
Robertson, Claire C. and Klein, Martin A. (eds.)
Women and Slavery in Africa. Madison, Wisconsin: University of Wisconsin Press. 1983. 380p.
Robertson, Claire C. and Klein, Martin A.
"Women's Importance in African Slave Systems." (In) Robertson, Claire C. and Klein, Martin A. (eds.). Women and Slavery in Africa. Madison, Wisconsin: University of Wisconsin Press. 1983. pp. 3-25.
Robertson, Claire C.
"The Death of Makola and Other Tragedies: Male Strategies Against a Female Dominated Distribution Network." Paper Presented at the Annual Meeting of the Canadian African Studies Association. Toronto, Ontario, Canada. May, 1982.
Roboff, Farron V. and Renwick, Hilary L.
"The Changing Role of Women in the Development of the Sahel." Paper Presented to the Annual Meeting of the African Studies Association. Paper #92. Boston, Massachusetts. 1976. 12p.
Rogers, Barbara
"Well, Um, I Suppose We Never Thought of it Like That...." Development. Volume 20 #3/4 1978. pp. 61-64.
Rogers, Barbara
"Women's Projects: New Segregation?" Africa Report. Volume 23 #3 May-June, 1978. pp. 48-50.
Rogers, Barbara
"Food, Fertility and Nuclear Mothers: How Development Can Increase Rather than Reduce the Social and Economic Burdens of African Women." Populi. Volume 5 #1 1978. pp. 23-27.
Rogers, Barbara
The Domestication of Women: Discrimination in Developing Societies. New York: St. Martin's Press. 1980. 200p.

Rogombe, Rose F.
"Equal Partners in Development." Africa Report. Volume 30 #2 March-April, 1985. pp. 17-20.
Romalis, Coleman and Romalis, Shelly
"Sexism, Racism and Technological Change: Two Cases of Minority Protest." International Journal of Women's Studies. Volume 6 May-June, 1983. pp. 270-287.
Rosenberg, E.M.
"Demographic Effects of Sex Differential Nutrition." (In) Jerome, Norge W. and Kandel, Randy F. and Pelto, Gretel H. (eds.). Nutritional Anthropology. Pleasantville, New York: Redgrave Publishing. 1980. pp. 181-201.
Rousseau-Mukenge, Ida
"Conceptualizations of African Women's Role in Development: A Search for New Directions." Journal of International Affairs. Volume 30 #2 Fall/Winter, 1976. pp. 261-268.
Russell, Diana E.H. and Vandeven, Nicole (eds.)
Crimes Against Women: Proceedings of the International Tribunal. Millbrae, California: Les Femmes. 1976. 298p.
Sabean, David W.
"The History of the Family in Africa and Europe: Some Comparative Perspectives." Journal of African History. Volume 24 #2 1983. pp. 163-171.
Sachs, Carolyn E.
Invisible Farmers: Women in Agricultural Production. Totowa, New Jersey: Rowman and Allen Held. 1983. 153p.
Sacks, Karen
Sisters and Wives: The Past and Future of Sexual Equality. Westport, Connecticut: Greenwood Press. Contributions in Women's Studies #10. 1979. 274p.
Sadik, Nafis
"Muslim Women Today." Populi. Volume 12 #1 1985. pp. 36-51.
Safilios-Rothschild, Constantina
Access of Rural Girls to Primary Education in the Third World: State of Art, Obstacles and Policy Recommendations. Washington, D.C.: U.S. Department of State. U.S. Agency for International Development. 1979. 31p.
Safilios-Rothschild, Constantina
Female Power, Autonomy and Demographic Change in the Third World. Geneva: International Labour Organization. The Role of Women and Demographic Change Research Program. 1980.
Safilios-Rothschild, Constantina
Can Agriculture in the Third World Modernize With Traditional Female Agricultural Labor? State College, Pennsylvania: Pennsylvania State University. Department of Sociology. 1981.
Sai, Fred T.
"Report of the Conference on the Medical and Social Aspects of Abortion in Africa." (In) Sai, F.T. (ed.). A

Strategy for Abortion Management. London: International Planned Parenthood Federation. 1978. pp 6-22.
Sai, Fred T.
Family Welfare and Development in Africa: Proceedings of the IPPF Africa Regional Conference, University of Ibadan. London: International Planned Parenthood Federation. Ibadan, Nigeria. Aug. 29-Sept. 3, 1977. 327p.
Salamone, Frank A.
"Gbagyi Witchcraft: A Reconsideration of S.F. Nadel's Theory of African Witchcraft." Paper Presented at the Annual Meeting of the African Studies Association. Paper #84. Los Angeles, California. 1979.
Sanderson, Lilian P.
Against the Mutilation of Women: The Struggle Against Unnecessary Suffering. London: Ithaca Press. 1981. 117p.
Sanjek, Roger
"New Perspectives on West African Women." Reviews in Anthropology. Volume 3 #2 March-April, 1976. pp. 115-134.
Schierling, Marla J.
"Primeval Women: A Yahwistic View of Women in Genesis 1-11:9." Journal of Theology for Southern Africa. #42 March, 1983.
Schoenmaeckers, Ronald C.
Current Fertility Behavior in Africa: Results From a Birth Interval Analysis of World Fertility Survey Data. Brussels, Belgium: Vrije Universiteit Brussel. Inter-University Program in Demography. IPD Working Paper 1985-4. 1985. 24p.
Schoenmaeckers, Ronald C.
The Child-Spacing Tradition and the Postpartum Taboo in Tropical Africa: Anthropological Evidence. Paper Prepared for the IUSSP Workshop on Child-Spacing in Tropical Africa: Tradition and Change. Brussels, Belgium: International Union for the Scientific Study of Population. April, 17-19, 1979.
Schoenmaeckers, Ronald C. and Shah, I.H. and Lesthaeghe, Ron J. and Tambashe, O.
"The Child-Spacing Tradition and the Postpartum Taboo in Tropical Africa: Anthropological Evidence." (In) Page, Hilary J. and Lesthaeghe, Ron (eds.). Child-Spacing in Tropical Africa: Traditions and Change. New York: Academic Press. 1981. pp. 25-71.
Schumacher, Ilsa and Buvinic, Mayra and Sebstad, Jennefer
Limits to Productivity: Improving Women's Access to Technology and Credit. Washington, D.C.: U.S. Department of State. U.S. Agency for International Development. Center for Research on Women. Office of Women and Development. May, 1980. 65p.
Schutjer, Wayne A. and Stokes, C. Shannon
"Agricultural Policies and Human Fertility: Some Emerging Connections." Population Research and Policy Review. Volume 1 October, 1982. pp. 225-244.

Schutjer, Wayne A. and Stokes, C. Shannon
The Human Fertility Implications of Food and Agricultural Policies in Less-Developed Countries. University Park, Pennsylvania: Pennsylvania State University. College of Agriculture. Agriculture Experiment Station Bulletin #835. January, 1982. 14p.
Schutjer, Wayne A. and Stokes, C. Shannon (eds.)
Rural Development and Human Fertility. New York: MacMillan. 1984. 380p.
Schwendinger, Julia and Schwendinger, Herman
"Rape, Sexual Inequality and Levels of Violence." Crime and Social Justice. Volume 16 Winter, 1981. pp. 3-31.
Seetharam, K.S. and Duza, M. Badrud and Sivamurthy, M.
"Nuptiality Patterns in Selected Urban Areas for Four Arab and African Cities." (In) Huzayyin, S.A. and Acsadi, G.T. (eds.). Family and Marriage in Some African and Asiatic Countries. Cairo, Egypt: Cairo Demographic Centre. CDC Research Monograph Series #6. 1976. pp. 311-323.
Seetharam, K.S. and Duza, M. Badrud
"Nuptiality and Fertility in Selected Areas of Four Arab and African Cities." (In) Huzayyin, S.A. and Acsadi, G.T. (eds.). Family and Marriage in Some African and Asiatic Countries. Cairo, Egypt: Cairo Demographic Centre. CDC Research Monograph Series #6. 1976. pp. 337-355.
Shaalan, Mohammed
"Clitoris Envy: A Psychodynamic Construct Instrumental in Female Circumcision." Paper Presented at the Seminar on Traditional Practices Affecting the Health of Women and Children. World Conference of the United Nations Decade for Women. New York: United Nations. Copenhagen, Denmark. July 14-30, 1980.
Shaalan, Mohammed
"Clitoris Envy: A Psychdynamic Construct Instrumental in Female Circumcision." Paper Presented at the Seminar on Traditional Practices Affecting the Health of Women and Children: Female Circumcision, Childhood Marriage, Nutritional Taboos, etc. Alexandria, Egypt: World Health Organization. Eastern Mediterranean Regional Office. Khartoum, Sudan. February 10-15, 1979.
Shazali, Hafez El
"Breast and Supplementary Feeding During Early Childhood." Paper Presented at the Seminar on Traditional Practices Affecting the Health of Women and Children: Female Circumcision, Childhood Marriage, Nutritional Taboos, etc. Alexandria, Egypt: World Health Organization. Eastern Mediterranean Regional Office. Khartoum, Sudan. February 10-15, 1979.
Siann, Gerda and Khalid, R.
"Muslim Traditions and Attitudes to Female Education." Journal of Adolescence. Volume 7 June, 1984. pp. 191-200.
Simms, Ruth
"The African Woman as Entrepreneur: Problems and

Perspectives on Their Roles." (In) Steady, Filomina C. (ed.). The Black Woman Cross-Culturally. Cambridge, Massachusetts: Schenkman Publishing. 1981. pp. 141-168.

Sindzingre, N.
"Plus and Minus--Concerning Female Circumcision." Cahiers d'Etudes Africaines. Volume 17 #1 1977. pp. 65-76.

Singleton, Michael
Contributions to the Rights and Wrongs of African Women. Brussels, Belgium: Pro Mundi Vita Dossiers. Africa Dossier #9. October, 1979. pp. 1-36.

Sivamurthy, M. and Seetharam, K.S.
"Age at First Marriage in Selected Areas of Four Arab and African Cities." (In) Huzayyin, S.A. and Acsadi, G.T. (eds). Family and Marriage in Some African and Asiatic Countries. Cairo, Egypt: Cairo Demographic Centre. CDC Research Monograph Series #6. 1976. pp. 285-309.

Skjonsberg, Else
Women and Food and the Social Sciences: Perspectives on African Food Production and Food Handling. Oslo, Norway: Mimeo. Available From the International Center for Research on Women, Washington, D.C. 1977.

Smith, Jane I. (ed.)
Women in Contemporary Muslim Societies. Lewisburg, Pennsylvania: Bucknell University Press. 1980. 264p.

Smith, Janet I.
"The Experience of Muslim Women: Considerations of Power and Authority." (In) Haddad, Yvonne Y. and Haines, Byron and Findly, Ellison (eds.). The Islamic Impact. Syracuse, New York: Syracuse University Press. 1984. pp. 89-112.

Smith, M.G.
"After Secondary Marriage What?" Ethnology. Volume 19 #3 July, 1980. pp. 265-278.

Sojourner, Sabrina
"From the House of Yemanja: The Goddess Heritage of Black Women." (In) Spretnak, Charlene (ed.). The Politics of Women's Spirituality: Essays on the Rise of Spiritual Power Within the Feminist Movement. Garden City, New Jersey: Anchor Books. 1982. pp. 57-63.

South African Congress of Trade Unions
"The Chains That Bind Black Women Workers." Workers Unity. #14 March, 1979.

Sow, Fatou
"Muslim Families in Contemporary Black Africa." Current Anthropology. Volume 26 December, 1985. pp. 563-570.

Soyinka, Susan
"Family and Fertility in the West African Novel." (In) Caldwell, John C. (ed.). The Persistence of High Fertility: Population Prospects in the Third World. Canberra, Australia: Australian National University. Department of Demography. Volume One. 1977. pp. 427-450.

Spencer, P.
"Polygyny as a Measure of Social Differentiation in

Africa." (In) Mitchell, J.C. (ed.). Numerical Techniques in Social Anthropology. Philadelphia, Pennsylvania: Institute for the Study of Human Issues. 1980.

Spitler, Manon L.
"Women--Africa." Common Ground. Volume 2 #1 January, 1976.

Staudt, Kathleen A.
"The Umoja Federation: Women's Cooptation Into a Local Power Structure." Western Political Quarterly. Volume 33 #2 June, 1980. pp. 278-290.

Staudt, Kathleen A.
"Victorian Womanhood in British Colonial Africa." Paper Presented to the Conference on the History of Women. St. Paul, Minnesota: College of St. Catherine. October 21-23, 1977.

Staudt, Kathleen A.
"Women in Development--Policy Strategies at the End of the Decade." Africa Report. Volume 30 #2 March-April, 1985. pp. 71-74.

Staudt, Kathleen A.
"Class and Sex in the Politics of Women Farmers." Journal of Politics. Volume 41 #2 May, 1979. pp. 492-512.

Staudt, Kathleen A.
"Agricultural Productivity Gaps: A Case Study of Male Preference in Government Policy Implementation." Development and Change. Volume 9 #3 July, 1978. pp. 439-458.

Staudt, Kathleen A.
Women's Politics and Capitalist Transformation in Subsaharan Africa. East Lansing, Michigan: Michigan State University. Office of Women in International Development. Working Paper #54. April, 1984.

Staudt, Kathleen A.
"Tracing Sex Differences in Donor Agricultural Programs." Paper Presented at the American Political Science Association Annual Meeting. Washington, D.C. 1979.

Staveley, Jennifer L.
"Prostitutes and Prostitution in Africa: The Development of Women's First Wage Earning Activity." M.A. Thesis: University of Waterloo. Waterloo, Ontario, Canada. 1977.

Steady, Filomina C.
Women in Africa. Cambridge, Massachusetts: Schenkman. 1983. 256p.

Steady, Filomina C.
The Black Woman Cross-Culturally. Cambridge, Massachusetts: Schenkman. 1981. 645p.

Steady, Filomina C.
"The Black Woman Cross-Culturally: An Overview." (In) Steady, Filomina C. (ed.). The Black Woman Cross-Culturally. Cambridge, Massachusetts: Schenkman Publishing. 1981. pp. 7-41.

Steckle, Jean M.
"Improving Food Utilization in Developing Countries." Canadian Home Economics Journal. Volume 27 #4 October, 1977. pp. 34-39.

Stokland, Torill and Vajrathon, Mallica and Davidson, Nicol
Creative Women in Changing Societies: A Quest for Alternatives. Dobbs Ferry, New York: Transnational Publishers. 1982. 173p.

Strobel, Margaret A.
"Women in Religion and in Secular Ideology." (In) Hay, Margaret J. and Stichter, Sharon (eds.). African Women South of the Sahara. New York: Longman. 1984. pp. 87-101.

Strobel, Margaret A.
"African Women." Signs. Volume 8 #1 1982. pp. 109-131.

Strodtbeck, Fred L.
"Intimacy in Conjugal Interaction and the Capacity to Plan." (In) Oppong, C. and Adaba, G. and Bekombo-Priso, M. and Mogey, J. (eds.). Marriage, Fertility and Parenthood in West Africa. Canberra, Australia: Australian National University. Department of Demography. Volume Two. 1978. pp. 747-763.

Sudarkasa, Niara
The Effects of 20th Century Social Change, Especially of Migration, on Women of West Africa. Tucson, Arizona: University of Arizona. Proceedings of the West Africa Conference. 1976. pp. 102-109.

Sudarkasa, Niara
"Female Employment and Family Organization in West Africa." (In) Steady, Filomina C. (ed.). The Black Woman Cross-Culturally. Cambridge, Massachusetts: Schenkman Publishing. 1981. pp. 49-64.

Sudarkasa, Niara
"Sex Roles, Education and Development in Africa." Anthropology and Education Quarterly. Volume 13 #3 Fall, 1982. pp. 279-288.

Sutlive, Vinson H. and Altshuler, Nathan and Zamora, Mario D.
Women and Politics in 20th Century Africa and Asia. Williamsburg, Virginia: College of William and Mary. Anthropology Department. Studies in Third World Societies. Publication #16. 1981. 160p.

Szklut, Jay
"Bride Wealth, An Alternate View." Behavior Science Research. Volume 16 #3/4 1981. pp. 225-247.

Taba, A.H.
"Female Circumcision." World Health. May, 1979. pp. 8-13.

Taba, A.H.
"Female Circumcision." (In) World Health Organization. Traditional Practices Affecting the Health of Women and Children: Female Circumcision, Childhood Marriage, Nutritional Taboos, etc. Report of a Seminar, Khartoum, Sudan, February 10-15, 1979. Alexandria, Egypt: WHO/EMRO Technical Publication #2. 1979. pp. 43-52.

Tadesse, Zenebeworke
"Studies on Rural Women in Africa: An Overview." (In) International Labour Organization (ILO). Rural Development and Women in Africa. Geneva: ILO. 1984. pp. 65-73.

Tadesse, Zenebeworke
"Africa--A New Look From the Inside." UNESCO Courier. Volume 33 #6 July, 1980. pp. 31-32.

Teilhetfisk, J.
"Djuka Women and Mens Art." African Arts. Volume 17 #2 1984. pp. 63+.

Tesha, Nancy
"Womens Role in Rearing Children and National Development." Paper Presented at the Workshop on Women's Studies and Development. Dar-es-Salaam, Tanzania: University of Dar-es-Salaam. Bureau of Resource Assessment and Land Use Planning. Paper #39. September 24-29, 1979. 3p.

Thea, Carolee
"Masks, Power and Sisterhood in an African Society." Heresies. Volume 12 #1 1982. pp. 106-111.

Thelejane, T.S.
"An African Girl and an African Woman in a Changing World." Paper Presented at the Seminar on the Changing Family in the African Context. Paris: United Nations Educational, Scientific and Cultural Organization. Maseru, Lesotho. 1984. 24p.

Thiam, Awa
"Women's Fight for the Abolition of Sexual Mutilation." International Social Science Journal. Volume 35 #4 1983. pp. 747-756.

Thornton, John
"Sexual Demography: The Impact of Slave Trade on Family Structure." (In) Robertson, Claire C. and Klein, Martin A. (eds.). Women and Slavery in Africa. Madison, Wisconsin: University of Wisconsin Press. 1983. pp. 39-48.

Tillion, Germaine
"Prehistoric Origins of the Condition of Women in Civilized Areas." International Social Science Journal. Volume 29 #4 1977. pp. 671-681.

Tillion, Germaine
The Republic of Cousins: Women's Oppression in Mediterranean Society. London: Al Saqi Books. Translated by Q. Hoare. 1983. 181p.

Tinker, Irene and Bramson, Michele B. (eds.)
Women and World Developmemt. New York: Praeger Publishers. 1976. 228p.

Tinker, Irene
New Technologies for Food Chain Activities: The Imperative of Equity for Women. Washington, D.C.: U.S. Department of State. U.S. Agency for International Development. Office of Women in Development. 1979. 43p.

Tinker, Irene
"New Technologies for Food Related Activities: An Equity Strategy." (In) Dauber, Roslyn and Cain, Melinda L. (eds.). Women and Technological Change in Developing Countries. Boulder, Colorado: Westview Press. 1981. pp. 51-88.

Tonkin, Elizabeth
"Women Excluded? Masking and Masquerading in West Africa." (In) Holden, P. (ed.). Women's Religious Experience. Totowa, New Jersey: Barnes and Noble. 1983. pp. 163-174.

Trager, Lillian
"Urban Market Women: Hoarders, Hagglers, Economic Heroines?" Paper Presented at the Annual Meeting of the African Studies Association. Paper #94. Los Angeles, California. Oct. 31-Nov. 3, 1979. 26p.

Traore, Aminata
"Evolving Relations Between Mothers and Children in Rural Africa." International Social Science Journal. Volume 31 #3 1979. pp. 486-491.

Turner, Edith
"Girl Into Woman." Anthropology and Humanism Quarterly. Volume 10 #2 1985. pp. 27-32.

U.S. Agency for International Development (U.S. AID)
Non-Formal Education--Women in Sahel. Washington, D.C.: U.S. Deapartment of State. U.S. AID. 1978. 23p.

U.S. Agency for International Development (U.S. AID)
International Directory of Women's Development Organizations. Washington, D.C.: U.S. Department of State. U.S. AID. Office of Women in Development. 1977. 311p.

U.S. Agency for International Development (U.S. AID)
The Productivity of Women in Developing Countries: Measurement Issues and Recommendations. Washington, D.C.: U.S. Department of State. U.S. AID. International Center for Research on Women. Office of Women in Development. 1980. 46p.

Uba, Sam
"Women Put the Case for Southern African Liberation." New African Development. March, 1977.

Uche, U.U.
"The Law, Family Welfare and Development in Africa: A Strategy for Future Action." (In) International Planned Parenthood Federation (IPPF). Proceedings of the IPPF Africa Regional Conference. London: IPPF. 1977. pp. 256-262.

Ukaegbu, Alfred O.
"Marriage Habits and Fertility of Women in Tropical Africa: A Socio-Cultural Perspective." (In) Dupaquier, J. and Helin, E. and Laslett, P. and Livi-Bacci, M. (eds.). Marriage and Remarriage in Populations of the Past. New York: Academic Press. Population and Social Structure: Advances in Historical Demography Series. 1981. pp. 127-137.

United Nations
Impact on Women of Socioeconomic Changes in Africa South of the Sahara: Project Proposal. Geneva: United Nations Research Institute for Social Development. Reference Center. 1979. 56p.

United Nations
Report of the World Conference to Review and Appraise the Achievements of the United Nations Decade for Women: Equality, Development and Peace. Nairobi, Kenya, July 15-26, 1985. New York: United Nations. 1986. 304p.

United Nations Centre on Transnational Corporations and International Labour Office (ILO)
Women Workers in Multinational Enterprises in Developing Countries: A Contribution to the United Nations Decade for Women. Geneva: ILO. 1985. 119p.

United Nations Ctr. for Social Dev. and Humanitarian Affairs
Water, Women and Development. New York: United Nations. February 19, 1977.

United Nations Economic Commission for Africa (UNECA)
"Women as Clientele of Non-Formal Education." Paper Presented to the Regional Symposium on Non-Formal Education for Rural Development. Addis Ababa, Ethiopia: UNECA. Aug. 28-Sept. 8, 1978. 12p.

United Nations Economic Commission for Africa (UNECA)
Some Fertility Indicators and Their Implications for Africa. Addis Ababa, Ethiopia: UNECA. African Population Studies Series #3. 1979. 51p.

United Nations Economic Commission for Africa (UNECA)
"Technical Co-Operation Among Developing Countries and Human Resource Development: The Experience of the African Training and Research Centre for Women of the Economic Commission for Africa." Paper Presented at the United Nations Conference on Technical Co-Operation Among Developing Countries. Addis Ababa, Ethiopia: UNECA. Buenos Aires, Argentina. 1978. 16p.

United Nations Economic Commission for Africa (UNECA)
"The Role of Women in Alternative Patterns of Development and Life-Styles in the Africa Region." Paper Presented at the Seminar on Alternative Patterns of Development and Lifestyles for the African Region. Addis Ababa, Ethiopia: UNECA. December 14, 1978. 16p.

United Nations Economic Commission for Africa (UNECA)
Women Population and Rural Development in Africa. Addis Ababa, Ethiopia: UNECA/FAO Women's Development Programme Unit. 1976.

United Nations Economic Commission for Africa (UNECA)
"Women in Development: Moving Away From Tradition." U.N. Chronicle. Volume 19 #11 December, 1982. pp. 105-106.

United Nations Economic Commission for Africa (UNECA)
African Women and Equality, Development and Peace: Strategy for 1980-85. Addis Ababa, Ethiopia: UNECA. Working Paper for Regional Prepatory Meeting of the UNECA Second Regional Conference for the Integration of Women in Development. Lusaka, Zambia. December 3-7, 1979.

United Nations Economic Commission for Africa (UNECA)
Family, Welfare and Development in Africa: Social Welfare Aspects of Family Planning. Addis Ababa, Ethiopia: UNECA. Social Development Section. Social Welfare Services in Africa #11. 1977. 133p.

United Nations Economic Commission for Africa (UNECA)
The Changing and Contemporary Role of Women in African Development. Addis Ababa, Ethiopia: UNECA. 1977.

United Nations Economic Commission for Africa (UNECA)
African Women Workers: Analysis of the Factors Affecting Women's Employment. Addis Ababa, Ethiopia: UNECA. African Training and Research Centre for Women. 1976. 53p.

United Nations Economic Commission for Africa (UNECA)
The Critical Needs of African Women and Appropriate Strategies in the Framework of the Gisenyi and Lusaka MULPOCS. Addis Ababa, Ethiopia: UNECA. 1981.

United Nations Economic Commission for Africa (UNECA)
"The Role of Women in the Solution of the Food Crisis in Africa (Implementation of the Lagos Plan of Action)." Paper Presented at the Regional Intergovernmental Preparatory Meeting for the World Conference to Review and Appraise the Achievements of the United Nations Decade for Women: Equality, Development and Peace/Third Regional Conference on the Integration of Women in Development, Arusha, Tanzania, October 8-12. Addis Ababa, Ethiopia: UNECA. 1984.

United Nations Educational, Scientific and Cultural Organ.
Comparative Report on the Role of Working Mothers in Early Childhood Education in Five Countries. Paris: UNESCO. 1978. 82p.

United Nations Educational, Scientific and Cultural Organ.
Final Report: Regional Workshop on Women's Crafts in Developing Countries. Paris: UNESCO. CREA #14. Katiola, Ivory Coast. 1983. 22p.

United States Department of Health and Human Services
Family Planning Methods and Practice: Africa. Atlanta, Georgia: U.S. Department of Health and Human Services. Centers for Disease Control. Center for Health Promotion and Education. 1983. 329p.

Ushewokunze, C.M.
"Reflections on Youth and Family Welfare Law in Africa." (In) International Planned Parenthood Federation (IPPF). Proceedings of the IPPF Africa Regional Conference. London: IPPF. 1977. pp. 182-190.

Valentine, C.H. and Revson, J.E.
"Cultural Traditions, Social Change, and Fertility in Sub-Saharan Africa." Journal of Modern African Studies. Volume 17 #3 September, 1979. pp. 453-472.

Van de Walle, Etienne
"Community Level Variable and Institutional Factors in the Study of African Nuptiality." (In) Casterline, John B. (ed.). The Collection and Analysis of Community Data. Voorburg, Netherlands: International Statistical Institute. 1985. pp. 103-111.

Waines, D.
"Through a Veil Darkly--The Study of Women in Muslim Societies." Comparative Studies in Society and History. Volume 24 #4 1982.
Wallace, Karen S.
"Women and Identity: A Black Francophone Female Perspective." Sage: A Scholarly Journal on Black Women. Volume 2 #1 1985. pp. 19-23.
Walle, Etienne V. and Kekouole, John
The Recent Evolution of African Marriage and Polygyny. Philadelphia, Pennsylvania: University of Pennsylvania. Population Studies Center. 1984.
Ware, Helen
"Security in the City: The Role of the Family in Urban West Africa." (In) Ruzicka, Lado T. (ed.). The Economic and Social Supports for High Fertility: Proceedings of the Conference Held in Canberra, November 16-18, 1976. Canberra, Australia: Australian National University. Development Studies Center. 1977. pp. 385-408.
Ware, Helen
"Women's Work and Fertility in Africa." (In) Kupinsky, Stanley (ed.). The Fertility of Working Women: A Synthesis of International Research. New York: Praeger Publishers. Praeger Special Studies in International Economics and Development. 1977. pp. 1-34.
Ware, Helen
"Economic Strategy and the Number of Children." (In) Caldwell, John C. (ed.). The Persistence of High Fertility: Population Prospects in the Third World. Canberra, Australia: Australian National University. Department of Demography. Volume Two. 1977. pp. 469-592.
Ware, Helen
Women, Education and Modernization of the Family in West Africa. Canberra, Australia: Australian National University. Department of Demography. Changing African Family Project Series. Monograph #7. 1981. 178p.
Ware, Helen
"Female and Male Life-Cycles." (In) Oppong, Christine (ed.). Female and Male in West Africa. London: George Allen and Unwin. 1983. pp. 6-31.
Ware, Helen
"Motivations for the Use of Birth Control: Evidence From West Africa." Demography. Volume 13 #4 November, 1976. pp. 479-494.
Wass, Betty M.
"The 'Kaba Sloht': Women's Dress and Ethnic Consciousness in Krio Society." Paper Presented at the Annual Meeting of the African Studies Association. Paper #92. Houston, Texas. 1977. 19p.
Watson, D.S.
"The Mutual Recognition of Ordained Ministries." Journal of Theology for Southern Africa. #23 June, 1978. pp. 56-70.

Weekes-Vagliani, Winifred
"Women, Food and Rural Development." (In) Rose, T. (ed.). Crisis and Recovery in Subsaharan Africa. Paris: OECD Development Center. 1985. pp. 104-110.

Wegner, J.R.
"The Status of Women in Jewish and Islamic Marriage and Divorce Law." Harvard Women's Law Journal. Volume 5 #1 1982.

Welch, Charles E. and Glick, Paul C.
"The Incidence of Polygamy in Contemporary Africa: A Research Note." Journal of Marriage and the Family. Volume 43 #1 February, 1981. pp. 191-192.

Westwood, Sally
Women and Power in Africa. Belfast, Maine: Porter. 1978.

White, Douglas R. and Bruton, Michael L. and Dow, Malcolm M.
"Sexual Division of Labor in African Agriculture: A Network Autocorrelation Analysis." American Anthropologist. Volume 83 #4 December, 1981. pp. 824-849.

White, Luise S.
"Women in the Changing African Family." (In) Hay, Margaret J. and Stichter, Sharon (eds.). African Women South of the Sahara. New York: Longman. 1984. pp. 53-68.

Whiting, Beatrice B.
"Rapid Social Change: Threat or Promise?" Ekistics. Volume 43 #255. February, 1977. pp. 64-68.

Whyte, Martin K.
The Status of Women in Preindustrial Societies. Princeton, New Jersey: Princeton University Press. 1978. 222p.

Whyte, Susan R.
"Men, Women and Misfortune in Bunyole." Man. Volume 16 #3 September, 1981. pp. 350-366.

Wilson, Monica H.
"Zig-Zag Change." Africa. Volume 46 #4 1976. pp. 399-409.

Winans, Edgar V.
"The Matter of Marauding Pigs." Anthropology U.C.L.A. Volume 8 #1/2 1976. pp. 45-59.

Wipper, Audrey
"Women's Voluntary Associations." (In) Hay, Margaret J. and Stichter, Sharon (eds.). African Women South of the Sahara. New York: Longman. 1984. pp. 69-86.

World Health Organization (WHO)
Traditional Practices Affecting the Health of Women and Children: Female Circumcision, Childhood Marriage, Nutritional Taboos, etc. Report of a Seminar, Khartoum, Sudan, February 10-15, 1979. Alexandria, Egypt: WHO. Eastern Mediterranean Regional Office. Technical Publication #2. 1979. 170p.

Wright, Marcia
"Bwanikwa: Consciousness and Protest Among Slave Women in Central Africa, 1886-1911." (In) Robertson, Claire C.

and Klein, Martin A. (eds.). Women and Slavery in Africa. Madison, Wisconsin: University of Wisconsin Press. 1983. pp. 246-267.

Wulf, Deirdre
"The Future of Family Planning in Sub-Saharan Africa." International Family Planning Perspectives. Volume 11 #1 March, 1985. pp. 1-8.

Youssef, Nadia H.
Women and Work in Developing Societies. Westport, Connecticut: Greenwood Press. 1976. 137p.

Youssef, Nadia H.
"The Status and Fertility Patterns of Muslim Women." (In) Beck, Lois and Keddie, Nikki R. (eds.). Women in the Muslim World. Cambridge, Massachusetts: Harvard University Press. 1978. pp. 69-99.

Youssef, Nadia H. and Buvinic, Mayra and Kudat, Ayse
Women in Migration: A Third World Focus. Washington, D.C.: U.S. Department of State. U.S. Agency for International Development. International Centre for Research on Women. Office of Women in Development. 1979. 151p.

Youssef, Nadia H.
"Interrelationship Between the Division of Labor in the Household, Women's Roles and Their Impact Upon Fertility." Paper Presented at the Informal Workshop on Women's Roles and Demographic Research Program. Geneva: International Labour Organization. November, 1978.

Youssef, Nadia H. and Hetler, Carol B.
"Establishing the Economic Condition of Woman-Headed Households in the Third World: A New Approach." (In) Buvinic, Mayra and Lycette, Margaret A. and McGreevey, William P. (eds.). Women and Poverty in the Third World. Baltimore, Maryland: Johns Hopkins University. 1983. pp. 216-243.

Youssef, Nadia H.
"Women and Agricultural Production in Muslim Societies." Studies in Comparative International Development. Volume 12 #1 Spring, 1977. pp. 41-58.

Zivetz, L.
The Impact of Rural Development on the Status of Women and its Consequences for Fertility in Africa. Submitted to the Research Triangle Institute and the Southeast Consortium for International Development. Chapel Hill, North Carolina. 1979.

Zoe-Obianga, Rose
"Resources in the Tradition for the Renewal of Community." Mid Stream. Volume 21 July, 1982. pp. 305-310.

Zoe-Obianga, Rose
"Resources in the Tradition for the Renewal of Community." (In) Parvey, Constance F. (ed.). The Community of Women and Men. Philadelphia, Pennsylvania: Fortress Press. 1983. pp. 68-73.

Development and Technology

Abdel Kader, Soha
"Research on the Status of Women, Development and Population Trends in Arab States: An Annotated Bibliography." (In) UNESCO. Bibliographic Guide to Studies on the Status of Women: Development and Population. Paris: United Nations Educational, Scientific and Cultural Organization. 1983. pp. 67-81.

Acsadi, George T.
"Effect of Economic Development on Fertility Trends in Africa." (In) Cairo Demographic Centre (CDC). Aspects of Population Change and Development in Some African and Asian Countries. Cairo, Egypt: CDC. CDC Research Monograph Series #9. 1984. pp. 57-105.

Adedeji, John A.
"Social Change and Women in African Sport." International Social Science Journal. Volume 34 #2 1982. pp. 210-218.

Adepoju, Aderanti
"Migration and Development in Tropical Africa: Some Research Priorities." African Affairs. Volume 76 #303 April, 1977. pp. 210-225.

Agarwal, Bina
"Women and Technological Change in Agriculture: The Asian and African Experience." (In) Ahmed, Iftikhar (ed.). Technology and Rural Women: Conceptual and Empirical Issues. Boston: George Allen and Unwin. 1985. pp. 67-114.

Ahmed, Iftikhar
"Technologies for Rural Women." Women at Work. #3 1977.

Ahmed, Iftikhar
"Technology and Rural Women in the Third World." International Labour Review. Volume 122 #4 July-August, 1983. pp. 493-505.

Ahmed, Iftikhar (ed.)
Technology and Rural Women: Conceptual and Empirical Issues. Boston: George Allen and Unwin. 1985. 383p.

Aidoo, Agnes A.
"Women and Development in Africa: Alternative Strategies for the Future." (In) Adedeji, A. and Shaw, T.M. (eds.). Economic Crisis in Africa: African Perspectives on Development Problems and Potentials. Boulder, Colorado: Lynne Rienner. 1985. pp. 201-217.

Amin, Samir
Imperialism and Unequal Development. New York: Monthly Review Press. 1977.

Amon-Nikoi, Gloria
"Women and Work in Africa." (In) Damachi, Ukandi G. and Diejomaoh, Victor P. Human Resources and African Development. New York: Praeger Publishers. 1978. pp. 188-219.

Anker, Richard
Demographic Change and the Role of Women: A Research Programme in Developing Countries. Geneva: International Labour Office. Population and Employment Working Paper #69. 1978. 27p.

Anokwa, C. Ofosu
"Higher Education in Home Economics: The Need for Collaboration." Paper Presented at the Workshop on the Role of Women and Home Economics in Rural Development in Africa. Rome: United Nations Food and Agricultural Organization. Alexandria, Egypt. October 17, 1983. 12p.

Anonymous
"African Women's Development Task Force." Rural Progress. Volume 1 #1 October, 1977. pp. 25-26.

Anonymous
"The Contribution of Women to the Development of the Pan African World." (In) Resolutions and Selected Speeches From the Sixth Pan African Congress. Dar-es-Salaam, Tanzania: Tanzania Publishing House. 1976. pp. 190-194.

Anonymous
"International Conference on the Role of Women in Liberation Struggles and Women in Development." IDOC Bulletin. #50/51 December-January, 1976. pp. 4-21.

Anonymous
"Official Documents: ILO Standards Relating to Women Workers; Equal Renumeration Convention: Situation in Africa." Women at Work. #2 1983.

Anonymous
"The Position of Women in Africa." Rural Progress. Volume 1 #3 1979. pp. 20-23.

Anonymous
Women and Family in Rural Development: An Annotated Bibliography. Rome: United Nations Food and Agriculture Organization. Documentation Centre and Population Documentation Centre. 1977. 66p.

Anonymous
"Women in Africa." Agenda. Volume 1 #2 February, 1978. pp. 1-7.

Anonymous
Women in Rural Development: Critical Issues. Geneva:

International Labour Organization. 1980. 51p.
Anonymous
"Women in Rural Development: Recommendations and Realities." Ceres. May-June, 1980. pp. 15-42.
Anonymous
"Workshop on Better Quality of Life for Rural Women Leaders." Rural Progress. Volume 2 #2 January, 1982. pp. 12-13.
Anyaoku, Emeka
"Changing Attitudes: A Cooperative Effort." Africa Report. Volume 30 #2 March, 1985. pp. 21-25.
Asare, Janet
"Making Life Easier for Africa's Rural Women." UNICEF News. #90 1976. pp. 20-23.
Ashworth, Georgina and May, Nicky (eds.)
Of Conjuring and Caring: Women in Development. London: Change. 1982. 28p.
Baffoun, Alya
"Women and Social Change in the Muslim Arab World." Women's Studies International Forum. Volume 5 #2 1982.
Balakrishnan, Revathi and Firebaugh, Francille M.
Roles of Women in Third World Economic Development From a Systems Perspective of Family Resource Management. Columbus, Ohio: Ohio State University. Department of Home Management and Housing. School of Home Economics. Working Papers #81-01. 1981. 39p.
Bay, Edna G. and Hafkin, Nancy J. (eds.)
"Women in Africa: Studies in Social and Economic Change." Stanford, California: Stanford University Press. 1976. 306p.
Bay, Edna G.
Women and Work in Africa. Boulder, Colorado: Westview Press. Westview Special Studies on Africa. 1982. 310p.
Beneria, Lourdes
"Conceptualizing the Labour Force: The Underestimation of Women's Economic Activities." Journal of Development Studies. Volume 17 #3 April, 1981. pp. 10-28.
Beneria, Lourdes
Women and Development: The Sexual Division of Labor in Rural Societies: A Study. New York: Praeger Publishers. Praeger Special Studies. 1982. 257p.
Beneria, Lourdes
"Conceptualizing the Labour Force: The Underestimation of Women's Economic Activities." (In) Nelson, Nici (ed.). African Women in the Development Process." Totowa, New Jersey: Frank Cass. 1981. pp. 10-28.
Bifani, Patricia
"Women and Development in Africa: A Tentative Approach Through Scenario Building." Journal of Eastern African Research and Development. Volume 15 1985. pp. 245-267.
Birdsall, Nancy and McGreevey, William P.
"The Second Sex in the Third World: Is Female Poverty a Development Issue?" Paper Prepared for the International Center for Research on Women Policy Roundtable. Washington, D.C. June 21, 1978.

Black, Naomi and Cottrell, Ann B.
Women and World Change: Equity Issues in Development. Beverly Hills, California: Sage Publications. Sage Focus Editions #38. 1981. 288p.

Blumberg, Rae
"Rural Women in Development: Veil of Invisibility, World of Work." International Journal of Intercultural Relations. Volume 3 #4 1979. pp. 447-472.

Blumberg, Rae
"Rural Women in Development." (In) Black, Naomi and Cottrell, Ann B. (eds.). Women and World Change: Equity Issues in Development. Beverly Hills, California: Sage Publications. 1981. pp. 32-56.

Boserup, Ester (ed.)
Traditional Division of Work Between the Sexes, A Source of Inequality: Research Symposium on Women and Decision Making: A Social Policy Priority. Geneva: International Institute for Labour Studies. Research Series #21. 1976. 32p.

Boulding, Elise
Women Peripheries and Food Production. (In) University of Arizona. Proceedings and Papers of the International Conference on Women and Food: Consortium for International Development. Tucson, Arizona: University of Arizona. 1978. pp. 22-44.

Boulding, Elise
"Productivity and Poverty of Third World Women: Problems in Measurement." (In) Buvinic, Mayra and Lycette, Margaret C. and McGreevey, William P. (eds.). Women and Poverty in the Third World. Baltimore, Maryland: Johns Hopkins University. 1983.

Broch-Due, Vigdis and Garfield, Patti
"Women and Pastoral Development: Some Research Priorities for the Social Sciences." (In) Galaty, John G. and Aronson, Dan and Salzman, Philip C. (eds.). The Future of Pastoral Peoples. Ottawa, Canada: International Development Research Centre. 1981. pp. 251-257.

Bujra, Janet M.
"Class, Gender and Capitalist Transformation in Africa." Africa Development. Volume 8 #3 1983. pp. 17-42.

Bukh, Jette
"Women in Food Production, Food Handling and Nutrition." Paper Presented to the Association of African Women for Research and Development (AAWORD) Workshop. Dakar, Senegal: AAWORD. December, 1977.

Burfisher, Mary E. and Horenstein, Nadine R.
"Incorporating Women Into Agricultural Development Planning: A Methodology." Paper Presented at the Annual Meeting of the African Studies Association. Paper #15. Washington, D.C. November 4-7, 1982.

Burke, Mary P.
"Women: The Missing Piece in the Development Puzzle." Agenda. Volume 1 #3 March, 1978. pp. 1-5.

Buvinic, Mayra
Women and World Development: An Annotated Bibliography.

Washington D.C.: Overseas Development Council. 1976. 162p.
Buvinic, Mayra and Youssef, Nadia H. and Schumacher, Ilsa
Women-Headed Households: The Ignored Factor in Development Planning. Washington D.C.: U.S. Department of State. U.S. Agency for International Development. International Center for Research on Women. Women in Development Office. March, 1978. 113p.
Buvinic, Mayra and Lycette, Margaret A. and McGreevey, William P.
Women and Poverty in the Third World. Baltimore, Maryland: Johns Hopkins University. Johns Hopkins Studies in Development. 1983. 329p.
Caldwell, John C.
"Towards a Restatement of Demographic Transition Theory: An Investigation of Conditions Before and at the Onset of Fertility Declining Employing Primarily African Experience and Data." Population and Development Review. Volume 2 #3 1976. pp. 321-366.
Callear, D.
Women and Coarse Grain Production in Africa. Expert Consultation on Women in Food Production. Rome: United Nations Food and Agriculture Organization. December 7, 1983. 13p.
Canady, Hortense
"Women in Development: The African Diaspora." Africa Report. Volume 30 #2 March-April, 1985. pp. 75.
Caplan, Patricia and Bujra, Janet M. (eds.)
Women United Women Divided: Comparative Studies of Ten Contemporary Cultures. Bloomington, Indiana: Indiana University Press. 1979. 288p.
Carew, Joy
"A Note on Women and Agricultural Technology in the Third World." Labour and Society. Volume 6 #3 July-September, 1981. pp. 279-285.
Carr, Marilyn
"Appropriate Technology for Rural African Women." Development Digest. Volume 20 #1 January, 1982. pp. 87-98.
Carr, Marilyn
Appropriate Technology for African Women. Addis Ababa, Ethiopia: United Nations Economic Commission for Africa. African Training and Research Center for Women. 1978. 105p.
Carr, Marilyn
"Technologies for Rural Women: Impact and Dissemination." (In) Ahmed, Iftikhar (ed.). Technology and Rural Women: Conceptual and Empirical Issues. Boston: George Allen and Unwin. 1985. pp. 115-153.
Carr, Marilyn
Technology and Rural Women in Africa. Addis Ababa, Ethiopia: United Nations Economic Commission for Africa. African Training and Research Center for Women. Joint Project With the International Labour Organization. ILO World Employment Programme Research Working Paper #61.

1980.
Carr, Marilyn
"Appropriate Technology for Women." Appropriate Technology. Volume 1 1979.
Carroll, Theodora F.
Women, Religion and Development in the Third World. New York: Praeger Publishers. 1983. 292p.
Case, Frederick
"Workers Movements: Revolution and Women's Consciousness in God's Bits of Wood." Canadian Journal of African Studies. Volume 15 #2 1981. pp. 272-292.
Castillo, Gelia T.
The Changing Role of Women in Rural Societies: A Summary of Trends and Issues. New York: Agricultural Development Council Inc. RTN Seminar Reports 12. February, 1977. 11p.
Caton, Douglas D.
Elements of the Food Production-Distribution System: An Overview on How Women Can Contribute. Proceedings and Papers of the International Conference on Women and Food Consortium for International Development. Tucson, Arizona: University of Arizona. 1978. pp. 45-61.
Caughman, Susan H.
Women at Work in Mali: The Case of the Markala Cooperative. Boston: Boston University. African Studies Center. Working Papers in African Studies #50. 1981. 72p.
Cernea, Michael M. (ed.).
Putting People First: Sociological Variables in Rural Development. New York: Oxford University Press. 1985. 430p.
Chan, S.
"Young Women and Development in Africa--Some Generally Unconsidered Considerations." Community Development Journal. Volume 18 #3 1983. pp. 257-262.
Chaney, Elsa M. and Simmons, Emmy and Staudt, Kathleen
Women in Development. Washington, D.C.: U.S. Department of State. U.S. Agency for International Development. Background Papers for the U.S. Delegation Attending the World Conference on Agrarian Reform and Rural Development. July, 1979. 40p.
Chaney, Elsa M.
Women in International Migration: Issues in Development Planning. Washington, D.C.: U.S. Department of State. U.S. Agency for International Development. Office of Women in Development. June, 1980.
Charlton, Sue E.
Women in Third World Development. Boulder, Colorado: Westview Press. 1984. 240p.
Claffey, Joan M. and Pigozzi, Mary J. and Axinn, Nancy W.
"Women in Development: A Selected Annotated Bibliography." International Journal of Intercultural Relations. Volume 3 1979.
Clark, Garcia
Fighting the African Food Crisis: Women Food Farmers and

Food Workers. New York: United Nations Development Fund for Women. 1985.
Cohen, Ronald and Knipp, Maggie
"Women and Change in West Africa: A Synthesis." Paper Presented at the Annual Meeting of the African Studies Association. Paper #16. Philadelphia, Pennsylvania. 1980.
Cohn, Steven and Wood, Robert and Haig, Richard
"U.S. Aid and Third World Women: The Impact of Peace Corps Programs." Economic Development and Cultural Change. Volume 29 #4 July, 1981. pp. 795-811.
Cook, Gayla
"Women in Africa: Working With African Women: Options for the West." Africa Report. Volume 26 #2 March-April, 1981. pp. 43-46.
Cook, Rebacca J.
"A Law on Family Welfare and Development in Africa." (In) International Planned Parenthood Federation (IPPF). Proceedings of the IPPF Africa Regional Conference. London: IPPF. 1977. pp. 241-246.
Creative Associates, Inc.
Participation of Women in the Economic Development Process: A Suggested Strategy for the African Bureau. Washington, D.C.: Creative Associates, Inc. 1980. 20p.
Cutrufelli, Maria R.
Women of Africa: Roots of Oppression. Totowa, New Jersey: Zed Press. 1983. 186p.
D'onofrio-Flores, Pamela M. and Pfafflin, Sheila M. (eds.)
Scientific-Technological Change and the Role of Women in Development. Boulder, Colorado: Westview Press. Published for the United Nations Institute for Training and Research. 1982. 206p.
Danforth, Sandra C.
Women and National Development. Monticello, Illinois: Vance Bibliographies. #P-916. February, 1982. 35p.
Date-Bah, Eugenia
"Rural Development and the Status of Women." Paper Presented at a Seminar on the Role of Population Factor in the Rural Development Strategy." Monrovia, Liberia. 1980.
Dauber, Roslyn and Cain, Melinda (eds.)
Women and Technological Change in Developing Countries. Boulder, Colorado: Westview Press. AAAS Selected Symposium #53. 1980. 266p.
Dawit, T.
"Mass Media and Rural Women in Africa." Assignment Children. Volume 38 #2 April-June, 1977. pp. 119-120.
De Graft-John, K.E.
"Issues in Family Welfare and Development in Africa." (In) International Planned Parenthood Federation (IPPF). Proceedings of the IPPF Africa Regional Conference. London: IPPF. 1977. pp. 33-45.
DeLancey, Virginia H.
"The Role of Credit Unions in Development for West African Women." Paper Presented at the Annual Meeting of

the African Studies Association. Paper #29. Bloomington, Indiana. October 21-24, 1981.

DeLancey, Virginia H.
"The Relationship Between Female Labor Force Participation and Fertility: Considerations of Role Compatibility in Research Methodology for Developing Countries." Paper Presented at the Annual Meeting of the African Studies Association. Paper #34. Los Angeles, California. 1979. 23p.

Dey, Jennie M.
Women in Food Production and Food Security in Africa. Rome: United Nations Food and Agriculture Organization. Women in Agriculture Series #3. 1984. 101p.

Dey, Jennie M.
"Women in African Rice Farming Systems." International Rice Commission Newsletter. Volume 32 #2 December, 1983. pp. 1-4.

Dey, Jennie M.
Women in Rice Farming Systems, Focus: Subsaharan Africa. Rome: United Nations Food and Agriculture Organization. Women in Agriculture Series #2. 1984. 106p.

Dey, Jennie M.
"Women in African Rice Farming Systems." (In) International Rice Research Institute. 'Women in Rice Farming': Proceedings of a Conference on Women in Rice Farming Systems. September 26-30, 1983. Brookfield, Vermont: Gower Publishing Co. 1985. pp. 419-444.

Dhamija, Jasleen
"Income-Generating Activities for Rural Women in Africa: Some Successes and Failures." (In) International Labour Organization (ILO). Rural Development and Women in Africa. Geneva: ILO. 1984. pp. 75-78.

Dhamija, Jasleen
"Technology as a Target to the Development of Women's Skills in Africa." Ceres. # 84 November, 1981. pp. 24-27.

Di Domenico, Catherine M. and Asuni, Judy and Scott, Jacqueline
"Family Welfare and Development in Africa." (In) International Planned Parenthood Federation (IPPF). Proceedings of the IPPF Africa Regional Conference, University of Ibadan. London: IPPF. 1976. pp. 283-284.

Dirasse, Laketch
The Critical Needs of African Women and Appropriate Strategies in the Framework of the Gisenyi and Lusaka MULPOCS. Addis Ababa, Ethiopia: United Nations Economic Commission for Africa. African Training and Research Centre for Women. 1981. 35p.

Dixon, Ruth B.
"Land, Labour and the Sex Composition of the Agricultural Labour Force: An International Comparison." Development and Change. Volume 14 #3 July, 1983. pp. 347-372.

Dixon, Ruth B.
Assessing the Impact of Development Projects on Women. Washington, D.C.: U.S. Department of State. U.S. Agency

for International Development. Office of Women in Development. AID Program Evaluation Discussion Paper #8. 1980. 105p.

Dixon, Ruth B.
"Jobs for Women in Rural Industry and Services." Paper Presented at the Conference on Agrarian Reform and Rural Development. Rome: United Nations Food and Agriculture Organization. Washington, D.C.: U.S. Department of State. U.S. Agency for International Development. Office of Women in Development. July, 1979.

Dixon, Ruth B.
"Seeing the Invisible Women Farmers in Africa: Improving Research and Data Collection Methods." (In) Monson, J. and Kalb, M. (eds.). Women as Food Producers in Developing Countries. Los Angeles: University of California-Los Angeles. African Studies Center and OEF International. 1985. pp. 19-35.

Dixon-Mueller, Ruth
Women's Work in the Third World Agriculture: Concepts and Indicators. Geneva: ILO. Women, Work and Development Series. Volume 9. 1985. 151p.

Due, Jean M. and Summary, Rebecca
"Constraints to Women and Development in Africa." Journal of Modern African Studies. Volume 20 #1 March, 1982. pp. 155-166.

Due, Jean M. and Summary, Rebecca
"Constraints to Women and Development in Africa." Paper Presented at the Annual Meeting of the African Studies Association. Paper #35. Los Angeles, California. 1979. 23p.

Due, Jean M. and Summary, Rebecca
Constraints to Women and Development in Africa. Urbana, Illinois: University of Illinois-Urbana-Champaign. Department of Agricultural Economics. Staff Paper Series E. Agricultural Economics 79-E-83. May, 1979. 27p.

Dulansey, Maryanne L.
Can Technology Help Women Feed Their Families? Post Harvest Storage, Processing and Cooking: Some Observations. Washington, D.C.: Consultants in Development. 1979. 9p.

Dulansey, Maryanne L.
Women in Development Program Concerns in Francophone Sahel: Report of a Workshop. Washington, D.C.: U.S. Department of State. U.S. Agency for International Development. Bobo-Dioulasso, Upper Volta. June 5-7, 1979. 11p.

El Bushra, Judy and Bekele, Abebech and Hammour, Fawzia
"Socio-Economic Development and Women Changing Status." Paper Presented to the Conference on Women and the Environment. Khartoum, Sudan: University of Khartoum. Institute of Environmental Studies. April 4-7, 1981.

Elias, Misrak
Training for Development Planning and Women, an African Perspective: Report on the Second Training Programme. Arusha, Tanzania: Eastern and Southern Africa Management

Institute. April 5-May 14, 1982. 55p.
Elias, Misrak
Training for Development Planning and Women: An African Perspective. Arusha, Tanzania: Eastern and Southern African Management Institute. Annual Report and Report of the First Training Programme. September 16, 1980-September 15, 1981. 1981.
Elson, Diane and Pearson, Ruth
"'Nimble Fingers Make Cheap Workers': An Analysis of Women's Employment in Third World Export Manufacturing." Feminist Review. Volume 7 Spring, 1981.
Ember, C.R.
"Relative Decline in Women's Contribution to Agriculture With Intensification." American Anthropologist. Volume 85 #2 June, 1983. pp. 285-304.
Emecheta, Buchi
"Building on Tradition: Can the Past Provide Direction for the Future." Paper Presented at the 'Women and Work Symposium #6'. Urbana, Illinois: University of Illinois. 1979.
Engberg, L.E.
"Emphasis on Economics--A Way to Strengthen the Relationship of Home Economics With Agriculture." Paper Presented at the Workshop on the Role of Women and Home Economics in Rural Development in Africa. Rome: United Nations Food and Agriculture Organization. Alexandria, Egypt. October 17, 1983. 10p.
Fapohunda, Eleanor R.
"Female and Male Work Profiles." (In) Oppong, Christine (ed.). Female and Male in West Africa. London: George Allen and Unwin. 1983. pp. 32-53.
Fatehally, Laeeq (ed.)
Women in the Third World. Bombay, India: Leslie Sawhny Programme. 1980. 155p.
Fortmann, Louise P.
Tillers of the Soil and Keepers of the Hearth: A Bibliographic Guide to Women and Rural Development. Ithaca, New York: Cornell University. Center for International Studies. Rural Development Committee. Bibliography Series #2. 1979. 53p.
Fortmann, Louise P.
"The Plight of the Invisible Farmer: The Effect of National Agricultural Policy on Women in Africa." (In) Dauber, Roslyn and Cain, Melinda L. Women and Technological Change in Developing Countries. Boulder, Colorado: Westview Press. 1981. pp. 205-214.
Fortmann, Louise P.
"A Role for Women in Agroforestry Projects." (In) United Nations Food and Agriculture Organization (FAO). 1983 Training for Agriculture and Rural Development. Rome: FAO. Economic and Social Development Series #31. 1984. pp. 21-26.
Fraker, Anne and Harrell-Bond, Barbara
"Feminine Influence." West Africa. December 17, 1979. pp. 2182-2186.

Franke, R.
"Mode of Production and Population Patterns: Policy Implications for West African Development." International Journal of Health Services. Volume 13 1981. pp. 361-387.

Fraser, Arvonne
Women in Development. Washington, D.C.: U.S. Department of State. U.S. Agency for International Development. Office of Women in Development. 1977. 12p.

Gallin, Rita and Spring, Anita (eds.).
Women Creating Wealth: Transforming Economic Development. Washington, D.C.: Association for Women in Development. 1985. 183p.

Gebre-Selassie, Alasebu
"The Situation of Women in Africa: A Review." Nairobi: UNICEF. Eastern Africa Regional Office. 1979. 65p.

Germain, Adrienne
"Poor Rural Women: A Policy Perspective." Journal of International Affairs. Volume 3 #2 Fall-Winter, 1976. 20p.

Germain. Adrienne
"Research on Women in Agricultural Production in Eastern and Southern Africa." Paper Presented at a Workshop on Women in Agricultural Production in Eastern and Southern Africa. Nairobi, Kenya. April 9-11, 1980.

Gilligan, John J.
"Importance of Third World Women." Rivista di Studi Politici Internazionali. Volume 45 #3 July-September, 1978.

Gladwin, Christina and Staudt, Kathleen A. and McMillan, Della
Reaffirming the Agricultural Role of Women: One Solution to the Food Crisis. (In) Association of Facilities of Agriculture in Africa. Proceedings of the Fifth General Conference on Food Security. Manzini, Swaziland. April, 1984.

Hafkin, Nancy J. and Bay, Edna G. (eds.)
Women in Africa: Studies in Social and Economic Change. Stanford, California: Stanford University Press. 1976. 306p.

Hafkin, Nancy J.
Women and Development in Africa: An Annotated Bibliography. Addis Ababa, Ethiopia: United Nations Economic Commisssion for Africa. African Training and Research Centre for Women. Bibliographic Series #1. 1977. 177p.

Hagan, A.L.
"The Role of Women in Rural Development: Some Critical Issues." (In) Mondjanagni, A.C. La Participation Populaire an Developpement en Afrique Noire. Paris: Karthala; Doula, Institut Pan Africain Pour Le Developpement. 1984. pp. 75-87.

Haile, Tsehaye
"Community Participation in Rural Water Supply Development." (In) International Development Research

Centre (IDRC). Rural Water Supply in Developing Countries Workshop on Training, Zomba, Malawi, August 5-12, 1980. Ottawa, Canada: IDRC. 1981. pp. 89-95.

Haq, Khadija (ed.)
Equality of Opportunity Within and Among Nations. New York: Praeger Publishers. Praeger Special Studies in International Economics and Development. 1977. 223p.

Harder, Gudrun M.
"Problems of Women in Developing Countries: A Selected Bibliography." Verfassung unp Recht in Ubersee. #10 1977. pp. 133-160.

Hawthorn, Geoffrey (ed.)
Population and Development: High and Low Fertility in Poorer Countries. London: Frank Cass. 1978. 210p.

Henn, Jeanne K.
"Feeding the Cities and Feeding the Peasants: What Role for Africa's Women Farmers." World Development. Volume 11 #12 1983.

Howard, Rhoda E.
"Women and the Crisis in Commonwealth Africa." International Political Science Review. Volume 6 #3 1985. pp. 287-296.

Huggard, Marianne
"The Rural Woman as a Food Producer: An Assessment of the Resolution on Women and Food From the World Food Conference in Rome, 1974." Paper Presented at the International Conference on Women and Food: Consortium for International Development. Tucson, Arizona. 10p. 1978.

International Center for Research on Women
Keeping Women Out: A Structural Analysis of Women's Employment in Developing Countries. Washington, D.C.: U.S. Department of State. U.S. Agency for International Development. Office on Women in Development. Bureau of Program and Policy Coordination. April, 1980.

International Center for Research on Women
The Productivity of Women in Developing Countries: Measurement Issues and Recommendtions. Washington, D.C.: U.S. Department of State. U.S. Agency for International Development. Office on Women in Development. 1980. 46p.

International Development Research Centre (IDRC)
Rural Water Supply in Developing Countries: Proccedings of a Workshop on Training. Ottawa, Canada: IDRC. Zomba, Malawi. August 5-12, 1981. 144p.

International Institute for Labour Studies (IILS) and Organization of African Unity (OAU)
Food Self-Sufficiency, Technological Autonomy, and Social Progress in Africa: A Research Guide. Geneva: IILS/Addis Ababa, Ethiopia: OAU. 1984. 144p.

International Labour Office (ILO)
Improved Village Technology for Women's Activities: A Manual for West Africa. London: ILO. 1985.

International Labour Organization (ILO)
Rural Development and Women in Africa: Papers of the ILO

Tripartite African Regional Seminar on Rural Development and Women, June 15-19, 1981. Geneva: ILO. Dakar, Senegal. 1984. 157p.

International Labour Organization (ILO)
Women, Technology and the Development Process. Paper Presented to the African Regional Meeting of UNCSTD. Geneva: ILO. Cairo, Egypt. July 24-29, 1978.

International Maize and Wheat Improvement Center (CIMMYT)
"CIMMYT's Experience With the User's Perspective in Technology Development." (In) Rockefeller Foundation (eds.). Women and Agricultural Technology: Relevance for Research. Volume 2-Experiences in International and National Research. New York: Rockefeller Foundation. 1985. pp. 13-26.

International Planned Parenthood Federation (IPPF)
Family Welfare and Development in Africa: Proceedings of the IPPF Africa Regional Conference, University of Ibadan. August 29-September 3, 1976. London: IPPF. Ibadan, Nigeria. 1977. 327p.

Javillonar, Gloria W.
Rural Development, Women's Roles and Fertility in Developing Countries: Review of the Literature. Chapel Hill, North Carolina: Research Triangle Institute. 1979. pp. 32-75.

Johnston, Bruce F. and Meyer, Anthony J.
"Nutrition, Health and Population in Strategies for Rural Development." Economic Development and Cultural Change. Volume 26 #1 October, 1977. pp. 1-23.

Johnston, Bruce F. and Meyer, Anthony J.
"Nutrition, Health and Population in Strategies for Rural Development." Nairobi: University of Nairobi. Institute for Development Studies. Discussion Paper #238. 1976. 45p.

Jorgensen, Kirsten
"Water Supply Projects in Africa: The Need to Involve the Main Users--Women." Ideas and Action Bulletin. #150 1983. pp. 14-18.

Kamba, Kate
"Fuel Wood and Energy Development for African Women." Paper Presented at the Workshop on Women in Agricultural Development. Addis Ababa, Ethiopia: United Nations Economic Commission for Africa. Awassa, Ethiopia. June 26, 1983. 13p.

Karanja, Wambui Wa
"Women and Work: A Study of Female and Male Attitudes in the Modern Sector of an African Metropolis." (In) Ware, Helen (ed.). Women, Education and Modernization of the Family in West Africa. Canberra, Australia: Australian National University. Department of Demography. Changing African Family Project Series. Monograph #7. 1978.

Kayongo-Male, Diana
"Helping Self-Help Groups Help Themselves: Training of Leaders of Women's Groups." Journal of Eastern African Research and Development. Volume 13 1983. pp. 88-103.

Kharas, Purveen
Women in Development--Africa: An Annotated Bibliography. Rome: United Nations Food and Agriculture Organization. 1978. 12p.

King-Akerele, O.
Traditional Palm Oil Processing, Women's Role and the Application of Appropriate Technology. Addis Ababa, Ethiopia: United Nations Economic Commission for Africa. Research Series. 1983.

Kisekka, Mere N.
"The Status of Women, Development and Population Trends in Africa: An Annotated Bibliography." Paper Presented at the Meeting of Experts on Research on the Status of Women, Development and Population Trends: Evaluation and Prospects. Paris: United Nations Educational, Scientific and Cultural Organization. 1980. 66p.

Kisekka, Mere N.
"Research on the Status of Women, Development and Population Trends in Africa: An Annotated Bibliography." (In) United Nations Educational, Scientific and Cultural Organization. Bibliographic Guide to Studies on the Status of Women: Development and Population. Paris: UNESCO. 1983. pp. 41-66.

Kitching, Gavin
"Proto-Industrialization and Demographic Change: A Thesis and Some Possible African Implications." Journal of African History. Volume 24 #2 1983. pp. 221-240.

Kizerbo, Joseph
"Women and the Energy Crisis in the Sahel Africa. From the Seminar on Fuel and Energy Development for African Women in Rural Areas, Bamako, Mali, December, 1980." Unasylva. Volume 33 #133 1981. pp. 5-10.

Kocher, James E.
"Socioeconomic Development and Fertility Change in Rural Africa." Paper Presented at the Annual Meeting of the African Studies Association. Paper #44. Boston, Massachusetts. 1976. 22p.

Kocher, James E.
"Supply-Demand Disequilibria and Fertility Change in Africa--Toward a More Appropriate Economic Approach." Social Biology. Volume 30 #1 1983. pp. 41-58.

Kwawu, J.
"The Role of Home Economics in Rural Development: A Focus on Family Planning." Paper Presented at the Workshop on the Role of Women and Home Economics in Rural Development in Africa. Rome: United Nations Food and Agricultural Organization. Alexandria, Egypt. October 17, 1983. 20p.

Lancaster, Chet S.
"Women, Horticulture and Society in Sub-Saharan Africa." American Anthropologist. Volume 78 #3 September, 1976. pp. 539-564.

Lewis, Barbara C.
"State/Society; Public/Private and Women: A Political Scientist's View." Paper Presented at the Annual Meeting

of the African Studies Association. Paper #75. Bloomington, Indiana. October 21-24, 1981.

Lewis, Barbara C. (ed.)
The Invisible Farmer: Women and the Crisis in Agriculture. Washington, D.C.: U.S. Department of State. U.S. Agency for International Development. Office of Women in Development. 1982. 456p.

Lewis, Shelby
"African Women and National Development." (In) Lindsay, Beverly (ed.). Comparative Perspectives of Third World Women: The Impact of Race, Sex and Class. New York: Praeger Publishers. 1980. pp. 36-54.

Lindsay, Beverly
"Women and National Development in Africa." Western Journal of Black Studies. Volume 1 #1 March, 1977. pp. 53-58.

Lindsay, Beverly (ed.)
Comparative Perspectives of Third World Women: The Impact of Race, Sex and Class. New York: Praeger Publishers. Praeger Special Studies. 1980. 318p.

Loutfi, Martha F.
Rural Women: Unequal Partners in Development. Geneva: International Labour Organization. 1982. 80p.

Mair, Lucille
"Adult Learning. Women and Development." Prospects 7. #2 1977. pp. 238-443.

Makundi, K. and Warioba, Evelyn
"Psychological Relationship Between Men and Women." Paper Presented at the Workshop on Women's Studies and Development. Dar-es-Salaam, Tanzania: University of Dar-es-Salaam. Bureau of Resource Assessment and Land Use Planning. Paper #27. September 24-29, 1979. 5p.

Marshall, Susan E.
"Politics and Female Status in North Africa: A Reconsideration of Development Theory." Economic Development and Cultural Change. Volume 32 #3 April, 1984. pp. 499-524.

Mason, Nondita
"Women and Development in Third World Writing." Populi. Volume 5 #4 1978. pp. 45-49.

Matsepe, Ivy F.
"Underdevelopment and African Women." Journal of Southern African Affairs. Volume 2 #2 April, 1977. pp. 135-143.

Matsepe-Casaburri, Ivy F.
Uneven Development and Political Consciousness Among African Women in Southern Africa. Lusaka, Zambia: United Nations Institute on Namibia. 1978.

Matsepe-Casaburri, Ivy F.
"Underdevelopment and African Women." Paper Presented at the Conference of the Southern Africa Research Group. College Park, Maryland: Southern Africa Research Group. September, 1976.

Max-Forson, Margaret
"The Role of Women and Youth in Development." Rural

Progress. Volume 1 #3 1979. pp. 28-30.
Max-Forson, Margaret
Progress and Obstacles in Achieving the Minimum Objectives of the World and Africa Plans of Action: A Critical Review. Report Presented to the Second Regional Conference on the Integration of Women in Development. Addis Ababa, Ethiopia: United Nations Economic Commission for Africa. Lusaka, Zambia. December 3-7, 1979. 56p.
Mbilinyi, Marjorie J.
"Women as Labor in Underdevelopment." Paper Presented at the Wellesley Conference on Women and Development. Wellesley, Massachusetts: Wellesley College. Wellesley Center for Research on Women. June, 1976.
McDowell, James and Hazzard, Virginia
"Village Technology and Women's Work in Eastern Africa." Assignment Children. Volume 36 Oct.-Dec., 1976. pp. 53-65.
McGrath, Mary J.
"What Private Institutions, Particularly Cooperative, Can do to Facilitate Full Participation of Women in Meeting Food and Nutrition Needs." (In) University of Arizona. Proceedings and Papers of the International Conference on Women and Food: Consortium for International Development. Tucson, Arizona: University of Arizona. 1978. pp. 145-153.
McKie, David
"Third World Women and Development: Ending the Women's Decade." International Perspectives. July-August, 1984. pp. 13-16.
Mitchnik, David A.
Improving Ways of Skill Acquisition of Women for Rural Employment in Some African Countries. Geneva: International Labour Organization. World Employment Programme Research. Education and Employment Research Project. Working Papers. February, 1977. 78p.
Monson, Jamie and Kalb, Marion
Women as Food Producers in Developing Countries. Los Angeles: University of California-Los Angeles. African Studies Center. African Studies Association. OEF International. 1985. 118p.
Moody, Elizabeth J.
Women and Development: A Select Bibliography. Pretoria, South Africa: Africa Institute of South Africa. Occasional Papers #43. 1979. 28p.
Moody, Elize
"Women: An Underrated Development Source." South African Journal of African Affairs. Volume 9 #2 1979. pp. 64-71.
Moss, G. and Dunn, M. and Nsarko, J.D.
"Home Economics in Rural Development in Africa: The Village Woman's Day." Paper Presented at the Workshop on the Role of Women and Home Economics in Rural Development in Africa. Rome: United Nations Food and Agricultural Organization. Alexandria, Egypt. 1983. 7p.

Muchena, Olivia N.
"Women in Southern Africa: Are Women Integrated Into Development?" Africa Report. Volume 28 #2 March-April, 1983. pp. 4-6.

Mullings, L.
"Women and Economic Change in Africa." (In) Hafkin, N. and Bay, Edna G. (eds.). Women in Africa: Studies in Social and Economic Change. Stanford, California: Stanford University Press. 1976. pp. 239-264.

Munuo, Edith
"Education for Equality." Paper Presented at the Workshop on Women's Studies and Development. Dar-es-Salaam, Tanzania: University of Dar-es-Salaam. Bureau of Resource Assessment and Land Use Planning. Paper #14. September 24-29, 1979. 19p.

Naali, Shamsahd
"Legal Provisions for Women's Participation in Cooperatives." Paper Presented at the Seminar on Women's Studies and Development. Dar-es-Salaam, Tanzania: University of Dar-es-Salaam. Bureau of Resource Assessment and Land Use Planning. Paper #15. September 24-29, 1979. 10p.

Nelson, Cynthia (ed.)
Women, Health and Development: Papers Presented at the 1976 Open University Seminar. Cairo, Egypt: American University of Cairo. Cairo Papers in Social Sciences. Volume One. Monograph One. 1977. 84p.

Nelson, Nici (ed.)
African Women in the Development Process. Totowa, New Jersey: F. Cass. 1981. 136p.

Newman, Jeanne S.
"Some Indicators of Women's Economic Roles in Sub-Saharan Africa." Paper Presented at the Annual Meeting of the American Statistical Association. Toronto, Ontario, Canada. August, 1983.

Newman, Jeanne S.
Women of the World: Sub-Saharan Africa. Washington, D.C.: U.S. Department of Commerce. U.S. Agency for International Development. Office of Women in Development. August, 1984. 200p.

Njoku, John E.
The Dawn of African Women. Hicksville, New York: Exposition Press. 1977. 96p.

Njoku, John E.
The World of the African Woman. Metuchen, New Jersey: Scarecrow Press. 1980. 132p.

Norem, R.H.
"The Integration of a Family Systems Perspective Into Farming Systems Projects." (In) Caldwell, John and Rojas, Mary (eds.). Family Systems and Farming Systems: A Second Annual Conference in the World of Women in Development Series. Blacksburg, Virginia: Virgnia Polytechnic Institute and State University. 1983.

North, Jeanne
"Women Participants in the Food Marketing System in West

Africa." (In) University of Arizona. Proceedings and Papers of the International Conference on Women and Food: Consortium for International Development. Tucson, Arizona: University of Arizona. 1978. pp. 103-111.

Nwanosike, Eugene O.
Women and Development: A Select Bibliography: A Select and Partially Annotated Bibliography. Buea, Cameroon: Regional Pan-African Institute for Development/West Africa. Bibliographic Series #10. 1980. 63p.

O'Barr, Jean F.
Third World Women: Factors in Their Changing Status. Durham, North Carolina: Duke University. Center for International Studies. Occasional Paper #2. 1976. 94p.

O'Barr, Jean F. (ed.)
Perspectives on Power: Women in Africa, Asia and Latin America. Durham, North Carolina: Duke University. Center for International Studies. Occasional Paper #13. 1982. 120p.

O'Kelly, Elizabeth
"Appropriate Technology for Women of the Developing Countries." Peace Corps Program and Training Journal. Volume 4 #6 1977.

O'Kelly, Elizabeth
Rural Women: Their Integration in Development Programmes and How Simple Intermediate Technologies Can Help Them. Available From the Author: 3 Cumberland Gardens, Lloyd Square, London, England WC1X 9AF. $4.00. 1978. 84p.

Obbo, Christine S. and Nelson, Nici
African Women: Their Struggle for Economic Independence. Westport, Connecticut: Lawrence Hill. 1980. 176p.

Ogundipe-Leslie, Molara
"African Women, Culture and Another Development." Journal of African Marxists. #5 February, 1984. pp. 77-92.

Okeyo, Achola P.
"African Women in Changing Rural Economies." Courier. Volume 57 Sept.-Oct., 1979. pp. 63-65.

Okeyo, Achola P.
The Role of Women in Changing Traditional Farming Systems. Paper Presented at the Workshop on Policies and Programmes for Increased Food and Agricultural Production in Traditional Subsistence Farms in Africa. Rome: United Nations Food and Agriculture Organization. Arusha, Tanzania. December 10, 1984. 27p.

Okeyo, Acholo P.
"Women and Africa: Reflections on Development Myths." Africa Report. Volume 26 #2 March-April, 1981. pp. 7-10.

Oloko, Olatunde
Modernization and Social Problems in Africa. Lagos, Nigeria: University of Lagos. United Nations Economic Commission for Africa. 1979.

Ooko-Ombaka, Oki
"An Assessment of National Machinery for Women." Assignment Children. #49/50 Spring, 1980.

Oomen-Myim, Marie A.
"Involvement of Rural Women in Decision-Making Within Smallscale Agricultural Projects." Paper Presented at the Workshop on Women's Studies and Development. Dar-es-Salaam, Tanzania: University of Dar-es-Salaam. Bureau of Resource Assessment and Land Use Planning. Paper #44. September 24-29, 1979. 7p.

Osseo-Asare, Fran S.
Towards a Strategy for the Integration of Women Into Development. University Park, Pennsylvania: Pennsylvania State University. 1982.

Overholt, C. and Anderson, M. and Cloud, K. and Austin, J.
Gender Roles in Development Projects: A Casebook. West Hartford: Connecticut: Kumarian Press. Kumarian Press Case Studies Series. 1985. 326p.

Pala, Achola O.
"Definitions of Women and Development: An African Perspective." Signs. Volume 3 #1 Autumn, 1977. pp. 9-13.

Pala, Achola O.
African Women in Rural Development: Research Trends and Priorities. Washington, D.C.: American Council on Education. Overseas Liaison Committee. OLC Paper #12. December, 1976. 35p.

Pala, Achola O. and Seidman, Ann
"A Proposed Model of the Status of Women in Africa." Paper Presented at the Conference on Women and Development. Wellesley, Massachusetts: Wellesley College. June, 1976.

Pala, Achola O.
"Definitions of Women and Development: An African Perspective." (In) Wellesley Editorial Committee. Women and National Development: The Complexities of Change. Chicago: University of Chicago Press. 1977. pp. 9-13.

Pala, Achola O.
"Definitions of Women and Development: An African Perspective." (In) Steady, Filomina C. (ed.). The Black Woman Cross-Culturally. Cambridge, Massachusetts: Schenkman Publishing. 1981. pp. 209-214.

Palmer, Ingrid
"Rural Women and the Basic Needs Approach." International Labour Review. Volume 115 #1 January-February, 1977. pp. 97-98.

Palmer, Ingrid
"Women in Rural Development." International Development Review. Volume 22 #2/3 1980. pp. 39-45.

Palmer, Ingrid
"The Role of Women in Agrarian Reform and Rural Development." (In) United Nations. Land Reform. Rome: United Nations Food and Agriculture Organization. 1979. pp. 57-70.

Palmer, Ingrid
'The Nemow Case', Case Studies of the Impact of Large Scale Development Projects on Women: A Series for Planners. New York: Population Council. International

Programs Working Paper #7. September, 1979. 92p.

Papanek, Hanna
"Development Planning for Women." (In) Wellesley Editorial Committee. Women and National Development: The Complexities of Change. Chicago: University of Chicago Press. 1977. pp. 14-21.

Pellow, Deborah
Marginality and Individual Consciousness: Women in Modernizing Africa. East Lansing, Michigan: Michigan State University. Office of Women in International Development. Working Paper #28. July, 1983. 33p.

Petty, Irene M.
"The Role of African Women in Identifying Needs for Labor Saving Devices." Prepared for the AAAS Workshop on Women and Development for UNCSTD. New York: United Nations. 1979.

Phillips, Beverly
Women in Rural Development: A Bibliography. Madison, Wisconsin: University of Wisconsin-Madison. Land Tenure Center Library. Training and Methods Series #29. 1979. 45p.

Phillott-Almeida, Ralphina
"Women and Water Resources Management for Socio-Economic Development in Africa: Health, Sanitation and Environmental Aspects." (In) United Nations Economic Commission for Africa (UNECA) (eds.). Regional Meeting on Socio-Economic and Policy Aspects of Water Management in Africa. Addis Ababa, Ethiopia: UNECA. June, 1986.

Reno, Barbara M.
Increasing Women's Credit Through Credit Unions in West Africa. Bilingual Seminar. Nairobi: Africa Co-Operative Savings and Credit Association. March 2-6, 1981. 43p.

Rihani, May
Development as if Women Mattered: An Annotated Bibliography With a Third World Focus. Washington, D.C.: Overseas Development Council. Occasional Paper #10. 1978. 137p.

Ritchie, Jean A.
"Training Women for Development in Africa." (In) United Nations Food and Agriculture Organization (FAO). Training for Agriculture and Rural Development, 1977. Rome: United Nations. FAO. Economic and Development Series #7. 1977. pp. 19-26.

Ritchie, Jean A.
"Impact of Changing Food Production. Processing and Marketing Systems on the Role of Women." (In) Proceedings of the World Conference. Ames, Iowa: Iowa State University Press. 1977. pp. 129-144.

Ritchie, Jean A.
General Conclusions on the Integration of Women in Agrarian Reform and Rural Development in Africa. Rome: United Nations Food and Agriculture Organization. 1978.

Ritchie, Jean A.
The Integration of Women in Agrarian Reform and Rural Development in English Speaking Countries of the African

Region. Rome: United Nations Food and Agriculture Organization. March, 1978. 95p.
Roark, Paula
Successful Rural Water Supply Projects and the Concerns of Women. Washington, D.C.: U.S. Department of State. U.S. Agency for International Development. Office of Women in Development. September, 1980. 66p.
Roboff, Farron V. and Renwick, Hilary L.
"The Changing Role of Women in the Development of the Sahel." Paper Presented to the Annual Meeting of the African Studies Association. Paper #92. Boston, Massachusetts 1976. 12p.
Rogers, Barbara
"What do Women Want?" Appropriate Technology. Volume 4 1979.
Rogers, Barbara
"Well, Um, I Suppose We Never Thought of it Like That...." Development. Volume 20 #3/4 1978. pp. 61-64.
Rogers, Barbara
"Women's Projects: New Segregation?" Africa Report. Volume 23 #3 May-June, 1978. pp. 48-50.
Rogers, Barbara
"Food, Fertility and Nuclear Mothers: How Development Can Increase Rather than Reduce the Social and Economic Burdens of African Women." Populi. Volume 5 #1 1978. pp. 23-27.
Rogers, Barbara
The Domestication of Women: Discrimination in Developing Societies. New York: St. Martin's Press. 1980. 200p.
Rogombe, Rose F.
"Equal Partners in Development." Africa Report. Volume 30 #2 March-April, 1985. pp. 17-20.
Romalis, Coleman and Romalis, Shelly
"Sexism, Racism and Technological Change: Two Cases of Minority Protest." International Journal of Women's Studies. Volume 6 May-June, 1983. pp. 270-287.
Rousseau-Mukenge, Ida
"Conceptualizations of African Women's Role in Development: A Search for New Directions." Journal of International Affairs. Volume 30 #2 Fall/Winter, 1976. pp. 261-268.
Rugh, Andrea B.
Women, Agriculture and Rural Development. Report Presented to the U.S. Agency for International Development Mission in Cairo, Egypt. Washington, D.C.: U.S. Department of State. U.S. Agency for International Development. 1979.
Sachak, N.
"Agricultural Research: Priorities for Women." (In) Bengtsson, Bo and Tedla, Getachew. Strengthening National Agricultural Research: Report From a SAREC Workshop, September 10-17, 1979. Stockholm, Sweden: Swedish Agency for Research Cooperation in Developing Countries. 1980. pp. 62-69.

Sachs, Carolyn E.
Invisible Farmers: Women in Agricultural Production. Totowa, New Jersey: Rowman and Allen Held. 1983. 153p.

Safilios-Rothschild, Constantina
The Role of Women in Modernizing Agricultural Systems. Washington, D.C.: U.S. Department of State. U.S. Agency for International Development. Office of Women in Development. May, 1981. 31p.

Safilios-Rothschild, Constantina
Can Agriculture in the Third World Modernize With Traditional Female Agricultural Labor? State College, Pennsylvania: Pennsylvania State University. Department of Sociology. 1981.

Sai, Fred T.
Family Welfare and Development in Africa: Proceedings of the IPPF Africa Regional Conference, University of Ibadan. London: International Planned Parenthood Federation. Ibadan, Nigeria. Aug. 29-Sept. 3, 1977. 327p.

Saleh, Saneya
"Professional Women and National Development: Women's Response to Migration." Paper Presented at the Open University Women Seminar Series on Women, Work and Social Change. Cairo, Egypt: American University of Cairo. May 16, 1977.

Saulniers, Suzanne S. and Rakowski, Cathy A.
Women in the Development Process: A Select Bibliography on Women in Sub-Saharan Africa and Latin America. Austin, Texas: University of Texas Press. Institute of Latin American Studies. 1977. 287p.

Savane, M.A.
"Women and Rural Development in Africa." (In) International Labour Organization (ILO). Women in Rural Development: Critical Issues. Geneva: ILO. 1980. pp. 26-32.

Scandinavian Institute of African Studies
Women in Africa and Development Assistance. Report From a Seminar. Uppsala, Sweden: Scandinavian Institute of African Studies. 1978. 55p.

Schick, Barbara
"Women: An Untapped Resource in a Hungry World." Agenda. Volume 1 #6 June, 1978. pp. 1-4.

Schumacher, Ilsa and Buvinic, Mayra and Sebstad, Jennefer
Limits to Productivity: Improving Women's Access to Technology and Credit. Washington, D.C.: U.S. Department of State. U.S. Agency for International Development. Center for Research on Women. Office of Women and Development. May, 1980. 65p.

Schuster, Ilsa M.
"Recent Research on Women in Development." Journal of Development Studies. Volume 18 #4 July, 1982. pp. 511-535.

Schutjer, Wayne A. and Stokes, C. Shannon
"Agricultural Policies and Human Fertility: Some Emerging Connections." Population Research and Policy Review.

Volume 1 October, 1982. pp. 225-244.
Schutjer, Wayne A. and Stokes, C. Shannon (eds.)
Rural Development and Human Fertility. New York: MacMillan. 1984. 380p.
Secretariat for Women in Development
Women in Development: A Resource List. Washington, D.C.: Secretariat for Women in Development. A Transcentury Publication. 1979. 86p.
Seidman, Ann
"Women and the Development of 'Underdevelopment': The African Experience." (In) Dauber, Roslyn and Cain, Melinda, L. (eds.). Women and Technological Change in Developing Countries. Boulder, Colorado: Westview Press. 1981. pp. 109-126.
Sembajwe, Israel S.
"A Note on Published National Data on Economic Activities and Women's Studies and Development." Paper Presented at the Workshop on Women's Studies and Development. Dar-es-Salaam, Tanzania: University of Dar-es-Salaam. Bureau of Resource Assessment and Land Use Planning. Paper #31. September 24-29, 1979. 6p.
Sen, G.
"Women Workers and the Green Revolution." (In) Beneria, Lourdes (ed.). Women and Development: The Sexual Division of Labor in Rural Societies. New York: Praeger Publishers. 1985.
Shaw, R. Paul
"Women's Employment in the Arab World: A Strategy of Selective Intervention." Development and Change. Volume 12 #2 April, 1981. pp. 237-272.
Shields, Nwanganga G.
"Fertility and Economic Development in Africa, 1950-1970: A Quantitative Analysis." Ph.D Dissertation: American University. Washington, D.C. 1976. 249p.
Simms, Ruth
"The African Woman as Entrepreneur: Problems and Perspectives on Their Roles." (In) Steady, Filomina C. (ed.). The Black Woman Cross-Culturally. Cambridge, Massachusetts: Schenkman Publishing. 1981. pp. 141-168.
Skjonsberg, Else
Women and Food and the Social Sciences: Perspectives on African Food Production and Food Handling. Oslo, Norway: Mimeo. Available From the International Center for Research on Women, Washington, D.C. 1977.
Spencer, Dunstan S.C.
Women in a Developing Economy: A West African Case Study. East Lansing, Michigan: Michigan State University. 1979. 134p.
Spitler, Manon L.
"Women--Africa." Common Ground. Volume 2 #1 January, 1976.
Stanley, Autumn
"From Africa to America: Black Women Inventors." (In) Zimmerman, Jan (ed.). The Technological Woman: Interfacing With Tomorrow. New York: Praeger Publishers.

Preager Special Studies. 1983. pp. 55-64.
Stanley, Joyce and Lundeen, Alisa
The Audio Cassette Listening Forums: A Participatory Women's Development Project. Washington, D.C.: U.S. Department of State. U.S. Agency for International Development. Office of Women in Development. 1979. 92p.
Staudt, Kathleen A.
Women's Organizations in Rural Development. Washington, D.C.: U.S. Department of State. U.S. Agency for International Development. Office of Women in Development. February, 1980. 71p.
Staudt, Kathleen A. and Jaquette, Jane S. (eds.)
Women in Developing Countries: A Policy Focus. New York: Haworth Press. 1983. 135p.
Staudt, Kathleen A.
"Women Farmers and Inequalities in Agricultural Services." Rural Africana. Volume 29 Winter, 1976. pp. 81-94.
Staudt, Kathleen A.
"Women in Development--Policy Strategies at the End of the Decade." Africa Report. Volume 30 #2 March-April, 1985. pp. 71-74.
Staudt, Kathleen A.
"Class and Sex in the Politics of Women Farmers." Journal of Politics. Volume 41 #2 May, 1979. pp. 492-512.
Staudt, Kathleen A.
"Women's Politics in Africa." Williamsburg, Virginia: College of William and Mary. Anthropology Department. Studies in Third World Societies Publication #16. June, 1981. pp. 1-28.
Staudt, Kathleen A.
Women and Participation in Rural Development: A Framework for Project Design and Policy-Oriented Research. Ithaca, New York: Cornell University. Center for International Studies. Rural Development Monograph #4. 1979. 78p.
Staudt, Kathleen A.
"Women Farmers and Inequities in Agricultural Services." (In) Bay, Edna G. (ed.). Women and Work in Africa. Boulder, Colorado: Westview Press. Westview Special Studies in Africa. 1982. pp. 207-224.
Staudt, Kathleen A.
"Organizing Rural Women in the Third World." Paper Presented at the Annual Meeting of the Western Political Science Association. March 27-29, 1980.
Staudt, Kathleen A.
"Agricultural Productivity Gaps: A Case Study of Male Preference in Government Policy Implementation." Development and Change. Volume 9 #3 July, 1978. pp. 439-458.
Staudt, Kathleen A.
Women's Politics and Capitalist Transformation in Subsaharan Africa. East Lansing, Michigan: Michigan State University. Office of Women in International

Development. Working Paper #54. April, 1984.
Staudt, Kathleen A.
"Tracing Sex Differences in Donor Agricultural Programs." Paper Presented at the American Political Science Association Annual Meeting. Washington, D.C. 1979.
Steady, Filomina C.
Women in Africa. Cambridge, Massachusetts: Schenkman. 1983. 256p.
Steady, Filomina C.
"African Women, Industrialization Another Development." Development Dialogue. #1/2 1982. pp. 51-64.
Steady, Filomina C.
The Black Woman Cross-Culturally. Cambridge, Massachusetts: Schenkman. 1981. 645p.
Steady, Filomina C.
"The Black Woman Cross-Culturally: An Overview." (In) Steady, Filomina C. (ed.). The Black Woman Cross-Culturally. Cambridge, Massachusetts: Schenkman Publishing. 1981. pp. 7-41.
Steel, William F.
"The Small-Scale Sector's Role in Growth, Income Distribution and Employment of Women." Paper Presented at the Annual Meeting of the African Studies Association. Paper #82. Houston, Texas. November 2-5, 1977. 20p.
Stephens, Betsy and Odell, M.
"Professional Women in Development Assistance." International Development Review. Volume 19 #2 1977. pp. 3-5.
Stokland, Torill and Vajrathon, Mallica and Davidson, Nicol
Creative Women in Changing Societies: A Quest for Alternatives. Dobbs Ferry, New York: Transnational Publishers. 1982. 173p.
Strobel, Margaret A.
"African Women." Signs. Volume 8 #1 1982. pp. 109-131.
Sudarkasa, Niara
"Sex Roles, Education and Development in Africa." Anthropology and Education Quarterly. Volume 13 #3 Fall, 1982. pp. 279-288.
Tabah, Leon
"Policy Implications of the Phenomenon of Rising Fertility in Response to Modernization." (In) Cairo Demographic Centre (CDC). Determinants of Fertility in Some African And Asian Countries. Cairo, Egypt: CDC. CDC Research Monograph Series #10. 1982. pp. 13-19.
Tadesse, Zenebeworke
"African Women in Rural Development: A New Group of African Women Researchers." Ideas and Action. #127 1979. pp. 7-10.
Tadesse, Zenebeworke
"Studies on Rural Women in Africa: An Overview." (In) International Labour Organization (ILO). Rural Development and Women in Africa. Geneva: ILO. 1984. pp. 65-73.
Tadesse, Zenebeworke
Women and Technological Development in Agriculture: An

Overview of the Problems in Developing Countries. New York: United Nations Institute for Training and Research. Science and Technology Working Paper Series #9. 1979.

Tadesse, Zenebeworke
"Africa--A New Look From the Inside." UNESCO Courier. Volume 33 #6 July, 1980. pp. 31-32.

Tadesse, Zenebeworke
"Women and Technology in Peripheral Countries: An Overview." (In) D'Onofrio-Flores, Pamela M. and Pfafflin, Sheila M. (eds.). Scientific-Technological Change and the Role of Women in Development. Boulder, Colorado: Westview Press. 1982. pp. 77-111.

Takata, Diana M.
"Private Volunteer Organizations and Women's Participation in African Development." Rural Africana. #21 Winter, 1985. pp. 65-80.

Takata, Diane M.
"Increasing Women's Participation in the African Development Process Through the Assistance of U.S. Private Voluntary Organizations." Paper Presented at the Annual Meeting of the African Studies Association. Paper #113. Washington, D.C. November 4-7, 1982.

Tau, Mildred M.
"Women: Critical to African Development." Africa Report. Volume 26 #2 March-April, 1981. pp. 4-6.

Tesha, Nancy
"Womens Role in Rearing Children and National Development." Paper Presented at the Workshop on Women's Studies and Development. Dar-es-Salaam, Tanzania: University of Dar-es-Salaam. Bureau of Resource Assessment and Land Use Planning. Paper #39. September 24-29, 1979. 3p.

Thadani, Veena N. and Todaro, Michael P.
Female Migration in Developing Countries: A Framework for Analysis. New York: Population Council. Center for Policy Studies. Working Papers #47. 1979. 48p.

Tinker, Irene and Bramson, Michele B. (eds.)
Women and World Developmemt. New York: Praeger Publishers. 1976. 228p.

Tinker, Irene
"Women and Africa: Policy Strategies for Women in the 1980's." Africa Report. Volume 26 #2 March-April, 1981. pp. 11-16.

Tinker, Irene
"The Adverse Impact of Development on Women." (In) Tinker, Irene (ed.). Women and World Development. New York: Praeger Publishers. 1976.

Tinker, Irene
New Technologies for Food Chain Activities: The Imperative of Equity for Women. Washington, D.C.: U.S. Department of State. U.S. Agency for International Development. Office of Women in Development. 1979. 43p.

Tinker, Irene
"New Technologies for Food Related Activities: An Equity

Strategy." (In) Dauber, Roslyn and Cain, Melinda L. (eds.). Women and Technological Change in Developing Countries. Boulder, Colorado: Westview Press. 1981. pp. 51-88.

Tomsic, Vida
"The Position and Role of Women in Development." Review of International Affairs. Volume 32 November 5, 1981. pp. 1-5.

Trager, Lillian
"Urban Market Women: Hoarders, Hagglers, Economic Heroines?" Paper Presented at the Annual Meeting of the African Studies Association. Paper #94. Los Angeles, California. Oct. 31-Nov. 3, 1979. 26p.

U.S. Agency for International Development (U.S. AID)
International Directory of Women's Development Organizations. Washington, D.C.: U.S. Department of State. U.S. AID. Office of Women in Development. 1977. 311p.

U.S. Agency for International Development (U.S. AID)
Training Women in the Sahel. Washington, D.C.: U.S. Department of State. U.S. AID. Office of Women in Development. 1978. 47p.

U.S. Agency for International Development (U.S. AID)
The Productivity of Women in Developing Countries: Measurement Issues and Recommendations. Washington, D.C.: U.S. Department of State. U.S. AID. International Center for Research on Women. Office of Women in Development. 1980. 46p.

U.S. Agency for International Development (U.S. AID)
Examples of Women in Development Programs in Sahel Francophone West Africa. Washington, D.C.: U.S. Department of State. U.S. AID. Office of Sahel and Francophone West Africa, Bureau for Africa. 1979. 27p.

Uba, Sam
"Women Put the Case for Southern African Liberation." New African Development. March, 1977.

Uche, U.U.
"The Law, Family Welfare and Development in Africa: A Strategy for Future Action." (In) International Planned Parenthood Federation (IPPF). Proceedings of the IPPF Africa Regional Conference. London: IPPF. 1977. pp. 256-262.

United Nations
Impact on Women of Socioeconomic Changes in Africa South of the Sahara: Project Proposal. Geneva: United Nations Research Institute for Social Development. Reference Center. 1979. 56p.

United Nations
Building New Knowledge Through Technical Cooperation Among Developing Countries: The Experience of the Association of African Women for Research and Development (AAWORD). New York: United Nations. March 6, 1980.

United Nations
Measures of Assistance for Women in Southern Africa. Paper Presented at the United Nations World Conference of

the United Nations Decade for Women: Equality, Development and Peace. New York: United Nations. Copenhagen, Denmark. July 14-30, 1980. 34p.

United Nations
Report of the World Conference to Review and Appraise the Achievements of the United Nations Decade for Women: Equality, Development and Peace. Nairobi, Kenya, July 15-26, 1985. New York: United Nations. 1986. 304p.

United Nations Centre on Transnational Corporations and International Labour Office (ILO)
Women Workers in Multinational Enterprises in Developing Countries: A Contribution to the United Nations Decade for Women. Geneva: ILO. 1985. 119p.

United Nations Ctr. for Social Dev. and Humanitarian Affairs
Water, Women and Development. New York: United Nations. February 19, 1977.

United Nations Economic Commission for Africa (UNECA)
"Women as Clientele of Non-Formal Education." Paper Presented to the Regional Symposium on Non-Formal Education for Rural Development. Addis Ababa, Ethiopia: UNECA. Aug. 28-Sept. 8, 1978. 12p.

United Nations Economic Commission for Africa (UNECA)
"Origin and Growth of the African Training and Research Centre for Women of the Economic Commission for Africa." Addis Ababa, Ethiopia: UNECA. September, 1977. 60p.

United Nations Economic Commission for Africa (UNECA)
"Technical Co-Operation Among Developing Countries and Human Resource Development: The Experience of the African Training and Research Centre for Women of the Economic Commission for Africa." Paper Presented at the United Nations Conference on Technical Co-Operation Among Developing Countries. Addis Ababa, Ethiopia: UNECA. Buenos Aires, Argentina. 1978. 16p.

United Nations Economic Commission for Africa (UNECA)
"The Role of Women in Alternative Patterns of Development and Life-Styles in the Africa Region." Paper Presented at the Seminar on Alternative Patterns of Development and Lifestyles for the African Region. Addis Ababa, Ethiopia: UNECA. December 14, 1978. 16p.

United Nations Economic Commission for Africa (UNECA)
The Role of Women in the Utilization of Science and Technology for Development: An ECA Contribution to the African Regional Meeting of the United Nations Conference on Science and Technology for Development (UNCSTD). Cairo, Egypt, July 24-29. Addis Ababa, Ethiopia: UNECA. African Training and Research Centre for Women. 1978. 62p.

United Nations Economic Commission for Africa (UNECA)
Women Population and Rural Development in Africa. Addis Ababa, Ethiopia: UNECA/FAO Women's Development Programme Unit. 1976.

United Nations Economic Commission for Africa (UNECA)
"Women in Development: Moving Away From Tradition." U.N. Chronicle. Volume 19 #11 December, 1982. pp. 105-106.

United Nations Economic Commission for Africa (UNECA) Summary of On-Going and Planned Projects of the United Nations Agencies and Organizations for the Integration of Women in Development in the African Region. Addis Ababa, Ethiopia: UNECA. 1980. 72p.

United Nations Economic Commission for Africa (UNECA) "Women in African Development." Paper Presented at the ACOSCA Bilingual Regional Seminar on Increasing Women's Access to Credit Unions in West Africa. Addis Ababa, Ethiopia: UNECA. Dakar, Senegal. March, 1981.

United Nations Economic Commission for Africa (UNECA) African Women and Equality, Development and Peace: Strategy for 1980-85. Addis Ababa, Ethiopia: UNECA. Working Paper for Regional Prepatory Meeting of the UNECA Second Regional Conference for the Integration of Women in Development. Lusaka, Zambia. December 3-7, 1979.

United Nations Economic Commission for Africa (UNECA) The New International Economic Order--What Role for Women in Africa? Addis Ababa, Ethiopia: UNECA. August, 1977. 54p.

United Nations Economic Commission for Africa (UNECA) Family, Welfare and Development in Africa: Social Welfare Aspects of Family Planning. Addis Ababa, Ethiopia: UNECA. Social Development Section. Social Welfare Services in Africa #11. 1977. 133p.

United Nations Economic Commission for Africa (UNECA) Establishment of Sub-Regional Machinery to Enhance the Role of Women in the Progress of Economic and Social Development in the Central African Sub-Region and to Promote and Guide the Activities of the ECA's Training and Research Centre for Women. Yaounde, Cameroon: MULPOC (Multi-National Operations Center for Central African Library). March, 1978.

United Nations Economic Commission for Africa (UNECA) ECA Five Year Programme on Pre-Vocational and Vocational Training of Girls and Women, Toward Their Full Participation in Development (1972-1976). Addis Ababa, Ethiopia: UNECA. 1976.

United Nations Economic Commission for Africa (UNECA) The Changing and Contemporary Role of Women in African Development. Addis Ababa, Ethiopia: UNECA. 1977.

United Nations Economic Commission for Africa (UNECA) African Women's Development Task Force. Addis Ababa, Ethiopia: UNECA. African Training and Research Centre for Women. 1976. 15p.

United Nations Economic Commission for Africa (UNECA) African Women Workers: Analysis of the Factors Affecting Women's Employment. Addis Ababa, Ethiopia: UNECA. African Training and Research Centre for Women. 1976. 53p.

United Nations Economic Commission for Africa (UNECA) Report: ECA/FAO Subregional Seminar on Fuelwood and Energy Development for African Women, April 18, 1983. Addis Ababa, Ethiopia: UNECA. Lusaka, Zambia. November, 1984. 25p.

United Nations Economic Commission for Africa (UNECA)
"National Machinery for the Integration of Women in Development in African Countries." Paper Presented to the Regional Conference on the Implementation of the National Regional and Worlds Plans of Action for the Integration of Women in Development. Addis Ababa, Ethiopia: UNECA. Nouakchott, Mauritania. 1977. 54p.

United Nations Economic Commission for Africa (UNECA)
The Critical Needs of African Women and Appropriate Strategies in the Framework of the Gisenyi and Lusaka MULPOCS. Addis Ababa, Ethiopia: UNECA. 1981.

United Nations Economic Commission for Africa (UNECA)
"The Role of Women in the Solution of the Food Crisis in Africa (Implementation of the Lagos Plan of Action)." Paper Presented at the Regional Intergovernmental Preparatory Meeting for the World Conference to Review and Appraise the Achievements of the United Nations Decade for Women: Equality, Development and Peace/Third Regional Conference on the Integration ofWomen in Development, Arusha, Tanzania, October 8-12. Addis Ababa, Ethiopia: UNECA. 1984.

United Nations Educational, Scientific and Cultural Organ.
Description of Projects Relevant to the Integration of Women in Development: Africa. Paris: UNESCO. May 16, 1979. 10p.

United Nations Educational, Scientific, and Cultural Organ.
Bibliographic Guide to Studies on the Status of Women: Development and Population Trends. Paris: UNESCO. Epping, England: Bowker. 1983. 284p.

United Nations Food and Agriculture Organization (FAO)
The State of Food and Agriculture; 1983: World Review: The Situation in Sub-Saharan Africa; Women in Developing Agriculture. New York: FAO. FAO Agriculture Series #16. 1984. 221p.

United Nations Food and Agriculture Organization (FAO)
Food Aid and the Role of Women in Development. Rome: FAO. 1976. 43p.

United Nations Food and Agriculture Organization (FAO)
The Role of Women in Population Dynamics Related to Food and Agriculture and Rural Development in Africa. Rome: FAO. United Nations Economic Commission for Africa. Women's Program Unit. Joint Agriculture Division. 1976.

United Nations Fund for Population Activities
Forum on Population and Development for Women Leaders From Sub-Saharan African Countries. New York: United Nations Fund for Population Activities. May 15-18, 1984. 39p.

United Nations Secretary-General
"Measures of Assistance for Women in Southern Africa: Report of the Secretary General." Paper Presented at the World Conference of the United Nations Decade for Women. New York: United Nations. Copenhagen, Denmark. July 14-30, 1980.

Van Allen, Judith
"African Women, 'Modernization' and National Liberation."

(In) Iglitzin, Lynne B. and Ross, Ruth (eds.). Women in the World. Santa Barbara, California: Clio Press. American Bibliographic Center. 1976. pp. 25-54.
Van der Horst, Sheila T.
Women as an Economic Force in Southern Africa. Rondebosch, South Africa: University of Cape Town. Abe Bailey Institute of Interracial Studies #18. 1977.
Vavrus, Linda G.
Women in Development: A Selected Annotated Bibliography and Resource Guide. East Lansing, Michigan: Michigan State University. Institute for International Studies in Education. Non-Formal Education Information Center. 1980. 69p.
Wadsworth, Gail M.
Women in Development: A Bibliography of Materials Available in the Library and Documentation Centre, Eastern and Southern African Management Institute. Arusha, Tanzania: Eastern and Southern African Management Institute. Library and Documentation Centre. February, 1982. 106p.
Waterman, Peter
"A New Focus in African Worker Studies: Promises, Problems, Dangers." Cahiers d'Etudes Africaines. Volume 24 #3 1984. pp. 343-361.
Weekes-Vagliani, Winifred and Grossat, Bernard
Women in Development: At the Right Time for the Right Reason. Paris: Organization for Economic Cooperation and Development. 1980. 330p.
Weekes-Vagliani, Winifred
"Women, Food and Rural Development." (In) Rose, T. (ed.). Crisis and Recovery in Subsaharan Africa. Paris: OECD Development Center. 1985. pp. 104-110.
Weisner, Thomas S. and Abbott, Susan
"Women, Modernity and Stress: Three Contrasting Contexts for Change in East Africa." Southwestern Journal of Anthropology. Volume 33 #4 Winter, 1977. pp. 421-451.
Whalen, Irene T.
Women and Livestock: The Impact of Technological Innovations on Women. Addis Ababa, Ethiopia: International Livestock Center, Africa. P/O Box 5689. 1984.
Whiting, Beatrice B.
"Rapid Social Change: Threat or Promise?" Ekistics. Volume 43 #255. February, 1977. pp. 64-68.
World Bank
Rural Development Projects: A Retrospective View of Bank Experience in Sub-Saharan Africa. Washington, D.C.: World Bank. Report #2242. October 13, 1978.
World Bank
Recognizing the 'Invisible' Woman in Development: The World Banks Experience. Washington, D.C.: World Bank. October, 1979. 33p.
World Health Organization (WHO)
Improving Ways of Skill Acquisition of Women for Rural Development in Some African Countries. Geneva: World

Health Organization. World Employment Programme Research Working Papers. WEP 2-18/WP 15. 1977. 76p.

Wright, Marcia
"Technology and Women's Control Over Production: Three Case Studies From East-Central Africa and Their Implications for Esther Boserup's Thesis About the Displacement of Women." Paper Presented at the Rockefeller Foundation Workshop on Women, Household and Human Capital Development in Low Income Countries. New York: Rockefeller Foundation. July, 1982.

Youssef, Nadia H.
Women and Work in Developing Societies. Westport, Connecticut: Greenwood Press. 1976. 137p.

Youssef, Nadia H.
"Women and Agricultural Production in Muslim Societies." Studies in Comparative International Development. Volume 12 #1 Spring, 1977. pp. 41-58.

Zivetz, L.
The Impact of Rural Development on the Status of Women and its Consequences for Fertility in Africa. Submitted to the Research Triangle Institute and the Southeast Consortium for International Development. Chapel Hill, North Carolina. 1979.

Economics

Acsadi, George T.
"Effect of Economic Development on Fertility Trends in Africa." (In) Cairo Demographic Centre (CDC). Aspects of Population Change and Development in Some African and Asian Countries. Cairo, Egypt: CDC. CDC Research Monograph Series #9. 1984. pp. 57-105.

Adedeji, John A.
"Social Change and Women in African Sport." International Social Science Journal. Volume 34 #2 1982. pp. 210-218.

Ahmed, Iftikhar
"Technologies for Rural Women." Women at Work. #3 1977.

Ahmed, Iftikhar
"Technology and Rural Women in the Third World." International Labour Review. Volume 122 #4 July-August, 1983. pp. 493-505.

Ahmed, Iftikhar (ed.)
Technology and Rural Women: Conceptual and Empirical Issues. Boston: George Allen and Unwin. 1985. 383p.

Aidoo, Agnes A.
"Women and Development in Africa: Alternative Strategies for the Future." (In) Adedeji, A. and Shaw, T.M. (eds.). Economic Crisis in Africa: African Perspectives on Development Problems and Potentials. Boulder, Colorado: Lynne Rienner. 1985. pp. 201-217.

Amin, Samir
Imperialism and Unequal Development. New York: Monthly Review Press. 1977.

Amon-Nikoi, Gloria
"Women and Work in Africa." (In) Damachi, Ukandi G. and Diejomaoh, Victor P. Human Resources and African Development. New York: Praeger Publishers. 1978. pp. 188-219.

Anker, Richard and Knowles, James C.
"A Micro-Analysis of Female Labour Force Participation in

Africa." (In) Standing, G. and Sheehan, G. (eds.). Labour Force Participation in Low Income Countries. Geneva: International Labour Office. 1978. pp. 137-163.

Anonymous
"African Women's Development Task Force." Rural Progress. Volume 1 #1 October, 1977. pp. 25-26.

Anonymous
"Official Documents: ILO Standards Relating to Women Workers; Equal Renumeration Convention: Situation in Africa." Women at Work. #2 1983.

Anonymous
"Two Views of Liberation." Agenda. Volume 1 #2 February, 1978. pp. 19-22.

Anonymous
"Women, Food and Nutrition in Africa: Economic Change and the Outlook for Nutrition." Food and Nutrition. Volume 10 #1 1984. pp. 71-79.

Anonymous
Women in Rural Development: Critical Issues. Geneva: International Labour Organization. 1980. 51p.

Anonymous
"Women in Rural Development: Recommendations and Realities." Ceres. May-June, 1980. pp. 15-42.

Balakrishnan, Revathi and Firebaugh, Francille M.
Roles of Women in Third World Economic Development From a Systems Perspective of Family Resource Management. Columbus, Ohio: Ohio State University. Department of Home Management and Housing. School of Home Economics. Working Papers #81-01. 1981. 39p.

Bay, Edna G. and Hafkin, Nancy J. (eds.)
Women in Africa: Studies in Social and Economic Change. Stanford, California: Stanford University Press. 1976. 306p.

Bay, Edna G.
Women and Work in Africa. Boulder, Colorado: Westview Press. Westview Special Studies on Africa. 1982. 310p.

Beneria, Lourdes
"Conceptualizing the Labour Force: The Underestimation of Women's Economic Activities." Journal of Development Studies. Volume 17 #3 April, 1981. pp. 10-28.

Beneria, Lourdes
"Reproduction, Production and the Sexual Division of Labour." Cambridge Journal of Economics. Volume 3 September, 1979. pp. 203-225.

Beneria, Lourdes
Women and Development: The Sexual Division of Labor in Rural Societies: A Study. New York: Praeger Publishers. Praeger Special Studies. 1982. 257p.

Beneria, Lourdes
"Reproduction, Production and the Sexual Division of Labour." Geneva: International Labour Office. World Employment Research Working Paper #2. 1978.

Beneria, Lourdes
"Conceptualizing the Labour Force: The Underestimation of Women's Economic Activities." (In) Nelson, Nici (ed.).

African Women in the Development Process." Totowa, New Jersey: Frank Cass. 1981. pp. 10-28.
Bifani, Patricia
"Women and Development in Africa: A Tentative Approach Through Scenario Building." Journal of Eastern African Research and Development. Volume 15 1985. pp. 245-267.
Birdsall, Nancy and McGreevey, William P.
"The Second Sex in the Third World: Is Female Poverty a Development Issue?" Paper Prepared for the International Center for Research on Women Policy Roundtable. Washington, D.C. June 21, 1978.
Black, Naomi and Cottrell, Ann B.
Women and World Change: Equity Issues in Development. Beverly Hills, California: Sage Publications. Sage Focus Editions #38. 1981. 288p.
Blumberg, Rae
"Rural Women in Development: Veil of Invisibility, World of Work." International Journal of Intercultural Relations. Volume 3 #4 1979. pp. 447-472.
Blumberg, Rae
"Rural Women in Development." (In) Black, Naomi and Cottrell, Ann B. (eds.). Women and World Change: Equity Issues in Development. Beverly Hills, California: Sage Publications. 1981. pp. 32-56.
Boserup, Ester
"Economic and Demographic Interrelationships in Sub-Saharan Africa." Population and Development Review. Volume 11 #3 September, 1985. pp. 383-397+.
Boulding, Elise
Women Peripheries and Food Production. (In) University of Arizona. Proceedings and Papers of the International Conference on Women and Food: Consortium for International Development. Tucson, Arizona: University of Arizona. 1978. pp. 22-44.
Boulding, Elise
"Productivity and Poverty of Third World Women: Problems in Measurement." (In) Buvinic, Mayra and Lycette, Margaret C. and McGreevey, William P. (eds.). Women and Poverty in the Third World. Baltimore, Maryland: Johns Hopkins University. 1983.
Brabin, Loretta
"Polygyny: An Indicator of Nutritional Stress in African Agricultural Societies." Africa. Volume 54 #1 1984. pp. 31-45.
Brown, Judith E.
"Polygyny and Family Planning in Sub-Saharan Africa." Studies in Family Planning. Volume 12 #8-9 August-September, 1981. pp. 322-326.
Bujra, Janet M.
"Class, Gender and Capitalist Transformation in Africa." Africa Development. Volume 8 #3 1983. pp. 17-42.
Burfisher, Mary E. and Horenstein, Nadine R.
"Incorporating Women Into Agricultural Development Planning: A Methodology." Paper Presented at the Annual Meeting of the African Studies Association. Paper #15.

Washington, D.C. November 4-7, 1982.
Buvinic, Mayra
Women and World Development: An Annotated Bibliography. Washington D.C.: Overseas Development Council. 1976. 162p.
Buvinic, Mayra and Youssef, Nadia H. and Schumacher, Ilsa
Women-Headed Households: The Ignored Factor in Development Planning. Washington D.C.: U.S. Department of State. U.S. Agency for International Development. International Center for Research on Women. Women in Development Office. March, 1978. 113p.
Buvinic, Mayra and Lycette, Margaret A. and McGreevey, William P.
Women and Poverty in the Third World. Baltimore, Maryland: Johns Hopkins University. Johns Hopkins Studies in Development. 1983. 329p.
Callear, D.
Women and Coarse Grain Production in Africa. Expert Consultation on Women in Food Production. Rome: United Nations Food and Agriculture Organization. December 7, 1983. 13p.
Canady, Hortense
"Women in Development: The African Diaspora." Africa Report. Volume 30 #2 March-April, 1985. pp. 75.
Caplan, Patricia and Bujra, Janet M. (eds.)
Women United Women Divided: Comparative Studies of Ten Contemporary Cultures. Bloomington, Indiana: Indiana University Press. 1979. 288p.
Caplan, Patricia
"Cognatic Descent, Islamic Law, and Women's Property on the East African Coast." (In) Hirschon, Renbee (ed.). Women and Property--Women as Property. New York: St. Martin's Press. 1983.
Carew, Joy
"A Note on Women and Agricultural Technology in the Third World." Labour and Society. Volume 6 #3 July-September, 1981. pp. 279-285.
Carr, Marilyn
"Appropriate Technology for Rural African Women." Development Digest. Volume 20 #1 January, 1982. pp. 87-98.
Carr, Marilyn
Appropriate Technology for African Women. Addis Ababa, Ethiopia: United Nations Economic Commission for Africa. African Training and Research Center for Women. 1978. 105p.
Carr, Marilyn
"Technologies for Rural Women: Impact and Dissemination." (In) Ahmed, Iftikhar (ed.). Technology and Rural Women: Conceptual and Empirical Issues. Boston: George Allen and Unwin. 1985. pp. 115-153.
Carr, Marilyn
Technology and Rural Women in Africa. Addis Ababa, Ethiopia: United Nations Economic Commission for Africa. African Training and Research Center for Women. Joint

Project With the International Labour Organization. ILO World Employment Programme Research Working Paper #61. 1980.
Carr, Marilyn
"Appropriate Technology for Women." Appropriate Technology. Volume 1 1979.
Castillo, Gelia T.
The Changing Role of Women in Rural Societies: A Summary of Trends and Issues. New York: Agricultural Development Council Inc. RTN Seminar Reports 12. February, 1977. 11p.
Caton, Douglas D.
Elements of the Food Production-Distribution System: An Overview on How Women Can Contribute. Proceedings and Papers of the International Conference on Women and Food Consortium for International Development. Tucson, Arizona: University of Arizona. 1978. pp. 45-61.
Caughman, Susan H.
Women at Work in Mali: The Case of the Markala Cooperative. Boston: Boston University. African Studies Center. Working Papers in African Studies #50. 1981. 72p.
Cernea, Michael M. (ed.).
Putting People First: Sociological Variables in Rural Development. New York: Oxford University Press. 1985. 430p.
Chan, S.
"Young Women and Development in Africa--Some Generally Unconsidered Considerations." Community Development Journal. Volume 18 #3 1983. pp. 257-262.
Chaney, Elsa M. and Simmons, Emmy and Staudt, Kathleen
Women in Development. Washington, D.C.: U.S. Department of State. U.S. Agency for International Development. Background Papers for the U.S. Delegation Attending the World Conference on Agrarian Reform and Rural Development. July, 1979. 40p.
Chaney, Elsa M.
Women in International Migration: Issues in Development Planning. Washington, D.C.: U.S. Department of State. U.S. Agency for International Development. Office of Women in Development. June, 1980.
Chaney, Elsa M. and Lewis, Martha W.
Women, Migration and the Decline of Smallholder Agriculture. Washington, D.C.: U.S. Department of State. U.S. Agency for International Development. Office of Women in Development. October, 1980.
Charlton, Sue E.
Women in Third World Development. Boulder, Colorado: Westview Press. 1984. 240p.
Claffey, Joan M. and Pigozzi, Mary J. and Axinn, Nancy W.
"Women in Development: A Selected Annotated Bibliography." International Journal of Intercultural Relations. Volume 3 1979.
Clark, Carolyn M.
Sexuality in the Workplace: Some African Examples. Santa

Cruz, California: University of California-Santa Cruz. 1981.
Cloud, Kathleen
"Sex Roles in Food Production and Distribution Systems in the Sahel." (In) Cowen, Ann B. (ed.). Proceedings and Papers of the International Conference on Women and Food: Consortium for International Development. Tucson, Arizona: University of Arizona. 1978. pp. 62-89.
Cloud, Kathleen
Sex Roles in Food Production and Food Distribution Systems in the Sahel. Washington, D.C.: U.S. Department of State. U.S. Agency for International Development. Office of Women in Development. 1977. 20p.
Cohen, Ronald and Knipp, Maggie
"Women and Change in West Africa: A Synthesis." Paper Presented at the Annual Meeting of the African Studies Association. Paper #16. Philadelphia, Pennsylvania. 1980.
Cohn, Steven and Wood, Robert and Haig, Richard
"U.S. Aid and Third World Women: The Impact of Peace Corps Programs." Economic Development and Cultural Change. Volume 29 #4 July, 1981. pp. 795-811.
Cook, Gayla
"Women in Africa: Working With African Women: Options for the West." Africa Report. Volume 26 #2 March-April, 1981. pp. 43-46.
Creative Associates, Inc.
Participation of Women in the Economic Development Process: A Suggested Strategy for the African Bureau. Washington, D.C.: Creative Associates, Inc. 1980. 20p.
D'onofrio-Flores, Pamela M. and Pfafflin, Sheila M. (eds.)
Scientific-Technological Change and the Role of Women in Development. Boulder, Colorado: Westview Press. Published for the United Nations Institute for Training and Research. 1982. 206p.
Danforth, Sandra C.
Women and National Development. Monticello, Illinois: Vance Bibliographies. #P-916. February, 1982. 35p.
Date-Bah, Eugenia
"Rural Development and the Status of Women." Paper Presented at a Seminar on the Role of Population Factor in the Rural Development Strategy." Monrovia, Liberia. 1980.
Dauber, Roslyn and Cain, Melinda (eds.)
Women and Technological Change in Developing Countries. Boulder, Colorado: Westview Press. AAAS Selected Symposium #53. 1980. 266p.
DeLancey, Virginia H.
"The Role of Credit Unions in Development for West African Women." Paper Presented at the Annual Meeting of the African Studies Association. Paper #29. Bloomington, Indiana. October 21-24, 1981.
DeLancey, Virginia H.
"The Relationship Between Female Labor Force Participation and Fertility: Considerations of Role

Compatibility in Research Methodology for Developing Countries." Paper Presented at the Annual Meeting of the African Studies Association. Paper #34. Los Angeles, California. 1979. 23p.

Dey, Jennie M.
Women in Food Production and Food Security in Africa. Rome: United Nations Food and Agriculture Organization. Women in Agriculture Series #3. 1984. 101p.

Dey, Jennie M.
"Women in African Rice Farming Systems." International Rice Commission Newsletter. Volume 32 #2 December, 1983. pp. 1-4.

Dey, Jennie M.
Women in Rice Farming Systems, Focus: Subsaharan Africa. Rome: United Nations Food and Agriculture Organization. Women in Agriculture Series #2. 1984. 106p.

Dey, Jennie M.
"Women in African Rice Farming Systems." (In) International Rice Research Institute. 'Women in Rice Farming': Proceedings of a Conference on Women in Rice Farming Systems. September 26-30, 1983. Brookfield, Vermont: Gower Publishing Co. 1985. pp. 419-444.

Dhamija, Jasleen
"Income-Generating Activities for Rural Women in Africa: Some Successes and Failures." (In) International Labour Organization (ILO). Rural Development and Women in Africa. Geneva: ILO. 1984. pp. 75-78.

Dhamija, Jasleen
"Technology as a Target to the Development of Women's Skills in Africa." Ceres. # 84 November, 1981. pp. 24-27.

Dirasse, Laketch
The Critical Needs of African Women and Appropriate Strategies in the Framework of the Gisenyi and Lusaka MULPOCS. Addis Ababa, Ethiopia: United Nations Economic Commission for Africa. African Training and Research Centre for Women. 1981. 35p.

Dixon, Ruth B.
"Land, Labour and the Sex Composition of the Agricultural Labour Force: An International Comparison." Development and Change. Volume 14 #3 July, 1983. pp. 347-372.

Dixon, Ruth B.
Assessing the Impact of Development Projects on Women. Washington, D.C.: U.S. Department of State. U.S. Agency for International Development. Office of Women in Development. AID Program Evaluation Discussion Paper #8. 1980. 105p.

Dixon, Ruth B.
"Jobs for Women in Rural Industry and Services." Paper Presented at the Conference on Agrarian Reform and Rural Development. Rome: United Nations Food and Agriculture Organization. Washington, D.C.: U.S. Department of State. U.S. Agency for International Development. Office of Women in Development. July, 1979.

Due, Jean M. and Summary, Rebecca
"Constraints to Women and Development in Africa." Journal of Modern African Studies. Volume 20 #1 March, 1982. pp. 155-166.

Due, Jean M. and Summary, Rebecca
"Constraints to Women and Development in Africa." Paper Presented at the Annual Meeting of the African Studies Association. Paper #35. Los Angeles, California. 1979. 23p.

Due, Jean M. and Summary, Rebecca
Constraints to Women and Development in Africa. Urbana, Illinois: University of Illinois-Urbana-Champaign. Department of Agricultural Economics. Staff Paper Series E. Agricultural Economics 79-E-83. May, 1979. 27p.

Dulansey, Maryanne L.
Can Technology Help Women Feed Their Families? Post Harvest Storage, Processing and Cooking: Some Observations. Washington, D.C.: Consultants in Development. 1979. 9p.

Dulansey, Maryanne L.
Women in Development Program Concerns in Francophone Sahel: Report of a Workshop. Washington, D.C.: U.S. Department of State. U.S. Agency for International Development. Bobo-Dioulasso, Upper Volta. June 5-7, 1979. 11p.

Eide, Wenche B. and Skjonsberg, Else and Pala, Achola O. and Bathily, Abjoulaye
"Women in Food Production, Food Handling and Nutrition With Special Emphasis on Africa." PAG Bulletin. Volume 7 #3/4 Sept.-Dec., 1977. pp. 40-49.

Eide, Wenche B. and Steady, Filomina C.
"Individual and Social Energy Flows: Bridging Nutritional and Anthropological Thinking About Women's Work in Rural Africa: Some Theoretical Considerations." (In) Jerome, Norge W. and Kandel, Randy F. and Pelto, Gretel H. (eds.). Nutritional Anthropology: Contemporary Approach to Diet and Culture. New York: Redgrave Publishing. 1980. pp. 61-84.

Eide, Wenche B. and Skjonsberg, Else and Bathily, Abjoulaye and Pala, Achola O. and Krystall, Abigail and Millwood, D.
Women in Food Production, Food Handling and Nutrition With Special Emphasis on Africa. Final Report. New York: United Nations. Protein-Calorie Advisory Group of the U.N. System. FAO Food and Nutrition Paper #8. June, 1977. 224p.

El Bushra, Judy and Bekele, Abebech and Hammour, Fawzia
"Socio-Economic Development and Women Changing Status." Paper Presented to the Conference on Women and the Environment. Khartoum, Sudan: University of Khartoum. Institute of Environmental Studies. April 4-7, 1981.

Elson, Diane and Pearson, Ruth
"'Nimble Fingers Make Cheap Workers': An Analysis of Women's Employment in Third World Export Manufacturing." Feminist Review. Volume 7 Spring, 1981.

Engberg, L.E.
"Emphasis on Economics--A Way to Strengthen the Relationship of Home Economics With Agriculture." Paper Presented at the Workshop on the Role of Women and Home Economics in Rural Development in Africa. Rome: United Nations Food and Agriculture Organization. Alexandria, Egypt. October 17, 1983. 10p.

Farooq, Ghazi M. and Simmons, George B. (eds.)
Fertility in Developing Countries: An Economic Perspective on Research and Policy Issues. New York: St. Martin's Press. 1985.

Fatehally, Laeeq (ed.)
Women in the Third World. Bombay, India: Leslie Sawhny Programme. 1980. 155p.

Fortmann, Louise P.
"The Plight of the Invisible Farmer: The Effect of National Agricultural Policy on Women in Africa." (In) Dauber, Roslyn and Cain, Melinda L. Women and Technological Change in Developing Countries. Boulder, Colorado: Westview Press. 1981. pp. 205-214.

Franke, R.
"Mode of Production and Population Patterns: Policy Implications for West African Development." International Journal of Health Services. Volume 13 1981. pp. 361-387.

Fraser, Arvonne
Women in Development. Washington, D.C.: U.S. Department of State. U.S. Agency for International Development. Office of Women in Development. 1977. 12p.

Gallin, Rita and Spring, Anita (eds.).
Women Creating Wealth: Transforming Economic Development. Washington, D.C.: Association for Women in Development. 1985. 183p.

Germain, Adrienne
"Poor Rural Women: A Policy Perspective." Journal of International Affairs. Volume 3 #2 Fall-Winter, 1976. 20p.

Gladwin, Christina and Staudt, Kathleen A. and McMillan, Della
Reaffirming the Agricultural Role of Women: One Solution to the Food Crisis. (In) Association of Facilities of Agriculture in Africa. Proceedings of the Fifth General Conference on Food Security. Manzini, Swaziland. April, 1984.

Grandmaison, C. LeCour
"Economic Contracts Between Married People in the West African Area." L'Homme. Volume 19 #3/4 July-December, 1979. pp. 159-170.

Gugler, Josef
"The Second Sex in Town." (In) Steady, Filomina C. (ed.). The Black Woman Cross-Culturally. Cambridge, Massachusetts: Schenkman Publishing. 1981. pp. 169-184.

Guyer, Jane I.
Women's Work in the Food Economy of the Cocoa Belt: A Comparison. Brookline, Massachusetts: Boston University.

African Studies Center. Working Paper #7. 1978. 34p.
Hafkin, Nancy J. and Bay, Edna G. (eds.)
Women in Africa: Studies in Social and Economic Change. Stanford, California: Stanford University Press. 1976. 306p.
Hagan, A.L.
"The Role of Women in Rural Development: Some Critical Issues." (In) Mondjanagni, A.C. La Participation Populaire an Developpement en Afrique Noire. Paris: Karthala; Doula, Institut Pan Africain Pour Le Developpement. 1984. pp. 75-87.
Haq, Khadija (ed.)
Equality of Opportunity Within and Among Nations. New York: Praeger Publishers. Praeger Special Studies in International Economics and Development. 1977. 223p.
Henn, Jeanne K.
"Feeding the Cities and Feeding the Peasants: What Role for Africa's Women Farmers." World Development. Volume 11 #12 1983.
Henn, Jeanne K.
"Women in the Rural Economy: Past, Present and Future." (In) Hay, Margaret J. and Stichter, Sharon (eds.). African Women South of the Sahara. New York: Longman. 1984. pp. 1-18.
Howard, Rhoda E.
"Women and the Crisis in Commonwealth Africa." International Political Science Review. Volume 6 #3 1985. pp. 287-296.
International Center for Research on Women
Women in Migration: A Third World Focus. Washington, D.C.: U.S. Department of State. U.S. Agency for International Development. Office of Women in Development. 1979.
International Center for Research on Women
Keeping Women Out: A Structural Analysis of Women's Employment in Developing Countries. Washington, D.C.: U.S. Department of State. U.S. Agency for International Development. Office on Women in Development. Bureau of Program and Policy Coordination. April, 1980.
International Center for Research on Women
The Productivity of Women in Developing Countries: Measurement Issues and Recommendtions. Washington, D.C.: U.S. Department of State. U.S. Agency for International Development. Office on Women in Development. 1980. 46p.
International Labour Organization (ILO)
Rural Development and Women in Africa: Papers of the ILO Tripartite African Regional Seminar on Rural Development and Women, June 15-19, 1981. Geneva: ILO. Dakar, Senegal. 1984. 157p.
International Labour Organization (ILO)
Women, Technology and the Development Process. Paper Presented to the African Regional Meeting of UNCSTD. Geneva: ILO. Cairo, Egypt. July 24-29, 1978.

Kamba, Kate
"Fuel Wood and Energy Development for African Women." Paper Presented at the Workshop on Women in Agricultural Development. Addis Ababa, Ethiopia: United Nations Economic Commission for Africa. Awassa, Ethiopia. June 26, 1983. 13p.

Kitching, Gavin
"Proto-Industrialization and Demographic Change: A Thesis and Some Possible African Implications." Journal of African History. Volume 24 #2 1983. pp. 221-240.

Kocher, James E.
"Socioeconomic Development and Fertility Change in Rural Africa." Paper Presented at the Annual Meeting of the African Studies Association. Paper #44. Boston, Massachusetts. 1976. 22p.

Kocher, James E.
"Supply-Demand Disequilibria and Fertility Change in Africa--Toward a More Appropriate Economic Approach." Social Biology. Volume 30 #1 1983. pp. 41-58.

Kurian, George and Ratna, Ghosh (eds.)
Women in the Family and the Economy: An International Comparative Survey. Westport, Connecticut: Greenwood Press. Contributions in Family Studies #5. 1981. 451p.

Kwawu, J.
"The Role of Home Economics in Rural Development: A Focus on Family Planning." Paper Presented at the Workshop on the Role of Women and Home Economics in Rural Development in Africa. Rome: United Nations Food and Agricultural Organization. Alexandria, Egypt. October 17, 1983. 20p.

Lewis, Barbara C.
"State/Society; Public/Private and Women: A Political Scientist's View." Paper Presented at the Annual Meeting of the African Studies Association. Paper #75. Bloomington, Indiana. October 21-24, 1981.

Lewis, Barbara C.
"Fertility and Employment: An Assessment of Role Incompatibility Among African Urban Women." (In) Bay, Edna G. Women and Work in Africa. Boulder, Colorado: Westview Press. Westview Special Studies. 1982. pp. 249-276.

Lewis, Barbara C. (ed.)
The Invisible Farmer: Women and the Crisis in Agriculture. Washington, D.C.: U.S. Department of State. U.S. Agency for International Development. Office of Women in Development. 1982. 456p.

Lewis, Shelby
"African Women and National Development." (In) Lindsay, Beverly (ed.). Comparative Perspectives of Third World Women: The Impact of Race, Sex and Class. New York: Praeger Publishers. 1980. pp. 36-54.

Lindsay, Beverly
"Women and National Development in Africa." Western Journal of Black Studies. Volume 1 #1 March, 1977. pp. 53-58.

Lindsay, Beverly (ed.)
Comparative Perspectives of Third World Women: The Impact of Race, Sex and Class. New York: Praeger Publishers. Praeger Special Studies. 1980. 318p.
Loutfi, Martha F.
Rural Women: Unequal Partners in Development. Geneva: International Labour Organization. 1982. 80p.
Lucas, D.
"Demographic Aspects of Women's Employment in Africa." Manpower and Unemployment Research. Volume 10 #1 April, 1977. pp. 31-38.
Marks, Shula and Unterhalter, Elaine
Women and the Migrant Labour System in Southern Africa. Lusaka, Zambia: United Nations Economic Commission for Africa. Multinational Programming and Operational Centre for Eastern and Central Africa. 1978. 15p.
Marshall, Susan E.
"Politics and Female Status in North Africa: A Reconsideration of Development Theory." Economic Development and Cultural Change. Volume 32 #3 April, 1984. pp. 499-524.
Matsepe, Ivy F.
"Underdevelopment and African Women." Journal of Southern African Affairs. Volume 2 #2 April, 1977. pp. 135-143.
Matsepe-Casaburri, Ivy F.
"Underdevelopment and African Women." Paper Presented at the Conference of the Southern Africa Research Group. College Park, Maryland: Southern Africa Research Group. September, 1976.
Max-Forson, Margaret
"The Role of Women and Youth in Development." Rural Progress. Volume 1 #3 1979. pp. 28-30.
Max-Forson, Margaret
Progress and Obstacles in Achieving the Minimum Objectives of the World and Africa Plans of Action: A Critical Review. Report Presented to the Second Regional Conference on the Integration of Women in Development. Addis Ababa, Ethiopia: United Nations Economic Commission for Africa. Lusaka, Zambia. December 3-7, 1979. 56p.
Mbilinyi, Marjorie J.
"The Changing Position of Women in the African Labour Force." (In) Shaw, Timothy M. and Aluko, Olajide (eds.). Africa Projected: From Recession to Renaissance by the Year 2000. London: MacMillan. 1985. pp. 170-186.
McFadden, Patricia
"Women Workers in Southern Africa." Journal of African Marxists. #4 September, 1983. pp. 54-62.
McGrath, Mary J.
"What Private Institutions, Particularly Cooperative, Can do to Facilitate Full Participation of Women in Meeting Food and Nutrition Needs." (In) University of Arizona. Proceedings and Papers of the International Conference on Women and Food: Consortium for International Development.

Tucson, Arizona: University of Arizona. 1978. pp. 145-153.
McKie, David
"Third World Women and Development: Ending the Women's Decade." International Perspectives. July-August, 1984. pp. 13-16.
Meghji, Zakia
"Nature of Female Urban Employment." Paper Presented at the Workshop on Women's Studies and Development. Dar-es-Salaam, Tanzania: University of Dar-es-Salaam. Bureau of Resource Assessment and Land Use Planning. Paper #37. September 24-29, 1979. 5p.
Meillassoux, Claude
Maidens, Meal and Money: Capitalism and the Domestic Community. Cambridge, New York: Cambridge University Press. 1981. 196p.
Mies, M.
"Consequences of Capitalist Penetration for Women's Subsistence Reproduction." Paper Presented at the Seminar on Underdevelopment and Subsistence Production in South East Africa. April, 1978.
Monson, Jamie and Kalb, Marion
Women as Food Producers in Developing Countries. Los Angeles: University of California-Los Angeles. African Studies Center. African Studies Association. OEF International. 1985. 118p.
Moody, Elize
"Women: An Underrated Development Source." South African Journal of African Affairs. Volume 9 #2 1979. pp. 64-71.
Moss, G. and Dunn, M. and Nsarko, J.D.
"Home Economics in Rural Development in Africa: The Village Woman's Day." Paper Presented at the Workshop on the Role of Women and Home Economics in Rural Development in Africa. Rome: United Nations Food and Agricultural Organization. Alexandria, Egypt. 1983. 7p.
Muchena, Olivia N.
"Women in Southern Africa: Are Women Integrated Into Development?" Africa Report. Volume 28 #2 March-April, 1983. pp. 4-6.
Mullings, L.
"Women and Economic Change in Africa." (In) Hafkin, N. and Bay, Edna G. (eds.). Women in Africa: Studies in Social and Economic Change. Stanford, California: Stanford University Press. 1976. pp. 239-264.
Murray, Colin G.
"Migrant Labour and Changing Family Structure in the Rural Periphery of Southern Africa." Journal of Southern African Studies. Volume 6 #2 1980. pp. 139-156.
Naali, Shamsahd
"Legal Provisions for Women's Participation in Cooperatives." Paper Presented at the Seminar on Women's Studies and Development. Dar-es-Salaam, Tanzania: University of Dar-es-Salaam. Bureau of Resource Assessment and Land Use Planning. Paper #15. September

24-29, 1979. 10p.
Nelson, Nici (ed.)
African Women in the Development Process. Totowa, New Jersey: F. Cass. 1981. 136p.
Newman, Jeanne S.
"Some Indicators of Women's Economic Roles in Sub-Saharan Africa." Paper Presented at the Annual Meeting of the American Statistical Association. Toronto, Ontario, Canada. August, 1983.
Newman, Jeanne S.
Women of the World: Sub-Saharan Africa. Washington, D.C.: U.S. Department of Commerce. U.S. Agency for International Development. Office of Women in Development. August, 1984. 200p.
Njoku, John E.
The Dawn of African Women. Hicksville, New York: Exposition Press. 1977. 96p.
Njoku, John E.
The World of the African Woman. Metuchen, New Jersey: Scarecrow Press. 1980. 132p.
North, Jeanne
"Women Participants in the Food Marketing System in West Africa." (In) University of Arizona. Proceedings and Papers of the International Conference on Women and Food: Consortium for International Development. Tucson, Arizona: University of Arizona. 1978. pp. 103-111.
O'Barr, Jean F.
Third World Women: Factors in Their Changing Status. Durham, North Carolina: Duke University. Center for International Studies. Occasional Paper #2. 1976. 94p.
O'Barr, Jean F. (ed.)
Perspectives on Power: Women in Africa, Asia and Latin America. Durham, North Carolina: Duke University. Center for International Studies. Occasional Paper #13. 1982. 120p.
Obbo, Christine S. and Nelson, Nici
African Women: Their Struggle for Economic Independence. Westport, Connecticut: Lawrence Hill. 1980. 176p.
Obbo, Christine S.
"Town Migration is Not for Women." Ph.D. Dissertation: University of Wisconsin-Madison. Madison, Wisconsin. 1977. 329p.
Okali, Christine
"The Changing Economic Position of Women in Rural Communities in West Africa." Africana Marburgensia. Volume 12 #1/2 1979. pp. 59-93.
Okeyo, Achola P.
"African Women in Changing Rural Economies." Courier. Volume 57 Sept.-Oct., 1979. pp. 63-65.
Okeyo, Achola P.
The Role of Women in Changing Traditional Farming

Systems. Paper Presented at the Workshop on Policies and Programmes for Increased Food and Agricultural Production in Traditional Subsistence Farms in Africa. Rome: United Nations Food and Agriculture Organization. Arusha, Tanzania. December 10, 1984. 27p.

Onyango, Philista P.M.
"The Working Mother and the Housemaid as a Substitute: Its Complications on the Children." Journal of Eastern African Research and Development. Volume 13 1983. pp. 24-31.

Ooko-Ombaka, Oki
"An Assessment of National Machinery for Women." Assignment Children. #49/50 Spring, 1980.

Osseo-Asare, Fran S.
Towards a Strategy for the Integration of Women Into Development. University Park, Pennsylvania: Pennsylvania State University. 1982.

Pala, Achola O.
"Definitions of Women and Development: An African Perspective." Signs. Volume 3 #1 Autumn, 1977. pp. 9-13.

Pala, Achola O.
African Women in Rural Development: Research Trends and Priorities. Washington, D.C.: American Council on Education. Overseas Liaison Committee. OLC Paper #12. December, 1976. 35p.

Pala, Achola O.
"Definitions of Women and Development: An African Perspective." (In) Wellesley Editorial Committee. Women and National Development: The Complexities of Change. Chicago: University of Chicago Press. 1977. pp. 9-13.

Pala, Achola O.
"Definitions of Women and Development: An African Perspective." (In) Steady, Filomina C. (ed.). The Black Woman Cross-Culturally. Cambridge, Massachusetts: Schenkman Publishing. 1981. pp. 209-214.

Palmer, Ingrid
The Impact of Male Out-Migration on Women in Farming. West Hartford, Connecticut: Kumarian Press. 1985. 78p.

Papanek, Hanna
"Development Planning for Women." (In) Wellesley Editorial Committee. Women and National Development: The Complexities of Change. Chicago: University of Chicago Press. 1977. pp. 14-21.

Phillott-Almeida, Ralphina
"Women and Water Resources Management for Socio-Economic Development in Africa: Health, Sanitation and Environmental Aspects." (In) United Nations Economic Commission for Africa (UNECA) (eds.). Regional Meeting on Socio-Economic and Policy Aspects of Water Management in Africa. Addis Ababa, Ethiopia: UNECA. June, 1985.

Reno, Barbara M.
Increasing Women's Credit Through Credit Unions in West

Africa. Bilingual Seminar. Nairobi: Africa Co-Operative Savings and Credit Association. March 2-6, 1981. 43p.
Reyna, Stephen P.
"Economics and Fertility: Waiting for the Demographic Transition in the Dry Zone of Francophone West Africa." (In) Caldwell, John C. (ed.). The Persistence of High Fertility: Population Prospects in the Third World." Canberra, Australia: Australian National University. Department of Demography. Volume One. 1977. pp. 393-426.
Ritchie, Jean A.
"Impact of Changing Food Production. Processing and Marketing Systems on the Role of Women." (In) Proceedings of the World Conference. Ames, Iowa: Iowa State University Press. 1977. pp. 129-144.
Roark, Paula
Successful Rural Water Supply Projects and the Concerns of Women. Washington, D.C.: U.S. Department of State. U.S. Agency for International Development. Office of Women in Development. September, 1980. 66p.
Robertson, Claire C.
"The Death of Makola and Other Tragedies: Male Strategies Against a Female Dominated Distribution Network." Paper Presented at the Annual Meeting of the Canadian African Studies Association. Toronto, Ontario, Canada. May, 1982.
Robertson, Claire C.
"Women in the Urban Economy." (In) Hay, Margaret J. and Stichter, Sharon (eds.). African Women South of the Sahara. New York: Longman. 1984. pp. 33-50.
Roboff, Farron V. and Renwick, Hilary L.
"The Changing Role of Women in the Development of the Sahel." Paper Presented to the Annual Meeting of the African Studies Association. Paper #92. Boston, Massachusetts. 1976. 12p.
Rogers, Barbara
"What do Women Want?" Appropriate Technology. Volume 4 1979.
Rogers, Barbara
"Women's Projects: New Segregation?" Africa Report. Volume 23 #3 May-June, 1978. pp. 48-50.
Rothschild, K.W.
"A Note on Female Labour Supply." Kyklos. Volume 33 1980. pp. 246-260.
Rousseau-Mukenge, Ida
"Conceptualizations of African Women's Role in Development: A Search for New Directions." Journal of International Affairs. Volume 30 #2 Fall/Winter, 1976. pp. 261-268.
Sachs, Carolyn E.
Invisible Farmers: Women in Agricultural Production. Totowa, New Jersey: Rowman and Allen Held. 1983. 153p.

Safilios-Rothschild, Constantina
The Role of Women in Modernizing Agricultural Systems. Washington, D.C.: U.S. Department of State. U.S. Agency for International Development. Office of Women in Development. May, 1981. 31p.

Saleh, Saneya
"Professional Women and National Development: Women's Response to Migration." Paper Presented at the Open University Women Seminar Series on Women, Work and Social Change. Cairo, Egypt: American University of Cairo. May 16, 1977.

Schumacher, Ilsa and Buvinic, Mayra and Sebstad, Jennefer
Limits to Productivity: Improving Women's Access to Technology and Credit. Washington, D.C.: U.S. Department of State. U.S. Agency for International Development. Center for Research on Women. Office of Women and Development. May, 1980. 65p.

Seidman, Ann
"Women and the Development of 'Underdevelopment': The African Experience." (In) Dauber, Roslyn and Cain, Melinda, L. (eds.). Women and Technological Change in Developing Countries. Boulder, Colorado: Westview Press. 1981. pp. 109-126.

Sembajwe, Israel S.
"A Note on Published National Data on Economic Activities and Women's Studies and Development." Paper Presented at the Workshop on Women's Studies and Development. Dar-es-Salaam, Tanzania: University of Dar-es-Salaam. Bureau of Resource Assessment and Land Use Planning. Paper #31. September 24-29, 1979. 6p.

Sen, G.
"Women Workers and the Green Revolution." (In) Beneria, Lourdes (ed.). Women and Development: The Sexual Division of Labor in Rural Societies. New York: Praeger Publishers. 1985.

Shaw, R. Paul
"Women's Employment in the Arab World: A Strategy of Selective Intervention." Development and Change. Volume 12 #2 April, 1981. pp. 237-272.

Shields, Nwanganga G.
"Fertility and Economic Development in Africa, 1950-1970: A Quantitative Analysis." Ph.D Dissertation: American University. Washington, D.C. 1976. 249p.

Simms, Ruth
"The African Woman as Entrepreneur: Problems and Perspectives on Their Roles." (In) Steady, Filomina C. (ed.). The Black Woman Cross-Culturally. Cambridge, Massachusetts: Schenkman Publishing. 1981. pp. 141-168.

South African Congress of Trade Unions
"The Chains That Bind Black Women Workers." Workers Unity. #14 March, 1979.

Spencer, Dunstan S.C.
Women in a Developing Economy: A West African Case Study. East Lansing, Michigan: Michigan State University. 1979. 134p.

Staudt, Kathleen A.
"The Umoja Federation: Women's Cooptation Into a Local Power Structure." Western Political Quarterly. Volume 33 #2 June, 1980. pp. 278-290.

Staudt, Kathleen A.
"Women Farmers and Inequalities in Agricultural Services." Rural Africana. Volume 29 Winter, 1976. pp. 81-94.

Staudt, Kathleen A.
"Women in Development--Policy Strategies at the End of the Decade." Africa Report. Volume 30 #2 March-April, 1985. pp. 71-74.

Staudt, Kathleen A.
"Women Farmers and Inequities in Agricultural Services." (In) Bay, Edna G. (ed.). Women and Work in Africa. Boulder, Colorado: Westview Press. Westview Special Studies in Africa. 1982. pp. 207-224.

Staudt, Kathleen A.
Women's Politics and Capitalist Transformation in Subsaharan Africa. East Lansing, Michigan: Michigan State University. Office of Women in International Development. Working Paper #54. April, 1984.

Steady, Filomina C.
Women in Africa. Cambridge, Massachusetts: Schenkman. 1983. 256p.

Steady, Filomina C.
"African Women, Industrialization Another Development." Development Dialogue. #1/2 1982. pp. 51-64.

Steady, Filomina C.
The Black Woman Cross-Culturally. Cambridge, Massachusetts: Schenkman. 1981. 645p.

Steady, Filomina C.
"The Black Woman Cross-Culturally: An Overview." (In) Steady, Filomina C. (ed.). The Black Woman Cross-Culturally. Cambridge, Massachusetts: Schenkman Publishing. 1981. pp. 7-41.

Steel, William F.
"The Small-Scale Sector's Role in Growth, Income Distribution and Employment of Women." Paper Presented at the Annual Meeting of the African Studies Association. Paper #82. Houston, Texas. November 2-5, 1977. 20p.

Tadesse, Zenebeworke
"African Women in Rural Development: A New Group of African Women Researchers." Ideas and Action. #127 1979. pp. 7-10.

Tadesse, Zenebeworke
"Studies on Rural Women in Africa: An Overview." (In)

International Labour Organization (ILO). Rural Development and Women in Africa. Geneva: ILO. 1984. pp. 65-73.

Tadesse, Zenebeworke
Women and Technological Development in Agriculture: An Overview of the Problems in Developing Countries. New York: United Nations Institute for Training and Research. Science and Technology Working Paper Series #9. 1979.

Takata, Diana M.
"Private Volunteer Organizations and Women's Participation in African Development." Rural Africana. #21 Winter, 1985. pp. 65-80.

Tau, Mildred M.
"Women: Critical to African Development." Africa Report. Volume 26 #2 March-April, 1981. pp. 4-6.

Thadani, Veena N. and Todaro, Michael P.
Female Migration in Developing Countries: A Framework for Analysis. New York: Population Council. Center for Policy Studies. Working Papers #47. 1979. 48p.

Tinker, Irene and Bramson, Michele B. (eds.)
Women and World Developmemt. New York: Praeger Publishers. 1976. 228p.

Tinker, Irene
"The Adverse Impact of Development on Women." (In) Tinker, Irene (ed.). Women and World Development. New York: Praeger Publishers. 1976.

Tomsic, Vida
"The Position and Role of Women in Development." Review of International Affairs. Volume 32 November 5, 1981. pp. 1-5.

Trager, Lillian
"Urban Market Women: Hoarders, Hagglers, Economic Heroines?" Paper Presented at the Annual Meeting of the African Studies Association. Paper #94. Los Angeles, California. Oct. 31-Nov. 3, 1979. 26p.

U.S. Agency for International Development (U.S. AID)
The Productivity of Women in Developing Countries: Measurement Issues and Recommendations. Washington, D.C.: U.S. Department of State. U.S. AID. International Center for Research on Women. Office of Women in Development. 1980. 46p.

U.S. Agency for International Development (U.S. AID)
Examples of Women in Development Programs in Sahel Francophone West Africa. Washington, D.C.: U.S. Department of State. U.S. AID. Office of Sahel and Francophone West Africa, Bureau for Africa. 1979. 27p.

United Nations Centre on Transnational Corporations and International Labour Office (ILO)
Women Workers in Multinational Enterprises in Developing Countries: A Contribution to the United Nations Decade for Women. Geneva: ILO. 1985. 119p.

United Nations Economic Commission for Africa (UNECA) "The Role of Women in Alternative Patterns of Development and Life-Styles in the Africa Region." Paper Presented at the Seminar on Alternative Patterns of Development and Lifestyles for the African Region. Addis Ababa, Ethiopia: UNECA. December 14, 1978. 16p.

United Nations Economic Commission for Africa (UNECA) "Women in Development: Moving Away From Tradition." U.N. Chronicle. Volume 19 #11 December, 1982. pp. 105-106.

United Nations Economic Commission for Africa (UNECA) Summary of On-Going and Planned Projects of the United Nations Agencies and Organizations for the Integration of Women in Development in the African Region. Addis Ababa, Ethiopia: UNECA. 1980. 72p.

United Nations Economic Commission for Africa (UNECA) "Women in African Development." Paper Presented at the ACOSCA Bilingual Regional Seminar on Increasing Women's Access to Credit Unions in West Africa. Addis Ababa, Ethiopia: UNECA. Dakar, Senegal. March, 1981.

United Nations Economic Commission for Africa (UNECA) The New International Economic Order--What Role for Women in Africa? Addis Ababa, Ethiopia: UNECA. August, 1977. 54p.

United Nations Economic Commission for Africa (UNECA) Establishment of Sub-Regional Machinery to Enhance the Role of Women in the Progress of Economic and Social Development in the Central African Sub-Region and to Promote and Guide the Activities of the ECA's Training and Research Centre for Women. Yaounde, Cameroon: MULPOC (Multi-National Operations Center for Central African Library). March, 1978.

United Nations Economic Commission for Africa (UNECA) ECA Five Year Programme on Pre-Vocational and Vocational Training of Girls and Women, Toward Their Full Participation in Development (1972-1976). Addis Ababa, Ethiopia: UNECA. 1976.

United Nations Economic Commission for Africa (UNECA) The Changing and Contemporary Role of Women in African Development. Addis Ababa, Ethiopia: UNECA. 1977.

United Nations Economic Commission for Africa (UNECA) African Women's Development Task Force. Addis Ababa, Ethiopia: UNECA. African Training and Research Centre for Women. 1976. 15p.

United Nations Economic Commission for Africa (UNECA) African Women Workers: Analysis of the Factors Affecting Women's Employment. Addis Ababa, Ethiopia: UNECA. African Training and Research Centre for Women. 1976. 53p.

United Nations Economic Commission for Africa (UNECA) Report: ECA/FAO Subregional Seminar on Fuelwood and Energy Development for African Women, April 18, 1983. Addis Ababa, Ethiopia: UNECA. Lusaka, Zambia. November, 1984. 25p.

United Nations Economic Commission for Africa (UNECA)
The Critical Needs of African Women and Appropriate Strategies in the Framework of the Gisenyi and Lusaka MULPOCS. Addis Ababa, Ethiopia: UNECA. 1981.

United Nations Educational, Scientific and Cultural Organ.
Final Report: Regional Workshop on Women's Crafts in Developing Countries. Paris: UNESCO. CREA #14. Katiola, Ivory Coast. 1983. 22p.

United Nations Food and Agriculture Organization (FAO)
The State of Food and Agriculture; 1983: World Review: The Situation in Sub-Saharan Africa; Women in Developing Agriculture. New York: FAO. FAO Agriculture Series #16. 1984. 221p.

United Nations Food and Agriculture Organization (FAO)
Food Aid and the Role of Women in Development. Rome: FAO. 1976. 43p.

United Nations Food and Agriculture Organization (FAO)
The Role of Women in Population Dynamics Related to Food and Agriculture and Rural Development in Africa. Rome: FAO. United Nations Economic Commission for Africa. Women's Program Unit. Joint Agriculture Division. 1976.

Van Allen, Judith
"African Women, 'Modernization' and National Liberation." (In) Iglitzin, Lynne B. and Ross, Ruth (eds.). Women in the World. Santa Barbara, California: Clio Press. American Bibliographic Center. 1976. pp. 25-54.

Van der Horst, Sheila T.
Women as an Economic Force in Southern Africa. Rondebosch, South Africa: University of Cape Town. Abe Bailey Institute of Interracial Studies #18. 1977.

Ware, Helen
"Economic Strategy and the Number of Children." (In) Caldwell, John C. (ed.). The Persistence of High Fertility: Population Prospects in the Third World. Canberra, Australia: Australian National University. Department of Demography. Volume Two. 1977. pp. 469-592.

Ware, Helen
"Motivations for the Use of Birth Control: Evidence From West Africa." Demography. Volume 13 #4 November, 1976. pp. 479-494.

Weekes-Vagliani, Winifred and Grossat, Bernard
Women in Development: At the Right Time for the Right Reason. Paris: Organization for Economic Cooperation and Development. 1980. 330p.

Wipper, Audrey
"Women's Voluntary Associations." (In) Hay, Margaret J. and Stichter, Sharon (eds.). African Women South of the Sahara. New York: Longman. 1984. pp. 69-86.

World Bank
Rural Development Projects: A Retrospective View of Bank Experience in Sub-Saharan Africa. Washington, D.C.: World Bank. Report #2242. October 13, 1978.

World Bank
Recognizing the 'Invisible' Woman in Development: The World Banks Experience. Washington, D.C.: World Bank. October, 1979. 33p.

Wright, Marcia
"Technology and Women's Control Over Production: Three Case Studies From East-Central Africa and Their Implications for Esther Boserup's Thesis About the Displacement of Women." Paper Presented at the Rockefeller Foundation Workshop on Women, Household and Human Capital Development in Low Income Countries. New York: Rockefeller Foundation. July, 1982.

Youssef, Nadia H. and Hetler, Carol B.
"Establishing the Economic Condition of Woman-Headed Households in the Third World: A New Approach." (In) Buvinic, Mayra and Lycette, Margaret A. and McGreevey, William P. (eds.). Women and Poverty in the Third World. Baltimore, Maryland: Johns Hopkins University. 1983. pp. 216-243.

Youssef, Nadia H.
"Women and Agricultural Production in Muslim Societies." Studies in Comparative International Development. Volume 12 #1 Spring, 1977. pp. 41-58.

Zivetz, L.
The Impact of Rural Development on the Status of Women and its Consequences for Fertility in Africa. Submitted to the Research Triangle Institute and the Southeast Consortium for International Development. Chapel Hill, North Carolina. 1979.

Education and Training

Abdel Kader, Soha
The Status of Research on Women in the Arab Region, 1960-1978. Paris: UNESCO. Division of Human Rights and Peace. January, 1979.

Agarwal, Bina
"Women and Technological Change in Agricultural Change: The Asian and African Experience." (In) Ahmed, I. (ed.). Technology and Rural Development: Conceptual and Empirical Issues. London: Allen and Unwin. 1985. pp. 67-114.

Aidoo, Agnes A.
"Women and Development in Africa: Alternative Strategies for the Future." (In) Adedeji, A. and Shaw, T.M. (eds.). Economic Crisis in Africa: African Perspectives on Development Problems and Potentials. Boulder, Colorado: Lynne Rienner. 1985. pp. 201-217.

Al-Qazza, Ayad
"Current Status of Research on Women in the Arab World." Middle Eastern Studies. Volume 14 #3 October, 1978. pp. 372-384.

Anokwa, C. Ofosu
"Higher Education in Home Economics: The Need for Collaboration." Paper Presented at the Workshop on the Role of Women and Home Economics in Rural Development in Africa. Rome: United Nations Food and Agricultural Organization. Alexandria, Egypt. October 17, 1983. 12p.

Anonymous
"Women in Rural Development: Recommendations and Realities." Ceres. May-June, 1980. pp. 15-42.

Asare, Janet
"Making Life Easier for Africa's Rural Women." UNICEF News. #90 1976. pp. 20-23.

Axinn, Nancy W.
Female Emancipation Versus Female Welfare. East Lansing, Michigan: Michigan State University. Institute for

International Studies in Education. College of Education. Non-Formal Education Information Center. 1979. 5p.

Barber, Elinor G.
"Some International Perspectives on Sex Differences in Education." Signs. Volume 4 #3 Spring, 1979. pp. 584-592.

Barthel, D.
"Women's Educational Experience Under Colonialism: Toward a Diachronic Model." Signs. Volume 11 Autumn, 1985. pp. 137-154.

Bell, Roseann C.
"Absence of the African Women Writer." CLA Journal. Volume 21 June, 1978. pp. 491-498.

Bowman, Mary J. and Anderson, C. Arnold
"The Participation of Women in Education in the Third World." Comparative Education Review. Volume 24 #2 Pt. 2 June, 1980. pp. S13-S32.

Bowman, Mary J. and Anderson, C. Arnold
"The Participation of Women in Education in the Third World." (In) Kelly, Gail P. and Elliott, Carolyn M. (eds.). Women's Education in the Third World. Albany, New York: State University of New York Press. 1982. pp. 11-30.

Bowman, Mary J. and Anderson, C. Arnold
The Participation of Women in Education in the Third World. New York: Ford Foundation. 1978. 278p.

Caldwell, Pat and Caldwell, John C.
"Population Change and Development in the ECWA Region." (In) Cairo Demographic Centre (CDC). Aspects of Population Change and Development in Some African and Asian Countries. Cairo, Egypt: CDC. CDC Research Monograph Series #9. 1984. pp. 43-56.

Caplan, Patricia and Bujra, Janet M. (eds.)
Women United Women Divided: Comparative Studies of Ten Contemporary Cultures. Bloomington, Indiana: Indiana University Press. 1979. 288p.

Carr, Marilyn
"Appropriate Technology for Rural African Women." Development Digest. Volume 20 #1 January, 1982. pp. 87-98.

Carr, Marilyn
Appropriate Technology for African Women. Addis Ababa, Ethiopia: United Nations Economic Commission for Africa. African Training and Research Center for Women. 1978. 105p.

Carr, Marilyn
"Technologies for Rural Women: Impact and Dissemination." (In) Ahmed, Iftikhar (ed.). Technology and Rural Women: Conceptual and Empirical Issues. Boston: George Allen and Unwin. 1985. pp. 115-153.

Carr, Marilyn
Technology and Rural Women in Africa. Addis Ababa, Ethiopia: United Nations Economic Commission for Africa. African Training and Research Center for Women. Joint

Project With the International Labour Organization. ILO World Employment Programme Research Working Paper #61. 1980.
Carr, Marilyn
"Appropriate Technology for Women." Appropriate Technology. Volume 1 1979.
Carter, Ann L.
"African Women and Career Counseling: A Model." Journal of Non-White Concerns in Personnel and Guidance. Volume 9 #1 October, 1980. pp. 23-33.
Caton, Douglas D.
Elements of the Food Production-Distribution System: An Overview on How Women Can Contribute. Proceedings and Papers of the International Conference on Women and Food Consortium for International Development. Tucson, Arizona: University of Arizona. 1978. pp. 45-61.
Cernea, Michael M. (ed.).
Putting People First: Sociological Variables in Rural Development. New York: Oxford University Press. 1985. 430p.
Chan, S.
"Young Women and Development in Africa--Some Generally Unconsidered Considerations." Community Development Journal. Volume 18 #3 1983. pp. 257-262.
Clark, Carolyn M.
Sexuality in the Workplace: Some African Examples. Santa Cruz, California: University of California-Santa Cruz. 1981.
Cohen, Ronald and Knipp, Maggie
"Women and Change in West Africa: A Synthesis." Paper Presented at the Annual Meeting of the African Studies Association. Paper #16. Philadelphia, Pennsylvania. 1980.
Cook, Gayla
"Women in Africa: Working With African Women: Options for the West." Africa Report. Volume 26 #2 March-April, 1981. pp. 43-46.
Cosminsky, Sheila
"The Role and Training of Traditional Midwives: Policy Implications for Maternal and Child Health Care." Paper Presented at the Annual Meeting of the African Studies Association. Paper #17. Houston, Texas. 1977. 25p.
Creative Associates, Inc.
Participation of Women in the Economic Development Process: A Suggested Strategy for the African Bureau. Washington, D.C.: Creative Associates, Inc. 1980. 20p.
D'onofrio-Flores, Pamela M. and Pfafflin, Sheila M. (eds.)
Scientific-Technological Change and the Role of Women in Development. Boulder, Colorado: Westview Press. Published for the United Nations Institute for Training and Research. 1982. 206p.
Dajani, Karen F.
"Magazine for Arab Women: Hawa." Journalism Quarterly. Spring, 1982. pp. 116-118.

Danforth, Sandra C.
Women and National Development. Monticello, Illinois: Vance Bibliographies. #P-916. February, 1982. 35p.

Derryck, Vivian L.
The Comparative Functionality of Formal and Non-Formal Education for Women: Final Report. Washington, D.C.: U.S. Department of State. U.S. Agency for International Development. January, 1979. 196p.

Dhamija, Jasleen
"Technology as a Target to the Development of Women's Skills in Africa." Ceres. # 84 November, 1981. pp. 24-27.

Dirasse, Laketch
"Approaches to the Study of Women in Africa: The Alternatives." (In) Ray, D.I. (ed.). Into the 80's: The Proceedings of 11th Annual Conference of the Canadian Association of African Studies. Vancouver, British Columbia, Canada: Tantalas Research Ltd. Volume Two. 1981. pp. 79-81.

Dirasse, Laketch
The Critical Needs of African Women and Appropriate Strategies in the Framework of the Gisenyi and Lusaka MULPOCS. Addis Ababa, Ethiopia: United Nations Economic Commission for Africa. African Training and Research Centre for Women. 1981. 35p.

Due, Jean M. and Summary, Rebecca
"Constraints to Women and Development in Africa." Journal of Modern African Studies. Volume 20 #1 March, 1982. pp. 155-166.

Due, Jean M. and Summary, Rebecca
"Constraints to Women and Development in Africa." Paper Presented at the Annual Meeting of the African Studies Association. Paper #35. Los Angeles, California. 1979. 23p.

Due, Jean M. and Summary, Rebecca
Constraints to Women and Development in Africa. Urbana, Illinois: University of Illinois-Urbana-Champaign. Department of Agricultural Economics. Staff Paper Series E. Agricultural Economics 79-E-83. May, 1979. 27p.

Elias, Misrak
Training for Development Planning and Women, an African Perspective: Report on the Second Training Programme. Arusha, Tanzania: Eastern and Southern Africa Management Institute. April 5-May 14, 1982. 55p.

Elias, Misrak
Training for Development Planning and Women: An African Perspective. Arusha, Tanzania: Eastern and Southern African Management Institute. Annual Report and Report of the First Training Programme. September 16, 1980-September 15, 1981. 1981.

Engberg, L.E.
"Emphasis on Economics--A Way to Strengthen the

Relationship of Home Economics With Agriculture." Paper Presented at the Workshop on the Role of Women and Home Economics in Rural Development in Africa. Rome: United Nations Food and Agriculture Organization. Alexandria, Egypt. October 17, 1983. 10p.

Epskamp, C.
Inequality in Female Access to Education in Developing Countries: A Bibliography. Hague, Netherlands: Centre for the Study of Education in Developing Countries. 1979. 42p.

Fatehally, Laeeq (ed.)
Women in the Third World. Bombay, India: Leslie Sawhny Programme. 1980. 155p.

Faulkner, Constance
"Women's Studies in the Muslim Middle East." Journal of Ethnic Studies. Volume 8 #3 Fall, 1980. pp. 67-76.

Fortmann, Louise P.
"A Role for Women in Agroforestry Projects." (In) United Nations Food and Agriculture Organization (FAO). 1983 Training for Agriculture and Rural Development. Rome: FAO. Economic and Social Development Series #31. 1984. pp. 21-26.

International Labour Office (ILO)
Improved Village Technology for Women's Activities: A Manual for West Africa. London: ILO. 1985.

Kayongo-Male, Diana
"Helping Self-Help Groups Help Themselves: Training of Leaders of Women's Groups." Journal of Eastern African Research and Development. Volume 13 1983. pp. 88-103.

Kelly, David H. and Kelly, Gail P.
"Education of Women in Developing Countries." Educational Documentation and Information: Bull. of the Intern. Bureau of Educ. Volume 56 #222 1st Quarter, 1982.

Kelly, David H. and Kelly, Gail P.
"Women and Schooling in the Third World: A Bibliography." (In) Kelly, Gail P. and Elliott, Carolyn M. (eds.). Women's Education in the Third World: Comparative Perspectives. Albany, New York: State University of New York Press. 1982. pp. 345-397.

Kelly, Gail P.
"Research on the Education of Women in the Third World: Problems and Perspectives." Women's Studies: International Quarterly. Volume 1 #4 1978. pp. 365-373.

Kelly, Gail P. and Elliott, Carolyn M. (eds.)
"Women's Education in the Third World: Comparative Perspectives." Albany, New York: State University of New York Press. 1982. 406p.

Kelly, Gail P. and Lulat, Younus
"Women and Schooling in the Third World: A Bibliography." Comparative Education Review. Volume 24 #2 June, 1980. pp. S224-S263.

Kwawu, J.
"The Role of Home Economics in Rural Development: A Focus on Family Planning." Paper Presented at the Workshop on the Role of Women and Home Economics in Rural Development in Africa. Rome: United Nations Food and Agricultural Organization. Alexandria, Egypt. October 17, 1983. 20p.

LeVine, Robert A. and Richman, Amy and Welles, Barbara and O'Rourke, Shelagh and Caron, James W.
Women's Education and Maternal Behavior in the Third World: A Report to the Ford Foundation. New York: Ford Foundation. 1978. 52p.

LeVine, Robert A.
"Influences of Women's Schooling on Maternal Behavior in the Third World." Comparative Education Review. Volume 24 #2 Part Two June, 1980. pp. S78-S105.

Lorimer, Thomas
Illustrative Statistics on Women in Selected Developing Countries. Washington, D.C.: U.S. Department of Commerce. Bureau of the Census. Prepared for the U.S. Agency for International Development. September, 1980. 24p.

M'bow, Amadou-Mahtar
"The United Nations Decade for Women: Towards a New Order With Regard to the Status of Women." Cultures. Volume 8 #4 1982.

Mair, Lucille
"Adult Learning. Women and Development." Prospects 7. #2 1977. pp. 238-443.

Mbilinyi, Marjorie J.
"Research Priorities in Women's Studies in Eastern Africa." Women's Studies International Forum. Volume 7 #4 1984. pp. 289-300.

McKie, David
"Third World Women and Development: Ending the Women's Decade." International Perspectives. July-August, 1984. pp. 13-16.

Mitchnik, David A.
Improving Ways of Skill Acquisition of Women for Rural Employment in Some African Countries. Geneva: International Labour Organization. World Employment Programme Research. Education and Employment Research Project. Working Papers. February, 1977. 78p.

Moris, J.R.
Reforming Agricultural Extension and Research Services in Africa. London: Overseas Development Institute. Discussion Paper #11. 1983.

Mortimer, Mildred P.
"Assie Djebar: A Feminist Movement." Paper Presented at the Annual Meeting of the African Studies Association. Paper #67. Boston, Massachusetts. 1976. 19p.

Moss, G. and Dunn, M. and Nsarko, J.D.
"Home Economics in Rural Development in Africa: The Village Woman's Day." Paper Presented at the Workshop on the Role of Women and Home Economics in Rural Development in Africa. Rome: United Nations Food and Agricultural Organization. Alexandria, Egypt. 1983. 7p.

Munuo, Edith
"Education for Equality." Paper Presented at the Workshop on Women's Studies and Development. Dar-es-Salaam, Tanzania: University of Dar-es-Salaam. Bureau of Resource Assessment and Land Use Planning. Paper #14. September 24-29, 1979. 19p.

Muriuki, Margaret N.
"The Role of Women in African Librarianship: The Next 25 Years." Paper Presented at the Standing Conference of Eastern, Central and Southern African Libraries. Lusaka, Zambia. October 4-9, 1976.

Ntiri, Daphne W.
"African Student Wives: Their Participation in Continuing Education." Lifelong Learning. Volume 3 #4 December, 1979. pp. 10-11+.

Nwagwu, Nicholas A.
"Equalization of Educational Opportunities in African Countries." Journal of Educational Administration. Volume 14 #2 October, 1976. pp. 270-278.

O'Barr, Jean F.
Third World Women: Factors in Their Changing Status. Durham, North Carolina: Duke University. Center for International Studies. Occasional Paper #2. 1976. 94p.

O'Kelly, Elizabeth
"Appropriate Technology for Women of the Developing Countries." Peace Corps Program and Training Journal. Volume 4 #6 1977.

O'Kelly, Elizabeth
Rural Women: Their Integration in Development Programmes and How Simple Intermediate Technologies Can Help Them. Available From the Author: 3 Cumberland Gardens, Lloyd Square, London, England WC1X 9AF. $4.00. 1978. 84p.

O'Shaughnessey, T.J.
"Growth of Educational Opportunity for Muslim Women, 1950-1973." Anthropos. Volume 73 #5/6 1978. pp. 887-901.

Rainey, Mary C.
"Non-Formal Education and Third World Women." Paper Presented at the International Conference on Human Lactation. New York: New York Academy of Science. March, 1977. 12p.

Ritchie, Jean A.
"Training Women for Development in Africa." (In) United Nations Food and Agriculture Organization (FAO).

Training for Agriculture and Rural Development, 1977. Rome: United Nations. FAO. Economic and Development Series #7. 1977. pp. 19-26.

Robertson, Claire
"A Growing Dilemma: Women and Change in African and Primary Education, 1958-1980." Journal of Eastern African Research and Development. Volume 15 1985. pp. 17-35.

Robertson, Claire C.
"The Nature and Effects of Differential Access to Education in a Society." Africa. Volume 47 #2 1977. pp. 208-219.

Robertson, Claire C.
"Women in the Urban Economy." (In) Hay, Margaret J. and Stichter, Sharon (eds.). African Women South of the Sahara. New York: Longman. 1984. pp. 33-50.

Rogers, Barbara
"Women's Projects: New Segregation?" Africa Report. Volume 23 #3 May-June, 1978. pp. 48-50.

Safilios-Rothschild, Constantina
Access of Rural Girls to Primary Education in the Third World: State of Art, Obstacles and Policy Recommendations. Washington, D.C.: U.S. Department of State. U.S. Agency for International Development. 1979. 31p.

Scandinavian Institute of African Studies
Women in Africa and Development Assistance. Report From a Seminar. Uppsala, Sweden: Scandinavian Institute of African Studies. 1978. 55p.

Schumacher, Ilsa and Buvinic, Mayra and Sebstad, Jennefer
Limits to Productivity: Improving Women's Access to Technology and Credit. Washington, D.C.: U.S. Department of State. U.S. Agency for International Development. Center for Research on Women. Office of Women and Development. May, 1980. 65p.

Sembajwe, Israel S.
"A Note on Published National Data on Economic Activities and Women's Studies and Development." Paper Presented at the Workshop on Women's Studies and Development. Dar-es-Salaam, Tanzania: University of Dar-es-Salaam. Bureau of Resource Assessment and Land Use Planning. Paper #31. September 24-29, 1979. 6p.

Siann, Gerda and Khalid, R.
"Muslim Traditions and Attitudes to Female Education." Journal of Adolescence. Volume 7 June, 1984. pp. 191-200.

Smock, Audrey C.
Women's Education in Developing Countries: Opportunities and Outcomes. New York: Praeger Publishers. Praeger Special Studies in Comparative Education. 1981. 293p.

Stanley, Joyce and Lundeen, Alisa
The Audio Cassette Listening Forums: A Participatory Women's Development Project. Washington, D.C.: U.S.

Department of State. U.S. Agency for International Development. Office of Women in Development. 1979. 92p.
Staudt, Kathleen A.
"Women in Development--Policy Strategies at the End of the Decade." Africa Report. Volume 30 #2 March-April, 1985. pp. 71-74.
Steady, Filomina C.
Women in Africa. Cambridge, Massachusetts: Schenkman. 1983. 256p.
Stephens, Betsy and Odell, M.
"Professional Women in Development Assistance." International Development Review. Volume 19 #2 1977. pp. 3-5.
Stokland, Torill and Vajrathon, Mallica and Davidson, Nicol
Creative Women in Changing Societies: A Quest for Alternatives. Dobbs Ferry, New York: Transnational Publishers. 1982. 173p.
Sudarkasa, Niara
"Sex Roles, Education and Development in Africa." Anthropology and Education Quarterly. Volume 13 #3 Fall, 1982. pp. 279-288.
Tadesse, Zenebeworke
Women and Technological Development in Agriculture: An Overview of the Problems in Developing Countries. New York: United Nations Institute for Training and Research. Science and Technology Working Paper Series #9. 1979.
Tadesse, Zenebeworke
"Women and Technology in Peripheral Countries: An Overview." (In) D'Onofrio-Flores, Pamela M. and Pfafflin, Sheila M. (eds.). Scientific-Technological Change and the Role of Women in Development. Boulder, Colorado: Westview Press. 1982. pp. 77-111.
Takata, Diane M.
"Increasing Women's Participation in the African Development Process Through the Assistance of U.S. Private Voluntary Organizations." Paper Presented at the Annual Meeting of the African Studies Association. Paper #113. Washington, D.C. November 4-7, 1982.
Thelejane, T.S.
"An African Girl and an African Woman in a Changing World." Paper Presented at the Seminar on the Changing Family in the African Context. Paris: United Nations Educational, Scientific and Cultural Organization. Maseru, Lesotho. 1984. 24p.
Tinker, Irene
New Technologies for Food Chain Activities: The Imperative of Equity for Women. Washington, D.C.: U.S. Department of State. U.S. Agency for International Development. Office of Women in Development. 1979. 43p.
Tinker, Irene
"New Technologies for Food Related Activities: An Equity

Strategy." (In) Dauber, Roslyn and Cain, Melinda L. (eds.). Women and Technological Change in Developing Countries. Boulder, Colorado: Westview Press. 1981. pp. 51-88.

U.S. Agency for International Development (U.S. AID) Non-Formal Education--Women in Sahel. Washington, D.C.: U.S. Department of State. U.S. AID. 1978. 23p.

U.S. Agency for International Development (U.S. AID) Training Women in the Sahel. Washington, D.C.: U.S. Department of State. U.S. AID. Office of Women in Development. 1978. 47p.

United Nations Building New Knowledge Through Technical Cooperation Among Developing Countries: The Experience of the Association of African Women for Research and Development (AAWORD). New York: United Nations. March 6, 1980.

United Nations Measures of Assistance for Women in Southern Africa. Paper Presented at the United Nations World Conference of the United Nations Decade for Women: Equality, Development and Peace. New York: United Nations. Copenhagen, Denmark. July 14-30, 1980. 34p.

United Nations Economic Commission for Africa (UNECA) "Women as Clientele of Non-Formal Education." Paper Presented to the Regional Symposium on Non-Formal Education for Rural Development. Addis Ababa, Ethiopia: UNECA. Aug. 28-Sept. 8, 1978. 12p.

United Nations Economic Commission for Africa (UNECA) "Origin and Growth of the African Training and Research Centre for Women of the Economic Commission for Africa." Addis Ababa, Ethiopia: UNECA. September, 1977. 60p.

United Nations Economic Commission for Africa (UNECA) "Technical Co-Operation Among Developing Countries and Human Resource Development: The Experience of the African Training and Research Centre for Women of the Economic Commission for Africa." Paper Presented at the United Nations Conference on Technical Co-Operation Among Developing Countries. Addis Ababa, Ethiopia: UNECA. Buenos Aires, Argentina. 1978. 16p.

United Nations Economic Commission for Africa (UNECA) "The Role of Women in Alternative Patterns of Development and Life-Styles in the Africa Region." Paper Presented at the Seminar on Alternative Patterns of Development and Lifestyles for the African Region. Addis Ababa, Ethiopia: UNECA. December 14, 1978. 16p.

United Nations Economic Commission for Africa (UNECA) The Role of Women in the Utilization of Science and Technology for Development: An ECA Contribution to the African Regional Meeting of the United Nations Conference on Science and Technology for Development (UNCSTD). Cairo, Egypt, July 24-29. Addis Ababa, Ethiopia: UNECA. African Training and Research Centre for Women. 1978. 62p.

United Nations Economic Commission for Africa (UNECA) Summary of On-Going and Planned Projects of the United Nations Agencies and Organizations for the Integration of Women in Development in the African Region. Addis Ababa, Ethiopia: UNECA. 1980. 72p.

United Nations Economic Commission for Africa (UNECA) Establishment of Sub-Regional Machinery to Enhance the Role of Women in the Progress of Economic and Social Development in the Central African Sub-Region and to Promote and Guide the Activities of the ECA's Training and Research Centre for Women. Yaounde, Cameroon: MULPOC (Multi-National Operations Center for Central African Library). March, 1978.

United Nations Economic Commission for Africa (UNECA) ECA Five Year Programme on Pre-Vocational and Vocational Training of Girls and Women, Toward Their Full Participation in Development (1972-1976). Addis Ababa, Ethiopia: UNECA. 1976.

United Nations Economic Commission for Africa (UNECA) "National Machinery for the Integration of Women in Development in African Countries." Paper Presented to the Regional Conference on the Implementation of the National Regional and Worlds Plans of Action for the Integration of Women in Development. Addis Ababa, Ethiopia: UNECA. Nouakchott, Mauritania. 1977. 54p.

United Nations Economic Commission for Africa (UNECA) The Critical Needs of African Women and Appropriate Strategies in the Framework of the Gisenyi and Lusaka MULPOCS. Addis Ababa, Ethiopia: UNECA. 1981.

United Nations Economic Commission for Africa (UNECA) "The Role of Women in the Solution of the Food Crisis in Africa (Implementation of the Lagos Plan of Action)." Paper Presented at the Regional Intergovernmental Preparatory Meeting for the World Conference to Review and Appraise the Achievements of the United Nations Decade for Women: Equality, Development and Peace/Third Regional Conference on the Integration of Women in Development, Arusha, Tanzania, October 8-12. Addis Ababa, Ethiopia: UNECA. 1984.

United Nations Educational, Scientific and Cultural Organ. Female Participation in Higher Education: Enrollment Trends, 1975-1982. Paris: UNESCO. Current Surveys and Research in Statistics. February, 1985. 92p.

United Nations Educational, Scientific and Cultural Organ. Description of Projects Relevant to the Integration of Women in Development: Africa. Paris: UNESCO. May 16, 1979. 10p.

United Nations Educational, Scientific and Cultural Organ. Comparative Report on the Role of Working Mothers in Early Childhood Education in Five Countries. Paris: UNESCO. 1978. 82p.

United Nations Secretary-General
"Measures of Assistance for Women in Southern Africa: Report of the Secretary General." Paper Presented at the World Conference of the United Nations Decade for Women. New York: United Nations. Copenhagen, Denmark. July 14-30, 1980.

Von Blanckenberg, P.
Agricultural Extension Systems in Some African Countries. Rome: United Nations Food and Agriculture Organization (FAO). FAO Economic and Social Development Paper. 1984.

Ware, Helen
Women, Education and Modernization of the Family in West Africa. Canberra, Australia: Australian National University. Department of Demography. Changing African Family Project Series. Monograph #7. 1981. 178p.

Wells, Julia C.
Women in Africa. Johannesburg: South African Council of Higher Education. 1979.

Whalen, Irene T.
Women and Livestock: The Impact of Technological Innovations on Women. Addis Ababa, Ethiopia: International Livestock Center, Africa. P/O Box 5689. 1984.

Whitehead, Clive
"The Education of Women and Girls: An Aspect of British Colonial Policy." Journal of Educational Administration. Volume 16 #2 1984. pp. 24-34.

World Health Organization (WHO)
Improving Ways of Skill Acquisition of Women for Rural Development in Some African Countries. Geneva: World Health Organization. World Employment Programme Research Working Papers. WEP 2-18/WP 15. 1977. 76p.

Wright, Marcia
"Technology and Women's Control Over Production: Three Case Studies From East-Central Africa and Their Implications for Esther Boserup's Thesis About the Displacement of Women." Paper Presented at the Rockefeller Foundation Workshop on Women, Household and Human Capital Development in Low Income Countries. New York: Rockefeller Foundation. July, 1982.

Employment and Labor

Adepoju, Aderanti
"Patterns of Migration by Sex." (In) Oppong, Christine (ed.). Female and Male in West Africa. London: George Allen and Unwin. 1983. pp. 54-66.

African-American Labor Center
"Pan-African Conference on the Role of Trade Union Women." Paper Presented at the Conference on the Role of Trade Union Women: Problems, Prospects, Programs." New York: African-American Labor Center. Nairobi, Kenya. July 17-27, 1977. 152p.

Agarwal, Bina
"Women and Technological Change in Agriculture: The Asian and African Experience." (In) Ahmed, Iftikhar (ed.). Technology and Rural Women: Conceptual and Empirical Issues. Boston: George Allen and Unwin. 1985. pp. 67-114.

Agarwal, Bina
"Women and Technological Change in Agricultural Change: The Asian and African Experience." (In) Ahmed, I. (ed.). Technology and Rural Development: Conceptual and Empirical Issues. London: Allen and Unwin. 1985. pp. 67-114.

Ahdab-Yehia, May
"Women, Employment and Fertility Trends in the Arab Middle East and North Africa." (In) Kupinsky, Stanley (ed.). The Fertility of Working Women: A Synthesis of International Research. New York: Praeger Publishers. Preager Special Studies in International Economics and Development. 1977. pp. 172-187.

Ahmed, Iftikhar
"Technology and Rural Women in the Third World." International Labour Review. Volume 122 #4 July-August, 1983. pp. 493-505.

Aidoo, Christina A.A.
"Images of Women." (In) University of Illinois (ed.). Women and Work in Africa, April 29-May 1, 1979,

University of Illinois, Urbana-Champaign: A Project of the Africn Studies Association. Urbana, Illinois: University of Illinois. 1979.

Allison, C.
"Women, Land, Labour and Survival: Getting Some Basic Facts Straight." IDS Bulletin. Volume 16 #3 1985. pp. 24-30.

Amon-Nikoi, Gloria
"Women and Work in Africa." (In) Damachi, Ukandi G. and Diejomaoh, Victor P. Human Resources and African Development. New York: Praeger Publishers. 1978. pp. 188-219.

Anker, Richard
Demographic Change and the Role of Women: A Research Programme in Developing Countries. Geneva: International Labour Office. Population and Employment Working Paper #69. 1978. 27p.

Anker, Richard and Knowles, James C.
"A Micro-Analysis of Female Labour Force Participation in Africa." (In) Standing, G. and Sheehan, G. (eds.). Labour Force Participation in Low Income Countries. Geneva: International Labour Office. 1978. pp. 137-163.

Anonymous
"African Women's Development Task Force." Rural Progress. Volume 1 #1 October, 1977. pp. 25-26.

Anonymous
"Official Documents: ILO Standards Relating to Women Workers; Equal Renumeration Convention: Situation in Africa." Women at Work. #2 1983.

Anonymous
Women in Rural Development: Critical Issues. Geneva: International Labour Organization. 1980. 51p.

Bay, Edna G. and Hafkin, Nancy J. (eds.)
"Women in Africa: Studies in Social and Economic Change." Stanford, California: Stanford University Press. 1976. 306p.

Bay, Edna G.
Women and Work in Africa. Boulder, Colorado: Westview Press. Westview Special Studies on Africa. 1982. 310p.

Beneria, Lourdes
"Conceptualizing the Labour Force: The Underestimation of Women's Economic Activities." Journal of Development Studies. Volume 17 #3 April, 1981. pp. 10-28.

Beneria, Lourdes
"Reproduction, Production and the Sexual Division of Labour." Cambridge Journal of Economics. Volume 3 September, 1979. pp. 203-225.

Beneria, Lourdes
Women and Development: The Sexual Division of Labor in Rural Societies: A Study. New York: Praeger Publishers. Praeger Special Studies. 1982. 257p.

Beneria, Lourdes
"Reproduction, Production and the Sexual Division of Labour." Geneva: International Labour Office. World Employment Research Working Paper #2. 1978.

Beneria, Lourdes
"Conceptualizing the Labour Force: The Underestimation of Women's Economic Activities." (In) Nelson, Nici (ed.). African Women in the Development Process." Totowa, New Jersey: Frank Cass. 1981. pp. 10-28.

Besha, R.M.
The Mass Media and Entertainment. Dar-es-Salaam, Tanzania: University of Dar-es-Salaam. Bureau of Resource Assessment and Land Use Planning. Workshop on Women's Studies and Development. Paper #34. September 24-29, 1979.

Boserup, Ester (ed.)
Traditional Division of Work Between the Sexes, A Source of Inequality: Research Symposium on Women and Decision Making: A Social Policy Priority. Geneva: International Institute for Labour Studies. Research Series #21. 1976. 32p.

Boulding, Elise
"Productivity and Poverty of Third World Women: Problems in Measurement." (In) Buvinic, Mayra and Lycette, Margaret C. and McGreevey, William P. (eds.). Women and Poverty in the Third World. Baltimore, Maryland: Johns Hopkins University. 1983.

Bujra, Janet M.
"Class, Gender and Capitalist Transformation in Africa." Africa Development. Volume 8 #3 1983. pp. 17-42.

Burke, Mary P.
"Women: The Missing Piece in the Development Puzzle." Agenda. Volume 1 #3 March, 1978. pp. 1-5.

Caldwell, Pat and Caldwell, John C.
"Population Change and Development in the ECWA Region." (In) Cairo Demographic Centre (CDC). Aspects of Population Change and Development in Some African and Asian Countries. Cairo, Egypt: CDC. CDC Research Monograph Series #9. 1984. pp. 43-56.

Carr, Marilyn
"Appropriate Technology for Rural African Women." Development Digest. Volume 20 #1 January, 1982. pp. 87-98.

Carr, Marilyn
Appropriate Technology for African Women. Addis Ababa, Ethiopia: United Nations Economic Commission for Africa. African Training and Research Center for Women. 1978. 105p.

Carr, Marilyn
"Technologies for Rural Women: Impact and Dissemination." (In) Ahmed, Iftikhar (ed.). Technology and Rural Women: Conceptual and Empirical Issues. Boston: George Allen and Unwin. 1985. pp. 115-153.

Carr, Marilyn
Technology and Rural Women in Africa. Addis Ababa, Ethiopia: United Nations Economic Commission for Africa. African Training and Research Center for Women. Joint

Project With the International Labour Organization. ILO World Employment Programme Research Working Paper #61. 1980.
Carr, Marilyn
"Appropriate Technology for Women." Appropriate Technology. Volume 1 1979.
Carter, Ann L.
"African Women and Career Counseling: A Model." Journal of Non-White Concerns in Personnel and Guidance. Volume 9 #1 October, 1980. pp. 23-33.
Case, Frederick
"Workers Movements: Revolution and Women's Consciousness in God's Bits of Wood." Canadian Journal of African Studies. Volume 15 #2 1981. pp. 272-292.
Caughman, Susan H.
Women at Work in Mali: The Case of the Markala Cooperative. Boston: Boston University. African Studies Center. Working Papers in African Studies #50. 1981. 72p.
Clark, Carolyn M.
Sexuality in the Workplace: Some African Examples. Santa Cruz, California: University of California-Santa Cruz. 1981.
Clark, Garcia
Fighting the African Food Crisis: Women Food Farmers and Food Workers. New York: United Nations Development Fund for Women. 1985.
Cutrufelli, Maria R.
Women of Africa: Roots of Oppression. Totowa, New Jersey: Zed Press. 1983. 186p.
Dauber, Roslyn and Cain, Melinda (eds.)
Women and Technological Change in Developing Countries. Boulder, Colorado: Westview Press. AAAS Selected Symposium #53. 1980. 266p.
DeLancey, Virginia H.
"The Role of Credit Unions in Development for West African Women." Paper Presented at the Annual Meeting of the African Studies Association. Paper #29. Bloomington, Indiana. October 21-24, 1981.
DeLancey, Virginia H.
"The Relationship Between Female Labor Force Participation and Fertility: Considerations of Role Compatibility in Research Methodology for Developing Countries." Paper Presented at the Annual Meeting of the African Studies Association. Paper #34. Los Angeles, California. 1979. 23p.
Dey, Jennie M.
Women in Food Production and Food Security in Africa. Rome: United Nations Food and Agriculture Organization. Women in Agriculture Series #3. 1984. 101p.
Dey, Jennie M.
"Women in African Rice Farming Systems." International Rice Commission Newsletter. Volume 32 #2 December, 1983. pp. 1-4.

Dey, Jennie M.
Women in Rice Farming Systems, Focus: Subsaharan Africa. Rome: United Nations Food and Agriculture Organization. Women in Agriculture Series #2. 1984. 106p.
Dey, Jennie M.
"Women in African Rice Farming Systems." (In) International Rice Research Institute. 'Women in Rice Farming': Proceedings of a Conference on Women in Rice Farming Systems. September 26-30, 1983. Brookfield, Vermont: Gower Publishing Co. 1985. pp. 419-444.
Dhamija, Jasleen
"Income-Generating Activities for Rural Women in Africa: Some Successes and Failures." (In) International Labour Organization (ILO). Rural Development and Women in Africa. Geneva: ILO. 1984. pp. 75-78.
Dhamija, Jasleen
"Technology as a Target to the Development of Women's Skills in Africa." Ceres. # 84 November, 1981. pp. 24-27.
Dixon, Ruth B.
"Women in Agriculture: Counting the Labor Force in Developing Countries." Population and Development Review. Volume 8 #3 September, 1982. pp. 539-566.
Dixon, Ruth B.
"Land, Labour and the Sex Composition of the Agricultural Labour Force: An International Comparison." Development and Change. Volume 14 #3 July, 1983. pp. 347-372.
Dixon, Ruth B.
"Jobs for Women in Rural Industry and Services." Paper Presented at the Conference on Agrarian Reform and Rural Development. Rome: United Nations Food and Agriculture Organization. Washington, D.C.: U.S. Department of State. U.S. Agency for International Development. Office of Women in Development. July, 1979.
Dixon, Ruth B.
"Seeing the Invisible Women Farmers in Africa: Improving Research and Data Collection Methods." (In) Monson, J. and Kalb, M. (eds.). Women as Food Producers in Developing Countries. Los Angeles: University of California-Los Angeles. African Studies Center and OEF International. 1985. pp. 19-35.
Dixon-Mueller, Ruth
Women's Work in the Third World Agriculture: Concepts and Indicators. Geneva: ILO. Women, Work and Development Series. Volume 9. 1985. 151p.
Eide, Wenche B. and Steady, Filomina C.
"Individual and Social Energy Flows: Bridging Nutritional and Anthropological Thinking About Women's Work in Rural Africa: Some Theoretical Considerations." (In) Jerome, Norge W. and Kandel, Randy F. and Pelto, Gretel H. (eds.). Nutritional Anthropology: Contemporary Approach to Diet and Culture. New York: Redgrave Publishing. 1980. pp. 61-84.
Elson, Diane and Pearson, Ruth
"'Nimble Fingers Make Cheap Workers': An Analysis of

Women's Employment in Third World Export Manufacturing." Feminist Review. Volume 7 Spring, 1981.
Ember, C.R.
"Relative Decline in Women's Contribution to Agriculture With Intensification." American Anthropologist. Volume 85 #2 June, 1983. pp. 285-304.
Emecheta, Buchi
"Building on Tradition: Can the Past Provide Direction for the Future." Paper Presented at the 'Women and Work Symposium #6'. Urbana, Illinois: University of Illinois. 1979.
Emecheta, Buchi
"Building on Tradition: Can the Past Provide for the Future?" (In) University of Illinois (eds.). Women and Work in Africa, April 29-May 1, 1979, University of Illinois, Urbana-Champaign: A Project of the African Studies Association. Urbana, Illinois: University of Illinois. 1979.
Fapohunda, Eleanor R.
"Female and Male Work Profiles." (In) Oppong, Christine (ed.). Female and Male in West Africa. London: George Allen and Unwin. 1983. pp. 32-53.
Franke, R.
"Mode of Production and Population Patterns: Policy Implications for West African Development." International Journal of Health Services. Volume 13 1981. pp. 361-387.
Gallin, Rita and Spring, Anita (eds.).
Women Creating Wealth: Transforming Economic Development. Washington, D.C.: Association for Women in Development. 1985. 183p.
Gladwin, Christina and Staudt, Kathleen A. and McMillan, Della
Reaffirming the Agricultural Role of Women: One Solution to the Food Crisis. (In) Association of Facilities of Agriculture in Africa. Proceedings of the Fifth General Conference on Food Security. Manzini, Swaziland. April, 1984.
Guenther, Mathias G.
"Bushman Hunters as Farm Labourers." Canadian Journal of African Studies. Volume 11 #2 1977.
Guyer, Jane I.
The Raw, the Cooked and the Half-Baked: A Note on the Division of Labor by Sex. Brookline, Massachusetts: Boston University. African Studies Center. Working Papers in African Studies #48. 1981. 12p.
Guyer, Jane I.
Women's Work in the Food Economy of the Cocoa Belt: A Comparison. Brookline, Massachusetts: Boston University. African Studies Center. Working Paper #7. 1978. 34p.
Guyot, Jean
Migrant Women Speak: Interviews. London: Search Press Ltd. for the Churches Committee on Migrant Workers. 1978. 164p.

Hagan, A.L.
"The Role of Women in Rural Development: Some Critical Issues." (In) Mondjanagni, A.C. La Participation Populaire an Developpement en Afrique Noire. Paris: Karthala; Doula, Institut Pan Africain Pour Le Developpement. 1984. pp. 75-87.

Hein, Catherine R.
Factory Employment, Marriage and Fertility: The Case of Mauritian Women. Geneva: International Labour Organization. World Employment Programme Research Working Paper #118. June, 1982. 57p.

Howard, Rhoda E.
"Women and the Crisis in Commonwealth Africa." International Political Science Review. Volume 6 #3 1985. pp. 287-296.

Huggard, Marianne
"The Rural Woman as a Food Producer: An Assessment of the Resolution on Women and Food From the World Food Conference in Rome, 1974." Paper Presented at the International Conference on Women and Food: Consortium for International Development. Tucson, Arizona. 10p. 1978.

Igbinovia, Patrick E.
"Prostitution in Black Africa." International Journal of Women's Studies. Volume 7 #5 Nov.-Dec., 1984. pp. 430-449.

International Center for Research on Women
Women in Migration: A Third World Focus. Washington, D.C.: U.S. Department of State. U.S. Agency for International Development. Office of Women in Development. 1979.

International Center for Research on Women
Keeping Women Out: A Structural Analysis of Women's Employment in Developing Countries. Washington, D.C.: U.S. Department of State. U.S. Agency for International Development. Office on Women in Development. Bureau of Program and Policy Coordination. April, 1980.

International Center for Research on Women
The Productivity of Women in Developing Countries: Measurement Issues and Recommendtions. Washington, D.C.: U.S. Department of State. U.S. Agency for International Development. Office on Women in Development. 1980. 46p.

International Labour Organization (ILO)
Women, Technology and the Development Process. Paper Presented to the African Regional Meeting of UNCSTD. Geneva: ILO. Cairo, Egypt. July 24-29, 1978.

Javillonar, Gloria W.
Rural Development, Women's Roles and Fertility in Developing Countries: Review of the Literature. Chapel Hill, North Carolina: Research Triangle Institute. 1979. pp. 32-75.

Karanja, Wambui Wa
"Women and Work: A Study of Female and Male Attitudes in the Modern Sector of an African Metropolis." (In) Ware,

Helen (ed.). Women, Education and Modernization of the Family in West Africa. Canberra, Australia: Australian National University. Department of Demography. Changing African Family Project Series. Monograph #7. 1978.

Kayongo-Male, Diana
"Helping Self-Help Groups Help Themselves: Training of Leaders of Women's Groups." Journal of Eastern African Research and Development. Volume 13 1983. pp. 88-103.

King-Akerele, O.
Traditional Palm Oil Processing, Women's Role and the Application of Appropriate Technology. Addis Ababa, Ethiopia: United Nations Economic Commission for Africa. Research Series. 1983.

Lewis, Barbara C.
"Fertility and Employment: An Assessment of Role Incompatibility Among African Urban Women." (In) Bay, Edna G. Women and Work in Africa. Boulder, Colorado: Westview Press. Westview Special Studies. 1982. pp. 249-276.

Lucas, D.
"Demographic Aspects of Women's Employment in Africa." Manpower and Unemployment Research. Volume 10 #1 April, 1977. pp. 31-38.

Marks, Shula and Unterhalter, Elaine
Women and the Migrant Labour System in Southern Africa. Lusaka, Zambia: United Nations Economic Commission for Africa. Multinational Programming and Operational Centre for Eastern and Central Africa. 1978. 15p.

Max-Forson, Margaret
"The Role of Women and Youth in Development." Rural Progress. Volume 1 #3 1979. pp. 28-30.

Mbilinyi, Marjorie J.
"The Changing Position of Women in the African Labour Force." (In) Shaw, Timothy M. and Aluko, Olajide (eds.). Africa Projected: From Recession to Renaissance by the Year 2000. London: MacMillan. 1985. pp. 170-186.

Mbilinyi, Marjorie J.
"Women as Labor in Underdevelopment." Paper Presented at the Wellesley Conference on Women and Development. Wellesley, Massachusetts: Wellesley College. Wellesley Center for Research on Women. June, 1976.

McDowell, James and Hazzard, Virginia
"Village Technology and Women's Work in Eastern Africa." Assignment Children. Volume 36 Oct.-Dec., 1976. pp. 53-65.

McFadden, Patricia
"Women Workers in Southern Africa." Journal of African Marxists. #4 September, 1983. pp. 54-62.

Meer, Fatima (ed.)
The African Woman at Home and in Gainful Employment. Collection of Unpublished Papers. 1980.

Meghji, Zakia
"Nature of Female Urban Employment." Paper Presented at the Workshop on Women's Studies and Development. Dar-es-Salaam, Tanzania: University of Dar-es-Salaam.

Bureau of Resource Assessment and Land Use Planning. Paper #37. September 24-29, 1979. 5p.
Meillassoux, Claude
Maidens, Meal and Money: Capitalism and the Domestic Community. Cambridge, New York: Cambridge University Press. 1981. 196p.
Mies, M.
"Consequences of Capitalist Penetration for Women's Subsistence Reproduction." Paper Presented at the Seminar on Underdevelopment and Subsistence Production in South East Africa. April, 1978.
Mitchnik, David A.
Improving Ways of Skill Acquisition of Women for Rural Employment in Some African Countries. Geneva: International Labour Organization. World Employment Programme Research. Education and Employment Research Project. Working Papers. February, 1977. 78p.
Monson, Jamie and Kalb, Marion
Women as Food Producers in Developing Countries. Los Angeles: University of California-Los Angeles. African Studies Center. African Studies Association. OEF International. 1985. 118p.
Moody, Elize
"Women: An Underrated Development Source." South African Journal of African Affairs. Volume 9 #2 1979. pp. 64-71.
Moris, J.R.
Reforming Agricultural Extension and Research Services in Africa. London: Overseas Development Institute. Discussion Paper #11. 1983.
Mullings, L.
"Women and Economic Change in Africa." (In) Hafkin, N. and Bay, Edna G. (eds.). Women in Africa: Studies in Social and Economic Change. Stanford, California: Stanford University Press. 1976. pp. 239-264.
Muriuki, Margaret N.
"The Role of Women in African Librarianship: The Next 25 Years." Paper Presented at the Standing Conference of Eastern, Central and Southern African Libraries. Lusaka, Zambia. October 4-9, 1976.
Murray, Colin G.
"Migrant Labour and Changing Family Structure in the Rural Periphery of Southern Africa." Journal of Southern African Studies. Volume 6 #2 1980. pp. 139-156.
N'ska, Leci
"The Discrimination Against Women in the Civil Service." Viva. Volume 7 #2 1981. pp. 15-17, 45.
Ndongko, T.
"Tradition and the Role of Women in Africa." Presence Africaine. Volume 99/100 1976. pp. 143-152.
Nelson, Nici (ed.)
African Women in the Development Process. Totowa, New Jersey: F. Cass. 1981. 136p.
Newman, Jeanne S.
"Some Indicators of Women's Economic Roles in Sub-Saharan

Africa." Paper Presented at the Annual Meeting of the American Statistical Association. Toronto, Ontario, Canada. August, 1983.
Njoku, John E.
The World of the African Woman. Metuchen, New Jersey: Scarecrow Press. 1980. 132p.
Obbo, Christine S.
"Town Migration is Not for Women." Ph.D. Dissertation: University of Wisconsin-Madison. Madison, Wisconsin. 1977. 329p.
Okeyo, Acholo P.
"Women and Africa: Reflections on Development Myths." Africa Report. Volume 26 #2 March-April, 1981. pp. 7-10.
Onyango, Philista P.M.
"The Working Mother and the Housemaid as a Substitute: Its Complications on the Children." Journal of Eastern African Research and Development. Volume 13 1983. pp. 24-31.
Oppong, Christine
Family Structure and Women's Reproductive and Productive Roles: Some Conceptual and Methodological Issues. Geneva: International Labour Office. The Role of Women and Demographic Change Research Program. 1980.
Oppong, Christine
"Family Structure and Women's Reproductive and Productive Roles: Some Conceptual and Methodological Issues." (In) Anker, Richard and Buvinic, Mayra and Youssef, N. (eds.). Women's Roles and Population Trends in the Third World. London: Croom Helm. 1982.
Osseo-Asare, Fran S.
Towards a Strategy for the Integration of Women Into Development. University Park, Pennsylvania: Pennsylvania State University. 1982.
Pagezy, Helen
"Some Aspects of Daily Work of Women Oto and Twa Living in Equatorial Forest Middle." L'Anthropolgie. Volume 80 #3 1976. pp. 465-906.
Pala, Achola O.
"Definitions of Women and Development: An African Perspective." Signs. Volume 3 #1 Autumn, 1977. pp. 9-13.
Pala, Achola O.
African Women in Rural Development: Research Trends and Priorities. Washington, D.C.: American Council on Education. Overseas Liaison Committee. OLC Paper #12. December, 1976. 35p.
Pala, Achola O.
"Definitions of Women and Development: An African Perspective." (In) Wellesley Editorial Committee. Women and National Development: The Complexities of Change. Chicago: University of Chicago Press. 1977. pp. 9-13.
Pala, Achola O.
"Definitions of Women and Development: An African Perspective." (In) Steady, Filomina C. (ed.). The Black

Woman Cross-Culturally. Cambridge, Massachusetts: Schenkman Publishing. 1981. pp. 209-214.
Palmer, Ingrid
"Rural Women and the Basic Needs Approach." International Labour Review. Volume 115 #1 January-February, 1977. pp. 97-98.
Palmer, Ingrid
"Women in Rural Development." International Development Review. Volume 22 #2/3 1980. pp. 39-45.
Palmer, Ingrid
"The Role of Women in Agrarian Reform and Rural Development." (In) United Nations. Land Reform. Rome: United Nations Food and Agriculture Organization. 1979. pp. 57-70.
Palmer, Ingrid
'The Nemow Case', Case Studies of the Impact of Large Scale Development Projects on Women: A Series for Planners. New York: Population Council. International Programs Working Paper #7. September, 1979. 92p.
Palmer, Ingrid
"Seasonality of Women's Work: Patterns and Trends." (In) University of Sussex. Papers From the Conference on Seasonal Dimensions to Rural Poverty. Brighton, England: Sussex University. Institute of Development Studies. July 3-6, 1978. 8p.
Palmer, Ingrid
The Impact of Male Out-Migration on Women in Farming. West Hartford, Connecticut: Kumarian Press. 1985. 78p.
Papanek, Hanna
"Development Planning for Women." (In) Wellesley Editorial Committee. Women and National Development: The Complexities of Change. Chicago: University of Chicago Press. 1977. pp. 14-21.
Peil, Margaret
"Urban Women in the Labor Force." Sociology of Work and Occupations. Volume 6 #4 November, 1979. pp. 482-501.
Petty, Irene M.
"The Role of African Women in Identifying Needs for Labor Saving Devices." Prepared for the AAAS Workshop on Women and Development for UNCSTD. New York: United Nations. 1979.
Regional Economic Reseach and Documentation Center (Lome)
"The Role of African Trade Union Women." Paper Presented at the Pan African Conference on the Role of African Trade Union Women." Lome, Togo: Regional Economic Research and Documentation Center. 1978. 25p.
Roberts, Pepe
"The Sexual Politics of Labor and the Household in Africa." (In) Guyer, Jane I. and Peters, Pauline E. (eds.). Conceptualizing the Household: Issues of Theory, Method and Application. Charlottesville, Virginia: Teleprint. Papers From a Workshop Held at Harvard University, November 2-4, 1984. 1984.
Robertson, Claire C.
"Women in the Urban Economy." (In) Hay, Margaret J. and

Stichter, Sharon (eds.). African Women South of the Sahara. New York: Longman. 1984. pp. 33-50.
Rothschild, K.W.
"A Note on Female Labour Supply." Kyklos. Volume 33 1980. pp. 246-260.
Rugh, Andrea B.
Women, Agriculture and Rural Development. Report Presented to the U.S. Agency for International Development Mission in Cairo, Egypt. Washington, D.C.: U.S. Department of State. U.S. Agency for International Development. 1979.
Safilios-Rothschild, Constantina
The Role of Women in Modernizing Agricultural Systems. Washington, D.C.: U.S. Department of State. U.S. Agency for International Development. Office of Women in Development. May, 1981. 31p.
Safilios-Rothschild, Constantina
Can Agriculture in the Third World Modernize With Traditional Female Agricultural Labor? State College, Pennsylvania: Pennsylvania State University. Department of Sociology. 1981.
Saleh, Saneya
"Professional Women and National Development: Women's Response to Migration." Paper Presented at the Open University Women Seminar Series on Women, Work and Social Change. Cairo, Egypt: American University of Cairo. May 16, 1977.
Savane, M.A.
"Women and Rural Development in Africa." (In) International Labour Organization (ILO). Women in Rural Development: Critical Issues. Geneva: ILO. 1980. pp. 26-32.
Schick, Barbara
"Women: An Untapped Resource in a Hungry World." Agenda. Volume 1 #6 June, 1978. pp. 1-4.
Schutjer, Wayne A. and Stokes, C. Shannon
The Human Fertility Implications of Food and Agricultural Policies in Less-Developed Countries. University Park, Pennsylvania: Pennsylvania State University. College of Agriculture. Agriculture Experiment Station Bulletin #835. January, 1982. 14p.
Schutjer, Wayne A. and Stokes, C. Shannon (eds.)
Rural Development and Human Fertility. New York: MacMillan. 1984. 380p.
Seidman, Ann
"Women and the Development of 'Underdevelopment': The African Experience." (In) Dauber, Roslyn and Cain, Melinda, L. (eds.). Women and Technological Change in Developing Countries. Boulder, Colorado: Westview Press. 1981. pp. 109-126.
Sen, G.
"Women Workers and the Green Revolution." (In) Beneria, Lourdes (ed.). Women and Development: The Sexual Division of Labor in Rural Societies. New York: Praeger Publishers. 1985.

Shaw, R. Paul
"Women's Employment in the Arab World: A Strategy of Selective Intervention." Development and Change. Volume 12 #2 April, 1981. pp. 237-272.
South African Congress of Trade Unions
"The Chains That Bind Black Women Workers." Workers Unity. #14 March, 1979.
Spencer, Dunstan S.C.
Women in a Developing Economy: A West African Case Study. East Lansing, Michigan: Michigan State University. 1979. 134p.
Stanley, Autumn
"From Africa to America: Black Women Inventors." (In) Zimmerman, Jan (ed.). The Technological Woman: Interfacing With Tomorrow. New York: Praeger Publishers. Preager Special Studies. 1983. pp. 55-64.
Staudt, Kathleen A.
"Women Farmers and Inequalities in Agricultural Services." Rural Africana. Volume 29 Winter, 1976. pp. 81-94.
Staudt, Kathleen A.
"Women Farmers and Inequities in Agricultural Services." (In) Bay, Edna G. (ed.). Women and Work in Africa. Boulder, Colorado: Westview Press. Westview Special Studies in Africa. 1982. pp. 207-224.
Staudt, Kathleen A.
"Organizing Rural Women in the Third World." Paper Presented at the Annual Meeting of the Western Political Science Association. March 27-29, 1980.
Staveley, Jennifer L.
"Prostitutes and Prostitution in Africa: The Development of Women's First Wage Earning Activity." M.A. Thesis: University of Waterloo. Waterloo, Ontario, Canada. 1977.
Steady, Filomina C.
"African Women, Industrialization Another Development." Development Dialogue. #1/2 1982. pp. 51-64.
Steel, William F.
"The Small-Scale Sector's Role in Growth, Income Distribution and Employment of Women." Paper Presented at the Annual Meeting of the African Studies Association. Paper #82. Houston, Texas. November 2-5, 1977. 20p.
Stephens, Betsy and Odell, M.
"Professional Women in Development Assistance." International Development Review. Volume 19 #2 1977. pp. 3-5.
Sudarkasa, Niara
The Effects of 20th Century Social Change, Especially of Migration, on Women of West Africa. Tucson, Arizona: University of Arizona. Proceedings of the West Africa Conference. 1976. pp. 102-109.
Sudarkasa, Niara
"Female Employment and Family Organization in West Africa." (In) Steady, Filomina C. (ed.). The Black

Woman Cross-Culturally. Cambridge, Massachusetts: Schenkman Publishing. 1981. pp. 49-64.

Sudarkasa, Niara
"Sex Roles, Education and Development in Africa." Anthropology and Education Quarterly. Volume 13 #3 Fall, 1982. pp. 279-288.

Tadesse, Zenebeworke
"African Women in Rural Development: A New Group of African Women Researchers." Ideas and Action. #127 1979. pp. 7-10.

Tadesse, Zenebeworke
"Studies on Rural Women in Africa: An Overview." (In) International Labour Organization (ILO). Rural Development and Women in Africa. Geneva: ILO. 1984. pp. 65-73.

Tadesse, Zenebeworke
Women and Technological Development in Agriculture: An Overview of the Problems in Developing Countries. New York: United Nations Institute for Training and Research. Science and Technology Working Paper Series #9. 1979.

Tadesse, Zenebeworke
"Women and Technology in Peripheral Countries: An Overview." (In) D'Onofrio-Flores, Pamela M. and Pfafflin, Sheila M. (eds.). Scientific-Technological Change and the Role of Women in Development. Boulder, Colorado: Westview Press. 1982. pp. 77-111.

Tau, Mildred M.
"Women: Critical to African Development." Africa Report. Volume 26 #2 March-April, 1981. pp. 4-6.

Thadani, Veena N. and Todaro, Michael P.
Female Migration in Developing Countries: A Framework for Analysis. New York: Population Council. Center for Policy Studies. Working Papers #47. 1979. 48p.

Tinker, Irene and Bramson, Michele B. (eds.)
Women and World Developmemt. New York: Praeger Publishers. 1976. 228p.

Tinker, Irene
"Women and Africa: Policy Strategies for Women in the 1980's." Africa Report. Volume 26 #2 March-April, 1981. pp. 11-16.

Tinker, Irene
"The Adverse Impact of Development on Women." (In) Tinker, Irene (ed.). Women and World Development. New York: Praeger Publishers. 1976.

Tomsic, Vida
"The Position and Role of Women in Development." Review of International Affairs. Volume 32 November 5, 1981. pp. 1-5.

U.S. Agency for International Development (U.S. AID)
The Productivity of Women in Developing Countries: Measurement Issues and Recommendations. Washington, D.C.: U.S. Department of State. U.S. AID. International Center for Research on Women. Office of Women in Development. 1980. 46p.

United Nations
Impact on Women of Socioeconomic Changes in Africa South of the Sahara: Project Proposal. Geneva: United Nations Research Institute for Social Development. Reference Center. 1979. 56p.

United Nations
Measures of Assistance for Women in Southern Africa. Paper Presented at the United Nations World Conference of the United Nations Decade for Women: Equality, Development and Peace. New York: United Nations. Copenhagen, Denmark. July 14-30, 1980. 34p.

United Nations Centre on Transnational Corporations and International Labour Office (ILO)
Women Workers in Multinational Enterprises in Developing Countries: A Contribution to the United Nations Decade for Women. Geneva: ILO. 1985. 119p.

United Nations Economic Commission for Africa (UNECA)
Women Population and Rural Development in Africa. Addis Ababa, Ethiopia: UNECA/FAO Women's Development Programme Unit. 1976.

United Nations Economic Commission for Africa (UNECA)
"Women in Development: Moving Away From Tradition." U.N. Chronicle. Volume 19 #11 December, 1982. pp. 105-106.

United Nations Economic Commission for Africa (UNECA)
The Changing and Contemporary Role of Women in African Development. Addis Ababa, Ethiopia: UNECA. 1977.

United Nations Economic Commission for Africa (UNECA)
African Women's Development Task Force. Addis Ababa, Ethiopia: UNECA. African Training and Research Centre for Women. 1976. 15p.

United Nations Economic Commission for Africa (UNECA)
African Women Workers: Analysis of the Factors Affecting Women's Employment. Addis Ababa, Ethiopia: UNECA. African Training and Research Centre for Women. 1976. 53p.

United Nations Educational, Scientific and Cultural Organ.
Description of Projects Relevant to the Integration of Women in Development: Africa. Paris: UNESCO. May 16, 1979. 10p.

United Nations Educational, Scientific and Cultural Organ.
Comparative Report on the Role of Working Mothers in Early Childhood Education in Five Countries. Paris: UNESCO. 1978. 82p.

United Nations Educational, Scientific and Cultural Organ.
Final Report: Regional Workshop on Women's Crafts in Developing Countries. Paris: UNESCO. CREA #14. Katiola, Ivory Coast. 1983. 22p.

Van der Horst, Sheila T.
Women as an Economic Force in Southern Africa. Rondebosch, South Africa: University of Cape Town. Abe Bailey Institute of Interracial Studies #18. 1977.

Von Blanckenberg, P.
Agricultural Extension Systems in Some African Countries. Rome: United Nations Food and Agriculture Organization (FAO). FAO Economic and Social Development Paper. 1984.

Ware, Helen
"Women's Work and Fertility in Africa." (In) Kupinsky, Stanley (ed.). The Fertility of Working Women: A Synthesis of International Research. New York: Praeger Publishers. Praeger Special Studies in International Economics and Development. 1977. pp. 1-34.

Waterman, Peter
"A New Focus in African Worker Studies: Promises, Problems, Dangers." Cahiers d'Etudes Africaines. Volume 24 #3 1984. pp. 343-361.

Whalen, Irene T.
Women and Livestock: The Impact of Technological Innovations on Women. Addis Ababa, Ethiopia: International Livestock Center, Africa. P/O Box 5689. 1984.

White, Douglas R. and Bruton, Michael L. and Dow, Malcolm M.
"Sexual Division of Labor in African Agriculture: A Network Autocorrelation Analysis." American Anthropologist. Volume 83 #4 December, 1981. pp. 824-849.

White, Luise S.
"Women in the Changing African Family." (In) Hay, Margaret J. and Stichter, Sharon (eds.). African Women South of the Sahara. New York: Longman. 1984. pp. 53-68.

World Bank
Recognizing the 'Invisible' Woman in Development: The World Banks Experience. Washington, D.C.: World Bank. October, 1979. 33p.

Youssef, Nadia H.
Women and Work in Developing Societies. Westport, Connecticut: Greenwood Press. 1976. 137p.

Youssef, Nadia H. and Buvinic, Mayra and Kudat, Ayse
Women in Migration: A Third World Focus. Washington, D.C.: U.S. Department of State. U.S. Agency for International Development. International Centre for Research on Women. Office of Women in Development. 1979. 151p.

Youssef, Nadia H.
"Interrelationship Between the Division of Labor in the Household, Women's Roles and Their Impact Upon Fertility." Paper Presented at the Informal Workshop on Women's Roles and Demographic Research Program. Geneva: International Labour Organization. November, 1978.

Equality and Liberation

Abdel Kader, Soha
The Status of Research on Women in the Arab Region, 1960-1978. Paris: UNESCO. Division of Human Rights and Peace. January, 1979.

Accad, Evelyne
"Complex Inter-Relation of Women's Liberation and Arab Nationalism in North African Novels Written by Women." Paper Presented at the Annual Meeting of the African Studies Association. Paper #1. Boston, Massachusetts. 1976. 16p.

Accad, Evelyne
"Interrelationship Between Arab Nationalism and Feminist Consciousness in the North African Novels Written by Women." Ba Shiru. Volume 8 #2 1977. pp. 3-12.

Anonymous
"International Conference on the Role of Women in Liberation Struggles and Women in Development." IDOC Bulletin. #50/51 December-January, 1976. pp. 4-21.

Anonymous
"Southern African Women Speak Out." Africa Report. Volume 28 #2 March-April, 1983. pp. 15-19.

Anonymous
"Two Views of Liberation." Agenda. Volume 1 #2 February, 1978. pp. 19-22.

Axinn, Nancy W.
Female Emancipation Versus Female Welfare. East Lansing, Michigan: Michigan State University. Institute for International Studies in Education. College of Education. Non-Formal Education Information Center. 1979. 5p.

Black, Naomi and Cottrell, Ann B.
Women and World Change: Equity Issues in Development. Beverly Hills, California: Sage Publications. Sage Focus Editions #38. 1981. 288p.

Boserup, Ester (ed.)
Traditional Division of Work Between the Sexes, A Source

of Inequality: Research Symposium on Women and Decision Making: A Social Policy Priority. Geneva: International Institute for Labour Studies. Research Series #21. 1976. 32p.

Boulware-Miller, Kay
"Female Circumcision: Challenges to the Practice as a Human Rights Violation." Harvard Women's Law Journal. Volume 8 Spring, 1985. pp. 155-177.

Bujra, Janet M.
"Female Solidarity and the Sexual Division of Labour." (In) Caplan, P. and Bujra, J. (eds.). Women United, Women Divided: Cross-Cultural Perspectives on Female Solidarity. London: Tavistock. 1978. pp. 13-45.

Case, Frederick
"Workers Movements: Revolution and Women's Consciousness in God's Bits of Wood." Canadian Journal of African Studies. Volume 15 #2 1981. pp. 272-292.

Frank, Katherine
"Feminist Criticism and the African Novel." African Literature Today. #14 1984. pp. 34-38.

Haq, Khadija (ed.)
Equality of Opportunity Within and Among Nations. New York: Praeger Publishers. Praeger Special Studies in International Economics and Development. 1977. 223p.

Howard, R.
"Women's Rights in English-Speaking Sub-Saharan Africa." (In) Welch, Claude E. and Meltzer, Ronald I. (eds.). Human Rights and Development in Africa. Albany, New York: State University of New York Press. 1984.

Kisekka, Mere N.
"On the Status of Women Within the Framework of the Liberation Movement." African Urban Notes. Volume 2 #3 Fall/Winter, 1976. pp. 65-74.

Koning, Karen L.
"Revolutionary Potential Among Arab Women Today." Mawazo. Volume 4 #4 1976. pp. 48-57.

Leland, Stephanie and Mutasa, Joyce and Willard, Fran
Women in Southern Africa: Struggles and Achievements--The U.N. Decade for Women Diary, July, 1985/86. London: Feminist International for Peace and Food. 1985. 120p.

Matsepe, Ivy F.
"Underdevelopment and African Women." Journal of Southern African Affairs. Volume 2 #2 April, 1977. pp. 135-143.

Matsepe, Ivy F.
"Women in the Struggle for Liberation." (In) Wiley, David and Isaacman, Allen (eds.). Southern Africa: Society, Economy and Liberation. East Lansing, Michigan: Michigan State University. African Studies Center. 1981.

Mbilinyi, Marjorie J.
"Women in Liberation Struggles." ISIS International Bulletin. April, 1977. pp. 8-10.

Munuo, Edith
"Education for Equality." Paper Presented at the

Workshop on Women's Studies and Development. Dar-es-Salaam, Tanzania: University of Dar-es-Salaam. Bureau of Resource Assessment and Land Use Planning. Paper #14. September 24-29, 1979. 19p.

Osseo-Asare, Fran S.
Towards a Strategy for the Integration of Women Into Development. University Park, Pennsylvania: Pennsylvania State University. 1982.

Roberts, Penelope
"Feminism in Africa: Feminism and Africa." Review of African Political Economy. #27/28 1984. pp. 175-184.

Rogombe, Rose F.
"Equal Partners in Development." Africa Report. Volume 30 #2 March-April, 1985. pp. 17-20.

Romalis, Coleman and Romalis, Shelly
"Sexism, Racism and Technological Change: Two Cases of Minority Protest." International Journal of Women's Studies. Volume 6 May-June, 1983. pp. 270-287.

Sacks, Karen
Sisters and Wives: The Past and Future of Sexual Equality. Westport, Connecticut: Greenwood Press. Contributions in Women's Studies #10. 1979. 274p.

Schultz, Bonnie J.
"Women and African Liberation--Miriam Makeba, An Interview." Africa Report. Volume 22 #1 January-February, 1977. pp. 10-14.

Singleton, Michael
Contributions to the Rights and Wrongs of African Women. Brussels, Belgium: Pro Mundi Vita Dossiers. Africa Dossier #9. October, 1979. pp. 1-36.

United Nations
Report of the World Conference to Review and Appraise the Achievements of the United Nations Decade for Women: Equality, Development and Peace. Nairobi, Kenya, July 15-26, 1985. New York: United Nations. 1986. 304p.

United Nations Economic Commission for Africa (UNECA)
African Women and Equality, Development and Peace: Strategy for 1980-85. Addis Ababa, Ethiopia: UNECA. Working Paper for Regional Prepatory Meeting of the UNECA Second Regional Conference for the Integration of Women in Development. Lusaka, Zambia. December 3-7, 1979.

Urdang, Stephanie
"Women in National Liberation Movements." (In) Hay, Margaret J. and Stichter, Sharon (eds.). African Women South of the Sahara. New York: Longman. 1984. pp. 156-169.

Van Allen, Judith
"African Women, 'Modernization' and National Liberation." (In) Iglitzin, Lynne B. and Ross, Ruth (eds.). Women in the World. Santa Barbara, California: Clio Press. American Bibliographic Center. 1976. pp. 25-54.

Weiss, R.
"Women in Liberation Movements." (In) Schild, U. (ed.). Jaw-Bone and Umbilical Cords: A Selection of Papers Presented at the Third Janheinz Jahn Symposium, 1979 and

the Fourth Jan einz Jahn Symposium, 1982. Berlin, Germany: Reimer. 1985. pp. 127-133.

White, E. Frances
"A Black Feminist in Africa." New England Journal of Black Studies. 1981. pp. 37-43.

White, E. Frances
"A Black Feminist in Africa." Paper Presented at the Annual Meeting of the African Studies Association. Paper #115. Philadelphia, Pennsylvania. 1980.

Wipper, Audrey
"Riot and Rebellion Among African Women: Three Examples of Women's Political Clout." (In) O'Barr, Jean (ed.). Perspectives on Power: Women in Africa, Asia and Latin America. Durham, North Carolina: Duke University. Center for International Studies. 1982. pp.50-72.

Family Life

Aborampah, Osei-Mensah
"Family Structure in African Fertility Studies: Some Conceptual and Methodological Issues." Current Bibliography on African Affairs. Volume 18 #4 1986. pp. 319-335.

Allison, C.
"Women, Land, Labour and Survival: Getting Some Basic Facts Straight." IDS Bulletin. Volume 16 #3 1985. pp. 24-30.

Allman, James
"Family Patterns, Women's Status and Fertility in Middle-East and North-Africa." International Journal of Sociology of the Family. Volume 8 #1 1978. pp. 19-35.

Allman, James
"Family Life, Women's Status, and Fertility: Middle East and North African Perspectives." (In) Allman, James (ed.). Women's Studies and Fertility in the Muslim World. New York: Praeger Publishers. Praeger Special Studies. 1978. pp. 24-47.

Allman, James (ed.)
Women's Status and Fertility in the Muslim World. New York: Praeger Publishers. Praeger Special Studies. 1978. 378p.

Anonymous
"The Contribution of Women to the Development of the Pan African World." (In) Resolutions and Selected Speeches From the Sixth Pan African Congress. Dar-es-Salaam, Tanzania: Tanzania Publishing House. 1976. pp. 190-194.

Anonymous
"Women, Food and Nutrition in Africa: Economic Change and the Outlook for Nutrition." Food and Nutrition. Volume 10 #1 1984. pp. 71-79.

Anonymous
Women and Family in Rural Development: An Annotated Bibliography. Rome: United Nations Food and Agriculture

Organization. Documentation Centre and Population Documentation Centre. 1977. 66p.

Attah, E.B.
Family Nucleation and Fertility Change in Tropical Africa: Background to the Demographic Transition. Atlanta, Georgia: Atlanta University. Department of Sociology. 1985.

Balakrishnan, Revathi and Firebaugh, Francille M.
Roles of Women in Third World Economic Development From a Systems Perspective of Family Resource Management. Columbus, Ohio: Ohio State University. Department of Home Management and Housing. School of Home Economics. Working Papers #81-01. 1981. 39p.

Bay, Edna G. and Hafkin, Nancy J. (eds.)
"Women in Africa: Studies in Social and Economic Change." Stanford, California: Stanford University Press. 1976. 306p.

Beddada, Belletech
"Traditional Practices in Relation to Pregnancy and Childbirth." Paper Presented at the Seminar on Traditional Practices Affecting the Health of Women and Children. World Conference of the United Nations Decade for Women. New York: United Nations. Copenhagen, Denmark. July 14-30, 1980.

Bingham, Marjorie W. and Gross, Susan H.
Women in Africa of the Sub-Sahara. Hudson, Wisconsin: Gem Publishers. Volume One: Ancient Times to the Twentieth Century. Volume Two: The Twentieth Century. 1982. 260p.

Bisilliat, Jeanne
"The Feminine Sphere in the Institutions of Songhay-Zarma." (In) Oppong, Christine (ed.). Female and Male in West Africa. London: George Allen and Unwin. 1983. pp. 99-106.

Boserup, Ester
"Economic and Demographic Interrelationships in Sub-Saharan Africa." Population and Development Review. Volume 11 #3 September, 1985. pp. 383-397+.

Bourguignon, Erika
A World of Women: Anthropological Studies of Women in the Societies of the World. New York: Praeger Publishers. Praeger Special Studies. 1980. 364p.

Brabin, Loretta
"Polygyny: An Indicator of Nutritional Stress in African Agricultural Societies." Africa. Volume 54 #1 1984. pp. 31-45.

Brown, Judith E.
"Polygyny and Family Planning in Sub-Saharan Africa." Studies in Family Planning. Volume 12 #8-9 August-September, 1981. pp. 322-326.

Bruner, Charlotte H.
"Been-To or Has-Been: A Dilemma for Today's African Women." Paper Presented at the African Literature Association Conference. 1976. 15p.

Bruner, Charlotte H.
"Been-To or Has-Been: A Dilemma for Today's African Women." Ba Shiru. Volume 8 #2 1977. pp. 23-31.
Bryant, Coralie
"Women Migrants, Urbanization and Social Change: An African Case." Paper Presented at the American Political Science Association Annual Meeting. Washington, D.C. September, 1977.
Bulatao, R.A.
"Transitions in the Value of Children and the Fertility Transition." Paper Presented at the Seminar on Determinants of Fertility Trends: Major Themes and New Directions for Research. International Union for the Scientific Study of Population. Bad Homburg, Germany. 1980.
Caldwell, John C. and Caldwell, Pat
"Demographic and Contraceptive Innovators: A Study of Transitional African Society." Journal of Biosocial Science. Volume 8 #4 October, 1976. pp. 347-366.
Caldwell, Pat and Caldwell, John C.
"Population Change and Development in the ECWA Region." (In) Cairo Demographic Centre (CDC). Aspects of Population Change and Development in Some African and Asian Countries. Cairo, Egypt: CDC. CDC Research Monograph Series #9. 1984. pp. 43-56.
Caldwell, Pat
"Issues of Marriage and Marital Change: Tropical Africa and the Middle East." (In) Huzayyin, S.A. and Acsadi, G.T. (eds.). Family and Marriage in Some African and Asiatic Countries. Cairo, Egypt: Cairo Demographic Centre. Research Monograph Series #6. 1976. pp. 325-335.
Casteinuovo, Shirley
"The Impact of Urbanization on the Family in Light of Recent Changes in African Family Law." Paper Presented at the Annual Meeting of the African Studies Association. Paper #11. Houston, Texas. 1977.
Chamie, Joseph
Polygamy Among Arabs. New York: United Nations. U.N. Population Division. 1985.
Chaney, Elsa M.
Women in International Migration: Issues in Development Planning. Washington, D.C.: U.S. Department of State. U.S. Agency for International Development. Office of Women in Development. June, 1980.
Chaney, Elsa M. and Lewis, Martha W.
Women, Migration and the Decline of Smallholder Agriculture. Washington, D.C.: U.S. Department of State. U.S. Agency for International Development. Office of Women in Development. October, 1980.
Chojnacka, Helena
"Polygyny and the Rate of Population Growth." Human Resources Research Bulletin. #78/05 1978. 34p.
Chojnacka, Helena
"Polygyny and the Rate of Population Growth." Population

Studies. Volume 34 #1 March, 1980. pp. 91-107.
Cook, Rebecca J.
"A Law on Family Welfare and Development in Africa." (In) International Planned Parenthood Federation (IPPF). Proceedings of the IPPF Africa Regional Conference. London: IPPF. 1977. pp. 241-246.
De Graft-John, K.E.
"Issues in Family Welfare and Development in Africa." (In) International Planned Parenthood Federation (IPPF). Proceedings of the IPPF Africa Regional Conference. London: IPPF. 1977. pp. 33-45.
Di Domenico, Catherine M. and Asuni, Judy and Scott, Jacqueline
"Family Welfare and Development in Africa." (In) International Planned Parenthood Federation (IPPF). Proceedings of the IPPF Africa Regional Conference, University of Ibadan. London: IPPF. 1976. pp. 283-284.
Duza, M. Badrud and Sivamurthy, M.
"Household Structure in Selected Urban Areas of Four Arab and African Cities." (In) Huzayyin, S.A. and Acsadi, G.T. (eds.). Family and Marriage in Some African and Asiatic Countries. Cairo, Egypt: Cairo Demographic Centre. Research Monograph Series #6. 1976. pp. 267-284.
Duza, M. Badrud and Seetharam, K.S. and Sivamurthy, M.
"Patterns of Family Cycles in Selected Areas of Four Arab and African Cities: Some Demographic Implications." (In) Huzayyin, S.A. and Acsadi, G.T. (eds.). Family and Marriage in Some African and Asiatic Countries. Cairo, Egypt: Cairo Demographic Centre. CDC Research Monograph Series #6. 1976. pp. 245-265.
Ekechi, Felix K.
"African Polygamy and Western Christian Ethnocentrism." Journal of African Studies. Volume 3 #3 August, 1976. pp. 329-349.
El Sadaawi, Nawal
The Hidden Face of Eve: Women in the Arab World. Boston: Beacon Press. 1982. 212p.
El-Khorazaty, Mohamed Nabil E.
"Regional Differences in Attitudes Toward Family Norms and Planning, 1979/80." Population Studies. Volume 12 #72 January-March, 1985. pp. 3-28.
Elwert, Georg
"Conflicts Inside and Outside the Household: A West African Case Study." (In) Smith, Joan (ed.). Households and the World Economy. Beverly Hills, California: Sage. 1984. pp. 272-296.
Esposito, John L.
Women in Muslim Family Law. Syracuse, New York: Syracuse University Press. Contemporary Issues in the Middle East Series. 1982. 172p.
Fernea, Elizabeth W.
Women and the Family in the Middle East: New Voices of Change. Austin, Texas: University of Texas Press. 1984. 368p.

Fortes, Meyer
"Parenthood, Marriage and Fertility in West Africa." Journal of Development Studies. Volume 14 #4 July, 1978. pp. 121-149.

Fortes, Meyer
"Family, Marriage and Fertility in West Africa." (In) Oppong, C. and Adaba, G. and Bekombo-Priso, M. and Mogey, J. (eds.). Marriage, Fertility and Parenthood in West Africa. Canberra, Australia: Australian National University Press. 1978. pp. 17-54.

Fortmann, Louise P.
Tillers of the Soil and Keepers of the Hearth: A Bibliographic Guide to Women and Rural Development. Ithaca, New York: Cornell University. Center for International Studies. Rural Development Committee. Bibliography Series #2. 1979. 53p.

Gilligan, John J.
"Importance of Third World Women." Rivista di Studi Politici Internazionali. Volume 45 #3 July-September, 1978.

Ginat, Joseph (ed.)
Women in Muslim Rural Society: Status and Role in Family Community. New Brunswick, New Jersey: Transition Books. 1981. 268p.

Goody, Esther N.
"Some Theoretical and Empirical Aspects of Parenthood in West Africa." (In) Oppong, C. and Adaba, G. and Bekombo-Priso, M. and Mogey, J. (eds.). Marriage, Fertility and Parenthood in West Africa. Canberra, Australia: Australian National University. Department of Demography. Volume One. 1978. pp. 227-272.

Goody, Esther N.
"Parental Strategies: Calculation or Sentiment: Fostering Practices Among West Africans." (In) Medick, Hans and Sabean, David W. (eds.). Interest and Emotion: Essays on the Study of Family and Kinship. Cambridge, New York: Cambridge University Press. 1984. pp. 266-277.

Goody, Jack
Production and Reproduction: A Comparative Study of the Domestic Domain. Cambridge, New York: Cambridge University Press. Cambridge Studies in Social Anthropology #17. 1976. 157p.

Gray, R.H.
"Birth Intervals, Postpartum Sexual Abstinence and Child Health." (In) Page, Hilary J. and Lesthaeghe, Ron (eds.). Child-Spacing in Tropical Africa: Traditions and Change. New York: Academic Press. 1981. pp. 93-109.

Guyer, Jane I.
The Raw, the Cooked and the Half-Baked: A Note on the Division of Labor by Sex. Brookline, Massachusetts: Boston University. African Studies Center. Working Papers in African Studies #48. 1981. 12p.

Guyer, Jane I.
"Household and Community in African Studies." African

Studies Review. Volume 24 #213 June-September, 1981. pp. 87-137.
Guyot, Jean
Migrant Women Speak: Interviews. London: Search Press Ltd. for the Churches Committee on Migrant Workers. 1978. 164p.
Hayani, Ibrahim
"The Changing Role of Arab Women." Convergence. Volume 13 #1 1980. pp. 136-142.
Hein, Catherine R.
Factory Employment, Marriage and Fertility: The Case of Mauritian Women. Geneva: International Labour Organization. World Employment Programme Research Working Paper #118. June, 1982. 57p.
Huzayyin, S.A. and Acsadi, George T. (eds.)
Family and Marriage in Some African and Asiatic Countries. Cairo, Egypt: Cairo Demographic Center. CDC Research Monograph Series #6. 1976. 570p.
International Center for Research on Women
Women in Migration: A Third World Focus. Washington, D.C.: U.S. Department of State. U.S. Agency for International Development. Office of Women in Development. 1979.
International Planned Parenthood Federation (IPPF)
Family Welfare and Development in Africa: Proceedings of the IPPF Africa Regional Conference, University of Ibadan. August 29-September 3, 1976. London: IPPF. Ibadan, Nigeria. 1977. 327p.
Joseph, Roger
"Sexual Dialectics and Strategy in Berber Marriage." Journal of Comparative Family Studies. Volume 7 #3 Autumn, 1976. pp. 471-481.
Karanja, Wambui Wa
"Women and Work: A Study of Female and Male Attitudes in the Modern Sector of an African Metropolis." (In) Ware, Helen (ed.). Women, Education and Modernization of the Family in West Africa. Canberra, Australia: Australian National University. Department of Demography. Changing African Family Project Series. Monograph #7. 1978.
Kayongo-Male, Diane
The Sociology of the African Family. New York: Longman. 1984. 124p.
Keenan, Jeremy
"Power and Wealth Are Cousins: Descent, Class and Marital Strategies Among the Kel Ahaggar." Africa. Volume 47 #3 1977. pp. 242-252.
Kerri, James
"Understanding the African Family: Persistence, Continuity and Change." Western Journal of Black Studies. Volume 3 #1 Spring, 1979. pp. 14-17.
Kisekka, Mere N.
"Polygyny and the Status of African Women." African Urban Notes. Volume 2 #3 Fall/Winter, 1976. pp. 21-42.
Kuper, Adam
"Symbolic Dimensions of the Southern Bantu Homestead."

Africa. Volume 50 #1 1980. pp. 8-23.
Kurian, George and Ratna, Ghosh (eds.)
Women in the Family and the Economy: An International Comparative Survey. Westport, Connecticut: Greenwood Press. Contributions in Family Studies #5. 1981. 451p.
Lancaster, Chet S.
"Women, Horticulture and Society in Sub-Saharan Africa." American Anthropologist. Volume 78 #3 September, 1976. pp. 539-564.
Levine, Nancy E.
"Nyinba Polyandry and the Allocation of Paternity." Journal of Comparative Family Studies. Volume 11 #3 Special Iss. August, 1980. pp. 283-298.
Levine, Nancy E. and Sangree, Walter H.
"Asian and African Systems of Polyandry." Journal of Comparative Family Studies. Volume 11 #3 Special Iss. August, 1980. pp. 385-410.
Levine, Nancy E. and Sangree, Walter H.
"Women With Many Husbands--Polyandrous Alliance and Marital Flexibility in Africa and Asia." Journal of Comparative Family Studies. Volume 11 #3 Special Iss. August, 1980.
Lindsay, Beverly (ed.)
Comparative Perspectives of Third World Women: The Impact of Race, Sex and Class. New York: Praeger Publishers. Praeger Special Studies. 1980. 318p.
Little, Kenneth L.
"Women's Strategies in Modern Marriage in Anglophone West Africa: An Ideological and Sociological Appraisal." Journal of Comparative Family Studies. Volume 8 #3 Autumn, 1977. pp. 341-356.
Little, Kenneth L.
"Women's Strategies in Modern Marriage in Anglophone West Africa: An Ideological and Sociological Appraisal." (In) Kurian, George (ed.). Cross-Cultural Perspectives of Mate Selection and Marriage. Westport, Connecticut: Greenwood Press. Contributions in Family Studies #3. 1979. pp. 202-217.
Lukutati, Bwembya
"The Concept of Parenthood in African Societies." (In) International Planned Parenthood Federation (IPPF). Proceedings of the IPPF Africa Regional Conference. London: IPPF. 1977. pp. 145-152.
Mabogunje, A.L.
"The Policy Implications of Changes in Child-Spacing Practices in Tropical Africa." (In) Page, Hilary J. and Lesthaeghe, Ron (eds.). Child-Spacing in Tropical Africa: Traditions and Changes. New York: Academic Press. 1981. pp. 303-316.
MacGaffey, Wyatt
"Lineage Structure, Marriage and the Family Amongst the Central Bantu." Journal of African History. Volume 24 #2 1983. pp. 173-187.
Marks, Shula and Rathbone, Richard
"The History of the Family in Africa: Introduction."

Journal of African History. Volume 24 #2 1983. pp. 145-161.
Martin-Cisse, Jeanne
"Family Problems in Africa." National Law Guild Practitioner. Volume 37 Winter, 1980. pp. 23-26.
Mbilinyi, Marjorie J.
"Patriarch Relations in the Peasant Household." Paper Presented at the Workshop on Women's Studies and Development. Dar-es-Salaam, Tanzania: University of Dar-es-Salaam. Bureau of Resource Assessment and Land Use Planning. Paper #20. September 24-29, 1979. 12p.
McSweeney, Brenda G.
"Collection and Analysis of Rural Women's Time Use." Studies in Family Planning. Volume 10 #11/12 Nov.-Dec., 1979. pp. 379+.
Meer, Fatima (ed.)
The African Woman at Home and in Gainful Employment. Collection of Unpublished Papers. 1980.
Murray, Colin G.
"Migrant Labour and Changing Family Structure in the Rural Periphery of Southern Africa." Journal of Southern African Studies. Volume 6 #2 1980. pp. 139-156.
Ndeti, K.
"Concept of Parenthood in Africa: An Exploratory Study of Complexity." (In) International Planned Parenthood Federation (IPPF). Proceedings of the IPPF Africa Regional Conference. London: IPPF. 1977. pp. 119-144.
Ndongko, T.
"Tradition and the Role of Women in Africa." Presence Africaine. Volume 99/100 1976. pp. 143-152.
Netting, Robert M. and Wilk, Richard R. and Arnold, Eric J, (eds.).
Households: Comparative and Historical Studies of the Domestic Group. Berkeley, California: University of California Press. 1984. 480p.
Norem, R.H.
"The Integration of a Family Systems Perspective Into Farming Systems Projects." (In) Caldwell, John and Rojas, Mary (eds.). Family Systems and Farming Systems: A Second Annual Conference in the World of Women in Development Series. Blacksburg, Virginia: Virgnia Polytechnic Institute and State University. 1983.
Nurse, G.T.
"Meity Endogamy and Anthropometric Variation Among the Maravi." Man. Volume 12 #3/4 December, 1977. pp. 397-404.
Okediji, Peter A.
"The Status of African Women in Family Planning." (In) Oppong, C. and Adaba, G. and Bekombo-Priso, M. and Mogey, J. (eds.). Marriage, Fertility and Parenthood in West Africa. Canberra, Australia: Australian National University. Department of Demography. Volume Two. 1978. pp. 673-676.
Okeyo, Achola P.
"Women in the Household Economy: Managing Multiple

Roles." Studies in Family Planning. Volume 10 #11/12 Nov.-Dec., 1979. pp. 337-343.

Onyango, Philista P.M.
"The Working Mother and the Housemaid as a Substitute: Its Complications on the Children." Journal of Eastern African Research and Development. Volume 13 1983. pp. 24-31.

Oppong, Christine
Family Structure and Women's Reproductive and Productive Roles: Some Conceptual and Methodological Issues. Geneva: International Labour Office. The Role of Women and Demographic Change Research Program. 1980.

Oppong, Christine
"Family Structure and Women's Reproductive and Productive Roles: Some Conceptual and Methodological Issues." (In) Anker, Richard and Buvinic, Mayra and Youssef, N. (eds.). Women's Roles and Population Trends in the Third World. London: Croom Helm. 1982.

Oppong, Christine and Adaba, Gemma and Bekomba-Priso, Manga and Mogey, J. (eds.)
Marriage, Fertility and Parenthood in West Africa. Canberra, Australia: Australian National University. Department of Demography. Changing African Family Project. Monograph #4. Two Volumes. 1978. 848p.

Oppong, Christine (ed.)
Female and Male in West Africa. Boston: George Allen and Unwin. 1983. 402p.

Oucho, John O.
"Socio-Economic Perspectives of Fertility Regulation in Traditional and Modern African Societies." (In) University of Nairobi. Papers of the Seminar on Oral Traditions: Past Growth and Future Development in East Africa. Nairobi: University of Nairobi. UNESCO Institute of African Affairs. Kisumu, Kenya. April 18-22, 1979. 18p.

Pagezy, Helen
"Some Aspects of Daily Work of Women Oto and Twa Living in Equatorial Forest Middle." L'Anthropolgie. Volume 80 #3 1976. pp. 465-906.

Paulme, Denise
"The Devouring Mother: Essay on the Morphology of African Tales." Journal of African Studies. Volume 4 Winter, 1977. pp. 480+.

Pauwels, Johan M.
"Nullity of Marriage and Divorce: Relevance of a Western Distinction to Modern African Law." (In) Roberts, Simon (ed.). Law and the Family in Africa. Hague, Netherlands: Mouton. 1977. pp. 225-239.

Peart, Nicola S.
"Civil or Christian Marriage and Customary Unions: The Legal Position of the 'Discarded' Spouse and Children." Comparative and International Law Journal of Southern Africa. Volume 16 #1 1983. pp. 39-64.

Peel, J.D.Y.
"The Changing Family in Modern Ijesha History." Paper

Presented at the Conference on the History of the Family in Africa. London: Cambridge University. School of Oriental and African Studies. September, 1981.

Roberts, Pepe
"The Sexual Politics of Labor and the Household in Africa." (In) Guyer, Jane I. and Peters, Pauline E. (eds.). Conceptualizing the Household: Issues of Theory, Method and Application. Charlottesville, Virginia: Teleprint. Papers From a Workshop Held at Harvard University, November 2-4, 1984. 1984.

Roberts, Simon (ed.)
Law and the Family in Africa. Hague, Netherlands: Mouton. 1977. 267p.

Roboff, Farron V. and Renwick, Hilary L.
"The Changing Role of Women in the Development of the Sahel." Paper Presented to the Annual Meeting of the African Studies Association. Paper #92. Boston, Massachusetts. 1976. 12p.

Rogers, Barbara
"Food, Fertility and Nuclear Mothers: How Development Can Increase Rather than Reduce the Social and Economic Burdens of African Women." Populi. Volume 5 #1 1978. pp. 23-27.

Rogers, Barbara
The Domestication of Women: Discrimination in Developing Societies. New York: St. Martin's Press. 1980. 200p.

Sabean, David W.
"The History of the Family in Africa and Europe: Some Comparative Perspectives." Journal of African History. Volume 24 #2 1983. pp. 163-171.

Sai, Fred T.
Family Welfare and Development in Africa: Proceedings of the IPPF Africa Regional Conference, University of Ibadan. London: International Planned Parenthood Federation. Ibadan, Nigeria. Aug. 29-Sept. 3, 1977. 327p.

Schwendinger, Julia and Schwendinger, Herman
"Rape, Sexual Inequality and Levels of Violence." Crime and Social Justice. Volume 16 Winter, 1981. pp. 3-31.

Smith, Jane I. (ed.)
Women in Contemporary Muslim Societies. Lewisburg, Pennsylvania: Bucknell University Press. 1980. 264p.

Smith, Janet I.
"The Experience of Muslim Women: Considerations of Power and Authority." (In) Haddad, Yvonne Y. and Haines, Byron and Findly, Ellison (eds.). The Islamic Impact. Syracuse, New York: Syracuse University Press. 1984. pp. 89-112.

Sow, Fatou
"Muslim Families in Contemporary Black Africa." Current Anthropology. Volume 26 December, 1985. pp. 563-570.

Spencer, P.
"Polygyny as a Measure of Social Differentiation in Africa." (In) Mitchell, J.C. (ed.). Numerical Techniques in Social Anthropology. Philadelphia,

Pennsylvania: Institute for the Study of Human Issues. 1980.
Sudarkasa, Niara
The Effects of 20th Century Social Change, Especially of Migration, on Women of West Africa. Tucson, Arizona: University of Arizona. Proceedings of the West Africa Conference. 1976. pp. 102-109.
Sudarkasa, Niara
"Female Employment and Family Organization in West Africa." (In) Steady, Filomina C. (ed.). The Black Woman Cross-Culturally. Cambridge, Massachusetts: Schenkman Publishing. 1981. pp. 49-64.
Tesha, Nancy
"Womens Role in Rearing Children and National Development." Paper Presented at the Workshop on Women's Studies and Development. Dar-es-Salaam, Tanzania: University of Dar-es-Salaam. Bureau of Resource Assessment and Land Use Planning. Paper #39. September 24-29, 1979. 3p.
Thadani, Veena N. and Todaro, Michael P.
Female Migration in Developing Countries: A Framework for Analysis. New York: Population Council. Center for Policy Studies. Working Papers #47. 1979. 48p.
Thelejane, T.S.
"An African Girl and an African Woman in a Changing World." Paper Presented at the Seminar on the Changing Family in the African Context. Paris: United Nations Educational, Scientific and Cultural Organization. Maseru, Lesotho. 1984. 24p.
Thornton, John
"Sexual Demography: The Impact of Slave Trade on Family Structure." (In) Robertson, Claire C. and Klein, Martin A. (eds.). Women and Slavery in Africa. Madison, Wisconsin: University of Wisconsin Press. 1983. pp. 39-48.
Tillion, Germaine
The Republic of Cousins: Women's Oppression in Mediterranean Society. London: Al Saqi Books. Translated by Q. Hoare. 1983. 181p.
Tinker, Irene and Bramson, Michele B. (eds.)
Women and World Developmemt. New York: Praeger Publishers. 1976. 228p.
Tinker, Irene
"Women and Africa: Policy Strategies for Women in the 1980's." Africa Report. Volume 26 #2 March-April, 1981. pp. 11-16.
Tinker, Irene
"The Adverse Impact of Development on Women." (In) Tinker, Irene (ed.). Women and World Development. New York: Praeger Publishers. 1976.
Tomsic, Vida
"The Position and Role of Women in Development." Review of International Affairs. Volume 32 November 5, 1981. pp. 1-5.

Traore, Aminata
"Evolving Relations Between Mothers and Children in Rural Africa." International Social Science Journal. Volume 31 #3 1979. pp. 486-491.

Uche, U.U.
"The Law, Family Welfare and Development in Africa: A Strategy for Future Action." (In) International Planned Parenthood Federation (IPPF). Proceedings of the IPPF Africa Regional Conference. London: IPPF. 1977. pp. 256-262.

United Nations
Impact on Women of Socioeconomic Changes in Africa South of the Sahara: Project Proposal. Geneva: United Nations Research Institute for Social Development. Reference Center. 1979. 56p.

United Nations Economic Commission for Africa (UNECA)
Women Population and Rural Development in Africa. Addis Ababa, Ethiopia: UNECA/FAO Women's Development Programme Unit. 1976.

United Nations Economic Commission for Africa (UNECA)
Family, Welfare and Development in Africa: Social Welfare Aspects of Family Planning. Addis Ababa, Ethiopia: UNECA. Social Development Section. Social Welfare Services in Africa #11. 1977. 133p.

United Nations Educational, Scientific and Cultural Organ.
Description of Projects Relevant to the Integration of Women in Development: Africa. Paris: UNESCO. May 16, 1979. 10p.

United Nations Educational, Scientific and Cultural Organ.
Comparative Report on the Role of Working Mothers in Early Childhood Education in Five Countries. Paris: UNESCO. 1978. 82p.

Ushewokunze, C.M.
"Reflections on Youth and Family Welfare Law in Africa." (In) International Planned Parenthood Federation (IPPF). Proceedings of the IPPF Africa Regional Conference. London: IPPF. 1977. pp. 182-190.

Valentine, C.H. and Revson, J.E.
"Cultural Traditions, Social Change, and Fertility in Sub-Saharan Africa." Journal of Modern African Studies. Volume 17 #3 September, 1979. pp. 453-472.

Waines, D.
"Through a Veil Darkly--The Study of Women in Muslim Societies." Comparative Studies in Society and History. Volume 24 #4 1982.

Walle, Etienne V. and Kekouole, John
The Recent Evolution of African Marriage and Polygyny. Philadelphia, Pennsylvania: University of Pennsylvania. Population Studies Center. 1984.

Ware, Helen
"Security in the City: The Role of the Family in Urban West Africa." (In) Ruzicka, Lado T. (ed.). The Economic and Social Supports for High Fertility: Proceedings of

the Conference Held in Canberra, November 16-18, 1976. Canberra, Australia: Australian National University. Development Studies Center. 1977. pp. 385-408.

Ware, Helen
"Women's Work and Fertility in Africa." (In) Kupinsky, Stanley (ed.). The Fertility of Working Women: A Synthesis of International Research. New York: Praeger Publishers. Praeger Special Studies in International Economics and Development. 1977. pp. 1-34.

Ware, Helen
"Economic Strategy and the Number of Children." (In) Caldwell, John C. (ed.). The Persistence of High Fertility: Population Prospects in the Third World. Canberra, Australia: Australian National University. Department of Demography. Volume Two. 1977. pp. 469-592.

Ware, Helen
Women, Education and Modernization of the Family in West Africa. Canberra, Australia: Australian National University. Department of Demography. Changing African Family Project Series. Monograph #7. 1981. 178p.

Welch, Charles E. and Glick, Paul C.
"The Incidence of Polygamy in Contemporary Africa: A Research Note." Journal of Marriage and the Family. Volume 43 #1 February, 1981. pp. 191-192.

White, Luise S.
"Women in the Changing African Family." (In) Hay, Margaret J. and Stichter, Sharon (eds.). African Women South of the Sahara. New York: Longman. 1984. pp. 53-68.

Youssef, Nadia H.
"Interrelationship Between the Division of Labor in the Household, Women's Roles and Their Impact Upon Fertility." Paper Presented at the Informal Workshop on Women's Roles and Demographic Research Program. Geneva: International Labour Organization. November, 1978.

Youssef, Nadia H. and Hetler, Carol B.
"Establishing the Economic Condition of Woman-Headed Households in the Third World: A New Approach." (In) Buvinic, Mayra and Lycette, Margaret A. and McGreevey, William P. (eds.). Women and Poverty in the Third World. Baltimore, Maryland: Johns Hopkins University. 1983. pp. 216-243.

Zivetz, L.
The Impact of Rural Development on the Status of Women and its Consequences for Fertility in Africa. Submitted to the Research Triangle Institute and the Southeast Consortium for International Development. Chapel Hill, North Carolina. 1979.

Family Planning and Contraception

Allman, James
"Family Patterns, Women's Status and Fertility in Middle-East and North-Africa." International Journal of Sociology of the Family. Volume 8 #1 1978. pp. 19-35.

Allman, James
"Family Life, Women's Status, and Fertility: Middle East and North African Perspectives." (In) Allman, James (ed.). Women's Studies and Fertility in the Muslim World. New York: Praeger Publishers. Praeger Special Studies. 1978. pp. 24-47.

Allman, James (ed.)
Women's Status and Fertility in the Muslim World. New York: Praeger Publishers. Praeger Special Studies. 1978. 378p.

Anker, Richard and Buvinic, Mayra and Youssef, Nadia H. (eds.)
Women's Roles and Population Trends in the Third World. London: Croon Helm Ltd. 1982. 288p.

Attah, E.B.
Family Nucleation and Fertility Change in Tropical Africa: Background to the Demographic Transition. Atlanta, Georgia: Atlanta University. Department of Sociology. 1985.

Beneria, Lourdes
"Reproduction, Production and the Sexual Division of Labour." Cambridge Journal of Economics. Volume 3 September, 1979. pp. 203-225.

Beneria, Lourdes
Reproduction, Production and the Sexual Division of Labour. Geneva: International Labour Office. World Employment Research Working Paper #2. 1978.

Blair, P.W.
The Health Needs of the World's Poor Women. (In) "Proceedings of the International Symposium on Women and Their Health." Washington D.C.: Equity Policy Center. June 8-11, 1980.

Bongaarts, John
"The Impact on Fertility of Traditional and Changing Child-Spacing Practices." (In) Page, Hilary J. and Lesthaeghe, Ron (eds.). Child-Spacing in Tropical Africa. New York: Academic Press. 1981. pp. 111-129.
Boserup, Ester
"Economic and Demographic Interrelationships in Sub-Saharan Africa." Population and Development Review. Volume 11 #3 September, 1985. pp. 383-397+.
Brown, Judith E.
"Polygyny and Family Planning in Sub-Saharan Africa." Studies in Family Planning. Volume 12 #8-9 August-September, 1981. pp. 322-326.
Cairo Demographic Centre (CDC)
Family and Marriage in Some African and Asian Countries. Cairo, Egypt: CDC. CDC Research Monograph Series #6. 1976.
Caldwell, John C. and Caldwell, Pat
"The Achieved Small Family: Early Fertility Transition in an African City." Studies in Family Planning. Volume 9 #1 January, 1978. pp. 2-18.
Caldwell, John C. and Caldwell, Pat
Cultural Forces Tending to Sustain High Fertility in Tropical Africa. Canberra, Australia: Australian National University. 1984.
Caldwell, John C. and Caldwell, Pat
"Demographic and Contraceptive Innovators: A Study of Transitional African Society." Journal of Biosocial Science. Volume 8 #4 October, 1976. pp. 347-366.
Caldwell, Pat
"Issues of Marriage and Marital Change: Tropical Africa and the Middle East." (In) Huzayyin, S.A. and Acsadi, G.T. (eds.). Family and Marriage in Some African and Asiatic Countries. Cairo, Egypt: Cairo Demographic Centre. Research Monograph Series #6. 1976. pp. 325-335.
Caldwell, Pat and Caldwell, John C.
"The Function of Child-Spacing in Traditional Societies and the Direction of Change." (In) Page, Hilary J. and Lesthaeghe, Ron (eds.). Child-Spacing in Tropical Africa: Traditions and Change. New York: Academic Press. 1981. pp. 73-92.
Chi, C. and Miller, E.R. and Fortney, J.A. and Bernard, Roger P.
"A Study of Abortion in Countries Where Abortions are Legally Restricted." Journal of Reproductive Medicine. Volume 18 #1 January, 1977. pp. 15-26.
Cook, Rebecca J.
"A Law on Family Welfare and Development in Africa." (In) International Planned Parenthood Federation (IPPF). Proceedings of the IPPF Africa Regional Conference. London: IPPF. 1977. pp. 241-246.
De Graft-John, K.E.
"Issues in Family Welfare and Development in Africa." (In) International Planned Parenthood Federation (IPPF).

Proceedings of the IPPF Africa Regional Conference. London: IPPF. 1977. pp. 33-45.

Dodds, Peter
"Family Planning in Africa." Africa Insight. Volume 15 #4 1985. pp. 256-261.

El-Khorazaty, Mohamed Nabil E.
"Regional Differences in Attitudes Toward Family Norms and Planning, 1979/80." Population Studies. Volume 12 #72 January-March, 1985. pp. 3-28.

Fortes, Meyer
"Parenthood, Marriage and Fertility in West Africa." Journal of Development Studies. Volume 14 #4 July, 1978. pp. 121-149.

Fortes, Meyer
"Family, Marriage and Fertility in West Africa." (In) Oppong, C. and Adaba, G. and Bekombo-Priso, M. and Mogey, J. (eds.). Marriage, Fertility and Parenthood in West Africa. Canberra, Australia: Australian National University Press. 1978. pp. 17-54.

Frank, Odile
The Demand for Fertility Control in Sub-Saharan Africa. New York: Population Council. Center for Policy Studies. Working Paper #117. November, 1985. 50p.

Frank, Odile
Child Fostering in Sub-Saharan Africa. New York: Population Council. Center for Policy Studies. 1984.

Gadalla, Saad M.
Population Policy and Family Planning Communication Strategies in the Arab States Region. Paris: UNESCO. Volume One: Summaries of Pertinent Literature and Research Studies. 1978.

Goody, Esther N.
"Some Theoretical and Empirical Aspects of Parenthood in West Africa." (In) Oppong, C. and Adaba, G. and Bekombo-Priso, M. and Mogey, J. (eds.). Marriage, Fertility and Parenthood in West Africa. Canberra, Australia: Australian National University. Department of Demography. Volume One. 1978. pp. 227-272.

Goody, Jack
Production and Reproduction: A Comparative Study of the Domestic Domain. Cambridge, New York: Cambridge University Press. Cambridge Studies in Social Anthropology #17. 1976. 157p.

Henn, Albert E.
Before Family Planning: The Implications of Infertility in Africa for Population Program Planning. Washington, D.C.: World Population Society Meeting. Mimeo. December, 1976.

Hosken, Fran P.
"A Crucial New Direction for International Family Planning." Humanist. Volume 44 #1 January-February, 1984.

Hosken, Fran P.
"Women and Health in East and West Africa: Family Planning and Female Cicumcision." Paper Presented at the

Seminar on Traditional Practices Affecting the Health of Women and Children. World Conference of the United Nations Decade for Women. New York: United Nations. Copenhagen, Denmark. July 14-30, 1980.

Hosken, Fran P.
"Women and Health in East and West Africa: Family Planning and Female Circumcision." Paper Presented at the Seminar on Traditional Practices Affecting the Health of Women and Children: Female Circumcision, Childhood Marriage, Nutritional Taboos, etc. Alexandria, Egypt: World Health Organization. Eastern Mediterranean Regional Office. Khartoum, Sudan. February 10-15, 1979.

International Planned Parenthood Federation (IPPF)
Family Welfare and Development in Africa: Proceedings of the IPPF Africa Regional Conference, University of Ibadan. August 29-September 3, 1976. London: IPPF. Ibadan, Nigeria. 1977. 327p.

Isley, R.
Medical, Socio-Cultural, Economic and Psychological Correlates of Childlessness in Africa. Research Triangle Park, North Carolina: Research Triangle Institute. RTI Concept Paper #24-CP-80-01. 1980.

Johnston, Bruce F. and Meyer, Anthony J.
"Nutrition, Health and Population in Strategies for Rural Development." Economic Development and Cultural Change. Volume 26 #1 October, 1977. pp. 1-23.

Johnston, Bruce F. and Meyer, Anthony J.
"Nutrition, Health and Population in Strategies for Rural Development." Nairobi: University of Nairobi. Institute for Development Studies. Discussion Paper #238. 1976. 45p.

Kabagambe, John C.
"Family Planning Concepts: Myths and Realities." (In) International Planned Parenthood Federation (IPPF). Proceedings of the IPPF Africa Regional Conference. London: IPPF. 1977. pp. 55+.

Kamanga, Kawaye
"The Dilemma of High Fertility in Sub-Saharan Africa." Ph.D Dissertation: University of Pittsburgh. Pittsburgh, Pennsylvania. 1985. 140p.

Kisekka, Mere N.
"Polygyny and the Status of African Women." African Urban Notes. Volume 2 #3 Fall/Winter, 1976. pp. 21-42.

Kwawu, J.
"The Role of Home Economics in Rural Development: A Focus on Family Planning." Paper Presented at the Workshop on the Role of Women and Home Economics in Rural Development in Africa. Rome: United Nations Food and Agricultural Organization. Alexandria, Egypt. October 17, 1983. 20p.

Lesthaeghe, Ron J. and Ohadike, Patrick O. and Kocher, James E. and Page, Hilary J.
"Child-Spacing and Fertility in Sub-Saharan Africa: An Overview of Issues." (In) Page, Hilary J. and Lesthaeghe, Ron (eds.). Child-Spacing in Tropical

Africa: Traditions and Change. New York: Academic Press. 1981. pp. 3-23.

Little, Kenneth L.
"Women's Strategies in Modern Marriage in Anglophone West Africa: An Ideological and Sociological Appraisal." Journal of Comparative Family Studies. Volume 8 #3 Autumn, 1977. pp. 341-356.

Little, Kenneth L.
"Women's Strategies in Modern Marriage in Anglophone West Africa: An Ideological and Sociological Appraisal." (In) Kurian, George (ed.). Cross-Cultural Perspectives of Mate Selection and Marriage. Westport, Connecticut: Greenwood Press. Contributions in Family Studies #3. 1979. pp. 202-217.

Mabogunje, A.L.
"The Policy Implications of Changes in Child-Spacing Practices in Tropical Africa." (In) Page, Hilary J. and Lesthaeghe, Ron (eds.). Child-Spacing in Tropical Africa: Traditions and Changes. New York: Academic Press. 1981. pp. 303-316.

Meumaun, Alfred K.
"Integration of Family Planning and Maternal and Child Health in Rural West Africa." Journal of Biosocial Science. Volume 8 #2 April, 1976. pp. 161-174.

Mott, Frank L. and Mott, Susan H.
"Household Fertility Decision-Making in a West African Setting: Do Male and Female Surveys Lead to Similar Interpretations?" Worthington, Ohio: Ohio State University. Center for Human Resource Research. 1984.

Musallam, B.
Sex and Society in Islam: Birth Control Before the 19th Century. Cambridge, New York: Cambridge University Press. Cambridge Studies in Islamic Civilization. 1983. 176p.

Nagi, Mostafa H. and Stockwell, Edward G.
"Muslim Fertility: Recent Trends and Future Outlook." Journal of South Asian and Middle Eastern Studies. Volume 6 #2 Winter, 1982. pp. 48-70.

Nagi, Mostafa H.
"Trends and Differentials in Moslem Fertility." Journal of Biosocial Science. Volume 16 #2 April, 1984. pp. 189-204.

Ndeti, K.
"Concept of Parenthood in Africa: An Exploratory Study of Complexity." (In) International Planned Parenthood Federation (IPPF). Proceedings of the IPPF Africa Regional Conference. London: IPPF. 1977. pp. 119-144.

Okediji, Frances Olu
"The Limitations of Family Planning Programmes in the Developing Nations." (In) Oppong, C. and Adaba, G. and Bekombo-Priso, M. and Mogey, J. (eds.). Marriage, Fertility and Parenthood in West Africa. Canberra, Australia: Australian National University. Department of Demography. Volume Two. 1978. pp. 617-639.

Okediji, Peter A.
"The Status of African Women in Family Planning." (In) Oppong, C. and Adaba, G. and Bekombo-Priso, M. and Mogey, J. (eds.). Marriage, Fertility and Parenthood in West Africa. Canberra, Australia: Australian National University. Department of Demography. Volume Two. 1978. pp. 673-676.

Okeyo, Achola P.
"Research Priorities: Women in Africa." Studies in Family Planning. Volume 10 #11/12 Nov.-Dec., 1979. pp. 401-404.

Okeyo, Achola P.
"Women in the Household Economy: Managing Multiple Roles." Studies in Family Planning. Volume 10 #11/12 Nov.-Dec., 1979. pp. 337-343.

Omran, Abdel R. and Johnston, Alan G.
Family Planning for Health in Africa. Chapel Hill, North Carolina: University of North Carolina. Carolina Population Center. 1984. 190p.

Oppong, Christine
Family Structure and Women's Reproductive and Productive Roles: Some Conceptual and Methodological Issues. Geneva: International Labour Office. The Role of Women and Demographic Change Research Program. 1980.

Oppong, Christine
"Family Structure and Women's Reproductive and Productive Roles: Some Conceptual and Methodological Issues." (In) Anker, Richard and Buvinic, Mayra and Youssef, N. (eds.). Women's Roles and Population Trends in the Third World. London: Croom Helm. 1982.

Oucho, John O.
"Socio-Economic Perspectives of Fertility Regulation in Traditional and Modern African Societies." (In) University of Nairobi. Papers of the Seminar on Oral Traditions: Past Growth and Future Development in East Africa. Nairobi: University of Nairobi. UNESCO Institute of African Affairs. Kisumu, Kenya. April 18-22, 1979. 18p.

Page, Hilary J. and Lesthaeghe, Ron J. (eds.)
Child-Spacing in Tropical Africa: Traditions and Change. New York: Academic Press. Studies in Population Series. 1981. 332p.

Paraiso, Maitre A.
"Family Planning Legislation in the Francophone Countries of Africa." (In) International Planned Parenthood Federation (IPPF). Proceedings of the IPPF Africa Regional Conference. London: IPPF. 1977. pp. 247-255.

Pratt, Edward O.
"Current Status of Family Planning in Africa." (In) International Planned Parenthood Federation (IPPF). Proceedings of the IPPF Africa Regional Conference. London: IPPF. 1977. pp. 61-65.

Rosenfield, A. and Maine, D. and Gorosh, M.E.
"Non Clinical Distribution of the Pill in the Developing

World." International Family Planning Perspectives. Volume 6 December, 1980. pp. 130-136.
Sai, Fred T.
"Report of the Conference on the Medical and Social Aspects of Abortion in Africa." (In) Sai, F.T. (ed.). A Strategy for Abortion Management. London: International Planned Parenthood Federation. 1978. pp 6-22.
Sai, Fred T.
Defining Family Health Needs, Standards of Care and Priorities, With Particular Reference to Family Planning. London: International Planned Parenthood Federation. 1977. 32p.
Sai, Fred T.
"The Place of Nutrition in Family Planning Programs in Africa." Paper Presented at the International Planned Parenthood Federation Refresher Course for Clinical Supervisors. Nairobi. November 24-28, 1980.
Sai, Fred T.
Family Welfare and Development in Africa: Proceedings of the IPPF Africa Regional Conference, University of Ibadan. London: International Planned Parenthood Federation. Ibadan, Nigeria. Aug. 29-Sept. 3, 1977. 327p.
Sala-Diakanda, Mpembele
"Problems of Infertility and Sub-Fertility in West and Central Africa." (In) International Union for the Scientific Study of Population (IUSSP). International Population Conference. Papers of the 19th General Conference. Liege, Belgium: IUSSP. Volume Three. 1981. pp. 643-666.
Schoenmaeckers, Ronald C.
The Child-Spacing Tradition and the Postpartum Taboo in Tropical Africa: Anthropological Evidence. Paper Prepared for the IUSSP Workshop on Child-Spacing in Tropical Africa: Tradition and Change. Brussels, Belgium: International Union for the Scientific Study of Population. April, 17-19, 1979.
Schoenmaeckers, Ronald C. and Shah, I.H. and Lesthaeghe, Ron J. and Tambashe, O.
"The Child-Spacing Tradition and the Postpartum Taboo in Tropical Africa: Anthropological Evidence." (In) Page, Hilary J. and Lesthaeghe, Ron (eds.). Child-Spacing in Tropical Africa: Traditions and Change. New York: Academic Press. 1981. pp. 25-71.
Seetharam, K.S. and Duza, M. Badrud
"Nuptiality and Fertility in Selected Areas of Four Arab and African Cities." (In) Huzayyin, S.A. and Acsadi, G.T. (eds.). Family and Marriage in Some African and Asiatic Countries. Cairo, Egypt: Cairo Demographic Centre. CDC Research Monograph Series #6. 1976. pp. 337-355.
Uba, Sam
"Women Put the Case for Southern African Liberation." New African Development. March, 1977.

Uche, U.U.
"The Law, Family Welfare and Development in Africa: A Strategy for Future Action." (In) International Planned Parenthood Federation (IPPF). Proceedings of the IPPF Africa Regional Conference. London: IPPF. 1977. pp. 256-262.

Ukaegbu, Alfred O.
"Marriage Habits and Fertility of Women in Tropical Africa: A Socio-Cultural Perspective." (In) Dupaquier, J. and Helin, E. and Laslett, P. and Livi-Bacci, M. (eds.). Marriage and Remarriage in Populations of the Past. New York: Academic Press. Population and Social Structure: Advances in Historical Demography Series. 1981. pp. 127-137.

United Nations Economic Commission for Africa (UNECA)
Family, Welfare and Development in Africa: Social Welfare Aspects of Family Planning. Addis Ababa, Ethiopia: UNECA. Social Development Section. Social Welfare Services in Africa #11. 1977. 133p.

United States Department of Health and Human Services
Family Planning Methods and Practice: Africa. Atlanta, Georgia: U.S. Department of Health and Human Services. Centers for Disease Control. Center for Health Promotion and Education. 1983. 329p.

Ware, Helen
"Security in the City: The Role of the Family in Urban West Africa." (In) Ruzicka, Lado T. (ed.). The Economic and Social Supports for High Fertility: Proceedings of the Conference Held in Canberra, November 16-18, 1976. Canberra, Australia: Australian National University. Development Studies Center. 1977. pp. 385-408.

Ware, Helen
"Economic Strategy and the Number of Children." (In) Caldwell, John C. (ed.). The Persistence of High Fertility: Population Prospects in the Third World. Canberra, Australia: Australian National University. Department of Demography. Volume Two. 1977. pp. 469-592.

Ware, Helen
"Motivations for the Use of Birth Control: Evidence From West Africa." Demography. Volume 13 #4 November, 1976. pp. 479-494.

Wulf, Deirdre
"The Future of Family Planning in Sub-Saharan Africa." International Family Planning Perspectives. Volume 11 #1 March, 1985. pp. 1-8.

Fertility and Infertility

Aborampah, Osei-Mensah
"Family Structure in African Fertility Studies: Some Conceptual and Methodological Issues." Current Bibliography on African Affairs. Volume 18 #4 1986. pp. 319-335.

Acsadi, George T.
"Effect of Economic Development on Fertility Trends in Africa." (In) Cairo Demographic Centre (CDC). Aspects of Population Change and Development in Some African and Asian Countries. Cairo, Egypt: CDC. CDC Research Monograph Series #9. 1984. pp. 57-105.

Adadevoh, B. Kwaku
"Sub-Fertility and Infertility in Africa." (In) International Planned Parenthood Federation (IPPF). Proceedings of the IPPF Africa Regional Conference. London: IPPF. 1977. pp. 80-84.

Adegbola, O.
"New Estimates of Fertility and Child Mortality in Africa, South of the Sahara." Population Studies(London). Volume 31 #3 1977. pp. 467-486.

Adepoju, Aderanti
"Migration and Development in Tropical Africa: Some Research Priorities." African Affairs. Volume 76 #303 April, 1977. pp. 210-225.

Ahdab-Yehia, May
"Women, Employment and Fertility Trends in the Arab Middle East and North Africa." (In) Kupinsky, Stanley (ed.). The Fertility of Working Women: A Synthesis of International Research. New York: Praeger Publishers. Preager Special Studies in International Economics and Development. 1977. pp. 172-187.

Alausa, O. and Osoba, A.O.
"The Role of Sexually Transmitted Diseases in Male Infertility in Tropical Africa." Nigerian Medical Journal. Volume 8 #3 May, 1978. pp. 225-229.

Allman, James
"Family Patterns, Women's Status and Fertility in Middle-East and North-Africa." International Journal of Sociology of the Family. Volume 8 #1 1978. pp. 19-35.

Allman, James
"Family Life, Women's Status, and Fertility: Middle East and North African Perspectives." (In) Allman, James (ed.). Women's Studies and Fertility in the Muslim World. New York: Praeger Publishers. Praeger Special Studies. 1978. pp. 24-47.

Allman, James
"The Demographic Transition in the Middle East and North Africa." International Journal of Middle East Studies. Volume 12 #3 November, 1980. pp. 277-301.

Allman, James
Natural Fertility in North Africa and the Middle-East. New York: Columbia University Press/U.S. AID. 1980.

Allman, James (ed.)
Women's Status and Fertility in the Muslim World. New York: Praeger Publishers. Praeger Special Studies. 1978. 378p.

Attah, E.B.
Family Nucleation and Fertility Change in Tropical Africa: Background to the Demographic Transition. Atlanta, Georgia: Atlanta University. Department of Sociology. 1985.

Belsey, Mark A.
"Biological Factors Other Than Nutrition and Lactation Which May Influence Natural Fertility: Additional Notes With Particular Reference to Sub-Saharan Africa." Paper Presented at the International Union for the Scientific Study of Population Seminar on Natural Fertility. Leige, Belgium: IUSSP. Paris, France. 1977.

Belsey, Mark A.
"Biological Factors Other Than Nutrition and Lactation Which May Influence Natural Fertility: Additional Notes With Particular Reference to Sub-Saharan Africa." (In) Leridon, Henri and Menken, Jane (eds.). Natural Fertility: Patterns and Determinants of Natural Fertility. Liege, Belgium: International Union for the Scientific Study of Population. 1979. pp. 253-272.

Belsey. Mark A.
"The Epidemiology of Infertility: A Review With Particular Reference to Sub-Saharan Africa." Bulletin of the World Health Organization. Volume 54 #3 1976. pp. 319-341.

Bongaarts, John and Frank, Odile and Lesthaeghe, Ron J.
"The Proximate Determinants of Fertility in Sub-Saharan Africa." Population and Developement Review. Volume 10 #3 September, 1984. pp. 511-538+.

Bongaarts, John
"The Impact on Fertility of Traditional and Changing Child-Spacing Practices." (In) Page, Hilary J. and Lesthaeghe, Ron (eds.). Child-Spacing in Tropical Africa. New York: Academic Press. 1981. pp. 111-129.

Boserup, Ester
"Economic and Demographic Interrelationships in Sub-Saharan Africa." Population and Development Review. Volume 11 #3 September, 1985. pp. 383-397+.

Bulatao, R.A.
"Transitions in the Value of Children and the Fertility Transition." Paper Presented at the Seminar on Determinants of Fertility Trends: Major Themes and New Directions for Research. International Union for the Scientific Study of Population. Bad Homburg, Germany. 1980.

Cairo Demographic Center (CDC)
Determinants of Fertility in Some African And Asian Countries. Cairo, Egypt: CDC. CDC Research Monograph Series #10. 1982. 698p.

Caldwell, John C. and Caldwell, Pat
"The Demographic Evidence for the Incidence and Cause of Abnormally Low Fertility in Tropical Africa." World Health Statistics Quarterly. Volume 36 #1 1983. pp. 2-34.

Caldwell, John C. and Caldwell, Pat
"The Achieved Small Family: Early Fertility Transition in an African City." Studies in Family Planning. Volume 9 #1 January, 1978. pp. 2-18.

Caldwell, John C.
Fertility in Africa. (In) Eberstadt, Nick (ed.). "Fertility Decline in the Less Developed Countries." New York: Praeger Publishers. Praeger Special Studies. 1981. pp. 97-118.

Caldwell, John C.
"Towards a Restatement of Demographic Transition Theory: An Investigation of Conditions Before and at the Onset of Fertility Declining Employing Primarily African Experience and Data." Population and Development Review. Volume 2 #3 1976. pp. 321-366.

Caldwell, John C. and Caldwell, Pat
Cultural Forces Tending to Sustain High Fertility in Tropical Africa. Canberra, Australia: Australian National University. 1984.

Caldwell, John C.
"Measuring Wealth Flows and the Rationality of Fertility: Thoughts and Plans Based in the First Place on African Work." (In) Ruzicka, Lado T. (ed.). The Economic and Social Supports for High Fertility: Proceedings of the Conference. Canberra, Australia: Australian National University. Development Studies Center. November 16-18, 1977. pp. 439-454.

Caldwell, Pat and Caldwell, John C.
"Population Change and Development in the ECWA Region." (In) Cairo Demographic Centre (CDC). Aspects of Population Change and Development in Some African and Asian Countries. Cairo, Egypt: CDC. CDC Research Monograph Series #9. 1984. pp. 43-56.

Cantrelle, Pierre and Ferry, Benoit and Mondot, J.
"Relationships Between Fertility and Mortality in

Tropical Africa." (In) Preston, Samuel H. (ed.). The Effects of Infant and Child Mortality on Fertility. New York: Academic Press. 1978. pp. 181-205.

Cates, W. and Farley, T.M. and Rowe, P.J.
"Worldwide Patterns of Infertility: Is Africa Different?" Lancet. #8455 September 14, 1985. pp. 596-598.

Cleveland, David
"Fertility and the Value of Children in Subsistence Agriculture: Savanna West Africa." Paper Presented at the Annual Meeting of the American Anthropological Association. Cincinnati, Ohio. November, 1979.

Clignet, Remi and Sween, Joyce A.
"Ethnicity and Fertility: Implications for Population Programs in Africa." Africa. Volume 48 #1 1978. pp. 47-65.

DeLancey, Virginia H.
"The Relationship Between Female Labor Force Participation and Fertility: Considerations of Role Compatibility in Research Methodology for Developing Countries." Paper Presented at the Annual Meeting of the African Studies Association. Paper #34. Los Angeles, California. 1979. 23p.

Eberstadt, Nick (ed.)
Fertility Decline in the Less Developed Countries. New York: Praeger Publishers. Praeger Special Studies. 1981. 370p.

Ekanem, Ita I.
"Prospects of Fertility Decline in Sub-Saharan Africa." Population Studies. #67 1979. pp. 174-196.

El-Badry, M.A.
"Determinants of Fertility in African and Asian Countries: An Introductory Overview." (In) Cairo Demographic Centre (CDC). Determinants of Fertility in Some African and Asian Countries." Cairo, Egypt: CDC. CDC Monograph Series #10. 1982. pp. 3-11.

Ember, C.R.
"Relative Decline in Women's Contribution to Agriculture With Intensification." American Anthropologist. Volume 85 #2 June, 1983. pp. 285-304.

Ewbank, Douglas C. and Mode, Charles J. and Pickens, Gary T.
Quantifying Implicit Fertility Forecasts for Africa. Philadelphia, Pennsylvania: University of Pennsylvania. Population Studies Center. 1984.

Farooq, Ghazi M. and Simmons, George B. (eds.)
Fertility in Developing Countries: An Economic Perspective on Research and Policy Issues. New York: St. Martin's Press. 1985.

Fortes, Meyer
"Parenthood, Marriage and Fertility in West Africa." Journal of Development Studies. Volume 14 #4 July, 1978. pp. 121-149.

Fortes, Meyer
"Family, Marriage and Fertility in West Africa." (In) Oppong, C. and Adaba, G. and Bekombo-Priso, M. and Mogey, J. (eds.). Marriage, Fertility and Parenthood in West

Africa. Canberra, Australia: Australian National University Press. 1978. pp. 17-54.

Frank, Odile
Infertility in Sub-Saharan Africa. New York: Population Council. Center for Population Studies. Working Working Paper #97. June, 1983. 107p.

Frank, Odile
"Infertility in Sub-Saharan Africa: Estimates and Implications." Population and Development Review. Volume 9 #1 March, 1983. pp. 137-144+.

Frank, Odile
The Demand for Fertility Control in Sub-Saharan Africa. New York: Population Council. Center for Policy Studies. Working Paper #117. November, 1985. 50p.

Guest, Iain
"Special Report: Infertility in Africa." People (London). Volume 5 #1 1978. pp. 23-34.

Gyepi-Garbrah, Benjamin and Nichols, Douglas J. and Kpedekpo, Gottlieb M.
Adolescent Fertility in Sub-Saharan Africa: An Overview. Boston: Pathfinder Fund. 1985. 51p.

Hawthorn, Geoffrey (ed.)
Population and Development: High and Low Fertility in Poorer Countries. London: Frank Cass. 1978. 210p.

Hein, Catherine R.
Factory Employment, Marriage and Fertility: The Case of Mauritian Women. Geneva: International Labour Organization. World Employment Programme Research Working Paper #118. June, 1982. 57p.

Henin, Roushdi A.
"Fertility, Infertility and Sub-Fertility in Eastern Africa." (In) International Union for the Scientic Study of Population (IUSSP). International Population Conference: Solicited Papers. Liege, Netherland: IUSSP. Volume Three. 1981. pp. 667-697.

Henn, Albert E.
Before Family Planning: The Implications of Infertility in Africa for Population Program Planning. Washington, D.C.: World Population Society Meeting. Mimeo. December, 1976.

Hosken, Fran P.
"Female Circumcision and Fertility in Africa." Women and Health. Volume 1 #6 Nov.-Dec., 1976. pp. 3-11.

Isley, R.
Medical, Socio-Cultural, Economic and Psychological Correlates of Childlessness in Africa. Research Triangle Park, North Carolina: Research Triangle Institute. RTI Concept Paper #24-CP-80-01. 1980.

Javillonar, Gloria W.
Rural Development, Women's Roles and Fertility in Developing Countries: Review of the Literature. Chapel Hill, North Carolina: Research Triangle Institute. 1979. pp. 32-75.

Kamanga, Kawaye
"The Dilemma of High Fertility in Sub-Saharan Africa."

Ph.D Dissertation: University of Pittsburgh. Pittsburgh, Pennsylvania. 1985. 140p.

Kazeze, Z.W.
"Review of Some Determinants of Fertility in Africa." (In) Cairo Demographic Centre (CDC). Determinants of Fertility in Some African and Asian Countries. Cairo, Egypt: CDC. CDC Research Monograph Series #10. 1982. pp. 391-414.

Kitching, Gavin
"Proto-Industrialization and Demographic Change: A Thesis and Some Possible African Implications." Journal of African History. Volume 24 #2 1983. pp. 221-240.

Kocher, James E.
"Socioeconomic Development and Fertility Change in Rural Africa." Paper Presented at the Annual Meeting of the African Studies Association. Paper #44. Boston, Massachusetts. 1976. 22p.

Kocher, James E.
"Supply-Demand Disequilibria and Fertility Change in Africa--Toward a More Appropriate Economic Approach." Social Biology. Volume 30 #1 1983. pp. 41-58.

Kpedekpo, Gottlieb M.
"Age Patterns of Fertility in Selected African Countries." Jimlar Mutane. Volume 1 #1 February, 1976. pp. 9-26.

Ladipo, O.A.
"The Role of Artificial Insemimation in the Management of Infertility." East African Medical Journal. Volume 56 #5 May, 1979. pp. 219-222.

LeVine, Robert A. and Dixon, Suzanne and LeVine, Sarah
"High Fertility in Africa: A Consideration of Causes and Consequences." Paper Presented at the Annual Meeting of the African Studies Association. Paper #48. Boston, Massachusetts. 1976. 18p.

Leke, R. and Nash, B.
"Biological and Socio-Cultural Aspects of Infertility and Subfertility in Africa." (In) United Nations Economic Commission for Africa (UNECA). Population Dynamics: Fertility and Mortality in Africa. Addis Ababa, Ethiopia: UNECA. May, 1981. pp. 488-498.

Lesthaeghe, Ron J.
"Fertility and its Proximate Determinants in Sub-Saharan Africa: The Record of the 1960's and 70's." Brussels, Belgium: Vrije Universiteit Brussel. Interuniversity Programme in Demography. IPD Working Paper #1984-2. 1984. 117p.

Lesthaeghe, Ron J. and Ohadike, Patrick O. and Kocher, James E. and Page, Hilary J.
"Child-Spacing and Fertility in Sub-Saharan Africa: An Overview of Issues." (In) Page, Hilary J. and Lesthaeghe, Ron (eds.). Child-Spacing in Tropical Africa: Traditions and Change. New York: Academic Press. 1981. pp. 3-23.

Lewis, Barbara C.
"Fertility and Employment: An Assessment of Role

Incompatibility Among African Urban Women." (In) Bay, Edna G. Women and Work in Africa. Boulder, Colorado: Westview Press. Westview Special Studies. 1982. pp. 249-276.
Lightbourne, Robert E.
"Desired Number of Births and Prospects for Fertility Decline in 40 Countries." International Family Planning Perspectives. Volume 11 #2 June, 1985. pp. 34-39.
Lwanga, C.
"Infertility and Sub-Fertility in Africa." (In) International Planned Parenthood Federation (IPPF). Proceedings of the IPPF Africa Regional Conference. London: IPPF. 1977. pp. 85-95.
McFalls, Joseph A. and McFalls, Marguerite H.
Disease and Fertility. Orlando, Florida: Academic Press Inc. 1984. 593p.
Mondot-Bernard, Jacqueline M.
Relationships Between Fertility, Child Mortality and Nutrition in Africa: Tentative Analysis. Paris: Development Center of the Organization for Economic Co-Operation and Development. Technical Papers Series. 1977. 105p.
Mott, Frank L. and Mott, Susan H.
"Household Fertility Decision-Making in a West African Setting: Do Male and Female Surveys Lead to Similar Interpretations?" Worthington, Ohio: Ohio State University. Center for Human Resource Research. 1984.
Nagi, Mostafa H. and Stockwell, Edward G.
"Muslim Fertility: Recent Trends and Future Outlook." Journal of South Asian and Middle Eastern Studies. Volume 6 #2 Winter, 1982. pp. 48-70.
Nagi, Mostafa H.
"Trends and Differentials in Moslem Fertility." Journal of Biosocial Science. Volume 16 #2 April, 1984. pp. 189-204.
Neupert, Ricardo F. and Macrae, Sheila M.
"The Unequal Distribution of Fertility in Developing Countries." (In) Cairo Demographic Centre (CDC). Determinants of Fertility in Some African and Asian Countries. Cairo, Egypt: CDC. CDC Research Monograph Series #10. 1982. pp. 37-47.
Omran, Abdel R. and Johnston, Alan G.
Family Planning for Health in Africa. Chapel Hill, North Carolina: University of North Carolina. Carolina Population Center. 1984. 190p.
Oppong, Christine
"Some Aspects of Anthropological Contributions to the Study of Fertility." (In) Farooq, G.M. and Simmons, G.B. (eds.). Fertility in Developing Countries: An Economic Perspective on Research and Policy Issues. New York: St. Martin's Press. 1985.
Oppong, Christine and Adaba, Gemma and Bekomba-Priso, Manga and Mogey, J. (eds.)
Marriage, Fertility and Parenthood in West Africa. Canberra, Australia: Australian National University.

Department of Demography. Changing African Family Project. Monograph #4. Two Volumes. 1978. 848p.

Oucho, John O.
"Socio-Economic Perspectives of Fertility Regulation in Traditional and Modern African Societies." (In) University of Nairobi. Papers of the Seminar on Oral Traditions: Past Growth and Future Development in East Africa. Nairobi: University of Nairobi. UNESCO Institute of African Affairs. Kisumu, Kenya. April 18-22, 1979. 18p.

Retel-Laurentin, Anne
"Appraising the Role of Certain Diseases in Sterility: An African Example." Population. Volume 33 #1 January-February, 1978. pp. 101-120.

Reyna, Stephen P.
"Economics and Fertility: Waiting for the Demographic Transition in the Dry Zone of Francophone West Africa." (In) Caldwell, John C. (ed.). The Persistence of High Fertility: Population Prospects in the Third World." Canberra, Australia: Australian National University. Department of Demography. Volume One. 1977. pp. 393-426.

Rogers, Barbara
"Food, Fertility and Nuclear Mothers: How Development Can Increase Rather than Reduce the Social and Economic Burdens of African Women." Populi. Volume 5 #1 1978. pp. 23-27.

Schoenmaeckers, Ronald C.
Current Fertility Behavior in Africa: Results From a Birth Interval Analysis of World Fertility Survey Data. Brussels, Belgium: Vrije Universiteit Brussel. Inter-University Program in Demography. IPD Working Paper 1985-4. 1985. 24p.

Schutjer, Wayne A. and Stokes, C. Shannon
"Agricultural Policies and Human Fertility: Some Emerging Connections." Population Research and Policy Review. Volume 1 October, 1982. pp. 225-244.

Schutjer, Wayne A. and Stokes, C. Shannon
The Human Fertility Implications of Food and Agricultural Policies in Less-Developed Countries. University Park, Pennsylvania: Pennsylvania State University. College of Agriculture. Agriculture Experiment Station Bulletin #835. January, 1982. 14p.

Schutjer, Wayne A. and Stokes, C. Shannon (eds.)
Rural Development and Human Fertility. New York: MacMillan. 1984. 380p.

Seetharam, K.S. and Duza, M. Badrud
"Nuptiality and Fertility in Selected Areas of Four Arab and African Cities." (In) Huzayyin, S.A. and Acsadi, G.T. (eds.). Family and Marriage in Some African and Asiatic Countries. Cairo, Egypt: Cairo Demographic Centre. CDC Research Monograph Series #6. 1976. pp. 337-355.

Shields, Nwanganga G.
"Fertility and Economic Development in Africa, 1950-1970:

A Quantitative Analysis." Ph.D Dissertation: American University. Washington, D.C. 1976. 249p.
Shorter, Frederic C.
"Casual Interpretation of Observed Fertility Change." (In) Cairo Demographic Centre (CDC). Determinants of Fertility in Some African and Asian Countries. Cairo, Egypt: CDC. CDC Research Monograph Series #10. 1982. pp. 21-36.
Soyinka, Susan
"Family and Fertility in the West African Novel." (In) Caldwell, John C. (ed.). The Persistence of High Fertility: Population Prospects in the Third World. Canberra, Australia: Australian National University. Department of Demography. Volume One. 1977. pp. 427-450.
Strodtbeck, Fred L.
"Intimacy in Conjugal Interaction and the Capacity to Plan." (In) Oppong, C. and Adaba, G. and Bekombo-Priso, M. and Mogey, J. (eds.). Marriage, Fertility and Parenthood in West Africa. Canberra, Australia: Australian National University. Department of Demography. Volume Two. 1978. pp. 747-763.
Tabah, Leon
"Policy Implications of the Phenomenon of Rising Fertility in Response to Modernization." (In) Cairo Demographic Centre (CDC). Determinants of Fertility in Some African And Asian Countries. Cairo, Egypt: CDC. CDC Research Monograph Series #10. 1982. pp. 13-19.
Tabutin, Dominique
"Fertility and Mortality in African Censuses Over the Last Twenty-Five Years." Population. Volume 39 March-April, 1984. pp. 295-312.
Ukaegbu, Alfred O.
"Marriage Habits and Fertility of Women in Tropical Africa: A Socio-Cultural Perspective." (In) Dupaquier, J. and Helin, E. and Laslett, P. and Livi-Bacci, M. (eds.). Marriage and Remarriage in Populations of the Past. New York: Academic Press. Population and Social Structure: Advances in Historical Demography Series. 1981. pp. 127-137.
United Nations Economic Commission for Africa (UNECA)
Some Fertility Indicators and Their Implications for Africa. Addis Ababa, Ethiopia: UNECA. African Population Studies Series #3. 1979. 51p.
Valentine, C.H. and Revson, J.E.
"Cultural Traditions, Social Change, and Fertility in Sub-Saharan Africa." Journal of Modern African Studies. Volume 17 #3 September, 1979. pp. 453-472.
Ward, Kathryn B.
Women in the Third World-System: Its Impact on Status and Fertility. New York: Praeger Publishers. 1984. 191p.
Ware, Helen
"Security in the City: The Role of the Family in Urban West Africa." (In) Ruzicka, Lado T. (ed.). The Economic and Social Supports for High Fertility: Proceedings of

the Conference Held in Canberra, November 16-18, 1976. Canberra, Australia: Australian National University. Development Studies Center. 1977. pp. 385-408.

Ware, Helen
"Women's Work and Fertility in Africa." (In) Kupinsky, Stanley (ed.). The Fertility of Working Women: A Synthesis of International Research. New York: Praeger Publishers. Praeger Special Studies in International Economics and Development. 1977. pp. 1-34.

Youssef, Nadia H.
"The Status and Fertility Patterns of Muslim Women." (In) Beck, Lois and Keddie, Nikki R. (eds.). Women in the Muslim World. Cambridge, Massachusetts: Harvard University Press. 1978. pp. 69-99.

Youssef, Nadia H.
"Interrelationship Between the Division of Labor in the Household, Women's Roles and Their Impact Upon Fertility." Paper Presented at the Informal Workshop on Women's Roles and Demographic Research Program. Geneva: International Labour Organization. November, 1978.

Health, Nutrition and Medicine

Adadevoh, B. Kwaku
"Sub-Fertility and Infertility in Africa." (In) International Planned Parenthood Federation (IPPF). Proceedings of the IPPF Africa Regional Conference. London: IPPF. 1977. pp. 80-84.

Adegbola, O.
"New Estimates of Fertility and Child Mortality in Africa, South of the Sahara." Population Studies(London). Volume 31 #3 1977. pp. 467-486.

Alausa, O. and Osoba, A.O.
"The Role of Sexually Transmitted Diseases in Male Infertility in Tropical Africa." Nigerian Medical Journal. Volume 8 #3 May, 1978. pp. 225-229.

Anonymous
"Mothers, Babies and Health." Agenda. Volume 1 #2 February, 1978. pp. 8-14.

Anonymous
"Women, Food and Nutrition in Africa: Economic Change and the Outlook for Nutrition." Food and Nutrition. Volume 10 #1 1984. pp. 71-79.

Anonymous
"Women Against Mutilation." Off Our Backs. Volume 9 December, 1979. pp. 7.

Appelbaum, P.C. and Ross, S.M. and Dhupelia, I. and Naeye, R.L.
"The Effect of Diet Supplementation and Addition of Zinc in Vitro on the Growth Supporting Property of Amniotic Fluid in African Women." American Journal of Obstetrics and Gynacology. Volume 135 #1 September, 1979. pp. 82-84.

Bates, C.J. and Whitehead, Roger G.
"The Effect of Vitamin C Supplementation on Lactating Women in Keneba, a West African Rural Community." International Journal of Vitamin Nutrition Research. Volume 53 #1 1982. pp. 68-76.

Bates, C.J. and Prentice, Andrew M. and Prentice, Ann and Whitehead, Roger G.
"Vitamin C Supplementation of Lactating Women in Keneba: A West African Rural Community." Proceedings of the Nutrition Society. Volume 41 #3 1982. pp. 124A.

Beddada, Belletech
"Traditional Practices in Relation to Pregnancy and Childbirth." Paper Presented at the Seminar on Traditional Practices Affecting the Health of Women and Children. World Conference of the United Nations Decade for Women. New York: United Nations. Copenhagen, Denmark. July 14-30, 1980.

Belsey, Mark A.
"Biological Factors Other Than Nutrition and Lactation Which May Influence Natural Fertility: Additional Notes With Particular Reference to Sub-Saharan Africa." Paper Presented at the International Union for the Scientific Study of Population Seminar on Natural Fertility. Leige, Belgium: IUSSP. Paris, France. 1977.

Belsey, Mark A.
"Biological Factors Other Than Nutrition and Lactation Which May Influence Natural Fertility: Additional Notes With Particular Reference to Sub-Saharan Africa." (In) Leridon, Henri and Menken, Jane (eds.). Natural Fertility: Patterns and Determinants of Natural Fertility. Liege, Belgium: International Union for the Scientific Study of Population. 1979. pp. 253-272.

Belsey. Mark A.
"The Epidemiology of Infertility: A Review With Particular Reference to Sub-Saharan Africa." Bulletin of the World Health Organization. Volume 54 #3 1976. pp. 319-341.

Blair, P.W.
The Health Needs of the World's Poor Women. (In) "Proceedings of the International Symposium on Women and Their Health." Washington D.C.: Equity Policy Center. June 8-11, 1980.

Bongaarts, John and Frank, Odile and Lesthaeghe, Ron J.
"The Proximate Determinants of Fertility in Sub-Saharan Africa." Population and Developement Review. Volume 10 #3 September, 1984. pp. 511-538+.

Boulware-Miller, Kay
"Female Circumcision: Challenges to the Practice as a Human Rights Violation." Harvard Women's Law Journal. Volume 8 Spring, 1985. pp. 155-177.

Bukh, Jette
"Women in Food Production, Food Handling and Nutrition." Paper Presented to the Association of African Women for Research and Development (AAWORD) Workshop. Dakar, Senegal: AAWORD. December, 1977.

Cairo Demographic Center (CDC)
Determinants of Fertility in Some African And Asian Countries. Cairo, Egypt: CDC. CDC Research Monograph Series #10. 1982. 698p.

Caldwell, John C. and Caldwell, Pat
"The Demographic Evidence for the Incidence and Cause of Abnormally Low Fertility in Tropical Africa." World Health Statistics Quarterly. Volume 36 #1 1983. pp. 2-34.

Caldwell, John C.
Fertility in Africa. (In) Eberstadt, Nick (ed.). Fertility Decline in the Less Developed Countries. New York: Praeger Publishers. Praeger Special Studies. 1981. pp. 97-118.

Caldwell, John C. and Caldwell, Pat
"Demographic and Contraceptive Innovators: A Study of Transitional African Society." Journal of Biosocial Science. Volume 8 #4 October, 1976. pp. 347-366.

Cantrelle, Pierre and Ferry, Benoit and Mondot, J.
"Relationships Between Fertility and Mortality in Tropical Africa." (In) Preston, Samuel H. (ed.). The Effects of Infant and Child Mortality on Fertility. New York: Academic Press. 1978. pp. 181-205.

Cates, W. and Farley, T.M. and Rowe, P.J.
"Worldwide Patterns of Infertility: Is Africa Different?" Lancet. #8455 September 14, 1985. pp. 596-598.

Chi, C. and Miller, E.R. and Fortney, J.A. and Bernard, Roger P.
"A Study of Abortion in Countries Where Abortions are Legally Restricted." Journal of Reproductive Medicine. Volume 18 #1 January, 1977. pp. 15-26.

Cook, Rebecca J. and Dickens, Bernard M.
"A Decade of International Change in Abortion Law: 1967-1977." American Journal of Public Health. Volume 68 #7 July, 1978. pp. 637-644.

Cosminsky, Sheila
"The Role and Training of Traditional Midwives: Policy Implications for Maternal and Child Health Care." Paper Presented at the Annual Meeting of the African Studies Association. Paper #17. Houston, Texas. 1977. 25p.

Cox, J.L.
"Postnatal Depression--A Comparison of African and Scottish Women." Social Psychiatry. Volume 18 #1 1983. pp. 25-28.

Di Domenico, Catherine M. and Asuni, Judy and Scott, Jacqueline
"Family Welfare and Development in Africa." (In) International Planned Parenthood Federation (IPPF). Proceedings of the IPPF Africa Regional Conference, University of Ibadan. London: IPPF. 1976. pp. 283-284.

Diallo, B.
"The Dream of Domination." World Health. April, 1985. pp. 26-28.

Eberstadt, Nick (ed.)
Fertility Decline in the Less Developed Countries. New York: Praeger Publishers. Praeger Special Studies. 1981. 370p.

Eide, Wenche B. and Skjonsberg, Else and Pala, Achola O. and Bathily, Abjoulaye
"Women in Food Production, Food Handling and Nutrition With Special Emphasis on Africa." PAG Bulletin. Volume 7 #3/4 Sept.-Dec., 1977. pp. 40-49.
Eide, Wenche B. and Steady, Filomina C.
"Individual and Social Energy Flows: Bridging Nutritional and Anthropological Thinking About Women's Work in Rural Africa: Some Theoretical Considerations." (In) Jerome, Norge W. and Kandel, Randy F. and Pelto, Gretel H. (eds.). Nutritional Anthropology: Contemporary Approach to Diet and Culture. New York: Redgrave Publishing. 1980. pp. 61-84.
Eide, Wenche B. and Skjonsberg, Else and Bathily, Abjoulaye and Pala, Achola O. and Krystall, Abigail and Millwood, D.
Women in Food Production, Food Handling and Nutrition With Special Emphasis on Africa. Final Report. New York: United Nations. Protein-Calorie Advisory Group of the U.N. System. FAO Food and Nutrition Paper #8. June, 1977. 224p.
Ekanem, Ita I.
"Prospects of Fertility Decline in Sub-Saharan Africa." Population Studies. #67 1979. pp. 174-196.
El-Badry, M.A.
"Determinants of Fertility in African and Asian Countries: An Introductory Overview." (In) Cairo Demographic Centre (CDC). Determinants of Fertility in Some African and Asian Countries." Cairo, Egypt: CDC. CDC Monograph Series #10. 1982. pp. 3-11.
Ember, C.R.
"Relative Decline in Women's Contribution to Agriculture With Intensification." American Anthropologist. Volume 85 #2 June, 1983. pp. 285-304.
Farmer, A.E. and Falkowski, W.F. (eds.)
"Maggot in the Salt: The Snake Factor and the Treatment of a Typical Psychosis in West African Women." British Journal of Psychiatry. Volume 146 April, 1985. pp. 446-447.
Fikry, M.
Traditional Maternal and Child Health Care and Related Problems in the Sahel: A Bibliographic Study. Washington, D.C.: U.S. Department of State. U.S. Agency for International Development. Sahel Development Project. 1977. 123p.
Frank, Odile
Infertility in Sub-Saharan Africa. New York: Population Council. Center for Population Studies. Working Working Paper #97. June, 1983. 107p.
Frank, Odile
"Infertility in Sub-Saharan Africa: Estimates and Implications." Population and Development Review. Volume 9 #1 March, 1983. pp. 137-144+.
Frank, Odile
The Demand for Fertility Control in Sub-Saharan Africa.

New York: Population Council. Center for Policy Studies. Working Paper #117. November, 1985. 50p.

Franke, R.
"Mode of Production and Population Patterns: Policy Implications for West African Development." International Journal of Health Services. Volume 13 1981. pp. 361-387.

Geletkanycz, Christine and Egan, Susan
Literature Review: The Practice of Female Circumcision. Washington, D.C.: U.S. Department of Health, Education and Welfare. Office of International Health. Mimeo. 1979.

Ghulam, L.J.
"Early Teenage Childbirth, Consequences of This for Child and Mother." Paper Presented at the Seminar on Traditional Practices Affecting the Health of Women and Children. World Conference of the United Nations Decade for Women. Copenhagen, Denmark. July 14-30, 1980.

Gordon, Gill
"Important Issues for Feminist Nutrition Research: A Case Study From the Savanna of West Africa." IDS Bulletin. Volume 15 #1 1984. pp. 38-44.

Gray, R.H.
"Birth Intervals, Postpartum Sexual Abstinence and Child Health." (In) Page, Hilary J. and Lesthaeghe, Ron (eds.). Child-Spacing in Tropical Africa: Traditions and Change. New York: Academic Press. 1981. pp. 93-109.

Guest, Iain
"Special Report: Infertility in Africa." People (London). Volume 5 #1 1978. pp. 23-34.

Gyepi-Garbrah, Benjamin and Nichols, Douglas J. and Kpedekpo, Gottlieb M.
Adolescent Fertility in Sub-Saharan Africa: An Overview. Boston: Pathfinder Fund. 1985. 51p.

Hamilton, Sahni and Popkin, Barry M. and Spicer, Deborah
Women and Nutrition in Third World Countries. New York: Praeger Publishers. 1984. 147p.

Hawthorn, Geoffrey (ed.)
Population and Development: High and Low Fertility in Poorer Countries. London: Frank Cass. 1978. 210p.

Henin, Roushdi A.
"Fertility, Infertility and Sub-Fertility in Eastern Africa." (In) International Union for the Scientic Study of Population (IUSSP). International Population Conference: Solicited Papers. Liege, Netherland: IUSSP. Volume Three. 1981. pp. 667-697.

Hill, Allan G. (ed.)
Population, Health and Nutrition in the Sahel: Issues in the Welfare of Selected West African Communities. Boston: KPI. 1985. 399p.

Hosken, Fran P.
"A Crucial New Direction for International Family Planning." Humanist. Volume 44 #1 January-February, 1984.

Hosken, Fran P.
"Women and Health: Genital And Sexual Mutilation of Females." International Journal of Women's Studies. Volume 3 #3 May-June, 1980. pp. 300-316.

Hosken, Fran P.
"The Violence of Power: The Genital Mutilation of Females." Heresies. Volume 6 #2 Summer, 1978. pp. 28-36.

Hosken, Fran P.
"Female Circumcision in Africa." Victimology. Volume 2 #3/4 1977. pp. 487-498.

Hosken, Fran P.
"Genital Mutilation of Women in Africa." Munger Africana Library Notes. #36 October, 1976. 21p.

Hosken, Fran P.
"Towards an Epidemiology of Genital Mutilation of Females in Africa." Paper Presented at the Annual Meeting of the African Studies Association. Paper #43. Baltimore, Maryland. 1978. 20p.

Hosken, Fran P.
The Hosken Report: Genital and Sexual Mutilation of Females. Lexington, Massachusetts: Women's International Network News. 1982. 327p.

Hosken, Fran P.
Female Sexual Mutilations: The Facts and Proposals for Action. Lexington, Massachusetts: Women's International Network News. 1980. 102p.

Hosken, Fran P.
"Female Genital Mutilation in the World Today: A Global Review." International Journal of Health Services. Volume 11 #3 1981. pp. 415-430.

Hosken, Fran P.
"Female Circumcision and Fertility in Africa." Women and Health. Volume 1 #6 Nov.-Dec., 1976. pp. 3-11.

Hosken, Fran P.
"The Epidemiology of Female Genital Mutilation." Tropical Doctor. July, 1978. pp. 150-156.

Hosken, Fran P.
"Women and Health in East and West Africa: Family Planning and Female Cicumcision." Paper Presented at the Seminar on Traditional Practices Affecting the Health of Women and Children. World Conference of the United Nations Decade for Women. New York: United Nations. Copenhagen, Denmark. July 14-30, 1980.

Hosken, Fran P.
"Women and Health in East and West Africa: Family Planning and Female Circumcision." Paper Presented at the Seminar on Traditional Practices Affecting the Health of Women and Children: Female Circumcision, Childhood Marriage, Nutritional Taboos, etc. Alexandria, Egypt: World Health Organization. Eastern Mediterranean Regional Office. Khartoum, Sudan. February 10-15, 1979.

Hosken, Fran P.
"Female Circumcision in the World of Today: A Global Review." Paper Presented at the Seminar on Traditional

Practices Affecting the Health of Women and Children. World Conference of the United Nations Decade for Women. New York: United Nations. Copenhagen, Denmark. July 14-30, 1980.

Hosken, Fran P.
"Female Circumcision in the World of Today: A Global View." Paper Presented at the Seminar on Traditional Practices Affecting the Health of Women and Children: Female Circumcision, Childhood Marriage, Nutritional Taboos, etc. Alexandria, Egypt: World Health Organization. Eastern Mediterranean Regional Office. Khartoum, Sudan. February 10-15, 1979.

Huelsman, Ben R.
"An Anthropological View of Clitoral and Other Female Genital Mutilations." (In) Lowery, T.P. and Lowery, T.S. (eds.). The Clitoris. St. Louis, Missouri: Warren H. Green. 1976. pp. 111-161.

International Development Research Centre (IDRC)
Nutritional Status of the Rural Population of the Sahel: Report of a Working Group, Paris, France, April 28-29, 1980. Ottawa, Canada: IDRC. 1981. 92p.

Isley, R.
Medical, Socio-Cultural, Economic and Psychological Correlates of Childlessness in Africa. Research Triangle Park, North Carolina: Research Triangle Institute. RTI Concept Paper #24-CP-80-01. 1980.

Jett, Joyce
The Role of Traditional Midwives in the Modern Health Sector in West and Central Africa. Washington, D.C.: U.S. Department of State. U.S. Agency for International Development. January, 1977. 150p.

Jett, Joyce
The Role of Traditional Midwives in the Modern Health Sector in West and Central Africa. Washington, D.C.: U.S. Department of State. U.S. Agency for International Development. January, 1977. 150p.

Johnson, B.C.
"Traditional Practices Affecting the Health of Women." Paper Presented at the Seminar on Traditional Practices Affecting the Health of Women and Children. World Conference of the United Nations Decade for Women. New York: United Nations. Copenhagen, Denmark. July 14-30, 1980.

Johnson, B.C.
"Traditional Practices Affecting the Health of Women." Paper Presented at the Seminar on Traditional Practices Affecting the Health of Women and Children. World Conference of the United Nations Decade for Women. New York: United Nations. Copenhagen, Denmark. July 14-30, 1980.

Johnston, Bruce F. and Meyer, Anthony J.
"Nutrition, Health and Population in Strategies for Rural Development." Economic Development and Cultural Change. Volume 26 #1 October, 1977. pp. 1-23.

Johnston, Bruce F. and Meyer, Anthony J.
"Nutrition, Health and Population in Strategies for Rural Development." Nairobi: University of Nairobi. Institute for Development Studies. Discussion Paper #238. 1976. 45p.
Jorgensen, Kirsten
"Water Supply Projects in Africa: The Need to Involve the Main Users--Women." Ideas and Action Bulletin. #150 1983. pp. 14-18.
Kamanga, Kawaye
"The Dilemma of High Fertility in Sub-Saharan Africa." Ph.D Dissertation: University of Pittsburgh. Pittsburgh, Pennsylvania. 1985. 140p.
Karoun, Haddad O.
"Adolescent Pregnancy and Childbirth." Paper Presented at the Seminar on Traditional Practices Affecting the Health and Children. World Conference of the United Nations Decade for Women. New York: United Nations. Copenhagen, Denmark. July 14-30, 1980.
Kazeze, Z.W.
"Review of Some Determinants of Fertility in Africa." (In) Cairo Demographic Centre (CDC). Determinants of Fertility in Some African and Asian Countries. Cairo, Egypt: CDC. CDC Research Monograph Series #10. 1982. pp. 391-414.
Keller, Bonnie B.
"Marriage and Medicine: Women's Search for Love and Luck." African Social Research. #26 December, 1978. pp. 489-505.
Kenton, J.
"Health of Women and Children in Africa." Midwives Chronicle. Volume 98 #1165 February, 1985. pp. 44-45.
Kouba, Leonard J. and Muasher, Judith
"Female Circumcision in Africa: An Overview." African Studies Review. Volume 28 #1 1985. pp. 95-110.
Kpedekpo, Gottlieb M.
"Age Patterns of Fertility in Selected African Countries." Jimlar Mutane. Volume 1 #1 February, 1976. pp. 9-26.
Kusin, Jane A. and Thiuri, B. and Lakhani, S.A. and Tmannetje, J.W.
"Anthropometric Changes During Pregnancy in Rural African Women." Tropical and Geographic Medicine. Volume 36 #1 1984. pp. 91-97.
Kuteyi, P.V.
"Nutritional Needs of the Child Especially in the First Year." Paper Presented at the Seminar on Traditional Practices Affecting the Health of Women and Children. World Conference of the United Nations Decade for Women. New York: United Nations. Copenhagen, Denmark. July 14-30, 1980.
Ladipo, O.A.
"The Role of Artificial Insemimation in the Management of Infertility." East African Medical Journal. Volume 56 #5 May, 1979. pp. 219-222.

Last, Murray
"Strategies Against Time." Sociology of Health and Illness. Volume 1 #3 December, 1979. pp. 306-317.

LeVine, Robert A. and Dixon, Suzanne and LeVine, Sarah
"High Fertility in Africa: A Consideration of Causes and Consequences." Paper Presented at the Annual Meeting of the African Studies Association. Paper #48. Boston, Massachusetts. 1976. 18p.

Leke, R. and Nash, B.
"Biological and Socio-Cultural Aspects of Infertility and Subfertility in Africa." (In) United Nations Economic Commission for Africa (UNECA). Population Dynamics: Fertility and Mortality in Africa. Addis Ababa, Ethiopia: UNECA. May, 1981. pp. 488-498.

Lesthaeghe, Ron J.
"Fertility and its Proximate Determinants in Sub-Saharan Africa: The Record of the 1960's and 70's." Brussels, Belgium: Vrije Universiteit Brussel. Interuniversity Programme in Demography. IPD Working Paper #1984-2. 1984. 117p.

Lewis, Barbara C.
"Fertility and Employment: An Assessment of Role Incompatibility Among African Urban Women." (In) Bay, Edna G. Women and Work in Africa. Boulder, Colorado: Westview Press. Westview Special Studies. 1982. pp. 249-276.

Lightbourne, Robert E.
"Desired Number of Births and Prospects for Fertility Decline in 40 Countries." International Family Planning Perspectives. Volume 11 #2 June, 1985. pp. 34-39.

Liskin, L.S.
"Complications of Abortion in Developing Countries." Population Reports. #F-7 July, 1980. pp. 107-155.

Lwanga, C.
"Infertility and Sub-Fertility in Africa." (In) International Planned Parenthood Federation (IPPF). Proceedings of the IPPF Africa Regional Conference. London: IPPF. 1977. pp. 85-95.

MacCormack, Carol P.
"Biological Events and Cultural Control." Signs. Volume 3 #1 Autumn, 1977. pp. 93-100.

Mahran, M.
"Medical Dangers of Female Circumcision." International Planned Parenthood Federation (IPPF) Medical Bulletin. Volume 15 #2 April, 1981.

Makundi, K. and Warioba, Evelyn
"Psychological Relationship Between Men and Women." Paper Presented at the Workshop on Women's Studies and Development. Dar-es-Salaam, Tanzania: University of Dar-es-Salaam. Bureau of Resource Assessment and Land Use Planning. Paper #27. September 24-29, 1979. 5p.

Mati, J.K. and Mbugua, S. and Ndavi, M.
"Control of Cancer of the Cervix: Feasibility of Screening for Premalignant Lesions in an African

Enviroment." IARC Science Publications. Volume 63 1984. pp. 451-463.
Mati, J.K.
"Focusing on Maternal Mortality and Morbidity." East African Medical Journal. Volume 57 #2 February, 1980. pp. 70-71.
Mati, J.K.
Abortion in Africa. (In) International Planned Parenthood Federation (IPPF). Proceedings of the IPPF Africa Regional Conference. London: IPPF. 1977. pp. 74-79.
Mbevi, Grace and Njoki, Margaret
"Traditional Practices in Relation to Child Health." Paper Presented at the Seminar on Traditional Practices Affecting the Health of Women and Children. World Conference of the United Nations Decade for Women. New York: United Nations. Copenhagen, Denmark. July 14-30, 1980.
McFalls, Joseph A. and McFalls, Marguerite H.
Disease and Fertility. Orlando, Florida: Academic Press Inc. 1984. 593p.
McLean, Scilla
"Female Genital Mutilation." ISIS Women's International Bulletin. #25 1982. pp. 26-32.
McLean, Scilla and Graham, Stella E.
Female Circumcision, Excision and Infibulation: The Fact and Proposals for Change. London: Minority Rights Group. Report #47. Second Revised Edition. 1985. 21p.
Meumaun, Alfred K.
"Integration of Family Planning and Maternal and Child Health in Rural West Africa." Journal of Biosocial Science. Volume 8 #2 April, 1976. pp. 161-174.
Mgone, C.S.
"Reproductive Behavior and Attitudes of African Mothers Following Birth of a Downs Syndrome Child." East African Medical Journal. Volume 59 #8 1982. pp. 555-559.
Moen, Elizabeth W.
Genital Mutilation: Everywoman's Problem. East Lansing, Michigan: Michigan State University. Office of Women in International Development. Working Paper #22. April, 1983.
Mojekwu, V. and Omojola, B. and Randriamanana, C.
"African Women Blaze a Trail." World Health. April, 1985. pp. 24-26.
Mondot-Bernard, Jacqueline M.
Relationships Between Fertility, Child Mortality and Nutrition in Africa: Tentative Analysis. Paris: Development Center of the Organization for Economic Co-Operation and Development. Technical Papers Series. 1977. 105p.
Monreal, T. and Nasah, B.T.
"Illegal Abortion in Selected African Capital Cities, 1976." (In) Sai, Fred T. (ed.). A Strategy for Abortion Management: A Report of the IPPF Africa Regional Workshop, March 20-23, 1978. London: International

Planned Parenthood Federation. Nairobi, Kenya. 1978. pp. 48-91.

Mukhtar, Behiza
"A Question of Our Children's Bodies: The Medical Injury Caused to a Girl by Circumcision." Paper Presented at the Conference on Islam and Family Planning. Sponsored by the International Planned Parenthood Federation. Banjul, Gambia. October 21-24, 1979. 7p.

Nelson, Cynthia (ed.)
Women, Health and Development: Papers Presented at the 1976 Open University Seminar. Cairo, Egypt: American University of Cairo. Cairo Papers in Social Sciences. Volume One. Monograph One. 1977. 84p.

Omran, Abdel R. and Johnston, Alan G.
Family Planning for Health in Africa. Chapel Hill, North Carolina: University of North Carolina. Carolina Population Center. 1984. 190p.

Osoba, A.O.
"Sexually Transmitted Diseases in Tropical Africa: A Review." British Journal of Veneral Diseases. Volume 57 #2 April, 1981. pp. 89-94.

Phillott-Almeida, Ralphina
"Women and Water Resources Management for Socio-Economic Development in Africa: Health, Sanitation and Environmental Aspects." (In) United Nations Economic Commission for Africa (UNECA) (eds.). Regional Meeting on Socio-Economic and Policy Aspects of Water Management in Africa. Addis Ababa, Ethiopia: UNECA. June, 1986.

Pieters, Guy and Lowenfels, A.
"Infibulation in the Horn of Africa." New York State Journal of Medicine. Volume 77 April, 1977. pp. 729-731.

Prentice, Andrew M. and Prentice, Ann and Lamb, W.H. and Lunn, P.G. and Austin, S.
"Metabolic Consequences of Fasting During Ramadan in Pregnant and Lactating Women." Human Nutrition. Clinical Nutrition. Volume 37 #4 July, 1983. pp. 283-294.

Prentice, Andrew M. and Cole, Tim J.
"Prenatal Dietary Supplementation of African Women and Birth-Weight." Lancet. #8323 March 5, 1983. pp. 489-492.

Rahal, K.
"In Face of the Bacterial Menace, Sex Inequality is Forgotten in Research." Impact of Science on Society. Volume 30 #1 January-March, 1980. pp. 43-45.

Ramachandran, K.V. and Venkatacharya, K. and Teklu, Tesfay
Fertility and Mortality Levels, Patterns and Trends in Some Anglophone African Countries. Legon, Ghana: United Nations Regional Institute for Population Studies. 1979. 78p.

Reinhardt, Michael C. and Ambroise-Thomas, P. and Cavallo-Serra, R. and Meylan, C. and Gautier, R.
"Malaria at Delivery in Abidjan." Helvetica Paediatrica Acta. Volume 33 Supp. 41 1978. pp. 65.

Retel-Laurentin, Anne
"Appraising the Role of Certain Diseases in Sterility: An African Example." Population. Volume 33 #1 January-February, 1978. pp. 101-120.
Richardson, Barbara D. and Pieters, Linda
"Menarche and Growth." American Journal of Clinical Nutrition. Volume 30 #12 December, 1977. pp. 2088-2091.
Rosenberg, E.M.
"Demographic Effects of Sex Differential Nutrition." (In) Jerome, Norge W. and Kandel, Randy F. and Pelto, Gretel H. (eds.). Nutritional Anthropology. Pleasantville, New York: Redgrave Publishing. 1980. pp. 181-201.
Rosenfield, A. and Maine, D. and Gorosh, M.E.
"Non Clinical Distribution of the Pill in the Developing World." International Family Planning Perspectives. Volume 6 December, 1980. pp. 130-136.
Ross, S.M. and Nel, E. and Naeye, R.L.
"Differing Effects of Low and High Bulk Maternal Dietary Supplements During Pregnancy." Early Human Development. Volume 10 #3/4 January, 1985. pp. 295-302.
Royston, E.
"The Prevalence of Nutritional Anemia in Women in Developing Countries: A Critical Review of Available Information." World Health Statistics Quarterly. Volume 35 #2 1982. pp. 52-91.
Sai, Fred T.
"Report of the Conference on the Medical and Social Aspects of Abortion in Africa." (In) Sai, F.T. (ed.). A Strategy for Abortion Management. London: International Planned Parenthood Federation. 1978. pp 6-22.
Sai, Fred T.
Defining Family Health Needs, Standards of Care and Priorities, With Particular Reference to Family Planning. London: International Planned Parenthood Federation. 1977. 32p.
Sai, Fred T.
"The Place of Nutrition in Family Planning Programs in Africa." Paper Presented at the International Planned Parenthood Federation Refresher Course for Clinical Supervisors. Nairobi. November 24-28, 1980.
Sala-Diakanda, Mpembele
"Problems of Infertility and Sub-Fertility in West and Central Africa." (In) International Union for the Scientific Study of Population (IUSSP). International Population Conference. Papers of the 19th General Conference. Liege, Belgium: IUSSP. Volume Three. 1981. pp. 643-666.
Sanderson, Lilian P.
Against the Mutilation of Women: The Struggle Against Unnecessary Suffering. London: Ithaca Press. 1981. 117p.
Seetharam, K.S. and Duza, M. Badrud
"Nuptiality and Fertility in Selected Areas of Four Arab

and African Cities." (In) Huzayyin, S.A. and Acsadi, G.T. (eds.). Family and Marriage in Some African and Asiatic Countries. Cairo, Egypt: Cairo Demographic Centre. CDC Research Monograph Series #6. 1976. pp. 337-355.

Shaalan, Mohammed
"Clitoris Envy: A Psychodynamic Construct Instrumental in Female Circumcision." Paper Presented at the Seminar on Traditional Practices Affecting the Health of Women and Children. World Conference of the United Nations Decade for Women. New York: United Nations. Copenhagen, Denmark. July 14-30, 1980.

Shaalan, Mohammed
"Clitoris Envy: A Psychdynamic Construct Instrumental in Female Circumcision." Paper Presented at the Seminar on Traditional Practices Affecting the Health of Women and Children: Female Circumcision, Childhood Marriage, Nutritional Taboos, etc. Alexandria, Egypt: World Health Organization. Eastern Mediterranean Regional Office. Khartoum, Sudan. February 10-15, 1979.

Shazali, Hafez El
"Breast and Supplementary Feeding During Early Childhood." Paper Presented at the Seminar on Traditional Practices Affecting the Health of Women and Children: Female Circumcision, Childhood Marriage, Nutritional Taboos, etc. Alexandria, Egypt: World Health Organization. Eastern Mediterranean Regional Office. Khartoum, Sudan. February 10-15, 1979.

Shorter, Frederic C.
"Casual Interpretation of Observed Fertility Change." (In) Cairo Demographic Centre (CDC). Determinants of Fertility in Some African and Asian Countries. Cairo, Egypt: CDC. CDC Research Monograph Series #10. 1982. pp. 21-36.

Sindzingre, N.
"Plus and Minus--Concerning Female Circumcision." Cahiers d'Etudes Africaines. Volume 17 #1 1977. pp. 65-76.

Taba, A.H.
"Female Circumcision." World Health. May, 1979. pp. 8-13.

Taba, A.H.
"Female Circumcision." (In) World Health Organization. Traditional Practices Affecting the Health of Women and Children: Female Circumcision, Childhood Marriage, Nutritional Taboos, etc. Report of a Seminar, Khartoum, Sudan, February 10-15, 1979. Alexandria, Egypt: WHO/EMRO Technical Publication #2. 1979. pp. 43-52.

Thiam, Awa
"Women's Fight for the Abolition of Sexual Mutilation." International Social Science Journal. Volume 35 #4 1983. pp. 747-756.

United Nations Economic Commission for Africa (UNECA)
Some Fertility Indicators and Their Implications for

Africa. Addis Ababa, Ethiopia: UNECA. African Population Studies Series #3. 1979. 51p.

United States Department of Health and Human Services
Family Planning Methods and Practice: Africa. Atlanta, Georgia: U.S. Department of Health and Human Services. Centers for Disease Control. Center for Health Promotion and Education. 1983. 329p.

Watkinson, M. and Rushton, D.I.
"Plasmodial Pigmentation of Placenta and Outcome of Pregnancy in West African Mothers." British Medical Journal. Volume 287 #6387 July 23, 1983. pp. 251-254.

Weisner, Thomas S. and Abbott, Susan
"Women, Modernity and Stress: Three Contrasting Contexts for Change in East Africa." Southwestern Journal of Anthropology. Volume 33 #4 Winter, 1977. pp. 421-451.

World Health Organization (WHO)
Traditional Practices Affecting the Health of Women and Children: Female Circumcision, Childhood Marriage, Nutritional Taboos, etc. Report of a Seminar, Khartoum, Sudan, February 10-15, 1979. Alexandria, Egypt: WHO. Eastern Mediterranean Regional Office. Technical Publication #2. 1979. 170p.

Wulf, Deirdre
"The Future of Family Planning in Sub-Saharan Africa." International Family Planning Perspectives. Volume 11 #1 March, 1985. pp. 1-8.

History

Adamson, Kay
"Approaches to the Study of Women in North Africa: As Reflected in Research of Various Scholars." Maghreb Review. Volume 3 #7-8 May-August, 1978. pp. 22-31.

Alpers, Edward
"The Story of Swema: Female Vulnerability in Nineteenth-Century East Africa." (In) Robertson, Claire C. and Klein, Martin A. (eds.). Women and Slavery in Africa. Madison, Wisconsin: University of Wisconsin Press. 1983. pp. 185-219.

Amin, Samir
Imperialism and Unequal Development. New York: Monthly Review Press. 1977.

Badran, Margot F.
"Middle East and North Africa: Women." Trends in History. Volume 1 #1 1979. pp. 123-129.

Barthel, D.
"Women's Educational Experience Under Colonialism: Toward a Diachronic Model." Signs. Volume 11 Autumn, 1985. pp. 137-154.

Berrian, Brenda F.
Bibliography of African Women Writers and Journalists (Ancient Egypt-1984). Washington, D.C.: Three Continents Press. 1985. 279p.

Bingham, Marjorie W. and Gross, Susan H.
Women in Africa of the Sub-Sahara. Hudson, Wisconsin: Gem Publishers. Volume One: Ancient Times to the Twentieth Century. Volume Two: The Twentieth Century. 1982. 260p.

Bisilliat, Jeanne
"The Feminine Sphere in the Institutions of Songhay-Zarma." (In) Oppong, Christine (ed.). Female and Male in West Africa. London: George Allen and Unwin. 1983. pp. 99-106.

Campbell, Penelope
"Presbyterian West African Missions: Women as Converts

and Agents of Social Change." Journal of Presbyterian History. Volume 56 #2 Summer, 1978. pp. 121-132.

De Sardan, Jean-Pierre O.
"The Songhay-Zarma Female Slave: Relations of Production and Ideological Status." (In) Robertson, Claire C. and Klein, Martin A. (eds.). Women and Slavery in Africa. Madison, Wisconsin: University of Wisconsin Press. 1983. pp. 130-143.

Denzer, LaRay
"Women in the West African Nationalist Movement From 1939-1950." Africana Research Review. Volume 7 #4 July, 1976. pp. 65-85.

Ekechi, Felix K.
"African Polygamy and Western Christian Ethnocentrism." Journal of African Studies. Volume 3 #3 August, 1976. pp. 329-349.

Fields, Karen E.
"Political Contingencies of Witchcraft in Colonial Central Africa." Canadian Journal of African Studies. Volume 16 #3 1982. pp. 567-593.

Hall, Richard
Lovers on the Nile: The Incredible African Journeys of Sam and Florence Baker. New York: Random House. 1980. 254p.

Hay, Margaret J. and Wright, Marcia (eds.)
African Women and the Law: Historical Perspectives. Boston, Masachusetts: Boston University. African Studies Center. Boston University Papers on Africa. Volume 7. 1982. 173p.

Henn, Jeanne K.
"Women in the Rural Economy: Past, Present and Future." (In) Hay, Margaret J. and Stichter, Sharon (eds.). African Women South of the Sahara. New York: Longman. 1984. pp. 1-18.

Imam, Ayesha M.
"The Presentation of African Women Through History." Paper Presented at the Meeting of Experts on Theoretical Frameworks and Methodological Approaches to Studies on the Role of Women in History as Actors in Economic, Social, Political and Ideological Processes. Paris: United Nations Educational, Scientific and Cultural Organization. 1984. 28p.

Jeffries, Rosalind
"The Image of Women in African Cave Art." Journal of African Civilizations. Volume 6 #1 1984. pp. 98-122.

Keim, Curtis A.
"Women in Slavery Among the Mangbetu, c. 1800-1910." (In) Robertson, Claire C. and Klein, Martin A. (eds.). Women and Slavery in Africa. Madison, Wisconsin: University of Wisconsin Press. 1983. pp. 144-159.

Kitching, Gavin
"Proto-Industrialization and Demographic Change: A Thesis and Some Possible African Implications." Journal of African History. Volume 24 #2 1983. pp. 221-240.

Ladner, Joyce A.
"Racism and Tradition: Black Womanhood in Historical Perspective." (In) Carroll, Berenice A. (ed.). Liberating Women's History. Chicago: University of Chicago Press. 1976. pp. 179-193.

Leis, Nancy B.
"West African Women and the Colonial Experience." Western Canadian Journal of Anthropology. Volume 6 #3 1976. pp. 123-132.

MacGaffey, Wyatt
"Lineage Structure, Marriage and the Family Amongst the Central Bantu." Journal of African History. Volume 24 #2 1983. pp. 173-187.

Marks, Shula and Rathbone, Richard
"The History of the Family in Africa: Introduction." Journal of African History. Volume 24 #2 1983. pp. 145-161.

Matsepe-Casaburri, Ivy F.
"Women in Southern Africa: Legacy of Exclusion." Africa Report. Volume 28 #2 March-April, 1983. pp. 7-10.

Meillassoux, Claude
"Female Slavery." (In) Robertson, Claire C. and Klein, Martin A. (eds.). Women and Slavery in Africa. Madison, Wisconsin: University of Wisconsin Press. 1983. pp. 49-66.

Morris, H.F.
"The Development of Statutory Marriage Law in 20th Century British Colonial Africa." Journal of African Law. Volume 23 #1 1979. pp. 37-64.

Musallam, B.
Sex and Society in Islam: Birth Control Before the 19th Century. Cambridge, New York: Cambridge University Press. Cambridge Studies in Islamic Civilization. 1983. 176p.

NGO Planning Committee
Forum '85: Final Report: Nairobi, Kenya. New York: NGO Planning Committee. 1985. 105p.

O'Barr, Jean F.
African Women in Politics. (In) Hay, Margaret J. and Stichter, Sharon (eds.). African Women South of the Sahara. New York: Longman. 1984. pp. 140-155.

Oliver, Caroline
Western Women in Colonial Africa. Westport, Connecticut: Greenwood Press. Contributions in Comparative Colonial Studies #12. 1982. 201p.

Ramachandran, K.V. and Venkatacharya, K. and Teklu, Tesfay
Fertility and Mortality Levels, Patterns and Trends in Some Anglophone African Countries. Legon, Ghana: United Nations Regional Institute for Population Studies. 1979. 78p.

Robertson, Claire C. and Klein, Martin A. (eds.)
Women and Slavery in Africa. Madison, Wisconsin: University of Wisconsin Press. 1983. 380p.

Robertson, Claire C. and Klein, Martin A.
"Women's Importance in African Slave Systems." (In)

Robertson, Claire C. and Klein, Martin A. (eds.). Women and Slavery in Africa. Madison, Wisconsin: University of Wisconsin Press. 1983. pp. 3-25.

Robertson, Claire C.
"The Death of Makola and Other Tragedies: Male Strategies Against a Female Dominated Distribution Network." Paper Presented at the Annual Meeting of the Canadian African Studies Association. Toronto, Ontario, Canada. May, 1982.

Sabean, David W.
"The History of the Family in Africa and Europe: Some Comparative Perspectives." Journal of African History. Volume 24 #2 1983. pp. 163-171.

Scobie, Edward
"African Women in Early Europe." Journal of African Civilizations. Volume 6 #1 1984. pp. 135-154.

Stanley, Autumn
"From Africa to America: Black Women Inventors." (In) Zimmerman, Jan (ed.). The Technological Woman: Interfacing With Tomorrow. New York: Praeger Publishers. Preager Special Studies. 1983. pp. 55-64.

Staudt, Kathleen A.
"Victorian Womanhood in British Colonial Africa." Paper Presented to the Conference on the History of Women. St. Paul, Minnesota: College of St. Catherine. October 21-23, 1977.

Strobel, Margaret A.
"African Women's History." History Teacher. Volume 15 #4 August, 1982. pp. 509-522.

Tadesse, Zenebeworke
"Breaking the Silence and Broadening the Frontiers of History: Notes on Recent Studies on African Women in History." Paper Presented at the Meeting of Experts on Theoretical Frameworks and Methodological Approaches to Studies on the Role of Women in History as Actors in Economic, Social, Political and Ideological Processes. Paris: United Nations Educational, Scientific and Cultural Organization. 1984. 15p.

Thornton, John
"Sexual Demography: The Impact of Slave Trade on Family Structure." (In) Robertson, Claire C. and Klein, Martin A. (eds.). Women and Slavery in Africa. Madison, Wisconsin: University of Wisconsin Press. 1983. pp. 39-48.

Tillion, Germaine
"Prehistoric Origins of the Condition of Women in Civilized Areas." International Social Science Journal. Volume 29 #4 1977. pp. 671-681.

United Nations
Report of the World Conference to Review and Appraise the Achievements of the United Nations Decade for Women: Equality, Development and Peace. Nairobi, Kenya, July 15-26, 1985. New York: United Nations. 1986. 304p.

White, E. Frances
"A Black Feminist in Africa." New England Journal of

Black Studies. 1981. pp. 37-43.
White, E. Frances
"A Black Feminist in Africa." Paper Presented at the Annual Meeting of the African Studies Association. Paper #115. Philadelphia, Pennsylvania. 1980.
Whitehead, Clive
"The Education of Women and Girls: An Aspect of British Colonial Policy." Journal of Educational Administration. Volume 16 #2 1984. pp. 24-34.
Wright, Marcia
"Bwanikwa: Consciousness and Protest Among Slave Women in Central Africa, 1886-1911." (In) Robertson, Claire C. and Klein, Martin A. (eds.). Women and Slavery in Africa. Madison, Wisconsin: University of Wisconsin Press. 1983. pp. 246-267.

Law and Legal Issues

Bennett, T.W. and Peart. Nicola S.
"The Dualism of Marriage Laws in Africa." ACTA Juridica. 1983. pp. 145-169.

Bujra, Janet M.
"Prostitution, Class and the State." (In) Sumner, Colin (ed.). Crime, Justice, and Underdevelopment. London: Heineman. Cambridge Studies in Criminology. #46. pp. 145-161. 1982.

Caplan, Patricia
"Cognatic Descent, Islamic Law, and Women's Property on the East African Coast." (In) Hirschon, Renbee (ed.). Women and Property--Women as Property. New York: St.Martin's Press. 1983.

Casteinuovo, Shirley
"The Impact of Urbanization on the Family in Light of Recent Changes in African Family Law." Paper Presented at the Annual Meeting of the African Studies Association. Paper #11. Houston, Texas. 1977.

Cook, Rebecca J.
"A Law on Family Welfare and Development in Africa." (In) International Planned Parenthood Federation (IPPF). Proceedings of the IPPF Africa Regional Conference. London: IPPF. 1977. pp. 241-246.

Cook, Rebecca J. and Dickens, Bernard N.
"Abortion Law in African Commonwealth Countries." Journal of African Law. Volume 25 #2 1981. pp. 60-79.

Dunbar, Roberta
"Legislative Reform and Muslim Family Law: Effects Upon Women's Rights in Africa South of the Sahara." Paper Presented at the Annual Meeting of the African Studies Association. Paper #25. Philadelphia, Pennsylvania. October 15-18, 1980.

Dwyer, Daisy H.
"Outside the Courts: Extra-Legal Strategies for the Subordination of Women." (In) Hay, Margaret J. and Wright, Marcia (eds.). African Women and the Law:

Historical Perspectives. Boston: Boston University. African Studies Center. Boston University Papers on Africa. Volume Seven. 1982. pp. 90-109.

Ensor, Linda and Cooper, Carole
The African Women's Handbook on the Law. Johannesburg: South African Institute of Race Relations. 1980. 41p.

Esposito, John L.
Women in Muslim Family Law. Syracuse, New York: Syracuse University Press. Contemporary Issues in the Middle East Series. 1982. 172p.

Hay, Margaret J. and Wright, Marcia (eds.)
African Women and the Law: Historical Perspectives. Boston, Masachusetts: Boston University. African Studies Center. Boston University Papers on Africa. Volume 7. 1982. 173p.

Howard, R.
"Women's Rights in English-Speaking Sub-Saharan Africa." (In) Welch, Claude E. and Meltzer, Ronald I. (eds.). Human Rights and Development in Africa. Albany, New York: State University of New York Press. 1984.

LeVine, Sarah
"Crime or Afflictions: Rape in an African Community." Culture, Medicine and Psychiatry. Volume 4 #2 1980.

Martin-Cisse, Jeanne
"Family Problems in Africa." National Law Guild Practitioner. Volume 37 Winter, 1980. pp. 23-26.

Morris, H.F.
"The Development of Statutory Marriage Law in 20th Century British Colonial Africa." Journal of African Law. Volume 23 #1 1979. pp. 37-64.

Naali, Shamsahd
"Legal Provisions for Women's Participation in Cooperatives." Paper Presented at the Seminar on Women's Studies and Development. Dar-es-Salaam, Tanzania: University of Dar-es-Salaam. Bureau of Resource Assessment and Land Use Planning. Paper #15. September 24-29, 1979. 10p.

Ndulo, Muna
"Liability of a Paramour in Damages for Adultery in Customary Law." African Social Research. #28 December, 1979. pp. 655-666.

Newman, Katherine S.
"Women and Law: Land Tenure in Africa." (In) Black, Naomi and Cottrell, Ann B. Women and World Change: Equity Issues in Development. Beverly Hills, California: Sage Publications. 1981. pp. 120-138.

Paraiso, Maitre A.
"Family Planning Legislation in the Francophone Countries of Africa." (In) International Planned Parenthood Federation (IPPF). Proceedings of the IPPF Africa Regional Conference. London: IPPF. 1977. pp. 247-255.

Pauwels, Johan M.
"Nullity of Marriage and Divorce: Relevance of a Western Distinction to Modern African Law." (In) Roberts, Simon (ed.). Law and the Family in Africa. Hague,

Netherlands: Mouton. 1977. pp. 225-239.

Peart, Nicola S.
"Civil or Christian Marriage and Customary Unions: The Legal Position of the 'Discarded' Spouse and Children." Comparative and International Law Journal of Southern Africa. Volume 16 #1 1983. pp. 39-64.

Roberts, Simon (ed.)
Law and the Family in Africa. Hague, Netherlands: Mouton. 1977. 267p.

Russell, Diana E.H. and Vandeven, Nicole (eds.)
Crimes Against Women: Proceedings of the International Tribunal. Millbrae, California: Les Femmes. 1976. 298p.

Singleton, Michael
Contributions to the Rights and Wrongs of African Women. Brussels, Belgium: Pro Mundi Vita Dossiers. Africa Dossier #9. October, 1979. pp. 1-36.

Thomas, Rosalind
"The Law in Southern Africa: Justice for All?" Africa Report. Volume 30 #2 March-April, 1985. pp. 59-63.

Uche, U.U.
"The Law, Family Welfare and Development in Africa: A Strategy for Future Action." (In) International Planned Parenthood Federation (IPPF). Proceedings of the IPPF Africa Regional Conference. London: IPPF. 1977. pp. 256-262.

Ushewokunze, C.M.
"Reflections on Youth and Family Welfare Law in Africa." (In) International Planned Parenthood Federation (IPPF). Proceedings of the IPPF Africa Regional Conference. London: IPPF. 1977. pp. 182-190.

Wegner, J.R.
"The Status of Women in Jewish and Islamic Marriage and Divorce Law." Harvard Women's Law Journal. Volume 5 #1 1982.

Literature

Accad, Evelyne
"The Theme of Sexual Oppression in the North African Novel." (In) Beck, Lois and Keddie, Nikki R. (eds.). Women in the Muslim World. Cambridge, Massachusetts: Harvard University Press. 1978. pp. 617-628.

Accad, Evelyne
"Complex Inter-Relation of Women's Liberation and Arab Nationalism in North African Novels Written by Women." Paper Presented at the Annual Meeting of the African Studies Association. Paper #1. Boston, Massachusetts. 1976. 16p.

Accad, Evelyne
"The Prostitute in Arab and North African Fiction." (In) Horn, Pierre L. and Pringle, Mary B. (eds.). The Image of the Prostitute in Modern Literature. New York: Ungar. 1984. pp. 63-75.

Accad, Evelyne
"Interrelationship Between Arab Nationalism and Feminist Consciousness in the North African Novels Written by Women." Ba Shiru. Volume 8 #2 1977. pp. 3-12.

Accad, Evelyne
Veil of Shame: The Role of Women in the Contemporary Fiction of North Africa and the Arab World. Sherbrooke, Canada: Editions Naaman. 1978. 182p.

Bell, Roseann C.
"Absence of the African Women Writer." CLA Journal. Volume 21 June, 1978. pp. 491-498.

Berrian, Brenda F.
"Bibliographies of Nine Female African Writers." Research in African Literatures. Volume 12 #2 Summer, 1981. pp. 214-236.

Berrian, Brenda F.
Bibliography of African Women Writers and Journalists (Ancient Egypt-1984). Washington, D.C.: Three Continents Press. 1985. 279p.

Brown, Lloyd W.
Women Writers in Black Africa. Westport, Connecticut: Greenwood Press. 1981. 204p.
Bruner, Charlotte H.
"Been-To or Has-Been: A Dilemma for Today's African Women." Paper Presented at the African Literature Association Conference. 1976. 15p.
Bruner, Charlotte H. (ed.)
Unwinding Threads: Writing by Women in Africa. Exeter, New Hampshire: Heinemann. African Writers Series. Volume 256. 1983. 208p.
Bruner, Charoltte H.
"Been-To or Has-Been: A Dilemma for Today's African Women." Ba Shiru. Volume 8 #2 1977. pp. 23-31.
Bruner, David K.
"Maryse Conde and the Woman-Writer Myth." Paper Presented at the African Literature Association Conference. 1977. 8p.
Christian, Barbara
"Alternative Versions of the Gendered Past: African Women Writers vs. Illich." Feminist Issues: A Journal of Feminist Social and Political Theory. Volume 3 #1 Spring, 1983. pp. 23-27.
Dajani, Karen F.
"Magazine for Arab Women: Hawa." Journalism Quarterly. Spring, 1982. pp. 116-118.
Dawit, T.
"Mass Media and Rural Women in Africa." Assignment Children. Volume 38 #2 April-June, 1977. pp. 119-120.
Douglas, Carol A.
"Ajowa Ifateyo: Speaking Up Front (Interview)." Off Our Backs. Volume 14 November, 1984. pp. 10-12.
Frank, Katherine
"Feminist Criticism and the African Novel." African Literature Today. #14 1984. pp. 34-38.
Grohs, G.
"Women and Politician in the Modern African Novel." (In) Schild, U. (ed.). Jaw-Bones and Umbilical Cords: A Selection of Papers Presented at the Third Janheinz Jahn Symposium, 1979 and the Fourth Janheinz Jahn Symposium, 1982. Berlin, Germany: Reimer. 1985. pp. 119-126.
Joseph, Terri B.
Poetry as a Strategy of Power: The Case of Riffian Berber Women. Signs. Volume 5 #3 Spring, 1980. pp. 418-434.
Kilson, Marion
"Women and African Literature." Journal of African Studies. Volume 4 #2 Summer, 1977. pp. 161-166.
LaPin, Deidre
"Women in African Literature." (In) Hay, Margaret J. and Stichter, Sharon (eds.). African Women South of the Sahara. New York: Longman. 1984. pp. 102-118.
Lawrence, Leota S.
"Women in Caribbean Literature--The African Presence." Phylon. Volume 44 #1 March, 1983. pp. 1-12.

Lee, S.
"The Image of the Woman in the African Folktale From the Sub-Saharan Francophone Area." Yale French Studies. #53 1976. pp. 19-28.
Linton, Marie A.
"The Image of the African Woman as Heroine in African Non-Vernacular Creative Writing." Paper Presented at the African Literature Association Conference. 1977. 16p.
Linton-Umeh, Marie A.
"An Exploratory Study of Images of Women in African Non-Vernacular Writing as Portrayed by Selected Contemporary African Authors." Ph.D Dissertation: Cornell University. Ithaca, New York. August, 1977. 107p.
Little, Kenneth L.
Sociology of Urban Women's Image in African Literature. Totowa, New Jersey: Rowman and Littlefield. 1980. 174p.
Martin, Ellen E.
"Allegory and the African Woman in the Old English Exodus." Journal of English and Germanic Philology. Volume 81 #1 January, 1982. pp. 1-15.
Mason, Nondita
"Women and Development in Third World Writing." Populi. Volume 5 #4 1978. pp. 45-49.
McCaffrey, Kathleen M.
"Images of Women in West African Literature and Film: A Struggle Against Dual Colonization." International Journal of Women's Studies. Volume 3 #1 January-February, 1980. pp. 76-88.
Mortimer, Mildred P.
"The Evolution of Assia Djebar's Feminist Conscience." (In) Wylie, Hal (ed.). Contemporary African Literature. Washington, D.C.: Three Continents. 1983. pp. 7-14.
Mortimer, Mildred P.
"Assie Djebar: A Feminist Movement." Paper Presented at the Annual Meeting of the African Studies Association. Paper #67. Boston, Massachusetts. 1976. 13p.
Mutiso, G.C.
"Women in African Literature." East Africa Journal. Volume 14 March, 1977. pp. 4-14.
Ngcobo, Lauretta
"Four Women Writers in Africa Today." South African Outlook. Volume 114 #1355 May, 1984. pp. 64-69.
Paulme, Denise
"The Devouring Mother: Essay on the Morphology of African Tales." Journal of African Studies. Volume 4 Winter, 1977. pp. 480+.
Smith, Pamela J.
"An Image of Women in Anglophone West African Literature." Paper Presented at the African Literature Association Conference. 1976. 11p.
Soyinka, Susan
"Family and Fertility in the West African Novel." (In) Caldwell, John C. (ed.). The Persistence of High Fertility: Population Prospects in the Third World.

Canberra, Australia: Australian National University. Department of Demography. Volume One. 1977. pp. 427-450.

Taivo, Olandele
Female Novelists of Modern Africa. London: MacMillan. 1984. 228p.

Wallace, Karen S.
"Women and Identity: A Black Francophone Female Perspective." Sage: A Scholarly Journal on Black Women. Volume 2 #1 1985. pp. 19-23.

Wilson, Elizabeth A.
"The Portrayal of Woman in the Works of Francophone Women Writers From West Africa and the French Caribbean." Ph.D Dissertation: Michigan State University. East Lansing, Michigan. 1985. 205p.

Marital Relations and Nuptiality

Abbott, Susan
"Full-Time Farmers and Week-End Wives, an Analysis of Altering Conjugal Roles." Journal of Marriage and the Family. Volume 38 #1 February, 1976. pp. 165-174.

Aborampah, Osei-Mensah
"Family Structure in African Fertility Studies: Some Conceptual and Methodological Issues." Current Bibliography on African Affairs. Volume 18 #4 1986. pp. 319-335.

Acsadi, George T.
"Effect of Economic Development on Fertility Trends in Africa." (In) Cairo Demographic Centre (CDC). Aspects of Population Change and Development in Some African and Asian Countries. Cairo, Egypt: CDC. CDC Research Monograph Series #9. 1984. pp. 57-105.

Adler, A.
"Avunculate and Matrilateral Marriage in Africa." L'Homme. Volume 16 October-December, 1976. pp. 7-28.

Anker, Richard and Buvinic, Mayra and Youssef, Nadia H. (eds.)
Women's Roles and Population Trends in the Third World. London: Croon Helm Ltd. 1982. 288p.

Appiah-Kubi, Kofi
"Monogamy: Is it Really So Christian?" African Women. #5 July-August, 1976. pp. 46-48.

Arens, W. and Arens, Diana A.
"Kinship and Marriage in a Polyethnic Community." Africa. Volume 48 1978. pp. 149-160.

Balakrishnan, Revathi and Firebaugh, Francille M.
Roles of Women in Third World Economic Development From a Systems Perspective of Family Resource Management. Columbus, Ohio: Ohio State University. Department of Home Management and Housing. School of Home Economics. Working Papers #81-01. 1981. 39p.

Beneria, Lourdes
"Reproduction, Production and the Sexual Division of

Labour." Cambridge Journal of Economics. Volume 3 September, 1979. pp. 203-225.

Beneria, Lourdes
"Reproduction, Production and the Sexual Division of Labour." Geneva: International Labour Office. World Employment Research Working Paper #2. 1978.

Bennett, T.W. and Peart. Nicola S.
"The Dualism of Marriage Laws in Africa." ACTA Juridica. 1983. pp. 145-169.

Bongaarts, John and Frank, Odile and Lesthaeghe, Ron J.
"The Proximate Determinants of Fertility in Sub-Saharan Africa." Population and Developement Review. Volume 10 #3 September, 1984. pp. 511-538+.

Bongaarts, John
"The Impact on Fertility of Traditional and Changing Child-Spacing Practices." (In) Page, Hilary J. and Lesthaeghe, Ron (eds.). Child-Spacing in Tropical Africa. New York: Academic Press. 1981. pp. 111-129.

Boserup, Ester
"Economic and Demographic Interrelationships in Sub-Saharan Africa." Population and Development Review. Volume 11 #3 September, 1985. pp. 383-397+.

Bourguignon, Erika
A World of Women: Anthropological Studies of Women in the Societies of the World. New York: Praeger Publishers. Praeger Special Studies. 1980. 364p.

Brabin, Loretta
"Polygyny: An Indicator of Nutritional Stress in African Agricultural Societies." Africa. Volume 54 #1 1984. pp. 31-45.

Brown, Judith E.
"Polygyny and Family Planning in Sub-Saharan Africa." Studies in Family Planning. Volume 12 #8-9 August-September, 1981. pp. 322-326.

Bruner, Charlotte H.
"Been-To or Has-Been: A Dilemma for Today's African Women." Paper Presented at the African Literature Association Conference. 1976. 15p.

Bruner, Charlotte H.
"Been-To or Has-Been: A Dilemma for Today's African Women." Ba Shiru. Volume 8 #2 1977. pp. 23-31.

Bryant, Coralie
"Women Migrants, Urbanization and Social Change: An African Case." Paper Presented at the American Political Science Association Annual Meeting. Washington, D.C. September, 1977.

Burton, Claire
"Woman Marriage in Africa: A Critical Study For Sex-Role Theory?" Australian and New Zealand Journal of Sociology. Volume 15 #2 July, 1979. pp. 65-71.

Cairo Demographic Centre (CDC)
Family and Marriage in Some African and Asian Countries. Cairo, Egypt: CDC. CDC Research Monograph Series #6. 1976.

Caldwell, John C. and Caldwell, Pat
Cultural Forces Tending to Sustain High Fertility in Tropical Africa. Canberra, Australia: Australian National University. 1984.

Caldwell, John C.
"Measuring Wealth Flows and the Rationality of Fertility: Thoughts and Plans Based in the First Place on African Work." (In) Ruzicka, Lado T. (ed.). The Economic and Social Supports for High Fertility: Proceedings of the Conference. Canberra, Australia: Australian National University. Development Studies Center. November 16-18, 1977. pp. 439-454.

Caldwell, Pat
"Issues of Marriage and Marital Change: Tropical Africa and the Middle East." (In) Huzayyin, S.A. and Acsadi, G.T. (eds.). Family and Marriage in Some African and Asiatic Countries. Cairo, Egypt: Cairo Demographic Centre. Research Monograph Series #6. 1976. pp. 325-335.

Caldwell, Pat and Caldwell, John C.
"The Function of Child-Spacing in Traditional Societies and the Direction of Change." (In) Page, Hilary J. and Lesthaeghe, Ron (eds.). Child-Spacing in Tropical Africa: Traditions and Change. New York: Academic Press. 1981. pp. 73-92.

Caplan, Patricia
"Cognatic Descent, Islamic Law, and Women's Property on the East African Coast." (In) Hirschon, Renbee (ed.). Women and Property--Women as Property. New York: St. Martin's Press. 1983.

Casajus, Dominique
"The Wedding Ritual Among the Kel Ferwan Tuaregs." Journal of the Anthropological Society of Oxford. Volume 14 #2 1983. pp. 227-257.

Casteinuovo, Shirley
"The Impact of Urbanization on the Family in Light of Recent Changes in African Family Law." Paper Presented at the Annual Meeting of the African Studies Association. Paper #11. Houston, Texas. 1977.

Castillo, Gelia T.
The Changing Role of Women in Rural Societies: A Summary of Trends and Issues. New York: Agricultural Development Council Inc. RTN Seminar Reports 12. February, 1977. 11p.

Chamie, Joseph and Weller, Robert H.
Levels, Trends and Differentials in Nuptiality in the Middle East and North Africa. Tallahassee, Florida: Florida State University. Center for the Study of Population. College of Social Sciences. Working Paper #83-02. 1983. 12p.

Chamie, Joseph and Weller, Robert H.
"Levels, Trends and Differentials in Nuptiality in the Middle East and North Africa." Genus. Volume 39 #1-4 January-December, 1983. pp. 213-231.

Chamie, Joseph
Polygamy Among Arabs. New York: United Nations. U.N. Population Division. 1985.
Chojnacka, Helena
"Polygyny and the Rate of Population Growth." Human Resources Research Bulletin. #78/05 1978. 34p.
Chojnacka, Helena
"Polygyny and the Rate of Population Growth." Population Studies. Volume 34 #1 March, 1980. pp. 91-107.
Cook, Rebecca J.
"A Law on Family Welfare and Development in Africa." (In) International Planned Parenthood Federation (IPPF). Proceedings of the IPPF Africa Regional Conference. London: IPPF. 1977. pp. 241-246.
Deheusch, L.
"The Good Usage of Wives and Cattle-Transformation of Marriage in Southern Africa." L'Homme. Volume 23 #4 1983.
Dodds, Peter
"Family Planning in Africa." Africa Insight. Volume 15 #4 1985. pp. 256-261.
Dunbar, Roberta
"Legislative Reform and Muslim Family Law: Effects Upon Women's Rights in Africa South of the Sahara." Paper Presented at the Annual Meeting of the African Studies Association. Paper #25. Philadelphia, Pennsylvania. October 15-18, 1980.
Duza, M. Badrud and Sivamurthy, M.
"Household Structure in Selected Urban Areas of Four Arab and African Cities." (In) Huzayyin, S.A. and Acsadi, G.T. (eds.). Family and Marriage in Some African and Asiatic Countries. Cairo, Egypt: Cairo Demographic Centre. Research Monograph Series #6. 1976. pp. 267-284.
Duza, M. Badrud and Seetharam, K.S. and Sivamurthy, M.
"Patterns of Family Cycles in Selected Areas of Four Arab and African Cities: Some Demographic Implications." (In) Huzayyin, S.A. and Acsadi, G.T. (eds.). Family and Marriage in Some African and Asiatic Countries. Cairo, Egypt: Cairo Demographic Centre. CDC Research Monograph Series #6. 1976. pp. 245-265.
Dwyer, Daisy H.
"Outside the Courts: Extra-Legal Strategies for the Subordination of Women." (In) Hay, Margaret J. and Wright, Marcia (eds.). African Women and the Law: Historical Perspectives. Boston: Boston University. African Studies Center. Boston University Papers on Africa. Volume Seven. 1982. pp. 90-109.
Ekechi, Felix K.
"African Polygamy and Western Christian Ethnocentrism." Journal of African Studies. Volume 3 #3 August, 1976. pp. 329-349.
El-Khorazaty, Mohamed Nabil E.
"Regional Differences in Attitudes Toward Family Norms

and Planning, 1979/80." Population Studies. Volume 12 #72 January-March, 1985. pp. 3-28.

Elwert, Georg
"Conflicts Inside and Outside the Household: A West African Case Study." (In) Smith, Joan (ed.). Households and the World Economy. Beverly Hills, California: Sage. 1984. pp. 272-296.

Epstein, Trude S.
Place of Social Anthropology in a Multidisciplinary Approach to the Study of Women's Roles and Status in Less Developed Countries. Geneva: International Labour Organization. 1978.

Esposito, John L.
Women in Muslim Family Law. Syracuse, New York: Syracuse University Press. Contemporary Issues in the Middle East Series. 1982. 172p.

Fernea, Elizabeth W.
Women and the Family in the Middle East: New Voices of Change. Austin, Texas: University of Texas Press. 1984. 368p.

Fortes, Meyer
"Parenthood, Marriage and Fertility in West Africa." Journal of Development Studies. Volume 14 #4 July, 1978. pp. 121-149.

Fortes, Meyer
"Family, Marriage and Fertility in West Africa." (In) Oppong, C. and Adaba, G. and Bekombo-Priso, M. and Mogey, J. (eds.). Marriage, Fertility and Parenthood in West Africa. Canberra, Australia: Australian National University Press. 1978. pp. 17-54.

Frank, Odile
Child Fostering in Sub-Saharan Africa. New York: Population Council. Center for Policy Studies. 1984.

Ginat, Joseph (ed.)
Women in Muslim Rural Society: Status and Role in Family Community. New Brunswick, New Jersey: Transition Books. 1981. 268p.

Goody, Esther N.
"Some Theoretical and Empirical Aspects of Parenthood in West Africa." (In) Oppong, C. and Adaba, G. and Bekombo-Priso, M. and Mogey, J. (eds.). Marriage, Fertility and Parenthood in West Africa. Canberra, Australia: Australian National University. Department of Demography. Volume One. 1978. pp. 227-272.

Goody, Esther N.
"Parental Strategies: Calculation or Sentiment: Fostering Practices Among West Africans." (In) Medick, Hans and Sabean, David W. (eds.). Interest and Emotion: Essays on the Study of Family and Kinship. Cambridge, New York: Cambridge University Press. 1984. pp. 266-277.

Goody, Jack
Production and Reproduction: A Comparative Study of the Domestic Domain. Cambridge, New York: Cambridge University Press. Cambridge Studies in Social Anthropology #17. 1976. 157p.

Grandmaison, C. LeCour
"Economic Contracts Between Married People in the West African Area." L'Homme. Volume 19 #3/4 July-December, 1979. pp. 159-170.

Gray, R.H.
"Birth Intervals, Postpartum Sexual Abstinence and Child Health." (In) Page, Hilary J. and Lesthaeghe, Ron (eds.). Child-Spacing in Tropical Africa: Traditions and Change. New York: Academic Press. 1981. pp. 93-109.

Guyer, Jane I.
The Raw, the Cooked and the Half-Baked: A Note on the Division of Labor by Sex. Brookline, Massachusetts: Boston University. African Studies Center. Working Papers in African Studies #48. 1981. 12p.

Guyer, Jane I.
"Household and Community in African Studies." African Studies Review. Volume 24 #213 June-September, 1981. pp. 87-137.

Guyot, Jean
Migrant Women Speak: Interviews. London: Search Press Ltd. for the Churches Committee on Migrant Workers. 1978. 164p.

Hadri, Gasim
"Opinions About Female Circumcision." Paper Presented at the Seminar on Traditional Practices Affecting the Health of Women and Children. World Conference of the United Nations Decade for Women. Copenhagen, Denmark. July 14-30, 1980.

Hafkin, Nancy J. and Bay, Edna G. (eds.)
Women in Africa: Studies in Social and Economic Change. Stanford, California: Stanford University Press. 1976. 306p.

Hanson, F. and Miller, F.
"The Wife's Brother's Wife and the Marriage Contract: A Structural Analysis." Bijdragen Tot de Taal-, Land-en Volkenkunde. Volume 133 #1 1977. pp. 11-22.

Hayani, Ibrahim
"The Changing Role of Arab Women." Convergence. Volume 13 #1 1980. pp. 136-142.

Hein, Catherine R.
Factory Employment, Marriage and Fertility: The Case of Mauritian Women. Geneva: International Labour Organization. World Employment Programme Research Working Paper #118. June, 1982. 57p.

Huzayyin, S.A. and Acsadi, George T. (eds.)
Family and Marriage in Some African and Asiatic Countries. Cairo, Egypt: Cairo Demographic Center. CDC Research Monograph Series #6. 1976. 570p.

Huzayyin, S.A.
"Marriage and Remarriage in Islam." (In) Dupaquier, J. and Helin, E. and Laslett, P. and Livi-Bacci, M. (eds.). Marriage and Remarriage in Populations of the Past. New York: Academic Press. Population and Social Structure: Advances in Historical Demography Series. 1981. pp. 95-109.

International Planned Parenthood Federation (IPPF)
Family Welfare and Development in Africa: Proceedings of the IPPF Africa Regional Conference, University of Ibadan. August 29-September 3, 1976. London: IPPF. Ibadan, Nigeria. 1977. 327p.

Isley, R.
Medical, Socio-Cultural, Economic and Psychological Correlates of Childlessness in Africa. Research Triangle Park, North Carolina: Research Triangle Institute. RTI Concept Paper #24-CP-80-01. 1980.

Joseph, Roger
"Sexual Dialectics and Strategy in Berber Marriage." Journal of Comparative Family Studies. Volume 7 #3 Autumn, 1976. pp. 471-481.

Kabagambe, John C.
"Family Planning Concepts: Myths and Realities." (In) International Planned Parenthood Federation (IPPF). Proceedings of the IPPF Africa Regional Conference. London: IPPF. 1977. pp. 55+.

Kazeze, Z.W.
"Review of Some Determinants of Fertility in Africa." (In) Cairo Demographic Centre (CDC). Determinants of Fertility in Some African and Asian Countries. Cairo, Egypt: CDC. CDC Research Monograph Series #10. 1982. pp. 391-414.

Keenan, Jeremy
"Power and Wealth Are Cousins: Descent, Class and Marital Strategies Among the Kel Ahaggar." Africa. Volume 47 #3 1977. pp. 242-252.

Keller, Bonnie B.
"Marriage by Elopment." African Social Research. #27 June, 1979. pp. 565-585.

Keller, Bonnie B.
"Marriage and Medicine: Women's Search for Love and Luck." African Social Research. #26 December, 1978. pp. 489-505.

Kerri, James
"Understanding the African Family: Persistence, Continuity and Change." Western Journal of Black Studies. Volume 3 #1 Spring, 1979. pp. 14-17.

Kisekka, Mere N.
"Polygyny and the Status of African Women." African Urban Notes. Volume 2 #3 Fall/Winter, 1976. pp. 21-42.

Kuper, Adam
"Cousin Marriage Among the Thembu?" African Affairs. Volume 40 #1 1981. pp. 41-42.

Kurian, George and Ratna, Ghosh (eds.)
Women in the Family and the Economy: An International Comparative Survey. Westport, Connecticut: Greenwood Press. Contributions in Family Studies #5. 1981. 451p.

Kwawu, J.
"The Role of Home Economics in Rural Development: A Focus on Family Planning." Paper Presented at the Workshop on the Role of Women and Home Economics in Rural Development in Africa. Rome: United Nations Food and Agricultural

Organization. Alexandria, Egypt. October 17, 1983. 20p.
LeVine, Robert A. and Dixon, Suzanne and LeVine, Sarah
"High Fertility in Africa: A Consideration of Causes and Consequences." Paper Presented at the Annual Meeting of the African Studies Association. Paper #48. Boston, Massachusetts. 1976. 18p.
Leke, R. and Nash, B.
"Biological and Socio-Cultural Aspects of Infertility and Subfertility in Africa." (In) United Nations Economic Commission for Africa (UNECA). Population Dynamics: Fertility and Mortality in Africa. Addis Ababa, Ethiopia: UNECA. May, 1981. pp. 488-498.
Lesthaeghe, Ron J.
Fertility and its Proximate Determinants in Sub-Saharan Africa: The Record of the 1960's and 70's. Brussels, Belgium: Vrije Universiteit Brussel. Interuniversity Programme in Demography. IPD Working Paper #1984-2. 1984. 117p.
Lesthaeghe, Ron J. and Ohadike, Patrick O. and Kocher, James E. and Page, Hilary J.
"Child-Spacing and Fertility in Sub-Saharan Africa: An Overview of Issues." (In) Page, Hilary J. and Lesthaeghe, Ron (eds.). Child-Spacing in Tropical Africa: Traditions and Change. New York: Academic Press. 1981. pp. 3-23.
Levine, Nancy E.
"Nyinba Polyandry and the Allocation of Paternity." Journal of Comparative Family Studies. Volume 11 #3 Special Iss. August, 1980. pp. 283-298.
Levine, Nancy E. and Sangree, Walter H.
"Asian and African Systems of Polyandry." Journal of Comparative Family Studies. Volume 11 #3 Special Iss. August, 1980. pp. 385-410.
Levine, Nancy E. and Sangree, Walter H.
"Women With Many Husbands--Polyandrous Alliance and Marital Flexibility in Africa and Asia." Journal of Comparative Family Studies. Volume 11 #3 Special Iss. August, 1980.
Lindsay, Beverly (ed.)
Comparative Perspectives of Third World Women: The Impact of Race, Sex and Class. New York: Praeger Publishers. Praeger Special Studies. 1980. 318p.
Little, Kenneth L.
"Women's Strategies in Modern Marriage in Anglophone West Africa: An Ideological and Sociological Appraisal." Journal of Comparative Family Studies. Volume 8 #3 Autumn, 1977. pp. 341-356.
Little, Kenneth L.
"Women's Strategies in Modern Marriage in Anglophone West Africa: An Ideological and Sociological Appraisal." (In) Kurian, George (ed.). Cross-Cultural Perspectives of Mate Selection and Marriage. Westport, Connecticut: Greenwood Press. Contributions in Family Studies #3. 1979. pp. 202-217.

Lukutati, Bwembya
"The Concept of Parenthood in African Societies." (In) International Planned Parenthood Federation (IPPF). Proceedings of the IPPF Africa Regional Conference. London: IPPF. 1977. pp. 145-152.

Mabogunje, A.L.
"The Policy Implications of Changes in Child-Spacing Practices in Tropical Africa." (In) Page, Hilary J. and Lesthaeghe, Ron (eds.). Child-Spacing in Tropical Africa: Traditions and Changes. New York: Academic Press. 1981. pp. 303-316.

MacGaffey, Wyatt
"Lineage Structure, Marriage and the Family Amongst the Central Bantu." Journal of African History. Volume 24 #2 1983. pp. 173-187.

Mati, J.K.
Abortion in Africa. (In) International Planned Parenthood Federation (IPPF). Proceedings of the IPPF Africa Regional Conference. London: IPPF. 1977. pp. 74-79.

Mbilinyi, Marjorie J.
"Patriarch Relations in the Peasant Household." Paper Presented at the Workshop on Women's Studies and Development. Dar-es-Salaam, Tanzania: University of Dar-es-Salaam. Bureau of Resource Assessment and Land Use Planning. Paper #20. September 24-29, 1979. 12p.

Moots, Patricia A. and Zak, Michele (eds.)
Women and the Politics of Culture: Studies in the Sexual Economy. New York: Longman. 1983. 452p.

Morris, H.F.
"The Development of Statutory Marriage Law in 20th Century British Colonial Africa." Journal of African Law. Volume 23 #1 1979. pp. 37-64.

Mott, Frank L. and Mott, Susan H.
"Household Fertility Decision-Making in a West African Setting: Do Male and Female Surveys Lead to Similar Interpretations?" Worthington, Ohio: Ohio State University. Center for Human Resource Research. 1984.

Murray, Colin G.
"Migrant Labour and Changing Family Structure in the Rural Periphery of Southern Africa." Journal of Southern African Studies. Volume 6 #2 1980. pp. 139-156.

Mushanga, Tibamanya M.
"Wife Victimization in East and Central Africa." Victimology. Volume 2 #3/4 1977. pp. 479-486.

Ndeti, K.
"Concept of Parenthood in Africa: An Exploratory Study of Complexity." (In) International Planned Parenthood Federation (IPPF). Proceedings of the IPPF Africa Regional Conference. London: IPPF. 1977. pp. 119-144.

Ndulo, Muna
"Liability of a Paramour in Damages for Adultery in Customary Law." African Social Research. #28 December, 1979. pp. 655-666.

Ntiri, Daphne W.
"African Student Wives: Their Participation in Continuing Education." Lifelong Learning. Volume 3 #4 December, 1979. pp. 10-11+.

Nurse, G.T.
"Meity Endogamy and Anthropometric Variation Among the Maravi." Man. Volume 12 #3/4 December, 1977. pp. 397-404.

O'Brien, Denise
"Female Husbands in Southern Bantu." (In) Schlegal, A. (ed.). Sexual Stratification: A Cross-Cultural View. New York: Columbia University Press. 1977. pp. 109-126.

Obbo, Christine S.
"Town Migration is Not for Women." Ph.D. Dissertation: University of Wisconsin-Madison. Madison, Wisconsin. 1977. 329p.

Obbo, Christine S.
"Dominant Male Ideology and Female Options: Three East African Case Studies." Africa. Volume 46 #4 1976. pp. 371-389.

Ogbu, John U.
"African Bridewealth and Women's Status." American Ethnologist. Volume 5 #2 May, 1978. pp. 241-262.

Okediji, Frances Olu
"The Limitations of Family Planning Programmes in the Developing Nations." (In) Oppong, C. and Adaba, G. and Bekombo-Priso, M. and Mogey, J. (eds.). Marriage, Fertility and Parenthood in West Africa. Canberra, Australia: Australian National University. Department of Demography. Volume Two. 1978. pp. 617-639.

Okediji, Peter A.
"The Status of African Women in Family Planning." (In) Oppong, C. and Adaba, G. and Bekombo-Priso, M. and Mogey, J. (eds.). Marriage, Fertility and Parenthood in West Africa. Canberra, Australia: Australian National University. Department of Demography. Volume Two. 1978. pp. 673-676.

Omran, Abdel R. and Johnston, Alan G.
Family Planning for Health in Africa. Chapel Hill, North Carolina: University of North Carolina. Carolina Population Center. 1984. 190p.

Oppong, Christine
Family Structure and Women's Reproductive and Productive Roles: Some Conceptual and Methodological Issues. Geneva: International Labour Office. The Role of Women and Demographic Change Research Program. 1980.

Oppong, Christine
A Synopsis of Seven Roles and Status of Women: An Outline of a Conceptual and Methodological Approach. Geneva: International Labour Organization. World Employment Programme. Research Working Paper. Mimeo. (Restricted) 1980.

Oppong, Christine
"Family Structure and Women's Reproductive and Productive Roles: Some Conceptual and Methodological Issues." (In)

Anker, Richard and Buvinic, Mayra and Youssef, N. (eds.). Women's Roles and Population Trends in the Third World. London: Croom Helm. 1982.

Oppong, Christine and Adaba, Gemma and Bekomba-Priso, Manga and Mogey, J. (eds.)
Marriage, Fertility and Parenthood in West Africa. Canberra, Australia: Australian National University. Department of Demography. Changing African Family Project. Monograph #4. Two Volumes. 1978. 848p.

Oppong, Christine (ed.)
Female and Male in West Africa. Boston: George Allen and Unwin. 1983. 402p.

Oucho, John O.
"Socio-Economic Perspectives of Fertility Regulation in Traditional and Modern African Societies." (In) University of Nairobi. Papers of the Seminar on Oral Traditions: Past Growth and Future Development in East Africa. Nairobi: University of Nairobi. UNESCO Institute of African Affairs. Kisumu, Kenya. April 18-22, 1979. 18p.

Page, Hilary J. and Lesthaeghe, Ron J. (eds.)
Child-Spacing in Tropical Africa: Traditions and Change. New York: Academic Press. Studies in Population Series. 1981. 332p.

Peart, Nicola S.
"Civil or Christian Marriage and Customary Unions: The Legal Position of the 'Discarded' Spouse and Children." Comparative and International Law Journal of Southern Africa. Volume 16 #1 1983. pp. 39-64.

Peel, J.D.Y.
"The Changing Family in Modern Ijesha History." Paper Presented at the Conference on the History of the Family in Africa. London: Cambridge University. School of Oriental and African Studies. September, 1981.

Peil, Margaret
African Urban Life: Components of Satisfaction. Birmingham, England: Birmingham University. Centre for West African Studies. 1982.

Pieters, Guy and Lowenfels, A.
"Infibulation in the Horn of Africa." New York State Journal of Medicine. Volume 77 April, 1977. pp. 729-731.

Pratt, Edward O.
"Current Status of Family Planning in Africa." (In) International Planned Parenthood Federation (IPPF). Proceedings of the IPPF Africa Regional Conference. London: IPPF. 1977. pp. 61-65.

Riesman, Paul
"Opulence and Pride in a Rite of Passage: A Comparison of the Weddings of Nobles and of Commoners in Fulani Society." Paper Presented at the Annual Meeting of the African Studies Association. Paper #102. Bloomington, Indiana. 1981.

Rogers, Barbara
"Food, Fertility and Nuclear Mothers: How Development Can

Increase Rather than Reduce the Social and Economic Burdens of African Women." Populi. Volume 5 #1 1978. pp. 23-27.

Rogers, Barbara
The Domestication of Women: Discrimination in Developing Societies. New York: St. Martin's Press. 1980. 200p.

Sacks, Karen
Sisters and Wives: The Past and Future of Sexual Equality. Westport, Connecticut: Greenwood Press. Contributions in Women's Studies #10. 1979. 274p.

Sai, Fred T.
"Report of the Conference on the Medical and Social Aspects of Abortion in Africa." (In) Sai, F.T. (ed.). A Strategy for Abortion Management. London: International Planned Parenthood Federation. 1978. pp 6-22.

Schoenmaeckers, Ronald C.
The Child-Spacing Tradition and the Postpartum Taboo in Tropical Africa: Anthropological Evidence. Paper Prepared for the IUSSP Workshop on Child-Spacing in Tropical Africa: Tradition and Change. Brussels, Belgium: International Union for the Scientific Study of Population. April, 17-19, 1979.

Schoenmaeckers, Ronald C. and Shah, I.H. and Lesthaeghe, Ron J. and Tambashe, O.
"The Child-Spacing Tradition and the Postpartum Taboo in Tropical Africa: Anthropological Evidence." (In) Page, Hilary J. and Lesthaeghe, Ron (eds.). Child-Spacing in Tropical Africa: Traditions and Change. New York: Academic Press. 1981. pp. 25-71.

Schwendinger, Julia and Schwendinger, Herman
"Rape, Sexual Inequality and Levels of Violence." Crime and Social Justice. Volume 16 Winter, 1981. pp. 3-31.

Seetharam, K.S. and Duza, M. Badrud and Sivamurthy, M.
"Nuptiality Patterns in Selected Urban Areas for Four Arab and African Cities." (In) Huzayyin, S.A. and Acsadi, G.T. (eds.). Family and Marriage in Some African and Asiatic Countries. Cairo, Egypt: Cairo Demographic Centre. CDC Research Monograph Series #6. 1976. pp. 311-323.

Seetharam, K.S. and Duza, M. Badrud
"Nuptiality and Fertility in Selected Areas of Four Arab and African Cities." (In) Huzayyin, S.A. and Acsadi, G.T. (eds.). Family and Marriage in Some African and Asiatic Countries. Cairo, Egypt: Cairo Demographic Centre. CDC Research Monograph Series #6. 1976. pp. 337-355.

Singleton, Michael
Contributions to the Rights and Wrongs of African Women. Brussels, Belgium: Pro Mundi Vita Dossiers. Africa Dossier #9. October, 1979. pp. 1-36.

Sivamurthy, M. and Seetharam, K.S.
"Age at First Marriage in Selected Areas of Four Arab and African Cities." (In) Huzayyin, S.A. and Acsadi, G.T.

(eds). Family and Marriage in Some African and Asiatic Countries. Cairo, Egypt: Cairo Demographic Centre. CDC Research Monograph Series #6. 1976. pp. 285-309.

Smith, Janet I.
"The Experience of Muslim Women: Considerations of Power and Authority." (In) Haddad, Yvonne Y. and Haines, Byron and Findly, Ellison (eds.). The Islamic Impact. Syracuse, New York: Syracuse University Press. 1984. pp. 89-112.

Smith, M.G.
"After Secondary Marriage What?" Ethnology. Volume 19 #3 July, 1980. pp. 265-278.

Spencer, P.
"Polygyny as a Measure of Social Differentiation in Africa." (In) Mitchell, J.C. (ed.). Numerical Techniques in Social Anthropology. Philadelphia, Pennsylvania: Institute for the Study of Human Issues. 1980.

Strodtbeck, Fred L.
"Intimacy in Conjugal Interaction and the Capacity to Plan." (In) Oppong, C. and Adaba, G. and Bekombo-Priso, M. and Mogey, J. (eds.). Marriage, Fertility and Parenthood in West Africa. Canberra, Australia: Australian National University. Department of Demography. Volume Two. 1978. pp. 747-763.

Sudarkasa, Niara
"Female Employment and Family Organization in West Africa." (In) Steady, Filomina C. (ed.). The Black Woman Cross-Culturally. Cambridge, Massachusetts: Schenkman Publishing. 1981. pp. 49-64.

Szklut, Jay
"Bride Wealth, An Alternate View." Behavior Science Research. Volume 16 #3/4 1981. pp. 225-247.

Tesha, Nancy
"Womens Role in Rearing Children and National Development." Paper Presented at the Workshop on Women's Studies and Development. Dar-es-Salaam, Tanzania: University of Dar-es-Salaam. Bureau of Resource Assessment and Land Use Planning. Paper #39. September 24-29, 1979. 3p.

Tillion, Germaine
The Republic of Cousins: Women's Oppression in Mediterranean Society. London: Al Saqi Books. Translated by Q. Hoare. 1983. 181p.

Ukaegbu, Alfred O.
"Marriage Habits and Fertility of Women in Tropical Africa: A Socio-Cultural Perspective." (In) Dupaquier, J. and Helin, E. and Laslett, P. and Livi-Bacci, M. (eds.). Marriage and Remarriage in Populations of the Past. New York: Academic Press. Population and Social Structure: Advances in Historical Demography Series. 1981. pp. 127-137.

United States Department of Health and Human Services
Family Planning Methods and Practice: Africa. Atlanta, Georgia: U.S. Department of Health and Human Services.

Centers for Disease Control. Center for Health Promotion and Education. 1983. 329p.
Ushewokunze, C.M.
"Reflections on Youth and Family Welfare Law in Africa." (In) International Planned Parenthood Federation (IPPF). Proceedings of the IPPF Africa Regional Conference. London: IPPF. 1977. pp. 182-190.
Valentine, C.H. and Revson, J.E.
"Cultural Traditions, Social Change, and Fertility in Sub-Saharan Africa." Journal of Modern African Studies. Volume 17 #3 September, 1979. pp. 453-472.
Van de Walle, Etienne
"Community Level Variable and Institutional Factors in the Study of African Nuptiality." (In) Casterline, John B. (ed.). The Collection and Analysis of Community Data. Voorburg, Netherlands: International Statistical Institute. 1985. pp. 103-111.
Waines, D.
"Through a Veil Darkly--The Study of Women in Muslim Societies." Comparative Studies in Society and History. Volume 24 #4 1982.
Walle, Etienne V. and Kekouole, John
The Recent Evolution of African Marriage and Polygyny. Philadelphia, Pennsylvania: University of Pennsylvania. Population Studies Center. 1984.
Ware, Helen
"Women's Work and Fertility in Africa." (In) Kupinsky, Stanley (ed.). The Fertility of Working Women: A Synthesis of International Research. New York: Praeger Publishers. Praeger Special Studies in International Economics and Development. 1977. pp. 1-34.
Ware, Helen
"Economic Strategy and the Number of Children." (In) Caldwell, John C. (ed.). The Persistence of High Fertility: Population Prospects in the Third World. Canberra, Australia: Australian National University. Department of Demography. Volume Two. 1977. pp. 469-592.
Ware, Helen
Women, Education and Modernization of the Family in West Africa. Canberra, Australia: Australian National University. Department of Demography. Changing African Family Project Series. Monograph #7. 1981. 178p.
Ware, Helen
"Motivations for the Use of Birth Control: Evidence From West Africa." Demography. Volume 13 #4 November, 1976. pp. 479-494.
Wegner, J.R.
"The Status of Women in Jewish and Islamic Marriage and Divorce Law." Harvard Women's Law Journal. Volume 5 #1 1982.
Welch, Charles E. and Glick, Paul C.
"The Incidence of Polygamy in Contemporary Africa: A Research Note." Journal of Marriage and the Family. Volume 43 #1 February, 1981. pp. 191-192.

White, Douglas R. and Bruton, Michael L. and Dow, Malcolm M. "Sexual Division of Labor in African Agriculture: A Network Autocorrelation Analysis." American Anthropologist. Volume 83 #4 December, 1981. pp. 824-849.

White, Luise S. "Women in the Changing African Family." (In) Hay, Margaret J. and Stichter, Sharon (eds.). African Women South of the Sahara. New York: Longman. 1984. pp. 53-68.

Whyte, Martin K. The Status of Women in Preindustrial Societies. Princeton, New Jersey: Princeton University Press. 1978. 222p.

Youssef, Nadia H. "Interrelationship Between the Division of Labor in the Household, Women's Roles and Their Impact Upon Fertility." Paper Presented at the Informal Workshop on Women's Roles and Demographic Research Program. Geneva: International Labour Organization. November, 1978.

Youssef, Nadia H. and Hetler, Carol B. "Establishing the Economic Condition of Woman-Headed Households in the Third World: A New Approach." (In) Buvinic, Mayra and Lycette, Margaret A. and McGreevey, William P. (eds.). Women and Poverty in the Third World. Baltimore, Maryland: Johns Hopkins University. 1983. pp. 216-243.

Zivetz, L. The Impact of Rural Development on the Status of Women and Its Consequences for Fertility in Africa. Submitted to the Research Triangle Institute and the Southeast Consortium for International Development. Chapel Hill, North Carolina. 1979.

Mass Media

Anonymous
"Women in East Africa Media Were 1% of Total: Now are 5% to 10%." Media Report to Women. Volume 8 January 1, 1980. pp. 6.

Besha, R.M.
The Mass Media and Entertainment. Dar-es-Salaam, Tanzania: University of Dar-es-Salaam. Bureau of Resource Assessment and Land Use Planning. Workshop on Women's Studies and Development. Paper #34. September 24-29, 1979.

Dawit, T.
"Mass Media and Rural Women in Africa." Assignment Children. Volume 38 #2 April-June, 1977. pp. 119-120.

Hall, Susan
"African Women on Film." Africa Report. Volume 22 #1 January-February, 1977. pp. 15-17.

Isaacs, Gayla C.
"Women in Southern Africa: The Media and the Ideal Woman." Africa Report. Volume 28 #2 March-April, 1983. pp. 48-51.

McCaffrey, Kathleen M.
"African Women on the Screen." Africa Report. Volume 26 #2 March-April, 1981. pp. 56-58.

McCaffrey, Kathleen M.
"Images of Women in West African Literature and Film: A Struggle Against Dual Colonization." International Journal of Women's Studies. Volume 3 #1 January-February, 1980. pp. 76-88.

Migration

Adepoju, Aderanti
"Patterns of Migration by Sex." (In) Oppong, Christine (ed.). Female and Male in West Africa. London: George Allen and Unwin. 1983. pp. 54-66.

Adepoju, Aderanti
"Migration and Development in Tropical Africa: Some Research Priorities." African Affairs. Volume 76 #303 April, 1977. pp. 210-225.

Bryant, Coralie
"Women Migrants, Urbanization and Social Change: An African Case." Paper Presented at the American Political Science Association Annual Meeting. Washington, D.C. September, 1977.

Chaney, Elsa M.
Women in International Migration: Issues in Development Planning. Washington, D.C.: U.S. Department of State. U.S. Agency for International Development. Office of Women in Development. June, 1980.

Chaney, Elsa M. and Lewis, Martha W.
Women, Migration and the Decline of Smallholder Agriculture. Washington, D.C.: U.S. Department of State. U.S. Agency for International Development. Office of Women in Development. October, 1980.

Guyot, Jean
Migrant Women Speak: Interviews. London: Search Press Ltd. for the Churches Committee on Migrant Workers. 1978. 164p.

International Center for Research on Women
Women in Migration: A Third World Focus. Washington, D.C.: U.S. Department of State. U.S. Agency for International Development. Office of Women in Development. 1979.

Marks, Shula and Unterhalter, Elaine
Women and the Migrant Labour System in Southern Africa. Lusaka, Zambia: United Nations Economic Commission for Africa. Multinational Programming and Operational Centre

for Eastern and Central Africa. 1978. 15p.
Murray, Colin G.
"Migrant Labour and Changing Family Structure in the Rural Periphery of Southern Africa." Journal of Southern African Studies. Volume 6 #2 1980. pp. 139-156.
Obbo, Christine S.
"Town Migration is Not for Women." Ph.D. Dissertation: University of Wisconsin-Madison. Madison, Wisconsin. 1977. 329p.
Palmer, Ingrid
The Impact of Male Out-Migration on Women in Farming. West Hartford, Connecticut: Kumarian Press. 1985. 78p.
Robertson, Claire C.
"Women in the Urban Economy." (In) Hay, Margaret J. and Stichter, Sharon (eds.). African Women South of the Sahara. New York: Longman. 1984. pp. 33-50.
Saleh, Saneya
"Professional Women and National Development: Women's Response to Migration." Paper Presented at the Open University Women Seminar Series on Women, Work and Social Change. Cairo, Egypt: American University of Cairo. May 16, 1977.
Sudarkasa, Niara
The Effects of 20th Century Social Change, Especially of Migration, on Women of West Africa. Tucson, Arizona: University of Arizona. Proceedings of the West Africa Conference. 1976. pp. 102-109.
Thadani, Veena N. and Todaro, Michael P.
Female Migration in Developing Countries: A Framework for Analysis. New York: Population Council. Center for Policy Studies. Working Papers #47. 1979. 48p.
Youssef, Nadia H. and Buvinic, Mayra and Kudat, Ayse
Women in Migration: A Third World Focus. Washington, D.C.: U.S. Department of State. U.S. Agency for International Development. International Centre for Research on Women. Office of Women in Development. 1979. 151p.

Miscellaneous

Accad, Evelyne
"The Prostitute in Arab and North African Fiction." (In) Horn, Pierre L. and Pringle, Mary B. (eds.). The Image of the Prostitute in Modern Literature. New York: Ungar. 1984. pp. 63-75.

Adedeji, John A.
"Social Change and Women in African Sport." International Social Science Journal. Volume 34 #2 1982. pp. 210-218.

Anker, Richard and Buvinic, Mayra and Youssef, Nadia H. (eds.)
Women's Roles and Population Trends in the Third World. London: Croon Helm Ltd. 1982. 288p.

Anker, Richard
Demographic Change and the Role of Women: A Research Programme in Developing Countries. Geneva: International Labour Office. Population and Employment Working Paper #69. 1978. 27p.

Attah, E.B.
Family Nucleation and Fertility Change in Tropical Africa: Background to the Demographic Transition. Atlanta, Georgia: Atlanta University. Department of Sociology. 1985.

Bujra, Janet M.
"Production, Property, Prostitution--Sexual Politics in Atu." Cahiers d'Etudes Africaines. Volume 17 #1 1977. pp. 13-40.

Bujra, Janet M.
"Prostitution, Class and the State." (In) Sumner, Colin (ed.). Crime, Justice, and Underdevelopment. London: Heineman. Cambridge Studies in Criminology. #46. 1982. pp. 145-161.

Caldwell, Pat and Caldwell, John C.
"Population Change and Development in the ECWA Region." (In) Cairo Demographic Centre (CDC). Aspects of Population Change and Development in Some African and

Asian Countries. Cairo, Egypt: CDC. CDC Research Monograph Series #9. 1984. pp. 43-56.
Chojnacka, Helena
"Polygyny and the Rate of Population Growth." Human Resources Research Bulletin. #78/05 1978. 34p.
Clignet, Remi and Sween, Joyce A.
"Ethnicity and Fertility: Implications for Population Programs in Africa." Africa. Volume 48 #1 1978. pp. 47-65.
Cohn, Steven and Wood, Robert and Haig, Richard
"U.S. Aid and Third World Women: The Impact of Peace Corps Programs." Economic Development and Cultural Change. Volume 29 #4 July, 1981. pp. 795-811.
Cook, Gayla
"Women in Africa: Working With African Women: Options for the West." Africa Report. Volume 26 #2 March-April, 1981. pp. 43-46.
Fabian, Johannes
"Popular Culture in Africa: Findings and Conjectures." Africa. Volume 48 #4 1978. pp. 315-334.
Gadalla, Saad M.
Population Policy and Family Planning Communication Strategies in the Arab States Region. Paris: UNESCO. Volume One: Summaries of Pertinent Literature and Research Studies. 1978.
Hawthorn, Geoffrey (ed.)
Population and Development: High and Low Fertility in Poorer Countries. London: Frank Cass. 1978. 210p.
Henn, Albert E.
Before Family Planning: The Implications of Infertility in Africa for Population Program Planning. Washington, D.C.: World Population Society Meeting. Mimeo. December, 1976.
Hill, Allan G (ed.)
Population, Health and Nutrition in the Sahel: Issues in the Welfare of Selected West African Communities. Boston: KPI. 1985. 399p.
Hosken, Fran P.
"Fran Hosken Reports on Women's Communication Networks in Africa." Media Report to Women. Volume 5 September 1, 1977. pp. 12.
Igbinovia, Patrick E.
"Prostitution in Black Africa." International Journal of Women's Studies. Volume 7 #5 Nov.-Dec., 1984. pp. 430-449.
Johnston, Bruce F. and Meyer, Anthony J.
"Nutrition, Health and Population in Strategies for Rural Development." Economic Development and Cultural Change. Volume 26 #1 October, 1977. pp. 1-23.
Johnston, Bruce F. and Meyer, Anthony J.
Nutrition, Health and Population in Strategies for Rural Development. Nairobi: University of Nairobi. Institute for Development Studies. Discussion Paper #238. 1976. 45p.

Kisekka, Mere N.
"The Status of Women, Development and Population Trends in Africa: An Annotated Bibliography." Paper Presented at the Meeting of Experts on Research on the Status of Women, Development and Population Trends: Evaluation and Prospects. Paris: United Nations Educational, Scientific and Cultural Organization. 1980. 66p.

Kisekka, Mere N.
"Research on the Status of Women, Development and Population Trends in Africa: An Annotated Bibliography." (In) United Nations Educational, Scientific and Cultural Organization. Bibliographic Guide to Studies on the Status of Women: Development and Population. Paris: UNESCO. 1983. pp. 41-66.

Kitching, Gavin
"Proto-Industrialization and Demographic Change: A Thesis and Some Possible African Implications." Journal of African History. Volume 24 #2 1983. pp. 221-240.

LeVine, Sarah
"Crime or Afflictions: Rape in an African Community." Culture, Medicine and Psychiatry. Volume 4 #2 1980.

Lucas, D.
"Demographic Aspects of Women's Employment in Africa." Manpower and Unemployment Research. Volume 10 #1 April, 1977. pp. 31-38.

Mazrui, Ali A.
"Military Technology and the Masculinity of War: An African Perspective." Impact of Science on Society. Volume 26 #1/2 January-April, 1976. pp. 71-75.

Muriuki, Margaret N.
"The Role of Women in African Librarianship: The Next 25 Years." Paper Presented at the Standing Conference of Eastern, Central and Southern African Libraries. Lusaka, Zambia. October 4-9, 1976.

Mushanga, Tibamanya M.
"Wife Victimization in East and Central Africa." Victimology. Volume 2 #3/4 1977. pp. 479-486.

Rosenberg, E.M.
"Demographic Effects of Sex Differential Nutrition." (In) Jerome, Norge W. and Kandel, Randy F. and Pelto, Gretel H. (eds.). Nutritional Anthropology. Pleasantville, New York: Redgrave Publishing. 1980. pp. 181-201.

Russell, Diana E.H. and Vandeven, Nicole (eds.)
Crimes Against Women: Proceedings of the International Tribunal. Millbrae, California: Les Femmes. 1976. 298p.

Schutjer, Wayne A. and Stokes, C. Shannon
"Agricultural Policies and Human Fertility: Some Emerging Connections." Population Research and Policy Review. Volume 1 October, 1982. pp. 225-244.

Schwendinger, Julia and Schwendinger, Herman
"Rape, Sexual Inequality and Levels of Violence." Crime and Social Justice. Volume 16 Winter, 1981. pp. 3-31.

MISCELLANEOUS

Staveley, Jennifer L.
"Prostitutes and Prostitution in Africa: The Development of Women's First Wage Earning Activity." M.A. Thesis: University of Waterloo. Waterloo, Ontario, Canada. 1977.

United Nations Educational, Scientific, and Cultural Organ.
Bibliographic Guide to Studies on the Status of Women: Development and Population Trends. Paris: UNESCO. Epping, England: Bowker. 1983. 284p.

United Nations Food and Agriculture Organization (FAO)
The Role of Women in Population Dynamics Related to Food and Agriculture and Rural Development in Africa. Rome: FAO. United Nations Economic Commission for Africa. Women's Program Unit. Joint Agriculture Division. 1976.

United Nations Fund for Population Activities
Forum on Population and Development for Women Leaders From Sub-Saharan African Countries. New York: United Nations Fund for Population Activities. May 15-18, 1984. 39p.

Ware, Helen
"Female and Male Life-Cycles." (In) Oppong, Christine (ed.). Female and Male in West Africa. London: George Allen and Unwin. 1983. pp. 6-31.

Nationalism

Accad, Evelyne
"Complex Inter-Relation of Women's Liberation and Arab Nationalism in North African Novels Written by Women." Paper Presented at the Annual Meeting of the African Studies Association. Paper #1. Boston, Massachusetts. 1976. 16p.

Accad, Evelyne
"Interrelationship Between Arab Nationalism and Feminist Consciousness in the North African Novels Written by Women." Ba Shiru. Volume 8 #2 1977. pp. 3-12.

Anonymous
"International Conference on the Role of Women in Liberation Struggles and Women in Development." IDOC Bulletin. #50/51 December-January, 1976. pp. 4-21.

Anonymous
"Southern African Women Speak Out." Africa Report. Volume 28 #2 March-April, 1983. pp. 15-19.

Anonymous
"Two Views of Liberation." Agenda. Volume 1 #2 February, 1978. pp. 19-22.

Case, Frederick
"Workers Movements: Revolution and Women's Consciousness in God's Bits of Wood." Canadian Journal of African Studies. Volume 15 #2 1981. pp. 272-292.

Denzer, LaRay
"Women in the West African Nationalist Movement From 1939-1950." Africana Research Review. Volume 7 #4 July, 1976. pp. 65-85.

Douglas, Carol A.
"Ajowa Ifateyo: Speaking Up Front (Interview)." Off Our Backs. Volume 14 November, 1984. pp. 10-12.

Fairbanks, Z.
"Fighting Women Go Home." New Statesman. Volume 101 April 17, 1981. pp. 14-15.

Kisekka, Mere N.
"On the Status of Women Within the Framework of the Liberation Movement." African Urban Notes. Volume 2 #3 Fall/Winter, 1976. pp. 65-74.

Matsepe, Ivy F.
"Women in the Struggle for Liberation." (In) Wiley, David and Isaacman, Allen (eds.). Southern Africa: Society, Economy and Liberation. East Lansing, Michigan: Michigan State University. African Studies Center. 1981.

Mbilinyi, Marjorie J.
"Women in Liberation Struggles." ISIS International Bulletin. April, 1977. pp. 8-10.

O'Barr, Jean F.
African Women in Politics. (In) Hay, Margaret J. and Stichter, Sharon (eds.). African Women South of the Sahara. New York: Longman. 1984. pp. 140-155.

Schultz, Bonnie J.
"Women and African Liberation--Miriam Makeba, An Interview." Africa Report. Volume 22 #1 January-February, 1977. pp. 10-14.

Uba, Sam
"Women Put the Case for Southern African Liberation." New African Development. March, 1977.

Urdang, Stephanie
"Women in National Liberation Movements." (In) Hay, Margaret J. and Stichter, Sharon (eds.). African Women South of the Sahara. New York: Longman. 1984. pp. 156-169.

Van Allen, Judith
"African Women, 'Modernization' and National Liberation." (In) Iglitzin, Lynne B. and Ross, Ruth (eds.). Women in the World. Santa Barbara, California: Clio Press. American Bibliographic Center. 1976. pp. 25-54.

Weiss, R.
"Women in Liberation Movements." (In) Schild, U. (ed.). Jaw-Bone and Umbilical Cords: A Selection of Papers Presented at the Third Janheinz Jahn Symposium, 1979 and the Fourth Jan einz Jahn Symposium, 1982. Berlin, Germany: Reimer. 1985. pp. 127-133.

Organizations

African-American Labor Center
"Pan-African Conference on the Role of Trade Union Women." Paper Presented at the Conference on the Role of Trade Union Women: Problems, Prospects, Programs." New York: African-American Labor Center. Nairobi, Kenya. July 17-27, 1977. 152p.

Anonymous
"African Women's Development Task Force." Rural Progress. Volume 1 #1 October, 1977. pp. 25-26.

DeLancey, Virginia H.
"The Role of Credit Unions in Development for West African Women." Paper Presented at the Annual Meeting of the African Studies Association. Paper #29. Bloomington, Indiana. October 21-24, 1981.

Hosken, Fran P.
"Fran Hosken Reports on Women's Communication Networks in Africa." Media Report to Women. Volume 5 September 1, 1977. pp. 12.

Kayongo-Male, Diana
"Helping Self-Help Groups Help Themselves: Training of Leaders of Women's Groups." Journal of Eastern African Research and Development. Volume 13 1983. pp. 88-103.

McGrath, Mary J.
"What Private Institutions, Particularly Cooperative, Can do to Facilitate Full Participation of Women in Meeting Food and Nutrition Needs." (In) University of Arizona. Proceedings and Papers of the International Conference on Women and Food: Consortium for International Development. Tucson, Arizona: University of Arizona. 1978. pp. 145-153.

NGO Planning Committee
Forum '85: Final Report: Nairobi, Kenya. New York: NGO Planning Committee. 1985. 105p.

Naali, Shamsahd
"Legal Provisions for Women's Participation in Cooperatives." Paper Presented at the Seminar on Women's Studies and Development. Dar-es-Salaam, Tanzania: University of Dar-es-Salaam. Bureau of Resource Assessment and Land Use Planning. Paper #15. September 24-29, 1979. 10p.

Regional Economic Reseach and Documentation Center (Lome)
"The Role of African Trade Union Women." Paper Presented at the Pan African Conference on the Role of African Trade Union Women. Lome, Togo: Regional Economic Research and Documentation Center. 1978. 25p.

Reno, Barbara M.
Increasing Women's Credit Through Credit Unions in West Africa. Bilingual Seminar. Nairobi: Africa Co-Operative Savings and Credit Association. March 2-6, 1981. 43p.

Staudt, Kathleen A.
"The Umoja Federation: Women's Cooptation Into a Local Power Structure." Western Political Quarterly. Volume 33 #2 June, 1980. pp. 278-290.

Staudt, Kathleen A.
Women's Organizations in Rural Development. Washington, D.C.: U.S. Department of State. U.S. Agency for International Development. Office of Women in Development. February, 1980. 71p.

Staudt, Kathleen A.
"Organizing Rural Women in the Third World." Paper Presented at the Annual Meeting of the Western Political Science Association. March 27-29, 1980.

Stephens, Betsy and Odell, M.
"Professional Women in Development Assistance." International Development Review. Volume 19 #2 1977. pp. 3-5.

Takata, Diana M.
"Private Volunteer Organizations and Women's Participation in African Development." Rural Africana. #21 Winter, 1985. pp. 65-80.

Takata, Diane M.
"Increasing Women's Participation in the African Development Process Through the Assistance of U.S. Private Voluntary Organizations." Paper Presented at the Annual Meeting of the African Studies Association. Paper #113. Washington, D.C. November 4-7, 1982.

U.S. Agency for International Development (U.S. AID)
International Directory of Women's Development Organizations. Washington, D.C.: U.S. Department of State. U.S. AID. Office of Women in Development. 1977. 311p.

United Nations
Building New Knowledge Through Technical Cooperation Among Developing Countries: The Experience of the Association of African Women for Research and Development (AAWORD). New York: United Nations. March 6, 1980.

United Nations
Measures of Assistance for Women in Southern Africa. Paper Presented at the United Nations World Conference of the United Nations Decade for Women: Equality, Development and Peace. New York: United Nations. Copenhagen, Denmark. July 14-30, 1980. 34p.

United Nations
Report of the World Conference to Review and Appraise the Achievements of the United Nations Decade for Women: Equality, Development and Peace. Nairobi, Kenya, July 15-26, 1985. New York: United Nations. 1986. 304p.

United Nations Economic Commission for Africa (UNECA)
Origin and Growth of the African Training and Research Centre for Women of the Economic Commission for Africa. Addis Ababa, Ethiopia: UNECA. September, 1977. 60p.

United Nations Economic Commission for Africa (UNECA)
Summary of On-Going and Planned Projects of the United Nations Agencies and Organizations for the Integration of Women in Development in the African Region. Addis Ababa, Ethiopia: UNECA. 1980. 72p.

United Nations Economic Commission for Africa (UNECA)
Establishment of Sub-Regional Machinery to Enhance the Role of Women in the Progress of Economic and Social Development in the Central African Sub-Region and to Promote and Guide the Activities of the ECA's Training and Research Centre for Women. Yaounde, Cameroon: MULPOC (Multi-National Operations Center for Central African Library). March, 1978.

United Nations Economic Commission for Africa (UNECA)
ECA Five Year Programme on Pre-Vocational and Vocational Training of Girls and Women, Toward Their Full Participation in Development (1972-1976). Addis Ababa, Ethiopia: UNECA. 1976.

United Nations Economic Commission for Africa (UNECA)
African Women's Development Task Force. Addis Ababa, Ethiopia: UNECA. African Training and Research Centre for Women. 1976. 15p.

United Nations Economic Commission for Africa (UNECA)
"National Machinery for the Integration of Women in Development in African Countries." Paper Presented to the Regional Conference on the Implementation of the National Regional and Worlds Plans of Action for the Integration of Women in Development. Addis Ababa, Ethiopia: UNECA. Nouakchott, Mauritania. 1977. 54p.

Weiss, R.
"Women in Liberation Movements." (In) Schild, U. (ed.). Jaw-Bone and Umbilical Cords: A Selection of Papers Presented at the Third Janheinz Jahn Symposium, 1979 and the Fourth Jan einz Jahn Symposium, 1982. Berlin, Germany: Reimer. 1985. pp. 127-133.

Wipper, Audrey
"Women's Voluntary Associations." (In) Hay, Margaret J. and Stichter, Sharon (eds.). African Women South of the Sahara. New York: Longman. 1984. pp. 69-86.

Politics and Government

Abbott, Susan
"In the End You Will Carry Me in Your Car--Sexual Politics in the Field." Women's Studies. Volume 10 #2 1983. pp. 161-178.

Amin, Samir
Imperialism and Unequal Development. New York: Monthly Review Press. 1977.

Anonymous
"International Conference on the Role of Women in Liberation Struggles and Women in Development." IDOC Bulletin. #50/51 December-January, 1976. pp. 4-21.

Anonymous
"Southern African Women Speak Out." Africa Report. Volume 28 #2 March-April, 1983. pp. 15-19.

Anonymous
"Workshop on Better Quality of Life for Rural Women Leaders." Rural Progress. Volume 2 #2 January, 1982. pp. 12-13.

Bujra, Janet M.
"Prostitution, Class and the State." (In) Sumner, Colin (ed.). Crime, Justice, and Underdevelopment. London: Heineman. Cambridge Studies in Criminology. #46. pp. 145-161. 1982.

Cohn, Steven and Wood, Robert and Haig, Richard
"U.S. Aid and Third World Women: The Impact of Peace Corps Programs." Economic Development and Cultural Change. Volume 29 #4 July, 1981. pp. 795-811.

Cook, Gayla
"Women in Africa: Working With African Women: Options for the West." Africa Report. Volume 26 #2 March-April, 1981. pp. 43-46.

Denzer, LaRay
"Women in the West African Nationalist Movement From 1939-1950." Africana Research Review. Volume 7 #4 July, 1976. pp. 65-85.

Douglas, Carol A.
"Ajowa Ifateyo: Speaking Up Front (Interview)." Off Our Backs. Volume 14 November, 1984. pp. 10-12.
Due, Jean M. and Summary, Rebecca
"Constraints to Women and Development in Africa." Journal of Modern African Studies. Volume 20 #1 March, 1982. pp. 155-166.
Due, Jean M. and Summary, Rebecca
"Constraints to Women and Development in Africa." Paper Presented at the Annual Meeting of the African Studies Association. Paper #35. Los Angeles, California. 1979. 23p.
Due, Jean M. and Summary, Rebecca
Constraints to Women and Development in Africa. Urbana, Illinois: University of Illinois-Urbana-Champaign. Department of Agricultural Economics. Staff Paper Series E. Agricultural Economics 79-E-83. May, 1979. 27p.
Dunbar, Roberta
"Legislative Reform and Muslim Family Law: Effects Upon Women's Rights in Africa South of the Sahara." Paper Presented at the Annual Meeting of the African Studies Association. Paper #25. Philadelphia, Pennsylvania. October 15-18, 1980.
Ekechi, Felix K.
"African Polygamy and Western Christian Ethnocentrism." Journal of African Studies. Volume 3 #3 August, 1976. pp. 329-349.
Fairbanks, Z.
"Fighting Women Go Home." New Statesman. Volume 101 April 17, 1981. pp. 14-15.
Fields, Karen E.
"Political Contingencies of Witchcraft in Colonial Central Africa." Canadian Journal of African Studies. Volume 16 #3 1982. pp. 567-593.
Fraker, Anne and Harrell-Bond, Barbara
"Feminine Influence." West Africa. December 17, 1979. pp. 2182-2186.
Grohs, G.
"Women and Politician in the Modern African Novel." (In) Schild, U. (ed.). Jaw-Bones and Umbilical Cords: A Selection of Papers Presented at the Third Janheinz Jahn Symposium, 1979 and the Fourth Janheinz Jahn Symposium, 1982. Berlin, Germany: Reimer. 1985. pp. 119-126.
Howard, Rhoda E.
"Women and the Crisis in Commonwealth Africa." International Political Science Review. Volume 6 #3 1985. pp. 287-296.
International Labour Organization (ILO)
Female Power, Autonomy and Demographic Change in the Third World. Geneva: ILO. The Role of Women and Demographic Change Ressearch Programme. 1980.
Johnson, B.C.
"Traditional Practices Affecting the Health of Women." Paper Presented at the Seminar on Traditional Practices Affecting the Health of Women and Children. World

Conference of the United Nations Decade for Women. New York: United Nations. Copenhagen, Denmark. July 14-30, 1980.

Kisekka, Mere N.
"On the Status of Women Within the Framework of the Liberation Movement." African Urban Notes. Volume 2 #3 Fall/Winter, 1976. pp. 65-74.

Konie, Gwendoline
"Women in Southern Africa: Gaining Political Power." Africa Report. Volume 28 #2 March-April, 1983. pp. 11-14.

Koning, Karen L.
"Revolutionary Potential Among Arab Women Today." Mawazo. Volume 4 #4 1976. pp. 48-57.

Leis, Nancy B.
"West African Women and the Colonial Experience." Western Canadian Journal of Anthropology. Volume 6 #3 1976. pp. 123-132.

Lewis, Barbara C.
"State/Society; Public/Private and Women: A Political Scientist's View." Paper Presented at the Annual Meeting of the African Studies Association. Paper #75. Bloomington, Indiana. October 21-24, 1981.

Marshall, Susan E.
"Politics and Female Status in North Africa: A Reconsideration of Development Theory." Economic Development and Cultural Change. Volume 32 #3 April, 1984. pp. 499-524.

Matsepe, Ivy F.
"Underdevelopment and African Women." Journal of Southern African Affairs. Volume 2 #2 April, 1977. pp. 135-143.

Matsepe, Ivy F.
"Women in the Struggle for Liberation." (In) Wiley, David and Isaacman, Allen (eds.). Southern Africa: Society, Economy and Liberation. East Lansing, Michigan: Michigan State University. African Studies Center. 1981.

Matsepe-Casaburri, Ivy F.
Uneven Development and Political Consciousness Among African Women in Southern Africa. Lusaka, Zambia: United Nations Institute on Namibia. 1978.

Mbilinyi, Marjorie J.
"Women in Liberation Struggles." ISIS International Bulletin. April, 1977. pp. 8-10.

N'ska, Leci
"The Discrimination Against Women in the Civil Service." Viva. Volume 7 #2 1981. pp. 15-17, 45.

O'Barr, Jean F.
"Pare Women: A Case of Political Involvement." Rural Africana. Volume 2 1976. pp. 121-134.

O'Barr, Jean F.
Third World Women: Factors in Their Changing Status. Durham, North Carolina: Duke University. Center for International Studies. Occasional Paper #2. 1976. 94p.

O'Barr, Jean F.
African Women in Politics. (In) Hay, Margaret J. and Stichter, Sharon (eds.). African Women South of the Sahara. New York: Longman. 1984. pp. 140-155.

O'Barr, Jean F. (ed.)
Perspectives on Power: Women in Africa, Asia and Latin America. Durham, North Carolina: Duke University. Center for International Studies. Occasional Paper #13. 1982. 120p.

Obbo, Christine S. and Nelson, Nici
African Women: Their Struggle for Economic Independence. Westport, Connecticut: Lawrence Hill. 1980. 176p.

Ogundipe-Leslie, Molara
"African Women, Culture and Another Development." Journal of African Marxists. #5 February, 1984. pp. 77-92.

Ooko-Ombaka, Oki
"An Assessment of National Machinery for Women." Assignment Children. #49/50 Spring, 1980.

Roberts, Penelope
"Feminism in Africa: Feminism and Africa." Review of African Political Economy. #27/28 1984. pp. 175-184.

Safilios-Rothschild, Constantina
Access of Rural Girls to Primary Education in the Third World: State of Art, Obstacles and Policy Recommendations. Washington, D.C.: U.S. Department of State. U.S. Agency for International Development. 1979. 31p.

Staudt, Kathleen A.
"The Umoja Federation: Women's Cooptation Into a Local Power Structure." Western Political Quarterly. Volume 33 #2 June, 1980. pp. 278-290.

Staudt, Kathleen A. and Jaquette, Jane S. (eds.)
Women in Developing Countries: A Policy Focus. New York: Haworth Press. 1983. 135p.

Staudt, Kathleen A.
"Class and Sex in the Politics of Women Farmers." Journal of Politics. Volume 41 #2 May, 1979. pp. 492-512.

Staudt, Kathleen A.
"Women's Politics in Africa." Williamsburg, Virginia: College of William and Mary. Anthropology Department. Studies in Third World Societies Publication #16. June, 1981. pp. 1-28.

Staudt, Kathleen A.
"Agricultural Productivity Gaps: A Case Study of Male Preference in Government Policy Implementation." Development and Change. Volume 9 #3 July, 1978. pp. 439-458.

Staudt, Kathleen A.
Women's Politics and Capitalist Transformation in Subsaharan Africa. East Lansing, Michigan: Michigan State University. Office of Women in International Development. Working Paper #54. April, 1984.

Sutlive, Vinson H. and Altshuler, Nathan and Zamora, Mario D.
Women and Politics in 20th Century Africa and Asia. Williamsburg, Virginia: College of William and Mary. Anthropology Department. Studies in Third World Societies. Publication #16. 1981. 160p.
Tabah, Leon
"Policy Implications of the Phenomenon of Rising Fertility in Response to Modernization." (In) Cairo Demographic Centre (CDC). Determinants of Fertility in Some African And Asian Countries. Cairo, Egypt: CDC. CDC Research Monograph Series #10. 1982. pp. 13-19.
U.S. Agency for International Development (U.S. AID)
International Directory of Women's Development Organizations. Washington, D.C.: U.S. Department of State. U.S. AID. Office of Women in Development. 1977. 311p.
United Nations Economic Commission for Africa (UNECA)
The New International Economic Order--What Role for Women in Africa? Addis Ababa, Ethiopia: UNECA. August, 1977. 54p.
United Nations Economic Commission for Africa (UNECA)
"National Machinery for the Integration of Women in Development in African Countries." Paper Presented to the Regional Conference on the Implementation of the National Regional and Worlds Plans of Action for the Integration of Women in Development. Addis Ababa, Ethiopia: UNECA. Nouakchott, Mauritania. 1977. 54p.
Urdang, Stephanie
"Women in National Liberation Movements." (In) Hay, Margaret J. and Stichter, Sharon (eds.). African Women South of the Sahara. New York: Longman. 1984. pp. 156-169.
Van Allen, Judith
"African Women, 'Modernization' and National Liberation." (In) Iglitzin, Lynne B. and Ross, Ruth (eds.). Women in the World. Santa Barbara, California: Clio Press. American Bibliographic Center. 1976. pp. 25-54.
Weiss, R.
"Women in Liberation Movements." (In) Schild, U. (ed.). Jaw-Bone and Umbilical Cords: A Selection of Papers Presented at the Third Janheinz Jahn Symposium, 1979 and the Fourth Jan einz Jahn Symposium, 1982. Berlin, Germany: Reimer. 1985. pp. 127-133.
Westwood, Sally
Women and Power in Africa. Belfast, Maine: Porter. 1978.
Wipper, Audrey
"Riot and Rebellion Among African Women: Three Examples of Women's Political Clout." (In) O'Barr, Jean (ed.). Perspectives on Power: Women in Africa, Asia and Latin America. Durham, North Carolina: Duke University. Center for International Studies. 1982. pp. 50-72.

Religion and Witchcraft

Appiah-Kubi, Kofi
"Monogamy: Is it Really So Christian?" African Women. #5 July-August, 1976. pp. 46-48.

Baffoun, Alya
"Women and Social Change in the Muslim Arab World." Women's Studies International Forum. Volume 5 #2 1982.

Baldwin, Lewis V.
"Black Women and African Union Methodism, 1813-1983." Methodist History. Volume 21 July, 1983. pp. 225-237.

Berger, Iris
"Rebels or Status Seekers? Women as Spirit Mediums in East Africa." (In) Hafkin, N.J. and Bay, Edna (eds.). Women in Africa: Studies in Social and Economic Change. Stanford, California: Stanford University Press. 1976. pp. 157-181.

Berger, Iris
"Women, Religion and Social Change: East and Central African Perspectives." Paper Presented at the Conference on Women and Development. Wellesley, Massachusetts: Wellesley College. Wellesley College Center for Research on Women. June 2-6, 1976. 25p.

Brandel, Syrier M.
"The Role of Women in African Independent Churches (Manyanos)." Missionalia. Volume 12 #1 April, 1984. pp. 13-18.

Caldwell, John C. and Caldwell, Pat
Cultural Forces Tending to Sustain High Fertility in Tropical Africa. Canberra, Australia: Australian National University. 1984.

Campbell, Penelope
"Presbyterian West African Missions: Women as Converts and Agents of Social Change." Journal of Presbyterian History. Volume 56 #2 Summer, 1978. pp. 121-132.

Caplan, Patricia
"Cognatic Descent, Islamic Law, and Women's Property on the East African Coast." (In) Hirschon, Renbee (ed.). Women and Property--Women as Property. New York: St.Martin's Press. 1983.

Carroll, Theodora F.
Women, Religion and Development in the Third World. New York: Praeger Publishers. 1983. 292p.

Catchpole, David R.
"The Fearful Silence of the Women at the Tomb: A Study in Markan Theology." Journal of Theology for Southern Africa. #18 March, 1977. pp. 3-10.

Davis, W.T.
"Rome and the Ordination of Women." West African Religion. Volume 17 #2 1978. pp. 3-8.

Dunbar, Roberta
"Legislative Reform and Muslim Family Law: Effects Upon Women's Rights in Africa South of the Sahara." Paper Presented at the Annual Meeting of the African Studies Association. Paper #25. Philadelphia, Pennsylvania. October 15-18, 1980.

Edwards, Felicity
"The Doctrine of God and the Feminine Principle." Journal of Theology for Southern Africa. #37 December, 1981. pp. 23-37.

Ekechi, Felix K.
"African Polygamy and Western Christian Ethnocentrism." Journal of African Studies. Volume 3 #3 August, 1976. pp. 329-349.

Elwert, Georg
"Conflicts Inside and Outside the Household: A West African Case Study." (In) Smith, Joan (ed.). Households and the World Economy. Beverly Hills, California: Sage. 1984. pp. 272-296.

Esposito, John L.
Women in Muslim Family Law. Syracuse, New York: Syracuse University Press. Contemporary Issues in the Middle East Series. 1982. 172p.

Faulkner, Constance
"Women's Studies in the Muslim Middle East." Journal of Ethnic Studies. Volume 8 #3 Fall, 1980. pp. 67-76.

Fields, Karen E.
"Political Contingencies of Witchcraft in Colonial Central Africa." Canadian Journal of African Studies. Volume 16 #3 1982. pp. 567-593.

Geletkanycz, Christine and Egan, Susan
Literature Review: The Practice of Female Circumcision. Washington, D.C.: U.S. Department of Health, Education and Welfare. Office of International Health. Mimeo. 1979.

Ginat, Joseph (ed.)
Women in Muslim Rural Society: Status and Role in Family Community. New Brunswick, New Jersey: Transition Books. 1981. 268p.

Green, Ronald M.
"Religion and Mortality in the African Traditional Setting." Journal of Religion in Africa. Volume 14 #1 1983. pp. 1-23.

Hadri, Gasim
"Opinions About Female Circumcision." Paper Presented at the Seminar on Traditional Practices Affecting the Health of Women and Children. World Conference of the United Nations Decade for Women. Copenhagen, Denmark. July 14-30, 1980.

Hayani, Ibrahim
"The Changing Role of Arab Women." Convergence. Volume 13 #1 1980. pp. 136-142.

Hinckley, Priscilla
"The Sowo Mask: Symbol of Sisterhood." Boston: Boston University. African Studies Center. Working Papers in African Studies #40. 1980.

Hoch-Smith, Judith and Spring, Anita (eds.)
Women in Ritual and Symbolic Roles. New York: Plenum Press. 1978. 289p.

Hussain, Freda (ed.)
Muslim Women. New York: St. Martin's Press. 1983. 240p.

Huzayyin, S.A.
"Marriage and Remarriage in Islam." (In) Dupaquier, J. and Helin, E. and Laslett, P. and Livi-Bacci, M. (eds.). Marriage and Remarriage in Populations of the Past. New York: Academic Press. Population and Social Structure: Advances in Historical Demography Series. 1981. pp. 95-109.

Jules-Rosette, Bennetta
"Changing Aspects of Women's Initiation in Southern Africa: An Exploratory Study." Canadian Journal of African Studies. Volume 13 #3 1980. pp. 389-406.

Jules-Rosette, Bennetta
Sources of Women's Leadership in an Indigenous African Church. Sociological Symposium. #17 Fall, 1976. pp. 69-89.

Kalugila, Leonidas
"Women in the Ministry of Priesthood in the Early Church: An Inquiry." Africa Theological Journal. Volume 14 #1 1985. pp. 35-45.

Kapalo, Ancilla
"African Sisters' Congregations: Realities of the Present Situation." (In) Fashole-Luke, Edward. Christianity in Independent Africa. London: R. Collings. 1978. pp. 122-135.

Kilson, Marion
"Women in African Traditional Religions." Journal of Religion in Africa. Volume 8 #2 1976. pp. 133-143.

Levine, Nancy E.
"Belief and Explanation in Nyinba Women's Witchcraft." Man. Volume 17 #2 1982.

Mahran, M.
"Medical Dangers of Female Circumcision." International Planned Parenthood Federation (IPPF) Medical Bulletin. Volume 15 #2 April, 1981.
McCall, Daniel
"Rank, Gender, Cult Affiliation Proclaimed in the Arts of Apparel: Reflections on Esie Sculpture." Paper Presented at the Annual Meeting of the African Studies Association. Paper #34. Bloomimgton, Indiana. 1981.
McLean, Scilla
"Female Genital Mutilation." ISIS Women's International Bulletin. #25 1982. pp. 26-32.
McLean, Scilla and Graham, Stella E.
Female Circumcision, Excision and Infibulation: The Fact and Proposals for Change. London: Minority Rights Group. Report #47. Second Revised Edition. 1985. 21p.
Mernissi, Fatima
"Women, Saints and Sanctuaries." Signs. Volume 3 #1 Autumn, 1977. pp. 101-112.
Mernissi, Fatima
"Women, Saints and Sanctuaries." (In) Wellesley Editorial Committee. Women and National Development: The Complexities of Change. Chicago: University of Chicago Press. 1977. pp. 101-112.
Moen, Elizabeth W.
Genital Mutilation: Everywoman's Problem. East Lansing, Michigan: Michigan State University. Office of Women in International Development. Working Paper #22. April, 1983.
Mukhtar, Behiza
"A Question of Our Children's Bodies: The Medical Injury Caused to a Girl by Circumcision." Paper Presented at the Conference on Islam and Family Planning. Sponsored by the International Planned Parenthood Federation. Banjul, Gambia. October 21-24, 1979. 7p.
Musallam, B.
Sex and Society in Islam: Birth Control Before the 19th Century. Cambridge, New York: Cambridge University Press. Cambridge Studies in Islamic Civilization. 1983. 176p.
Nagi, Mostafa H. and Stockwell, Edward G.
"Muslim Fertility: Recent Trends and Future Outlook." Journal of South Asian and Middle Eastern Studies. Volume 6 #2 Winter, 1982. pp. 48-70.
Nagi, Mostafa H.
"Trends and Differentials in Moslem Fertility." Journal of Biosocial Science. Volume 16 #2 April, 1984. pp. 189-204.
Ndeti, K.
"Concept of Parenthood in Africa: An Exploratory Study of Complexity." (In) International Planned Parenthood Federation (IPPF). Proceedings of the IPPF Africa Regional Conference. London: IPPF. 1977. pp. 119-144.

O'Shaughnessey, T.J.
"Growth of Educational Opportunity for Muslim Women, 1950-1973." Anthropos. Volume 73 #5/6 1978. pp. 887-901.

Oduyoye, Mercy Amba
"Feminism: A Pre-Condition for a Christian Anthropology." Africa Theological Journal. Volume 11 #3 1982. pp. 193-208.

Peart, Nicola S.
"Civil or Christian Marriage and Customary Unions: The Legal Position of the 'Discarded' Spouse and Children." Comparative and International Law Journal of Southern Africa. Volume 16 #1 1983. pp. 39-64.

Pernet, Henry
"Masks and Women: Toward a Reappraisal." History of Religions. Volume 22 #1 August, 1982. pp. 45-59.

Porter, J.R. and Albert, A.A.
"Subculture or Assimilation? A Cross-Cultural Analysis of Religion and Women's Role." Journal of the Scientific Study of Religion. Volume 16 #4 December, 1977. pp. 345-359.

Prentice, Andrew M. and Prentice, Ann and Lamb, W.H. and Lunn, P.G. and Austin, S.
"Metabolic Consequences of Fasting During Ramadan in Pregnant and Lactating Women." Human Nutrition. Clinical Nutrition. Volume 37 #4 July, 1983. pp. 283-294.

Ravenhill, Phillip L.
"The Interpretation of Symbolism in Wan Female Initiation." Africa. Volume 48 #1 1978. pp. 66-78.

Riesman, Paul
"Opulence and Pride in a Rite of Passage: A Comparison of the Weddings of Nobles and of Commoners in Fulani Society." Paper Presented at the Annual Meeting of the African Studies Association. Paper #102. Bloomington, Indiana. 1981.

Sadik, Nafis
"Muslim Women Today." Populi. Volume 12 #1 1985. pp. 36-51.

Salamone, Frank A.
"Gbagyi Witchcraft: A Reconsideration of S.F. Nadel's Theory of African Witchcraft." Paper Presented at the Annual Meeting of the African Studies Association. Paper #84. Los Angeles, California. 1979.

Schierling, Marla J.
"Primeval Women: A Yahwistic View of Women in Genesis 1-11:9." Journal of Theology for Southern Africa. #42 March, 1983.

Siann, Gerda and Khalid, R.
"Muslim Traditions and Attitudes to Female Education." Journal of Adolescence. Volume 7 June, 1984. pp. 191-200.

Singleton, Michael
Contributions to the Rights and Wrongs of African Women. Brussels, Belgium: Pro Mundi Vita Dossiers. Africa Dossier #9. October, 1979. pp. 1-36.

Smith, Jane I. (ed.)
Women in Contemporary Muslim Societies. Lewisburg, Pennsylvania: Bucknell University Press. 1980. 264p.

Smith, Janet I.
"The Experience of Muslim Women: Considerations of Power and Authority." (In) Haddad, Yvonne Y. and Haines, Byron and Findly, Ellison (eds.). The Islamic Impact. Syracuse, New York: Syracuse University Press. 1984. pp. 89-112.

Sojourner, Sabrina
"From the House of Yemanja: The Goddess Heritage of Black Women." (In) Spretnak, Charlene (ed.). The Politics of Women's Spirituality: Essays on the Rise of Spiritual Power Within the Feminist Movement. Garden City, New Jersey: Anchor Books. 1982. pp. 57-63.

Sow, Fatou
"Muslim Families in Contemporary Black Africa." Current Anthropology. Volume 26 December, 1985. pp. 563-570.

Strobel, Margaret A.
"Women in Religion and in Secular Ideology." (In) Hay, Margaret J. and Stichter, Sharon (eds.). African Women South of the Sahara. New York: Longman. 1984. pp. 87-101.

Tonkin, Elizabeth
"Women Excluded? Masking and Masquerading in West Africa." (In) Holden, P. (ed.). Women's Religious Experience. Totowa, New Jersey: Barnes and Noble. 1983. pp. 163-174.

Turner, Edith
"Girl Into Woman." Anthropology and Humanism Quarterly. Volume 10 #2 1985. pp. 27-32.

Watson, D.S.
"The Mutual Recognition of Ordained Ministries." Journal of Theology for Southern Africa. #23 June, 1978. pp. 56-70.

Wegner, J.R.
"The Status of Women in Jewish and Islamic Marriage and Divorce Law." Harvard Women's Law Journal. Volume 5 #1 1982.

Youssef, Nadia H.
"The Status and Fertility Patterns of Muslim Women." (In) Beck, Lois and Keddie, Nikki R. (eds.). Women in the Muslim World. Cambridge, Massachusetts: Harvard University Press. 1978. pp. 69-99.

Youssef, Nadia H.
"Women and Agricultural Production in Muslim Societies." Studies in Comparative International Development. Volume 12 #1 Spring, 1977. pp. 41-58.

Zoe-Obianga, Rose
"Resources in the Tradition for the Renewal of Community." Mid Stream. Volume 21 July, 1982. pp. 305-310.

Zoe-Obianga, Rose
"Resources in the Tradition for the Renewal of Community." (In) Parvey, Constance F. (ed.). The Community of Women and Men. Philadelphia, Pennsylvania: Fortress Press. 1983. pp. 68-73.

Research

Abdel Kader, Soha
"Research on the Status of Women, Development and Population Trends in Arab States: An Annotated Bibliography." (In) UNESCO. Bibliographic Guide to Studies on the Status of Women: Development and Population. Paris: United Nations Educational, Scientific and Cultural Organization. 1983. pp. 67-81.

Abdel Kader, Soha
The Status of Research on Women in the Arab Region, 1960-1978. Paris: UNESCO. Division of Human Rights and Peace. January, 1979.

Adamson, Kay
"Approaches to the Study of Women in North Africa: As Reflected in Research of Various Scholars." Maghreb Review. Volume 3 #7-8 May-August, 1978. pp. 22-31.

Adepoju, Aderanti
"Migration and Development in Tropical Africa: Some Research Priorities." African Affairs. Volume 76 #303 April, 1977. pp. 210-225.

Al-Qazza, Ayad
"Current Status of Research on Women in the Arab World." Middle Eastern Studies. Volume 14 #3 October, 1978. pp. 372-384.

Al-Qazza, Ayad
Women in the Middle East and North Africa: An Annotated Bibliography. Austin, Texas: University of Texas Press. Center for Middle Eastern Studies. Middle East Monograph #2. 1977. 179p.

Anker, Richard
Demographic Change and the Role of Women: A Research Programme in Developing Countries. Geneva: International Labour Office. Population and Employment Working Paper #69. 1978. 27p.

Anonymous
"Women in Southern Africa: Statistical Profile." Africa Report. Volume 28 #2 March-April, 1983. pp. 52-53.

Anonymous
"Women in Southern Africa: Bibliography." Africa Report. Volume 28 #2 March-April, 1983. pp. 54-55.

Anonymous
Women and Family in Rural Development: An Annotated Bibliography. Rome: United Nations Food and Agriculture Organization. Documentation Centre and Population Documentation Centre. 1977. 66p.

Berrian, Brenda F.
"Bibliographies of Nine Female African Writers." Research in African Literatures. Volume 12 #2 Summer, 1981. pp. 214-236.

Bifani, Patricia
"Women and Development in Africa: A Tentative Approach Through Scenario Building." Journal of Eastern African Research and Development. Volume 15 1985. pp. 245-267.

Boserup, Ester (ed.)
Traditional Division of Work Between the Sexes, A Source of Inequality: Research Symposium on Women and Decision Making: A Social Policy Priority. Geneva: International Institute for Labour Studies. Research Series #21. 1976. 32p.

Broch-Due, Vigdis and Garfield, Patti
"Women and Pastoral Development: Some Research Priorities for the Social Sciences." (In) Galaty, John G. and Aronson, Dan and Salzman, Philip C. (eds.). The Future of Pastoral Peoples. Ottawa, Canada: International Development Research Centre. 1981. pp. 251-257.

Bukh, Jette
"Women in Food Production, Food Handling and Nutrition." Paper Presented to the Association of African Women for Research and Development (AAWORD) Workshop. Dakar, Senegal: AAWORD. December, 1977.

Bullwinkle, Davis A.
"Women and Their Role in African Society: The Literature of the 70's." Current Bibliography on African Affairs. Volume 15 #4 1982. pp. 69-98.

Buvinic, Mayra
Women and World Development: An Annotated Bibliography. Washington D.C.: Overseas Development Council. 1976. 162p.

Claffey, Joan M. and Pigozzi, Mary J. and Axinn, Nancy W.
"Women in Development: A Selected Annotated Bibliography." International Journal of Intercultural Relations. Volume 3 1979.

DeLancey, Virginia H.
"The Relationship Between Female Labor Force Participation and Fertility: Considerations of Role

Compatibility in Research Methodology for Developing Countries." Paper Presented at the Annual Meeting of the African Studies Association. Paper #34. Los Angeles, California. 1979. 23p.

Dirasse, Laketch
"Approaches to the Study of Women in Africa: The Alternatives." (In) Ray, D.I. (ed.). Into the 80's: The Proceedings of 11th Annual Conference of the Canadian Association of African Studies. Vancouver, British Columbia, Canada: Tantalas Research Ltd. Volume Two. 1981. pp. 79-81.

Dixon, Ruth B.
"Seeing the Invisible Women Farmers in Africa: Improving Research and Data Collection Methods." (In) Monson, J. and Kalb, M. (eds.). Women as Food Producers in Developing Countries. Los Angeles: University of California-Los Angeles. African Studies Center and OEF International. 1985. pp. 19-35.

Farooq, Ghazi M. and Simmons, George B. (eds.)
Fertility in Developing Countries: An Economic Perspective on Research and Policy Issues. New York: St. Martin's Press. 1985.

Faulkner, Constance
"Women's Studies in the Muslim Middle East." Journal of Ethnic Studies. Volume 8 #3 Fall, 1980. pp. 67-76.

Gadalla, Saad M.
Population Policy and Family Planning Communication Strategies in the Arab States Region. Paris: UNESCO. Volume One: Summaries of Pertinent Literature and Research Studies. 1978.

Germain. Adrienne
"Research on Women in Agricultural Production in Eastern and Southern Africa." Paper Presented at a Workshop on Women in Agricultural Production in Eastern and Southern Africa. Nairobi, Kenya. April 9-11, 1980.

Gordon, Gill
"Important Issues for Feminist Nutrition Research: A Case Study From the Savanna of West Africa." IDS Bulletin. Volume 15 #1 1984. pp. 38-44.

Hafkin, Nancy J.
Women and Development in Africa: An Annotated Bibliography. Addis Ababa, Ethiopia: United Nations Economic Commisssion for Africa. African Training and Research Centre for Women. Bibliographic Series #1. 1977. 177p.

Harder, Gudrun M.
"Problems of Women in Developing Countries: A Selected Bibliography." Verfassung unp Recht in Ubersee. #10 1977. pp. 133-160.

International Institute for Labour Studies (IILS) and Organization of African Unity (OAU)
Food Self-Sufficiency, Technological Autonomy, and Social

Progress in Africa: A Research Guide. Geneva: IILS/Addis Ababa, Ethiopia: OAU. 1984. 144p.

International Maize and Wheat Improvement Center (CIMMYT)
"CIMMYT's Experience With the User's Perspective in Technology Development." (In) Rockefeller Foundation (eds.). Women and Agricultural Technology: Relevance for Research. Volume 2-Experiences in International and National Research. New York: Rockefeller Foundation. 1985. pp. 13-26.

Kelly, David H. and Kelly, Gail P.
"Women and Schooling in the Third World: A Bibliography." (In) Kelly, Gail P. and Elliott, Carolyn M. (eds.). Women's Education in the Third World: Comparative Perspectives. Albany, New York: State University of New York Press. 1982. pp. 345-397.

Kelly, Gail P.
"Research on the Education of Women in the Third World: Problems and Perspectives." Women's Studies: International Quarterly. Volume 1 #4 1978. pp. 365-373.

Kelly, Gail P. and Lulat, Younus
"Women and Schooling in the Third World: A Bibliography." Comparative Education Review. Volume 24 #2 June, 1980. pp. S224-S263.

Kharas, Purveen
Women in Development--Africa: An Annotated Bibliography. Rome: United Nations Food and Agriculture Organization. 1978. 12p.

Kisekka, Mere N.
"The Status of Women, Development and Population Trends in Africa: An Annotated Bibliography." Paper Presented at the Meeting of Experts on Research on the Status of Women, Development and Population Trends: Evaluation and Prospects. Paris: United Nations Educational, Scientific and Cultural Organization. 1980. 66p.

Kisekka, Mere N.
"Research on the Status of Women, Development and Population Trends in Africa: An Annotated Bibliography." (In) United Nations Educational, Scientific and Cultural Organization. Bibliographic Guide to Studies on the Status of Women: Development and Population. Paris: UNESCO. 1983. pp. 41-66.

Leland, Stephanie and Mutasa, Joyce and Willard, Fran
Women in Southern Africa: Struggles and Achievements--The U.N. Decade for Women Diary, July, 1985/86. London: Feminist International for Peace and Food. 1985. 120p.

Lorimer, Thomas
Illustrative Statistics on Women in Selected Developing Countries. Washington, D.C.: U.S. Department of Commerce. Bureau of the Census. Prepared for the U.S. Agency for International Development. September, 1980. 24p.

Mbilinyi, Marjorie J.
"Research Priorities in Women's Studies in Eastern Africa." Women's Studies International Forum. Volume 7 #4 1984. pp. 289-300.

Moody, Elizabeth J.
Women and Development: A Select Bibliography. Pretoria, South Africa: Africa Institute of South Africa. Occasional Papers #43. 1979. 28p.

Moris, J.R.
Reforming Agricultural Extension and Research Services in Africa. London: Overseas Development Institute. Discussion Paper #11. 1983.

NGO Planning Committee
Forum '85: Final Report: Nairobi, Kenya. New York: NGO Planning Committee. 1985. 105p.

Nwanosike, Eugene O.
Women and Development: A Select Bibliography: A Select and Partially Annotated Bibliography. Buea, Cameroon: Regional Pan-African Institute for Development/West Africa. Bibliographic Series #10. 1980. 63p.

Okeyo, Achola P.
"Research Priorities: Women in Africa." Studies in Family Planning. Volume 10 #11/12 Nov.-Dec., 1979. pp. 401-404.

Pala, Achola O.
African Women in Rural Development: Research Trends and Priorities. Washington, D.C.: American Council on Education. Overseas Liaison Committee. OLC Paper #12. December, 1976. 35p.

Pellow, Deborah
"Recent Studies on African Women." African Studies Review. Volume 20 #1 April, 1977. pp. 117-126.

Phillips, Beverly
Women in Rural Development: A Bibliography. Madison, Wisconsin: University of Wisconsin-Madison. Land Tenure Center Library. Training and Methods Series #29. 1979. 45p.

Rahal, K.
"In Face of the Bacterial Menace, Sex Inequality is Forgotten in Research." Impact of Science on Society. Volume 30 #1 January-March, 1980. pp. 43-45.

Rassam, Amal
"Towards a Theoretical Framework for the Study of Women in the Arab World." Cultures. Volume 8 #3 1982.

Rihani, May
Development as if Women Mattered: An Annotated Bibliography With a Third World Focus. Washington, D.C.: Overseas Development Council. Occasional Paper #10. 1978. 137p.

Ritchie, Maureen
Women's Studies: A Checklist of Bibliographies. London: Mansell. 1980. 107p.

Sachak, N.
"Agricultural Research: Priorities for Women." (In) Bengtsson, Bo and Tedla, Getachew. Strengthening National Agricultural Research: Report From a SAREC Workshop, September 10-17, 1979. Stockholm, Sweden: Swedish Agency for Research Cooperation in Developing Countries. 1980. pp. 62-69.

Safilios-Rothschild, Constantina
The State of Statistics on Women in Agriculture in the Third World. New York: United Nations. 1983.

Saulniers, Suzanne S. and Rakowski, Cathy A.
Women in the Development Process: A Select Bibliography on Women in Sub-Saharan Africa and Latin America. Austin, Texas: University of Texas Press. Institute of Latin American Studies. 1977. 287p.

Schuster, Ilsa M.
"Recent Research on Women in Development." Journal of Development Studies. Volume 18 #4 July, 1982. pp. 511-535.

Secretariat for Women in Development
Women in Development: A Resource List. Washington, D.C.: Secretariat for Women in Development. A Transcentury Publication. 1979. 86p.

Sembajwe, Israel S.
"A Note on Published National Data on Economic Activities and Women's Studies and Development." Paper Presented at the Workshop on Women's Studies and Development. Dar-es-Salaam, Tanzania: University of Dar-es-Salaam. Bureau of Resource Assessment and Land Use Planning. Paper #31. September 24-29, 1979. 6p.

Skjonsberg, Else
Women and Food and the Social Sciences: Perspectives on African Food Production and Food Handling. Oslo, Norway: Mimeo. Available From the International Center for Research on Women, Washington, D.C. 1977.

Staudt, Kathleen A.
Women and Participation in Rural Development: A Framework for Project Design and Policy-Oriented Research. Ithaca, New York: Cornell University. Center for International Studies. Rural Development Monograph #4. 1979. 78p.

Stichter, Sharon B.
"Some Selected Statistics on African Women." (In) Hay, Margaret J. and Stichter, Sharon (eds.). African Women South of the Sahara. New York: Longman. 1984. pp. 188-194.

Tadesse, Zenebework
"Research Trends on Women in Sub-Saharan Africa." Paper Presented at the Meeting of Experts on Research and Teaching Related to Women: Evaluation and Prospects. Paris: United Nations Educational, Scientific and Cultural Organization. May, 1980. 12p.

Tadesse, Zenebeworke
Survey of Principal Social Science Research on Women in Sub-Saharan Africa. Unpublished Manuscript. 1979.

Tadesse, Zenebeworke
"African Women in Rural Development: A New Group of African Women Researchers." Ideas and Action. #127 1979. pp. 7-10.

Tadesse, Zenebeworke
"Breaking the Silence and Broadening the Frontiers of History: Notes on Recent Studies on African Women in History." Paper Presented at the Meeting of Experts on Theoretical Frameworks and Methodological Approaches to Studies on the Role of Women in History as Actors in Economic, Social, Political and Ideological Processes. Paris: United Nations Educational, Scientific and Cultural Organization. 1984. 15p.

Tinker, Irene
"Women and Africa: Policy Strategies for Women in the 1980's." Africa Report. Volume 26 #2 March-April, 1981. pp. 11-16.

United Nations
Building New Knowledge Through Technical Cooperation Among Developing Countries: The Experience of the Association of African Women for Research and Development (AAWORD). New York: United Nations. March 6, 1980.

United Nations
Report of the World Conference to Review and Appraise the Achievements of the United Nations Decade for Women: Equality, Development and Peace. Nairobi, Kenya, July 15-26, 1985. New York: United Nations. 1986. 304p.

United Nations Economic Commission for Africa (UNECA)
An Inventory of Social Science Research on Women's Roles and Status in Sub-Saharan Africa Since 1960. (Draft) Addis Ababa, Ethiopia: UNECA. 1982.

United Nations Economic Commission for Africa (UNECA)
"Origin and Growth of the African Training and Research Centre for Women of the Economic Commission for Africa." Addis Ababa, Ethiopia: UNECA. September, 1977. 60p.

United Nations Educational, Scientific and Cultural Organ.
Female Participation in Higher Education: Enrollment Trends, 1975-1982. Paris: UNESCO. Current Surveys and Research in Statistics. February, 1985. 92p.

United Nations Educational, Scientific, and Cultural Organ.
Bibliographic Guide to Studies on the Status of Women: Development and Population Trends. Paris: UNESCO. Epping, England: Bowker. 1983. 284p.

Vavrus, Linda G.
Women in Development: A Selected Annotated Bibliography and Resource Guide. East Lansing, Michigan: Michigan State University. Institute for International Studies in Education. Non-Formal Education Information Center. 1980. 69p.

Wadsworth, Gail M.
Women in Development: A Bibliography of Materials Available in the Library and Documentation Centre, Eastern and Southern African Management Institute. Arusha, Tanzania: Eastern and Southern African Management Institute. Library and Documentation Centre. February, 1982. 106p.

Ware, Helen
"Women's Work and Fertility in Africa." (In) Kupinsky, Stanley (ed.). The Fertility of Working Women: A Synthesis of International Research. New York: Praeger Publishers. Praeger Special Studies in International Economics and Development. 1977. pp. 1-34.

Waterman, Peter
"A New Focus in African Worker Studies: Promises, Problems, Dangers." Cahiers d'Etudes Africaines. Volume 24 #3 1984. pp. 343-361.

Welch, Charles E. and Glick, Paul C.
"The Incidence of Polygamy in Contemporary Africa: A Research Note." Journal of Marriage and the Family. Volume 43 #1 February, 1981. pp. 191-192.

Sex Roles

Abbott, Susan
"In the End You Will Carry Me in Your Car--Sexual Politics in the Field." Women's Studies. Volume 10 #2 1983. pp. 161-178.

Abbott, Susan
"Full-Time Farmers and Week-End Wives, an Analysis of Altering Conjugal Roles." Journal of Marriage and the Family. Volume 38 #1 February, 1976. pp. 165-174.

Accad, Evelyne
"The Theme of Sexual Oppression in the North African Novel." (In) Beck, Lois and Keddie, Nikki R. (eds.). Women in the Muslim World. Cambridge, Massachusetts: Harvard University Press. 1978. pp. 617-628.

Adler, A.
"Avunculate and Matrilateral Marriage in Africa." L'Homme. Volume 16 October-December, 1976. pp. 7-28.

Agarwal, Bina
"Women and Technological Change in Agricultural Change: The Asian and African Experience." (In) Ahmed, I. (ed.). Technology and Rural Development: Conceptual and Empirical Issues. London: Allen and Unwin. 1985. pp. 67-114.

Aguta, M.O. and Exedij, F.O. (eds.)
Changing Status of Women in Africa. Addis Ababa, Ethiopia: United Nations Economic Commission for Africa. African Training and Research Centre for Women. 1978.

Aidoo, Agnes A.
"Women and Development in Africa: Alternative Strategies for the Future." (In) Adedeji, A. and Shaw, T.M. (eds.). Economic Crisis in Africa: African Perspectives on Development Problems and Potentials. Boulder, Colorado: Lynne Rienner. 1985. pp. 201-217.

Aidoo, Christina A.A.
"Images of Women." (In) University of Illinois (ed.). Women and Work in Africa, April 29-May 1, 1979, University of Illinois, Urbana-Champaign: A Project of

the Africn Studies Association. Urbana, Illinois: University of Illinois. 1979.

Allison, C.
"Women, Land, Labour and Survival: Getting Some Basic Facts Straight." IDS Bulletin. Volume 16 #3 1985. pp. 24-30.

Allman, James
"Family Patterns, Women's Status and Fertility in Middle-East and North-Africa." International Journal of Sociology of the Family. Volume 8 #1 1978. pp. 19-35.

Allman, James
"Family Life, Women's Status, and Fertility: Middle East and North African Perspectives." (In) Allman, James (ed.). Women's Studies and Fertility in the Muslim World. New York: Praeger Publishers. Praeger Special Studies. 1978. pp. 24-47.

Allman, James (ed.)
Women's Status and Fertility in the Muslim World. New York: Praeger Publishers. Praeger Special Studies. 1978. 378p.

Amon-Nikoi, Gloria
"Women and Work in Africa." (In) Damachi, Ukandi G. and Diejomaoh, Victor P. Human Resources and African Development. New York: Praeger Publishers. 1978. pp. 188-219.

Anker, Richard and Buvinic, Mayra and Youssef, Nadia H. (eds.)
Women's Roles and Population Trends in the Third World. London: Croon Helm Ltd. 1982. 288p.

Anonymous
"International Conference on the Role of Women in Liberation Struggles and Women in Development." IDOC Bulletin. #50/51 December-January, 1976. pp. 4-21.

Arens, W. and Arens, Diana A.
"Kinship and Marriage in a Polyethnic Community." Africa. Volume 48 1978. pp. 149-160.

Ashworth, Georgina and May, Nicky (eds.)
Of Conjuring and Caring: Women in Development. London: Change. 1982. 28p.

Axinn, Nancy W.
Female Emancipation Versus Female Welfare. East Lansing, Michigan: Michigan State University. Institute for International Studies in Education. College of Education. Non-Formal Education Information Center. 1979. 5p.

Balakrishnan, Revathi and Firebaugh, Francille M.
Roles of Women in Third World Economic Development From a Systems Perspective of Family Resource Management. Columbus, Ohio: Ohio State University. Department of Home Management and Housing. School of Home Economics. Working Papers #81-01. 1981. 39p.

Beddada, Belletech
"Traditional Practices in Relation to Pregnancy and Childbirth." Paper Presented at the Seminar on Traditional Practices Affecting the Health of Women and

Children. World Conference of the United Nations Decade for Women. New York: United Nations. Copenhagen, Denmark. July 14-30, 1980.

Beneria, Lourdes
"Reproduction, Production and the Sexual Division of Labour." Cambridge Journal of Economics. Volume 3 September, 1979. pp. 203-225.

Beneria, Lourdes
Women and Development: The Sexual Division of Labor in Rural Societies: A Study. New York: Praeger Publishers. Praeger Special Studies. 1982. 257p.

Beneria, Lourdes
"Reproduction, Production and the Sexual Division of Labour." Geneva: International Labour Office. World Employment Research Working Paper #2. 1978.

Bennett, T.W. and Peart. Nicola S.
"The Dualism of Marriage Laws in Africa." ACTA Juridica. 1983. pp. 145-169.

Bisilliat, Jeanne
"The Feminine Sphere in the Institutions of Songhay-Zarma." (In) Oppong, Christine (ed.). Female and Male in West Africa. London: George Allen and Unwin. 1983. pp. 99-106.

Blumberg, Rae
"Rural Women in Development: Veil of Invisibility, World of Work." International Journal of Intercultural Relations. Volume 3 #4 1979. pp. 447-472.

Blumberg, Rae
"Rural Women in Development." (In) Black, Naomi and Cottrell, Ann B. (eds.). Women and World Change: Equity Issues in Development. Beverly Hills, California: Sage Publications. 1981. pp. 32-56.

Bongaarts, John
"The Impact on Fertility of Traditional and Changing Child-Spacing Practices." (In) Page, Hilary J. and Lesthaeghe, Ron (eds.). Child-Spacing in Tropical Africa. New York: Academic Press. 1981. pp. 111-129.

Boserup, Ester (ed.)
Traditional Division of Work Between the Sexes, A Source of Inequality: Research Symposium on Women and Decision Making: A Social Policy Priority. Geneva: International Institute for Labour Studies. Research Series #21. 1976. 32p.

Boulding, Elise
Women Peripheries and Food Production. (In) University of Arizona. Proceedings and Papers of the International Conference on Women and Food: Consortium for International Development. Tucson, Arizona: University of Arizona. 1978. pp. 22-44.

Brabin, Loretta
"Polygyny: An Indicator of Nutritional Stress in African Agricultural Societies." Africa. Volume 54 #1 1984. pp. 31-45.

Bujra, Janet M.
"Production, Property, Prostitution--Sexual Politics in

Atu." Cahiers d'Etudes Africaines. Volume 17 #1 1977. pp. 13-40.
Bujra, Janet M.
"Class, Gender and Capitalist Transformation in Africa." Africa Development. Volume 8 #3 1983. pp. 17-42.
Bujra, Janet M.
"Female Solidarity and the Sexual Division of Labour." (In) Caplan, P. and Bujra, J. (eds.). Women United, Women Divided: Cross-Cultural Perspectives on Female Solidarity. London: Tavistock. 1978. pp. 13-48.
Burton Claire
"Woman Marriage in Africa: A Critical Study For Sex-Role Theory?" Australian and New Zealand Journal of Sociology. Volume 15 #2 July, 1979. pp. 65-71.
Buvinic, Mayra and Youssef, Nadia H. and Schumacher, Ilsa
Women-Headed Households: The Ignored Factor in Development Planning. Washington D.C.: U.S. Department of State. U.S. Agency for International Development. International Center for Research on Women. Women in Development Office. March, 1978. 113p.
Caldwell, John C. and Caldwell, Pat
Cultural Forces Tending to Sustain High Fertility in Tropical Africa. Canberra, Australia: Australian National University. 1984.
Caldwell, Pat
"Issues of Marriage and Marital Change: Tropical Africa and the Middle East." (In) Huzayyin, S.A. and Acsadi, G.T. (eds.). Family and Marriage in Some African and Asiatic Countries. Cairo, Egypt: Cairo Demographic Centre. Research Monograph Series #6. 1976. pp. 325-335.
Caplan, Patricia and Bujra, Janet M. (eds.)
Women United Women Divided: Comparative Studies of Ten Contemporary Cultures. Bloomington, Indiana: Indiana University Press. 1979. 288p.
Casajus, Dominique
"The Wedding Ritual Among the Kel Ferwan Tuaregs." Journal of the Anthropological Society of Oxford. Volume 14 #2 1983. pp. 227-257.
Castillo, Gelia T.
The Changing Role of Women in Rural Societies: A Summary of Trends and Issues. New York: Agricultural Development Council Inc. RTN Seminar Reports 12. February, 1977. 11p.
Caton, Douglas D.
Elements of the Food Production-Distribution System: An Overview on How Women Can Contribute. Proceedings and Papers of the International Conference on Women and Food Consortium for International Development. Tucson, Arizona: University of Arizona. 1978. pp. 45-61.
Chamie, Joseph and Weller, Robert H.
Levels, Trends and Differentials in Nuptiality in the Middle East and North Africa. Tallahassee, Florida: Florida State University. Center for the Study of

Population. College of Social Sciences. Working Paper #83-02. 1983. 12p.
Chamie, Joseph and Weller, Robert H.
"Levels, Trends and Differentials in Nuptiality in the Middle East and North Africa." Genus. Volume 39 #1-4 January-December, 1983. pp. 213-231.
Chamie, Joseph
Polygamy Among Arabs. New York: United Nations. U.N. Population Division. 1985.
Chaney, Elsa M.
Women in International Migration: Issues in Development Planning. Washington, D.C.: U.S. Department of State. U.S. Agency for International Development. Office of Women in Development. June, 1980.
Chaney, Elsa M. and Lewis, Martha W.
Women, Migration and the Decline of Smallholder Agriculture. Washington, D.C.: U.S. Department of State. U.S. Agency for International Development. Office of Women in Development. October, 1980.
Clark, Carolyn M.
Sexuality in the Workplace: Some African Examples. Santa Cruz, California: University of California-Santa Cruz. 1981.
Clark, Garcia
Fighting the African Food Crisis: Women Food Farmers and Food Workers. New York: United Nations Development Fund for Women. 1985.
Cloud, Kathleen
"Sex Roles in Food Production and Distribution Systems in the Sahel." (In) Cowen, Ann B. (ed.). Proceedings and Papers of the International Conference on Women and Food: Consortium for International Development. Tucson, Arizona: University of Arizona. 1978. pp. 62-89.
Cloud, Kathleen
Sex Roles in Food Production and Food Distribution Systems in the Sahel. Washington, D.C.: U.S. Department of State. U.S. Agency for International Development. Office of Women in Development. 1977. 20p.
Cook, Rebecca J.
"A Law on Family Welfare and Development in Africa." (In) International Planned Parenthood Federation (IPPF). Proceedings of the IPPF Africa Regional Conference. London: IPPF. 1977. pp. 241-246.
Cosminsky, Sheila
"The Role and Training of Traditional Midwives: Policy Implications for Maternal and Child Health Care." Paper Presented at the Annual Meeting of the African Studies Association. Paper #17. Houston, Texas. 1977. 25p.
Cutrufelli, Maria R.
Women of Africa: Roots of Oppression. Totowa, New Jersey: Zed Press. 1983. 186p.
Dahlberg, Frances (ed.)
Woman the Gatherer. New Haven, Connecticut: Yale University Press. 1981. 250p.

De Graft-John, K.E.
"Issues in Family Welfare and Development in Africa." (In) International Planned Parenthood Federation (IPPF). Proceedings of the IPPF Africa Regional Conference. London: IPPF. 1977. pp. 33-45.

DeLancey, Virginia H.
"The Relationship Between Female Labor Force Participation and Fertility: Considerations of Role Compatibility in Research Methodology for Developing Countries." Paper Presented at the Annual Meeting of the African Studies Association. Paper #34. Los Angeles, California. 1979. 23p.

Deheusch, L.
"The Good Usage of Wives and Cattle-Transformation of Marriage in Southern Africa." L'Homme. Volume 23 #4 1983.

Dey, Jennie M.
Women in Food Production and Food Security in Africa. Rome: United Nations Food and Agriculture Organization. Women in Agriculture Series #3. 1984. 101p.

Dey, Jennie M.
"Women in African Rice Farming Systems." International Rice Commission Newsletter. Volume 32 #2 December, 1983. pp. 1-4.

Dey, Jennie M.
Women in Rice Farming Systems, Focus: Subsaharan Africa. Rome: United Nations Food and Agriculture Organization. Women in Agriculture Series #2. 1984. 106p.

Dey, Jennie M.
"Women in African Rice Farming Systems." (In) International Rice Research Institute. 'Women in Rice Farming': Proceedings of a Conference on Women in Rice Farming Systems. September 26-30, 1983. Brookfield, Vermont: Gower Publishing Co. 1985. pp. 419-444.

Dhamija, Jasleen
"Income-Generating Activities for Rural Women in Africa: Some Successes and Failures." (In) International Labour Organization (ILO). Rural Development and Women in Africa. Geneva: ILO. 1984. pp. 75-78.

Di Domenico, Catherine M. and Asuni, Judy and Scott, Jacqueline
"Family Welfare and Development in Africa." (In) International Planned Parenthood Federation (IPPF). Proceedings of the IPPF Africa Regional Conference, University of Ibadan. London: IPPF. 1976. pp. 283-284.

Dirasse, Laketch
The Critical Needs of African Women and Appropriate Strategies in the Framework of the Gisenyi and Lusaka MULPOCS. Addis Ababa, Ethiopia: United Nations Economic Commission for Africa. African Training and Research Centre for Women. 1981. 35p.

Dixon, Ruth B.
"Women in Agriculture: Counting the Labor Force in Developing Countries." Population and Development Review. Volume 8 #3 September, 1982. pp. 539-566.

Dixon, Ruth B.
"Land, Labour and the Sex Composition of the Agricultural Labour Force: An International Comparison." Development and Change. Volume 14 #3 July, 1983. pp. 347-372.

Dixon, Ruth B.
Assessing the Impact of Development Projects on Women. Washington, D.C.: U.S. Department of State. U.S. Agency for International Development. Office of Women in Development. AID Program Evaluation Discussion Paper #8. 1980. 105p.

Dixon, Ruth B.
"Seeing the Invisible Women Farmers in Africa: Improving Research and Data Collection Methods." (In) Monson, J. and Kalb, M. (eds.). Women as Food Producers in Developing Countries. Los Angeles: University of California-Los Angeles. African Studies Center and OEF International. 1985. pp. 19-35.

Dixon-Mueller, Ruth
Women's Work in the Third World Agriculture: Concepts and Indicators. Geneva: ILO. Women, Work and Development Series. Volume 9. 1985. 151p.

Donhoff, Christoph G.
"The Women of Africa." Africa Insight. Volume 12 #1 1982. pp. 25-26.

Due, Jean M. and Summary, Rebecca
"Constraints to Women and Development in Africa." Journal of Modern African Studies. Volume 20 #1 March, 1982. pp. 155-166.

Due, Jean M. and Summary, Rebecca
"Constraints to Women and Development in Africa." Paper Presented at the Annual Meeting of the African Studies Association. Paper #35. Los Angeles, California. 1979. 23p.

Due, Jean M. and Summary, Rebecca
Constraints to Women and Development in Africa. Urbana, Illinois: University of Illinois-Urbana-Champaign. Department of Agricultural Economics. Staff Paper Series E. Agricultural Economics 79-E-83. May, 1979. 27p.

Dulansey, Maryanne L.
Can Technology Help Women Feed Their Families? Post Harvest Storage, Processing and Cooking: Some Observations. Washington, D.C.: Consultants in Development. 1979. 9p.

Dunbar, Roberta
"Legislative Reform and Muslim Family Law: Effects Upon Women's Rights in Africa South of the Sahara." Paper Presented at the Annual Meeting of the African Studies Association. Paper #25. Philadelphia, Pennsylvania. October 15-18, 1980.

Duza, M. Badrud and Sivamurthy, M.
"Household Structure in Selected Urban Areas of Four Arab and African Cities." (In) Huzayyin, S.A. and Acsadi, G.T. (eds.). Family and Marriage in Some African and

Asiatic Countries. Cairo, Egypt: Cairo Demographic Centre. Research Monograph Series #6. 1976. pp. 267-284.

Duza, M. Badrud and Seetharam, K.S. and Sivamurthy, M. "Patterns of Family Cycles in Selected Areas of Four Arab and African Cities: Some Demographic Implications." (In) Huzayyin, S.A. and Acsadi, G.T. (eds.). Family and Marriage in Some African and Asiatic Countries. Cairo, Egypt: Cairo Demographic Centre. CDC Research Monograph Series #6. 1976. pp. 245-265.

Dwyer, Daisy H. "Outside the Courts: Extra-Legal Strategies for the Subordination of Women." (In) Hay, Margaret J. and Wright, Marcia (eds.). African Women and the Law: Historical Perspectives. Boston: Boston University. African Studies Center. Boston University Papers on Africa. Volume Seven. 1982. pp. 90-109.

Edwards, Felicity "The Doctrine of God and the Feminine Principle." Journal of Theology for Southern Africa. #37 December, 1981. pp. 23-37.

Eide, Wenche B. and Skjonsberg, Else and Pala, Achola O. and Bathily, Abjoulaye "Women in Food Production, Food Handling and Nutrition With Special Emphasis on Africa." PAG Bulletin. Volume 7 #3/4 Sept.-Dec., 1977. pp. 40-49.

Eide, Wenche B. and Steady, Filomina C. "Individual and Social Energy Flows: Bridging Nutritional and Anthropological Thinking About Women's Work in Rural Africa: Some Theoretical Considerations." (In) Jerome, Norge W. and Kandel, Randy F. and Pelto, Gretel H. (eds.). Nutritional Anthropology: Contemporary Approach to Diet and Culture. New York: Redgrave Publishing. 1980. pp. 61-84.

Eide, Wenche B. and Skjonsberg, Else and Bathily, Abjoulaye and Pala, Achola O. and Krystall, Abigail and Millwood, D. Women in Food Production, Food Handling and Nutrition With Special Emphasis on Africa. Final Report. New York: United Nations. Protein-Calorie Advisory Group of the U.N. System. FAO Food and Nutrition Paper #8. June, 1977. 224p.

Ekechi, Felix K. "African Polygamy and Western Christian Ethnocentrism." Journal of African Studies. Volume 3 #3 August, 1976. pp. 329-349.

El Bushra, Judy and Bekele, Abebech and Hammour, Fawzia "Socio-Economic Development and Women Changing Status." Paper Presented to the Conference on Women and the Environment. Khartoum, Sudan: University of Khartoum. Institute of Environmental Studies. April 4-7, 1981.

El Sadaawi, Nawal The Hidden Face of Eve: Women in the Arab World. Boston: Beacon Press. 1982. 212p.

El-Khorazaty, Mohamed Nabil E. "Regional Differences in Attitudes Toward Family Norms

and Planning, 1979/80." Population Studies. Volume 12 #72 January-March, 1985. pp. 3-28.
Elwert, Georg
"Conflicts Inside and Outside the Household: A West African Case Study." (In) Smith, Joan (ed.). Households and the World Economy. Beverly Hills, California: Sage. 1984. pp. 272-296.
Ember, C.R.
"Relative Decline in Women's Contribution to Agriculture With Intensification." American Anthropologist. Volume 85 #2 June, 1983. pp. 285-304.
Emecheta, Buchi
"Building on Tradition: Can the Past Provide for the Future?" (In) University of Illinois (eds.). Women and Work in Africa, April 29-May 1, 1979, University of Illinois, Urbana-Champaign: A Project of the African Studies Association. Urbana, Illinois: University of Illinois. 1979.
Epskamp, C.
Inequality in Female Access to Education in Developing Countries: A Bibliography. Hague, Netherlands: Centre for the Study of Education in Developing Countries. 1979. 42p.
Epstein, Trude S.
Place of Social Anthropology in a Multidisciplinary Approach to the Study of Women's Roles and Status in Less Developed Countries. Geneva: International Labour Organization. 1978.
Esposito, John L.
Women in Muslim Family Law. Syracuse, New York: Syracuse University Press. Contemporary Issues in the Middle East Series. 1982. 172p.
Fernea, Elizabeth W.
Women and the Family in the Middle East: New Voices of Change. Austin, Texas: University of Texas Press. 1984. 368p.
Fortes, Meyer
"Parenthood, Marriage and Fertility in West Africa." Journal of Development Studies. Volume 14 #4 July, 1978. pp. 121-149.
Fortes, Meyer
"Family, Marriage and Fertility in West Africa." (In) Oppong, C. and Adaba, G. and Bekombo-Priso, M. and Mogey, J. (eds.). Marriage, Fertility and Parenthood in West Africa. Canberra, Australia: Australian National University Press. 1978. pp. 17-54.
Fortmann, Louise P.
Tillers of the Soil and Keepers of the Hearth: A Bibliographic Guide to Women and Rural Development. Ithaca, New York: Cornell University. Center for International Studies. Rural Development Committee. Bibliography Series #2. 1979. 53p.
Franke, R.
"Mode of Production and Population Patterns: Policy Implications for West African Development."

International Journal of Health Services. Volume 13 1981. pp. 361-387.

Ginat, Joseph (ed.)
Women in Muslim Rural Society: Status and Role in Family Community. New Brunswick, New Jersey: Transition Books. 1981. 268p.

Gladwin, Christina and Staudt, Kathleen A. and McMillan, Della
Reaffirming the Agricultural Role of Women: One Solution to the Food Crisis. (In) Association of Facilities of Agriculture in Africa. Proceedings of the Fifth General Conference on Food Security. Manzini, Swaziland. April, 1984.

Goody, Jack
Production and Reproduction: A Comparative Study of the Domestic Domain. Cambridge, New York: Cambridge University Press. Cambridge Studies in Social Anthropology #17. 1976. 157p.

Grandmaison, C. LeCour
"Economic Contracts Between Married People in the West African Area." L'Homme. Volume 19 #3/4 July-December, 1979. pp. 159-170.

Gugler, Josef
"The Second Sex in Town." (In) Steady, Filomina C. (ed.). The Black Woman Cross-Culturally. Cambridge, Massachusetts: Schenkman Publishing. 1981. pp. 169-184.

Guyer, Jane I.
The Raw, the Cooked and the Half-Baked: A Note on the Division of Labor by Sex. Brookline, Massachusetts: Boston University. African Studies Center. Working Papers in African Studies #48. 1981. 12p.

Guyer, Jane I.
Women's Work in the Food Economy of the Cocoa Belt: A Comparison. Brookline, Massachusetts: Boston University. African Studies Center. Working Paper #7. 1978. 34p.

Guyot, Jean
Migrant Women Speak: Interviews. London: Search Press Ltd. for the Churches Committee on Migrant Workers. 1978. 164p.

Halperin, Rhoda
Ecology and Mode of Production: Seasonal Variation and the Division of Labor by Sex Among Hunter-Gatherers. Cincinnati, Ohio: University of Cincinnati. Department of Anthropology. 1979.

Hanson, F. and Miller, F.
"The Wife's Brother's Wife and the Marriage Contract: A Structural Analysis." Bijdragen Tot de Taal-, Land-en Volkenkunde. Volume 133 #1 1977. pp. 11-22.

Hayani, Ibrahim
"The Changing Role of Arab Women." Convergence. Volume 13 #1 1980. pp. 136-142.

Henn, Jeanne K.
"Feeding the Cities and Feeding the Peasants: What Role for Africa's Women Farmers." World Development. Volume 11 #12 1983.

Henn, Jeanne K.
"Women in the Rural Economy: Past, Present and Future." (In) Hay, Margaret J. and Stichter, Sharon (eds.). African Women South of the Sahara. New York: Longman. 1984. pp. 1-18.
Hoch-Smith, Judith and Spring, Anita (eds.)
Women in Ritual and Symbolic Roles. New York: Plenum Press. 1978. 289p.
Howard, R.
"Women's Rights in English-Speaking Sub-Saharan Africa." (In) Welch, Claude E. and Meltzer, Ronald I. (eds.). Human Rights and Development in Africa. Albany, New York: State University of New York Press. 1984.
Howard, Rhoda E.
"Women and the Crisis in Commonwealth Africa." International Political Science Review. Volume 6 #3 1985. pp. 287-296.
Huggard, Marianne
"The Rural Woman as a Food Producer: An Assessment of the Resolution on Women and Food From the World Food Conference in Rome, 1974." Paper Presented at the International Conference on Women and Food: Consortium for International Development. Tucson, Arizona. 10p. 1978.
Huzayyin, S.A. and Acsadi, George T. (eds.)
Family and Marriage in Some African and Asiatic Countries. Cairo, Egypt: Cairo Demographic Center. CDC Research Monograph Series #6. 1976. 570p.
Igbinovia, Patrick E.
"Prostitution in Black Africa." International Journal of Women's Studies. Volume 7 #5 Nov.-Dec., 1984. pp. 430-449.
International Center for Research on Women
The Productivity of Women in Developing Countries: Measurement Issues and Recommendtions. Washington, D.C.: U.S. Department of State. U.S. Agency for International Development. Office on Women in Development. 1980. 46p.
International Development Research Centre (IDRC)
Rural Water Supply in Developing Countries: Proccedings of a Workshop on Training. Ottawa, Canada: IDRC. Zomba, Malawi. August 5-12, 1981. 144p.
International Institute for Labour Studies (IILS) and Organization of African Unity (OAU)
Food Self-Sufficiency, Technological Autonomy, and Social Progress in Africa: A Research Guide. Geneva: IILS/Addis Ababa, Ethiopia: OAU. 1984. 144p.
International Labour Organization (ILO)
Female Power, Autonomy and Demographic Change in the Third World. Geneva: ILO. The Role of Women and Demographic Change Ressearch Programme. 1980.
International Planned Parenthood Federation (IPPF)
Family Welfare and Development in Africa: Proceedings of the IPPF Africa Regional Conference, University of

Ibadan. August 29-September 3, 1976. London: IPPF. Ibadan, Nigeria. 1977. 327p.
Javillonar, Gloria W.
Rural Development, Women's Roles and Fertility in Developing Countries: Review of the Literature. Chapel Hill, North Carolina: Research Triangle Institute. 1979. pp. 32-75.
Jett, Joyce
The Role of Traditional Midwives in the Modern Health Sector in West and Central Africa. Washington, D.C.: U.S. Department of State. U.S. Agency for International Development. January, 1977. 150p.
Jewsiewicki, B.
"Lineage Mode of Production: Social Inequalities in Equatorial Central Africa." (In) Crummey, Donald and Steward, C.C. (eds.). Modes of Production in Africa: The Precolonial Era. Beverly Hills, California: Sage Publications. 1981. pp. 93-114.
Jorgensen, Kirsten
"Water Supply Projects in Africa: The Need to Involve the Main Users--Women." Ideas and Action Bulletin. #150 1983. pp. 14-18.
Joseph, Roger
"Sexual Dialectics and Strategy in Berber Marriage." Journal of Comparative Family Studies. Volume 7 #3 Autumn, 1976. pp. 471-481.
Joseph, Terri B.
"Poetry as a Strategy of Power: The Case of Riffian Berber Women." Signs. Volume 5 #3 Spring, 1980. pp. 418-434.
Kabagambe, John C.
"Family Planning Concepts: Myths and Realities." (In) International Planned Parenthood Federation (IPPF). Proceedings of the IPPF Africa Regional Conference. London: IPPF. 1977. pp. 55+.
Kamba, Kate
"Fuel Wood and Energy Development for African Women." Paper Presented at the Workshop on Women in Agricultural Development. Addis Ababa, Ethiopia: United Nations Economic Commission for Africa. Awassa, Ethiopia. June 26, 1983. 13p.
Karanja, Wambui Wa
"Women and Work: A Study of Female and Male Attitudes in the Modern Sector of an African Metropolis." (In) Ware, Helen (ed.). Women, Education and Modernization of the Family in West Africa. Canberra, Australia: Australian National University. Department of Demography. Changing African Family Project Series. Monograph #7. 1978.
Keenan, Jeremy
"Power and Wealth Are Cousins: Descent, Class and Marital Strategies Among the Kel Ahaggar." Africa. Volume 47 #3 1977. pp. 242-252.
Keenan, Jeremy
"The Tuareg Veil." Middle East Studies. Volume 13 #1 January, 1977. pp. 3-13.

Keller, Bonnie B.
"Marriage and Medicine: Women's Search for Love and Luck." African Social Research. #26 December, 1978. pp. 489-505.

Kerri, James
"Understanding the African Family: Persistence, Continuity and Change." Western Journal of Black Studies. Volume 3 #1 Spring, 1979. pp. 14-17.

King-Akerele, O.
Traditional Palm Oil Processing, Women's Role and the Application of Appropriate Technology. Addis Ababa, Ethiopia: United Nations Economic Commission for Africa. Research Series. 1983.

Kisekka, Mere N.
"Polygyny and the Status of African Women." African Urban Notes. Volume 2 #3 Fall/Winter, 1976. pp. 21-42.

Kisekka, Mere N.
"On the Status of Women Within the Framework of the Liberation Movement." African Urban Notes. Volume 2 #3 Fall/Winter, 1976. pp. 65-74.

Kizerbo, Joseph
"Women and the Energy Crisis in the Sahel Africa. From the Seminar on Fuel and Energy Development for African Women in Rural Areas, Bamako, Mali, December, 1980." Unasylva. Volume 33 #133 1981. pp. 5-10.

Kocher, James E.
"Socioeconomic Development and Fertility Change in Rural Africa." Paper Presented at the Annual Meeting of the African Studies Association. Paper #44. Boston, Massachusetts. 1976. 22p.

Kocher, James E.
"Supply-Demand Disequilibria and Fertility Change in Africa--Toward a More Appropriate Economic Approach." Social Biology. Volume 30 #1 1983. pp. 41-58.

Kuper, Adam
"Symbolic Dimensions of the Southern Bantu Homestead." Africa. Volume 50 #1 1980. pp. 8-23.

Kuper, Adam
"Cousin Marriage Among the Thembu?" African Affairs. Volume 40 #1 1981. pp. 41-42.

Kurian, George and Ratna, Ghosh (eds.)
Women in the Family and the Economy: An International Comparative Survey. Westport, Connecticut: Greenwood Press. Contributions in Family Studies #5. 1981. 451p.

Kurian, George and Ratna, Ghosh (eds.)
Women in the Family and the Economy: An International Comparative Survey. Westport, Connecticut: Greenwood Press. Contributions in Family Studies #5. 1981. 451p.

Kwawu, J.
"The Role of Home Economics in Rural Development: A Focus on Family Planning." Paper Presented at the Workshop on the Role of Women and Home Economics in Rural Development in Africa. Rome: United Nations Food and Agricultural Organization. Alexandria, Egypt. October 17, 1983. 20p.

Lancaster, Chet S.
"Women, Horticulture and Society in Sub-Saharan Africa." American Anthropologist. Volume 78 #3 September, 1976. pp. 539-564.

LeVine, Robert A. and Richman, Amy and Welles, Barbara and O'Rourke, Shelagh and Caron, James W.
Women's Education and Maternal Behavior in the Third World: A Report to the Ford Foundation. New York: Ford Foundation. 1978. 52p.

LeVine, Robert A.
"Influences of Women's Schooling on Maternal Behavior in the Third World." Comparative Education Review. Volume 24 #2 Part Two June, 1980. pp. S78-S105.

Leke, R. and Nash, B.
"Biological and Socio-Cultural Aspects of Infertility and Subfertility in Africa." (In) United Nations Economic Commission for Africa (UNECA). Population Dynamics: Fertility and Mortality in Africa. Addis Ababa, Ethiopia: UNECA. May, 1981. pp. 488-498.

Lesthaeghe, Ron J. and Ohadike, Patrick O. and Kocher, James E. and Page, Hilary J.
"Child-Spacing and Fertility in Sub-Saharan Africa: An Overview of Issues." (In) Page, Hilary J. and Lesthaeghe, Ron (eds.). Child-Spacing in Tropical Africa: Traditions and Change. New York: Academic Press. 1981. pp. 3-23.

Levine, Nancy E.
"Nyinba Polyandry and the Allocation of Paternity." Journal of Comparative Family Studies. Volume 11 #3 Special Iss. August, 1980. pp. 283-298.

Levine, Nancy E. and Sangree, Walter H.
"Asian and African Systems of Polyandry." Journal of Comparative Family Studies. Volume 11 #3 Special Iss. August, 1980. pp. 385-410.

Levine, Nancy E. and Sangree, Walter H.
"Women With Many Husbands--Polyandrous Alliance and Marital Flexibility in Africa and Asia." Journal of Comparative Family Studies. Volume 11 #3 Special Iss. August, 1980.

Lewis, Barbara C.
"Fertility and Employment: An Assessment of Role Incompatibility Among African Urban Women." (In) Bay, Edna G. Women and Work in Africa. Boulder, Colorado: Westview Press. Westview Special Studies. 1982. pp. 249-276.

Lewis, Barbara C. (ed.)
The Invisible Farmer: Women and the Crisis in Agriculture. Washington, D.C.: U.S. Department of State. U.S. Agency for International Development. Office of Women in Development. 1982. 456p.

Little, Kenneth L.
"Women's Strategies in Modern Marriage in Anglophone West Africa: An Ideological and Sociological Appraisal." Journal of Comparative Family Studies. Volume 8 #3 Autumn, 1977. pp. 341-356.

Little, Kenneth L.
"Women's Strategies in Modern Marriage in Anglophone West Africa: An Ideological and Sociological Appraisal." (In) Kurian, George (ed.). Cross-Cultural Perspectives of Mate Selection and Marriage. Westport, Connecticut: Greenwood Press. Contributions in Family Studies #3. 1979. pp. 202-217.

Loutfi, Martha F.
Rural Women: Unequal Partners in Development. Geneva: International Labour Organization. 1982. 80p.

Lukutati, Bwembya
"The Concept of Parenthood in African Societies." (In) International Planned Parenthood Federation (IPPF). Proceedings of the IPPF Africa Regional Conference. London: IPPF. 1977. pp. 145-152.

Mabogunje, A.L.
"The Policy Implications of Changes in Child-Spacing Practices in Tropical Africa." (In) Page, Hilary J. and Lesthaeghe, Ron (eds.). Child-Spacing in Tropical Africa: Traditions and Changes. New York: Academic Press. 1981. pp. 303-316.

MacGaffey, Wyatt
"Lineage Structure, Marriage and the Family Amongst the Central Bantu." Journal of African History. Volume 24 #2 1983. pp. 173-187.

McCall, Daniel
"Rank, Gender, Cult Affiliation Proclaimed in the Arts of Apparel: Reflections on Esie Sculpture." Paper Presented at the Annual Meeting of the African Studies Association. Paper #34. Bloomimgton, Indiana. 1981.

McDowell, James and Hazzard, Virginia
"Village Technology and Women's Work in Eastern Africa." Assignment Children. Volume 36 Oct.-Dec., 1976. pp. 53-65.

McSweeney, Brenda G.
"Collection and Analysis of Rural Women's Time Use." Studies in Family Planning. Volume 10 #11/12 Nov.-Dec., 1979. pp. 379+.

Meer, Fatima (ed.)
The African Woman at Home and in Gainful Employment. Collection of Unpublished Papers. 1980.

Minces, Juliette
The House of Obedience: Women in Arab Society. London: Zed Press. Westport, Connecticut: Lawrence Hill. 1982. 114p.

Moots, Patricia A. and Zak, Michele (eds.)
Women and the Politics of Culture: Studies in the Sexual Economy. New York: Longman. 1983. 452p.

Netting, Robert M. and Wilk, Richard R. and Arnold, Eric J, (eds.).
Households: Comparative and Historical Studies of the Domestic Group. Berkeley, California: University of California Press. 1984. 480p.

Norem, R.H.
"The Integration of a Family Systems Perspective Into

Farming Systems Projects." (In) Caldwell, John and Rojas, Mary (eds.). Family Systems and Farming Systems: A Second Annual Conference in the World of Women in Development Series. Blacksburg, Virginia: Virgnia Polytechnic Institute and State University. 1983.

Ntiri, Daphne W. (ed.)
One is Not a Woman--One Becomes....The African Woman in a Transitional Society. Troy, Michigan: Bedford Publishers. 1982. 137p.

O'Brien, Denise
"Female Husbands in Southern Bantu." (In) Schlegal, A. (ed.). Sexual Stratification: A Cross-Cultural View. New York: Columbia University Press. 1977. pp. 109-126.

Obbo, Christine S.
"Dominant Male Ideology and Female Options: Three East African Case Studies." Africa. Volume 46 #4 1976. pp. 371-389.

Okeyo, Achola P.
"Women in the Household Economy: Managing Multiple Roles." Studies in Family Planning. Volume 10 #11/12 Nov.-Dec., 1979. pp. 337-343.

Okeyo, Achola P.
The Role of Women in Changing Traditional Farming Systems. Paper Presented at the Workshop on Policies and Programmes for Increased Food and Agricultural Production in Traditional Subsistence Farms in Africa. Rome: United Nations Food and Agriculture Organization. Arusha, Tanzania. December 10, 1984. 27p.

Oppong, Christine
A Synopsis of Seven Roles and Status of Women: An Outline of a Conceptual and Methodological Approach. Geneva: International Labour Organization. World Employment Programme. Research Working Paper. Mimeo. (Restricted) 1980.

Oppong, Christine and Adaba, Gemma and Bekomba-Priso, Manga and Mogey, J. (eds.)
Marriage, Fertility and Parenthood in West Africa. Canberra, Australia: Australian National University. Department of Demography. Changing African Family Project. Monograph #4. Two Volumes. 1978. 848p.

Oppong, Christine (ed.)
Female and Male in West Africa. Boston: George Allen and Unwin. 1983. 402p.

Overholt, C. and Anderson, M. and Cloud, K. and Austin, J.
Gender Roles in Development Projects: A Casebook. West Hartford: Connecticut: Kumarian Press. Kumarian Press Case Studies Series. 1985. 326p.

Pagezy, Helen
"Some Aspects of Daily Work of Women Oto and Twa Living in Equatorial Forest Middle." L'Anthropolgie. Volume 80 #3 1976. pp. 465-906.

Pellow, Deborah and Spitzer, Leo
"Sexual Identity as a Basis for Marginality." Paper

Presented at the Annual Meeting of the African Studies Association. Paper #87. Philadelphia, Pennsylvania. 1980.

Roberts, Pepe
"The Sexual Politics of Labor and the Household in Africa." (In) Guyer, Jane I. and Peters, Pauline E. (eds.). Conceptualizing the Household: Issues of Theory, Method and Application. Charlottesville, Virginia: Teleprint. Papers From a Workshop Held at Harvard University, November 2-4, 1984. 1984.

Rogers, Barbara
"Food, Fertility and Nuclear Mothers: How Development Can Increase Rather than Reduce the Social and Economic Burdens of African Women." Populi. Volume 5 #1 1978. pp. 23-27.

Rogers, Barbara
The Domestication of Women: Discrimination in Developing Societies. New York: St. Martin's Press. 1980. 200p.

Sacks, Karen
Sisters and Wives: The Past and Future of Sexual Equality. Westport, Connecticut: Greenwood Press. Contributions in Women's Studies #10. 1979. 274p.

Safilios-Rothschild, Constantina
Female Power, Autonomy and Demographic Change in the Third World. Geneva: International Labour Organization. The Role of Women and Demographic Change Research Program. 1980.

Safilios-Rothschild, Constantina
Can Agriculture in the Third World Modernize With Traditional Female Agricultural Labor? State College, Pennsylvania: Pennsylvania State University. Department of Sociology. 1981.

Schwendinger, Julia and Schwendinger, Herman
"Rape, Sexual Inequality and Levels of Violence." Crime and Social Justice. Volume 16 Winter, 1981. pp. 3-31.

Sen, G.
"Women Workers and the Green Revolution." (In) Beneria, Lourdes (ed.). Women and Development: The Sexual Division of Labor in Rural Societies. New York: Praeger Publishers. 1985.

Simms, Ruth
"The African Woman as Entrepreneur: Problems and Perspectives on Their Roles." (In) Steady, Filomina C. (ed.). The Black Woman Cross-Culturally. Cambridge, Massachusetts: Schenkman Publishing. 1981. pp. 141-168.

Smith, Jane I. (ed.)
Women in Contemporary Muslim Societies. Lewisburg, Pennsylvania: Bucknell University Press. 1980. 264p.

Smith, Janet I.
"The Experience of Muslim Women: Considerations of Power and Authority." (In) Haddad, Yvonne Y. and Haines, Byron and Findly, Ellison (eds.). The Islamic Impact. Syracuse, New York: Syracuse University Press. 1984. pp. 89-112.

Staudt, Kathleen A.
"Tracing Sex Differences in Donor Agricultural Programs." Paper Presented at the American Political Science Association Annual Meeting. Washington, D.C. 1979.

Sudarkasa, Niara
"Sex Roles, Education and Development in Africa." Anthropology and Education Quarterly. Volume 13 #3 Fall, 1982. pp. 279-288.

Tillion, Germaine
The Republic of Cousins: Women's Oppression in Mediterranean Society. London: Al Saqi Books. Translated by Q. Hoare. 1983. 181p.

United Nations
Report of the World Conference to Review and Appraise the Achievements of the United Nations Decade for Women: Equality, Development and Peace. Nairobi, Kenya, July 15-26, 1985. New York: United Nations. 1986. 304p.

United Nations Centre on Transnational Corporations and International Labour Office (ILO)
Women Workers in Multinational Enterprises in Developing Countries: A Contribution to the United Nations Decade for Women. Geneva: ILO. 1985. 119p.

United Nations Economic Commission for Africa (UNECA)
An Inventory of Social Science Research on Women's Roles and Status in Sub-Saharan Africa Since 1960. (Draft) Addis Ababa, Ethiopia: UNECA. 1982.

Valentine, C.H. and Revson, J.E.
"Cultural Traditions, Social Change, and Fertility in Sub-Saharan Africa." Journal of Modern African Studies. Volume 17 #3 September, 1979. pp. 453-472.

Waines, D.
"Through a Veil Darkly--The Study of Women in Muslim Societies." Comparative Studies in Society and History. Volume 24 #4 1982.

Wallace, Karen S.
"Women and Identity: A Black Francophone Female Perspective." Sage: A Scholarly Journal on Black Women. Volume 2 #1 1985. pp. 19-23.

Waterman, Peter
"A New Focus in African Worker Studies: Promises, Problems, Dangers." Cahiers d'Etudes Africaines. Volume 24 #3 1984. pp. 343-361.

Weekes-Vagliani, Winifred
"Women, Food and Rural Development." (In) Rose, T. (ed.). Crisis and Recovery in Subsaharan Africa. Paris: OECD Development Center. 1985. pp. 104-110.

White, Douglas R. and Bruton, Michael L. and Dow, Malcolm M.
"Sexual Division of Labor in African Agriculture: A Network Autocorrelation Analysis." American Anthropologist. Volume 83 #4 December, 1981. pp. 824-849.

Whyte, Martin K.
The Status of Women in Preindustrial Societies. Princeton, New Jersey: Princeton University Press. 1978. 222p.

Youssef, Nadia H.
"Interrelationship Between the Division of Labor in the Household, Women's Roles and Their Impact Upon Fertility." Paper Presented at the Informal Workshop on Women's Roles and Demographic Research Program. Geneva: International Labour Organization. November, 1978.

Youssef, Nadia H. and Hetler, Carol B.
"Establishing the Economic Condition of Woman-Headed Households in the Third World: A New Approach." (In) Buvinic, Mayra and Lycette, Margaret A. and McGreevey, William P. (eds.). Women and Poverty in the Third World. Baltimore, Maryland: Johns Hopkins University. 1983. pp. 216-243.

Youssef, Nadia H.
"Women and Agricultural Production in Muslim Societies." Studies in Comparative International Development. Volume 12 #1 Spring, 1977. pp. 41-58.

Sexual Mutilation/Circumcision

Anonymous
"Women Against Mutilation." off our backs. Volume 9 December, 1979. pp. 7.

Boulware-Miller, Kay
"Female Circumcision: Challenges to the Practice as a Human Rights Violation." Harvard Women's Law Journal. Volume 8 Spring, 1985. pp. 155-177.

El Sadaawi, Nawal
The Hidden Face of Eve: Women in the Arab World. Boston: Beacon Press. 1982. 212p.

Geletkanycz, Christine and Egan, Susan
Literature Review: The Practice of Female Circumcision. Washington, D.C.: U.S. Department of Health, Education and Welfare. Office of International Health. Mimeo. 1979.

Hadri, Gasim
"Opinions About Female Circumcision." Paper Presented at the Seminar on Traditional Practices Affecting the Health of Women and Children. World Conference of the United Nations Decade for Women. Copenhagen, Denmark. July 14-30, 1980.

Hosken, Fran P.
"Women and Health: Genital And Sexual Mutilation of Females." International Journal of Women's Studies. Volume 3 #3 May-June, 1980. pp. 300-316.

Hosken, Fran P.
"The Violence of Power: The Genital Mutilation of Females." Heresies. Volume 6 #2 Summer, 1978. pp. 28-36.

Hosken, Fran P.
"Female Circumcision in Africa." Victimology. Volume 2 #3/4 1977. pp. 487-498.

Hosken, Fran P.
"Genital Mutilation of Women in Africa." Munger Africana Library Notes. #36 October, 1976. 21p.

Hosken, Fran P.
"Towards an Epidemiology of Genital Mutilation of Females in Africa." Paper Presented at the Annual Meeting of the African Studies Association. Paper #43. Baltimore, Maryland. 1978. 20p.

Hosken, Fran P.
The Hosken Report: Genital and Sexual Mutilation of Females. Lexington, Massachusetts: Women's International Network News. 1982. 327p.

Hosken, Fran P.
Female Sexual Mutilations: The Facts and Proposals for Action. Lexington, Massachusetts: Women's International Network News. 1980. 102p.

Hosken, Fran P.
"Female Genital Mutilation in the World Today: A Global Review." International Journal of Health Services. Volume 11 #3 1981. pp. 415-430.

Hosken, Fran P.
"Female Circumcision and Fertility in Africa." Women and Health. Volume 1 #6 Nov.-Dec., 1976. pp. 3-11.

Hosken, Fran P.
"The Epidemiology of Female Genital Mutilation." Tropical Doctor. July, 1978. pp. 150-156.

Hosken, Fran P.
"Women and Health in East and West Africa: Family Planning and Female Cicumcision." Paper Presented at the Seminar on Traditional Practices Affecting the Health of Women and Children. World Conference of the United Nations Decade for Women. New York: United Nations. Copenhagen, Denmark. July 14-30, 1980.

Hosken, Fran P.
"Women and Health in East and West Africa: Family Planning and Female Circumcision." Paper Presented at the Seminar on Traditional Practices Affecting the Health of Women and Children: Female Circumcision, Childhood Marriage, Nutritional Taboos, etc. Alexandria, Egypt: World Health Organization. Eastern Mediterranean Regional Office. Khartoum, Sudan. February 10-15, 1979.

Hosken, Fran P.
"Female Circumcision in the World of Today: A Global Review." Paper Presented at the Seminar on Traditional Practices Affecting the Health of Women and Children. World Conference of the United Nations Decade for Women. New York: United Nations. Copenhagen, Denmark. July 14-30, 1980.

Hosken, Fran P.
"Female Circumcision in the World of Today: A Global View." Paper Presented at the Seminar on Traditional Practices Affecting the Health of Women and Children: Female Circumcision, Childhood Marriage, Nutritional Taboos, etc. Alexandria, Egypt: World Health Organization. Eastern Mediterranean Regional Office. Khartoum, Sudan. February 10-15, 1979.

Huelsman, Ben R.
"An Anthropological View of Clitoral and Other Female Genital Mutilations." (In) Lowery, T.P. and Lowery, T.S. (eds.). The Clitoris. St. Louis, Missouri: Warren H. Green. 1976. pp. 111-161.

Johnson, B.C.
"Traditional Practices Affecting the Health of Women." Paper Presented at the Seminar on Traditional Practices Affecting the Health of Women and Children. World Conference of the United Nations Decade for Women. New York: United Nations. Copenhagen, Denmark. July 14-30, 1980.

Kouba, Leonard J. and Muasher, Judith
"Female Circumcision in Africa: An Overview." African Studies Review. Volume 28 #1 1985. pp. 95-110.

Mahran, M.
"Medical Dangers of Female Circumcision." International Planned Parenthood Federation (IPPF) Medical Bulletin. Volume 15 #2 April, 1981.

McLean, Scilla
"Female Genital Mutilation." ISIS Women's International Bulletin. #25 1982. pp. 26-32.

McLean, Scilla and Graham, Stella E.
Female Circumcision, Excision and Infibulation: The Fact and Proposals for Change. London: Minority Rights Group. Report #47. Second Revised Edition. 1985. 21p.

Moen, Elizabeth W.
Genital Mutilation: Everywoman's Problem. East Lansing, Michigan: Michigan State University. Office of Women in International Development. Working Paper #22. April, 1983.

Mukhtar, Behiza
"A Question of Our Children's Bodies: The Medical Injury Caused to a Girl by Circumcision." Paper Presented at the Conference on Islam and Family Planning. Sponsored by the International Planned Parenthood Federation. Banjul, Gambia. October 21-24, 1979. 7p.

Pieters, Guy and Lowenfels, A.
"Infibulation in the Horn of Africa." New York State Journal of Medicine. Volume 77 April, 1977. pp. 729-731.

Sanderson, Lilian P.
Against the Mutilation of Women: The Struggle Against Unnecessary Suffering. London: Ithaca Press. 1981. 117p.

Shaalan, Mohammed
"Clitoris Envy: A Psychodynamic Construct Instrumental in Female Circumcision." Paper Presented at the Seminar on Traditional Practices Affecting the Health of Women and Children. World Conference of the United Nations Decade for Women. New York: United Nations. Copenhagen, Denmark. July 14-30, 1980.

Shaalan, Mohammed
"Clitoris Envy: A Psychdynamic Construct Instrumental in Female Circumcision." Paper Presented at the Seminar on Traditional Practices Affecting the Health of Women and Children: Female Circumcision, Childhood Marriage, Nutritional Taboos, etc. Alexandria, Egypt: World Health Organization. Eastern Mediterranean Regional Office. Khartoum, Sudan. February 10-15, 1979.

Sindzingre, N.
"Plus and Minus--Concerning Female Circumcision." Cahiers d'Etudes Africaines. Volume 17 #1 1977. pp. 65-76.

Taba, A.H.
"Female Circumcision." World Health. May, 1979. pp. 8-13.

Taba, A.H.
"Female Circumcision." (In) World Health Organization. Traditional Practices Affecting the Health of Women and Children: Female Circumcision, Childhood Marriage, Nutritional Taboos, etc. Report of a Seminar, Khartoum, Sudan, February 10-15, 1979. Alexandria, Egypt: WHO/EMRO Technical Publication #2. 1979. pp. 43-52.

Thiam, Awa
"Women's Fight for the Abolition of Sexual Mutilation." International Social Science Journal. Volume 35 #4 1983. pp. 747-756.

World Health Organization (WHO)
Traditional Practices Affecting the Health of Women and Children: Female Circumcision, Childhood Marriage, Nutritional Taboos, etc. Report of a Seminar, Khartoum, Sudan, February 10-15, 1979. Alexandria, Egypt: WHO. Eastern Mediterranean Regional Office. Technical Publication #2. 1979. 170p.

Wright, Marcia
"Bwanikwa: Consciousness and Protest Among Slave Women in Central Africa, 1886-1911." (In) Robertson, Claire C. and Klein, Martin A. (eds.). Women and Slavery in Africa. Madison, Wisconsin: University of Wisconsin Press. 1983. pp. 246-267.

Slavery

Adebayo, Adedeji
"The Prospects of Family Planning in Africa." (In) International Planned Parenthood Federation (IPPF). Proceedings of the IPPF Africa Regional Conference. London: IPPF. 1977. pp. 46-54.

De Sardan, Jean-Pierre O.
"The Songhay-Zarma Female Slave: Relations of Production and Ideological Status." (In) Robertson, Claire C. and Klein, Martin A. (eds.). Women and Slavery in Africa. Madison, Wisconsin: University of Wisconsin Press. 1983. pp. 130-143.

Keim, Curtis A.
"Women in Slavery Among the Mangbetu, c. 1800-1910." (In) Robertson, Claire C. and Klein, Martin A. (eds.). Women and Slavery in Africa. Madison, Wisconsin: University of Wisconsin Press. 1983. pp. 144-159.

Mbevi, Grace
"Child Marriage and Early Teenage Childbirth." Paper Presented at the Seminar on Traditional Practices Affecting the Health of Women and Children. World Conference of the United Nations Decade for Women. New York: United Nations. Copenhagen, Denmark. July 14-30, 1980.

Meillassoux, Claude
"Female Slavery." (In) Robertson, Claire C. and Klein, Martin A. (eds.). Women and Slavery in Africa. Madison, Wisconsin: University of Wisconsin Press. 1983. pp. 49-66.

Nash, June
"Women in Development: Dependence and Exploitation." Development and Change. Volume 8 #2 April, 1977. pp. 161-182.

Robertson, Claire C. and Klein, Martin A. (eds.)
Women and Slavery in Africa. Madison, Wisconsin: University of Wisconsin Press. 1983. 380p.

Robertson, Claire C. and Klein, Martin A.
"Women's Importance in African Slave Systems." (In) Robertson, Claire C. and Klein, Martin A. (eds.). Women and Slavery in Africa. Madison, Wisconsin: University of Wisconsin Press. 1983. pp. 3-25.

Thornton, John
"Sexual Demography: The Impact of Slave Trade on Family Structure." (In) Robertson, Claire C. and Klein, Martin A. (eds.). Women and Slavery in Africa. Madison, Wisconsin: University of Wisconsin Press. 1983. pp. 39-48.

Status of Women

Abdel Kader, Soha
"Research on the Status of Women, Development and Population Trends in Arab States: An Annotated Bibliography." (In) UNESCO. Bibliographic Guide to Studies on the Status of Women: Development and Population. Paris: United Nations Educational, Scientific and Cultural Organization. 1983. pp. 67-81.

Abdel Kader, Soha
The Status of Research on Women in the Arab Region, 1960-1978. Paris: UNESCO. Division of Human Rights and Peace. January, 1979.

Accad, Evelyne
"Interrelationship Between Arab Nationalism and Feminist Consciousness in the North African Novels Written by Women." Ba Shiru. Volume 8 #2 1977. pp. 3-12.

Aguta, M.O. and Exedij, F.O. (eds.)
Changing Status of Women in Africa. Addis Ababa, Ethiopia: United Nations Economic Commission for Africa. African Training and Research Centre for Women. 1978.

Aidoo, Christina A.
"Images of Women." Paper Presented at the Women and Work in Africa Symposium #6. Urbana, Illinois: University of Ilinois. April 29, 1979.

Al-Qazza, Ayad
"Current Status of Research on Women in the Arab World." Middle Eastern Studies. Volume 14 #3 October, 1978. pp. 372-384.

Allman, James
"Family Patterns, Women's Status and Fertility in Middle-East and North-Africa." International Journal of Sociology of the Family. Volume 8 #1 1978. pp. 19-35.

Allman, James
"Family Life, Women's Status, and Fertility: Middle East and North African Perspectives." (In) Allman, James

(ed.). Women's Studies and Fertility in the Muslim World. New York: Praeger Publishers. Praeger Special Studies. 1978. pp. 24-48.

Allman, James (ed.)
Women's Status and Fertility in the Muslim World. New York: Praeger Publishers. Praeger Special Studies. 1978. 378p.

Anonymous
"International Conference on the Role of Women in Liberation Struggles and Women in Development." IDOC Bulletin. #50/51 December-January, 1976. pp. 4-21.

Anonymous
"The Position of Women in Africa." Rural Progress. Volume 1 #3 1979. pp. 20-23.

Anonymous
"Southern African Women Speak Out." Africa Report. Volume 28 #2 March-April, 1983. pp. 15-19.

Anonymous
"Two Views of Liberation." Agenda. Volume 1 #2 February, 1978. pp. 19-22.

Anyaoku, Emeka
"Changing Attitudes: A Cooperative Effort." Africa Report. Volume 30 #2 March, 1985. pp. 21-25.

Axinn, Nancy W.
Female Emancipation Versus Female Welfare. East Lansing, Michigan: Michigan State University. Institute for International Studies in Education. College of Education. Non-Formal Education Information Center. 1979. 5p.

Baffoun, Alya
"Women and Social Change in the Muslim Arab World." Women's Studies International Forum. Volume 5 #2 1982.

Caplan, Patricia and Bujra, Janet M. (eds.)
Women United Women Divided: Comparative Studies of Ten Contemporary Cultures. Bloomington, Indiana: Indiana University Press. 1979. 288p.

Caplan, Patricia
"Cognatic Descent, Islamic Law, and Women's Property on the East African Coast." (In) Hirschon, Renbee (ed.). Women and Property--Women as Property. New York: St.Martin's Press. 1983.

Castillo, Gelia T.
The Changing Role of Women in Rural Societies: A Summary of Trends and Issues. New York: Agricultural Development Council Inc. RTN Seminar Reports 12. February, 1977. 11p.

Danforth, Sandra C.
Women and National Development. Monticello, Illinois: Vance Bibliographies. #P-916. February, 1982. 35p.

Date-Bah, Eugenia
"Rural Development and the Status of Women." Paper Presented at a Seminar on the Role of Population Factor in the Rural Development Strategy." Monrovia, Liberia. 1980.

Dhamija, Jasleen
"Technology as a Target to the Development of Women's Skills in Africa." Ceres. # 84 November, 1981. pp. 24-27.

Donhoff, Christoph G.
"The Women of Africa." Africa Insight. Volume 12 #1 1982. pp. 25-26.

Dunbar, Roberta
"Legislative Reform and Muslim Family Law: Effects Upon Women's Rights in Africa South of the Sahara." Paper Presented at the Annual Meeting of the African Studies Association. Paper #25. Philadelphia, Pennsylvania. October 15-18, 1980.

El Bushra, Judy and Bekele, Abebech and Hammour, Fawzia
"Socio-Economic Development and Women Changing Status." Paper Presented to the Conference on Women and the Environment. Khartoum, Sudan: University of Khartoum. Institute of Environmental Studies. April 4-7, 1981.

Epstein, Trude S.
Place of Social Anthropology in a Multidisciplinary Approach to the Study of Women's Roles and Status in Less Developed Countries. Geneva: International Labour Organization. 1978.

Fairbanks, Z.
"Fighting Women Go Home." New Statesman. Volume 101 April 17, 1981. pp. 14-15.

Fatehally, Laeeq (ed.)
Women in the Third World. Bombay, India: Leslie Sawhny Programme. 1980. 155p.

Fraker, Anne and Harrell-Bond, Barbara
"Feminine Influence." West Africa. December 17, 1979. pp. 2182-2186.

Frank, Katherine
"Feminist Criticism and the African Novel." African Literature Today. #14 1984. pp. 34-38.

Gebre-Selassie, Alasebu
"The Situation of Women in Africa: A Review." Nairobi: UNICEF. Eastern Africa Regional Office. 1979. 65p.

Gilligan, John J.
"Importance of Third World Women." Rivista di Studi Politici Internazionali. Volume 45 #3 July-September, 1978.

Ginat, Joseph (ed.)
Women in Muslim Rural Society: Status and Role in Family Community. New Brunswick, New Jersey: Transition Books. 1981. 268p.

Haq, Khadija (ed.)
Equality of Opportunity Within and Among Nations. New York: Praeger Publishers. Praeger Special Studies in International Economics and Development. 1977. 223p.

Howard, Rhoda E.
"Women and the Crisis in Commonwealth Africa." International Political Science Review. Volume 6 #3 1985. pp. 287-296.

Imam, Ayesha M.
"The Presentation of African Women Through History." Paper Presented at the Meeting of Experts on Theoretical Frameworks and Methodological Approaches to Studies on the Role of Women in History as Actors in Economic, Social, Political and Ideological Processes. Paris: United Nations Educational, Scientific and Cultural Organization. 1984. 28p.

International Labour Organization (ILO)
Female Power, Autonomy and Demographic Change in the Third World. Geneva: ILO. The Role of Women and Demographic Change Ressearch Programme. 1980.

Kisekka, Mere N.
"Polygyny and the Status of African Women." African Urban Notes. Volume 2 #3 Fall/Winter, 1976. pp. 21-42.

Kisekka, Mere N.
"On the Status of Women Within the Framework of the Liberation Movement." African Urban Notes. Volume 2 #3 Fall/Winter, 1976. pp. 65-74.

Kisekka, Mere N.
"The Status of Women, Development and Population Trends in Africa: An Annotated Bibliography." Paper Presented at the Meeting of Experts on Research on the Status of Women, Development and Population Trends: Evaluation and Prospects. Paris: United Nations Educational, Scientific and Cultural Organization. 1980. 66p.

Kisekka, Mere N.
"Research on the Status of Women, Development and Population Trends in Africa: An Annotated Bibliography." (In) United Nations Educational, Scientific and Cultural Organization. Bibliographic Guide to Studies on the Status of Women: Development and Population. Paris: UNESCO. 1983. pp. 41-66.

Konie, Gwendoline
"Women in Southern Africa: Gaining Political Power." Africa Report. Volume 28 #2 March-April, 1983. pp. 11-14.

Koning, Karen L.
"Revolutionary Potential Among Arab Women Today." Mawazo. Volume 4 #4 1976. pp. 48-57.

M'bow, Amadou-Mahtar
"The United Nations Decade for Women: Towards a New Order With Regard to the Status of Women." Cultures. Volume 8 #4 1982.

Marshall, Susan E.
"Politics and Female Status in North Africa: A Reconsideration of Development Theory." Economic Development and Cultural Change. Volume 32 #3 April, 1984. pp. 499-524.

Matsepe, Ivy F.
"Women in the Struggle for Liberation." (In) Wiley, David and Isaacman, Allen (eds.). Southern Africa: Society, Economy and Liberation. East Lansing, Michigan: Michigan State University. African Studies Center. 1981.

Matsepe-Casaburri, Ivy F.
"Women in Southern Africa: Legacy of Exclusion." Africa Report. Volume 28 #2 March-April, 1983. pp. 7-10.
Meghdessian, S.R.
The Status of Arab Women: A Select Bibliography. Westport, Connecticut: Greenwood Press. 1980. 176p.
Mikhail, Mona
Images of Arab Women: Fact and Fiction. Washington, D.C.: Three Continents Press. 1979. 137p.
Minces, Juliette
The House of Obedience: Women in Arab Society. London: Zed Press. Westport, Connecticut: Lawrence Hill. 1982. 114p.
NGO Planning Committee
Forum '85: Final Report: Nairobi, Kenya. New York: NGO Planning Committee. 1985. 105p.
Nash, June
"Women in Development: Dependence and Exploitation." Development and Change. Volume 8 #2 April, 1977. pp. 161-182.
Njoku, John E.
The Dawn of African Women. Hicksville, New York: Exposition Press. 1977. 96p.
Ogbu, John U.
"African Bridewealth and Women's Status." American Ethnologist. Volume 5 #2 May, 1978. pp. 241-262.
Okanlawon, Tunde
Deterioration of Collective Identity: The Case of Women. Papers of the International Congress of African Studies. 1978. 8p.
Okonjo, Kemene
"Women in Contemporary Africa." (In) Mojekwu, Christopher C. and Uchendu, Victor C. and Hoey, Leo F. (eds.). African Society, Culture and Politics: An Introduction to African Studies. Washington, D.C.: University Press of America. 1978. pp. 201-214.
Oloko, Olatunde
Modernization and Social Problems in Africa. Lagos, Nigeria: University of Lagos. United Nations Economic Commission for Africa. 1979.
Ooko-Ombaka, Oki
"An Assessment of National Machinery for Women." Assignment Children. #49/50 Spring, 1980.
Oppong, Christine
A Synopsis of Seven Roles and Status of Women: An Outline of a Conceptual and Methodological Approach. Geneva: International Labour Organization. World Employment Programme. Research Working Paper. Mimeo. (Restricted) 1980.
Pala, Achola O. and Seidman, Ann
"A Proposed Model of the Status of Women in Africa." Paper Presented at the Conference on Women and Development. Wellesley, Massachusetts: Wellesley College. June, 1976.

Peil, Margaret
African Urban Life: Components of Satisfaction. Birmingham, England: Birmingham University. Centre for West African Studies. 1982.

Pellow, Deborah
Marginality and Individual Consciousness: Women in Modernizing Africa. East Lansing, Michigan: Michigan State University. Office of Women in International Development. Working Paper #28. July, 1983. 33p.

Pellow, Deborah and Spitzer, Leo
"Sexual Identity as a Basis for Marginality." Paper Presented at the Annual Meeting of the African Studies Association. Paper #87. Philadelphia, Pennsylvania. 1980.

Peters, Emrys L.
"The Status of Women in Four Middle East Communities." (In) Beck, Lois and Keddie, Nikki R. (eds.). Women in the Muslim World. Cambridge, Massachusetts: Harvard University Press. 1978. pp. 311-350.

Raccagni, Michelle
The Modern Arab Women: A Bibliography. Metuchen, New Jersey: Scarecrow Press. 1978. 262p.

Ritchie, Jean A.
"Impact of Changing Food Production. Processing and Marketing Systems on the Role of Women." (In) Proceedings of the World Conference. Ames, Iowa: Iowa State University Press. 1977. pp. 129-144.

Ritchie, Jean A.
The Integration of Women in Agrarian Reform and Rural Development in English Speaking Countries of the African Region. Rome: United Nations Food and Agriculture Organization. March, 1978. 95p.

Rizika, J.
"After the Decade." Africa Report. Volume 30 #5 Sept.-Oct., 1985. pp. 75-81.

Sadik, Nafis
"Muslim Women Today." Populi. Volume 12 #1 1985. pp. 36-51.

Steady, Filomina C.
"African Women at the End of the Decade." Africa Report. Volume 30 #2 March-April, 1985. pp. 4-7.

Thelejane, T.S.
"An African Girl and an African Woman in a Changing World." Paper Presented at the Seminar on the Changing Family in the African Context. Paris: United Nations Educational, Scientific and Cultural Organization. Maseru, Lesotho. 1984. 24p.

United Nations
Report of the World Conference to Review and Appraise the Achievements of the United Nations Decade for Women: Equality, Development and Peace. Nairobi, Kenya, July 15-26, 1985. New York: United Nations. 1986. 304p.

United Nations Economic Commission for Africa (UNECA)
An Inventory of Social Science Research on Women's Roles

and Status in Sub-Saharan Africa Since 1960. (Draft) Addis Ababa, Ethiopia: UNECA. 1982.

United Nations Economic Commission for Africa (UNECA)
"The Role of Women in the Solution of the Food Crisis in Africa (Implementation of the Lagos Plan of Action)." Paper Presented at the Regional Intergovernmental Preparatory Meeting for the World Conference to Review and Appraise the Achievements of the United Nations Decade for Women: Equality, Development and Peace/Third Regional Conference on the Integration of Women in Development, Arusha, Tanzania, October 8-12. Addis Ababa, Ethiopia: UNECA. 1984.

United Nations Educational, Scientific, and Cultural Organ.
Bibliographic Guide to Studies on the Status of Women: Development and Population Trends. Paris: UNESCO. Epping, England: Bowker. 1983. 284p.

Urdang, Stephanie
"Women in National Liberation Movements." (In) Hay, Margaret J. and Stichter, Sharon (eds.). African Women South of the Sahara. New York: Longman. 1984. pp. 156-169.

Ward, Kathryn B.
Women in the Third World-System: Its Impact on Status and Fertility. New York: Praeger Publishers. 1984. 191p.

Weekes-Vagliani, Winifred and Grossat, Bernard
Women in Development: At the Right Time for the Right Reason. Paris: Organization for Economic Cooperation and Development. 1980. 330p.

Whyte, Martin K.
The Status of Women in Preindustrial Societies. Princeton, New Jersey: Princeton University Press. 1978. 222p.

Youssef, Nadia H.
"The Status and Fertility Patterns of Muslim Women." (In) Beck, Lois and Keddie, Nikki R. (eds.). Women in the Muslim World. Cambridge, Massachusetts: Harvard University Press. 1978. pp. 69-99.

Zivetz, L.
The Impact of Rural Development on the Status of Women and its Consequences for Fertility in Africa. Submitted to the Research Triangle Institute and the Southeast Consortium for International Development. Chapel Hill, North Carolina. 1979.

Urbanization

Lewis, Barbara C.
"Fertility and Employment: An Assessment of Role Incompatibility Among African Urban Women." (In) Bay, Edna G. Women and Work in Africa. Boulder, Colorado: Westview Press. Westview Special Studies. 1982. pp. 249-276.

Little, Kenneth L.
Sociology of Urban Women's Image in African Literature. Totowa, New Jersey: Rowman and Littlefield. 1980. 174p.

Nash, June
"Women in Development: Dependence and Exploitation." Development and Change. Volume 8 #2 April, 1977. pp. 161-182.

Peil, Margaret
African Urban Life: Components of Satisfaction. Birmingham, England: Birmingham University. Centre for West African Studies. 1982.

Peil, Margaret
"Urban Women in the Labor Force." Sociology of Work and Occupations. Volume 6 #4 November, 1979. pp. 482-501.

Trager, Lillian
"Urban Market Women: Hoarders, Hagglers, Economic Heroines?" Paper Presented at the Annual Meeting of the African Studies Association. Paper #94. Los Angeles, California. Oct. 31-Nov. 3, 1979. 26p.

Ware, Helen
"Security in the City: The Role of the Family in Urban West Africa." (In) Ruzicka, Lado T. (ed.). The Economic and Social Supports for High Fertility: Proceedings of the Conference Held in Canberra, November 16-18, 1976. Canberra, Australia: Australian National University. Development Studies Center. 1977. pp. 385-408.

Women and Their Children

Anonymous
"Mothers, Babies and Health." Agenda. Volume 1 #2 February, 1978. pp. 8-14.

Bulatao, R.A.
"Transitions in the Value of Children and the Fertility Transition." Paper Presented at the Seminar on Determinants of Fertility Trends: Major Themes and New Directions for Research. International Union for the Scientific Study of Population. Bad Homburg, Germany. 1980.

Buvinic, Mayra and Youssef, Nadia H. and Schumacher, Ilsa
Women-Headed Households: The Ignored Factor in Development Planning. Washington D.C.: U.S. Department of State. U.S. Agency for International Development. International Center for Research on Women. Women in Development Office. March, 1978. 113p.

Cleveland, David
"Fertility and the Value of Children in Subsistence Agriculture: Savanna West Africa." Paper Presented at the Annual Meeting of the American Anthropological Association. Cincinnati, Ohio. November, 1979.

Cosminsky, Sheila
"The Role and Training of Traditional Midwives: Policy Implications for Maternal and Child Health Care." Paper Presented at the Annual Meeting of the African Studies Association. Paper #17. Houston, Texas. 1977. 25p.

Ghulam, L.J.
"Early Teenage Childbirth, Consequences of This for Child and Mother." Paper Presented at the Seminar on Traditional Practices Affecting the Health of Women and Children. World Conference of the United Nations Decade for Women. Copenhagen, Denmark. July 14-30, 1980.

Goody, Esther N.
"Parental Strategies: Calculation or Sentiment: Fostering Practices Among West Africans." (In) Medick, Hans and

Sabean, David W. (eds.). Interest and Emotion: Essays on the Study of Family and Kinship. Cambridge, New York: Cambridge University Press. 1984. pp. 266-277.
Karoun, Haddad O.
"Adolescent Pregnancy and Childbirth." Paper Presented at the Seminar on Traditional Practices Affecting the Health and Children. World Conference of the United Nations Decade for Women. New York: United Nations. Copenhagen, Denmark. July 14-30, 1980.
Kenton, J.
"Health of Women and Children in Africa." Midwives Chronicle. Volume 98 #1165 February, 1985. pp. 44-45.
Kuteyi, P.V.
"Nutritional Needs of the Child Especially in the First Year." Paper Presented at the Seminar on Traditional Practices Affecting the Health of Women and Children. World Conference of the United Nations Decade for Women. New York: United Nations. Copenhagen, Denmark. July 14-30, 1980.
LeVine, Robert A.
"Influences of Women's Schooling on Maternal Behavior in the Third World." Comparative Education Review. Volume 24 #2 Part Two June, 1980. pp. S78-S105.
Mbevi, Grace and Njoki, Margaret
"Traditional Practices in Relation to Child Health." Paper Presented at the Seminar on Traditional Practices Affecting the Health of Women and Children. World Conference of the United Nations Decade for Women. New York: United Nations. Copenhagen, Denmark. July 14-30, 1980.
Mgone, C.S.
"Reproductive Behavior and Attitudes of African Mothers Following Birth of a Downs Syndrome Child." East African Medical Journal. Volume 59 #8 1982. pp. 555-559.
Mukhtar, Behiza
"A Question of Our Children's Bodies: The Medical Injury Caused to a Girl by Circumcision." Paper Presented at the Conference on Islam and Family Planning. Sponsored by the International Planned Parenthood Federation. Banjul, Gambia. October 21-24, 1979. 7p.
Onyango, Philista P.M.
"The Working Mother and the Housemaid as a Substitute: Its Complications on the Children." Journal of Eastern African Research and Development. Volume 13 1983. pp. 24-31.
Oppong, Christine and Adaba, Gemma and Bekomba-Priso, Manga and Mogey, J. (eds.)
Marriage, Fertility and Parenthood in West Africa. Canberra, Australia: Australian National University. Department of Demography. Changing African Family Project. Monograph #4. Two Volumes. 1978. 848p.
Rogers, Barbara
"Food, Fertility and Nuclear Mothers: How Development Can Increase Rather than Reduce the Social and Economic

Burdens of African Women." Populi. Volume 5 #1 1978. pp. 23-27.

Tesha, Nancy
"Womens Role in Rearing Children and National Development." Paper Presented at the Workshop on Women's Studies and Development. Dar-es-Salaam, Tanzania: University of Dar-es-Salaam. Bureau of Resource Assessment and Land Use Planning. Paper #39. September 24-29, 1979. 3p.

Traore, Aminata
"Evolving Relations Between Mothers and Children in Rural Africa." International Social Science Journal. Volume 31 #3 1979. pp. 486-491.

United Nations Educational, Scientific and Cultural Organ.
Comparative Report on the Role of Working Mothers in Early Childhood Education in Five Countries. Paris: UNESCO. 1978. 82p.

Appendix A
Directory of National, Regional and International Organizations Affiliated with African Women's Projects and Programs

AFRICAN LITERATURE ASSO.
C/O PETER NAZARETH
DEPARTMENT OF ENGLISH
IOWA UNIVERSITY
IOWA CITY, IOWA 52242

AFRICAN NATIONAL CONGRESS
P.O. BOX 31797
LUSAKA, ZAMBIA

AFRICAN REGIONAL
CO-ORDINATING COMMITTEE
FOR THE INTEGRATION OF
WOMEN IN DEVELOPMENT
C/O ECONOMIC COMMISSION
FOR AFRICA
P.O. BOX 3001
ADDIS ABABA, ETHIOPIA

AFRICAN STUDIES ASSO.
UNIV. OF CALIFORNIA-
LOS ANGELES
255 KINSEY HALL
405 HILGARD AVE.
LOS ANGELES, CALIFORNIA
90024

AFRICAN WOMEN'S CENTER
ATLANTA UNIVERSITY
1706 STOKES AVE.
ATLANTA, GEORGIA 30310

AFRICAN WOMEN'S DEVELOPMENT
TASK FORCE
C/O ATRCW
ECONOMIC COMMISSION FOR
AFRICA
P.O. BOX 3001
ADDIS ABABA, ETHIOPIA

AFRICAN WOMEN'S NETWORK FOR
DEVELOPMENT
APPLE/US. AID
P.O. BOX 4625
ACCRA, GHANA

ALL AFRICAN CONFERENCE OF
CHURCHES
P.O. BOX 14205
NAIROBI, KENYA

AMERICAN ANTHRO. ASSO.
1703 NEW HAMPSHIRE AVE. NW
WASHINGTON, D.C. 20009

AMERICAN PUBLIC HEALTH
ASSO.
1015 15TH STREET, N.W.
WASHINGTON, D.C. 20005

ANGOLAN WOMEN ORGANIZATION
AVENIDA COMANDANTO GIKS 199
LUANDA, ANGOLA

APPENDIX A

ARAB WOMEN'S ORGANIZATION
P.O. BOX 926775
AMMAN, JORDON

ARAB WOMEN'S SOLIDARITY
ASSO.
25 MOURAD STREET
GIZA, EGYPT

ASSOCIATED COUNTRY WOMEN
OF THE WORLD
50 WARWICK SQUARE
LONDON SW1V 2AJ

ASSO. FOR THE ADVANCEMENT
OF WOMEN IN AFRICA
P.O. BOX 35500
KABWE, ZAMBIA

ASSO. OF AFRICAN WOMEN
FOR RESEARCH AND DEVELOPMENT
(AAWORD)
C.O. CODESRIA
B.P. 3304
DAKAR, SENEGAL

ASSO. OF WOMEN'S
CLUBS
64 SELOUS AVENUE
7TH STREET
HARARE, ZIMBABWE

BLACK WOMEN'S ECONOMIC
DEVELOPMENT ASSO. (BWEDA)
P.O. BOX 3419 NORTH-END,
PORT ELIZABETH,
SOUTH AFRICA

BLACK WOMEN UNITE (BWU)
ETKON HOUSE
WANDERERS STREET
JOHANNESBURG

BOSTON UNIVERSITY
AFRICAN STUDIES CENTER
125 BAY STREET
BOSTON, MASSACHUSETTS 02215

BOTSWANA. MINISTRY OF
AGRICULTURE
PRIVATE BAG 003
GABORONE, BOTSWANA

BOTSWANA CENTRAAL
STATISTICS OFFICE
BAG 008
GABORONE, BOTSWANA

BOTSWANA COUNCIL OF
WOMEN (BCW)
P.O. 339
GABORONE, BOTSWANA

BOTSWANA WOMEN'S AFFAIRS
UNIT
MINISTRY OF LABOUR AND
HOME AFFAIRS
PRIVATE BAG 002
GABORONE, BOTSWANA

CAIRO DEMOGRAPHIC CENTRE
6 SHARI WILLCOCKS
ZAMALEK, EGYPT

CANADIAN COUNCIL FOR
INTERN. COOPERATION
200 RUE ISABELLA,
SUITE 300
OTTAWA, ONTARIO K1S IV7
CANADA

CENTER FOR APPLIED
RELIGION AND EDUCATION
(CARE)
EASTERN AREA OFFICE
BOX 418
ENUGU, NIGERIA

CHURCH WOMEN OF KENYA
P.O. BOX 21360
NAIROBI, KENYA

COLLEGE OF ADULT AND
DISTANCE EDUCATION
ALTHABASCA UNIVERSITY
INTERN. COUNCIL-DISTANCE
EDUCATION/WOMEN'S INTERN.
NETWORK
P.O. BOX 56011
NAIROBI, KENYA

APPENDIX A

DEPARTMENT OF DEMOGRAPHY
AUSTRALIAN NATIONAL UNIVERSITY
G.P.O. BOX 4
A.C.T. AUSTRALIA 2601

EASTERN AND SOUTHERN AFRICAN MANAGEMENT INSTITUTE (ESAM)
P.O. BOX 3030
ARUSHA, TANZANIA

E.L.C./EQUITY POLICY CTR.
KENYA NGO COMMITTEE
ENVIRONMENTAL LIAISON CTR.
BOX 72461
NAIROBI, KENYA

EPISCOPAL CHURCH OF U.S.A.
OVERSEAS DEVELOPMENT OFFICE
2736 CARTER FARM COURT
ALEXANDRIA, VIRGINIA 22306

EQUITY POLICY CENTER/E.L.C.
KENYA NGO COMMITTEE
2001 S. STREET
WASHINGTON, D.C. 20009

FAMILY PLANNING ASSO. OF KENYA
P.O. BOX 30581
NAIROBI, KENYA

FEDERATION OF GHANA BUSINESS AND PROFESSIONAL WOMEN
NKULENU INDUSTRIES LTD.
BOX 36, LEGON
ACCRA, GHANA

GENERAL ARAB WOMEN'S FEDERATION
HAY AL-MAGHREB
BAGDAD, IRAQ

GLOBAL FUTURES NETWORK
428 ELWOOD AVE.
HAWTHORNE, NEW YORK 10532

INSTITUTE FOR DEVELOPMENT STUDIES
UNIVERSITY OF NAIROBI
P.O. BOX 30197
NAIROBI, KENYA

INTERN. ALLIANCE OF WOMEN
128 BUCKINGHAM PALACE ROAD
LONDON SW1W 9SH

INTERN. CENTER FOR RESEARCH ON WOMEN (ICRW)
1717 MASSACHUSETTS AVE. N.W.
SUITE 500
WASHINGTON, D.C.

INTERN. COMMITTEE OF SOLIDARITY WITH THE STRUGGLE OF WOMEN IN SOUTH AFRICA AND NAMIBIA
C/O EDITH BALLANTYNE
WILPF, 1 ROUTE DE VAREMBE
CP 28, CH-1211
GENEVA 20

INTERN. CO-OPERATIVE ALLIANCE
15 ROUTE DES MORILLONS
1218 GENEVA

INTERNATIONAL COUNCIL OF AFRICAN WOMEN
145 HANCOCK STREET
BROOKLYN, NEW YORK 11216

INTERN. COUNCIL OF AFRICAN WOMEN (ICAW)
BOX 8676
WASHINGTON, D.C. 20011

INTERN. COUNCIL OF WOMEN (ICW)
GENERAL SECRETARY
13 RUE CAUMARTIN
75009 PARIS

APPENDIX A

INTERN. DEVELOPMENT
RESEARCH CTR. (IDRC)
P.O. BOX 8500
OTTAWA, ONTARIO
CANADA ON KIG 3H9

INTERN. FEDERATION
OF AGRICULTURAL PRODUCERS
VIA YSER 14
00198 ROME

INTERN. FEDERATION OF
HOME ECONOMICS
KENYATTA UNIVERSITY
COLLEGE
P.O. BOX 43844
NAIROBI, KENYA

INTERN. LABOUR
ORGANIZATION
4 ROUTE DES MORILLONS
GENEVA 22

INTERN. LEAGUE FOR
HUMAN RIGHTS
R.D.I.
GLENMORE, PENNSYLVANIA
19343

INTERN. PLANNED PARENTHOOD
FEDERATION (IPPF)
18-20 LOWER REGENT STREET
LONDON SW1Y 4PW

INTERN. RESCUE COMMITTEE
95 RUE DE RENNE
PARIS 75006

INTERN. SOCIOLOGICAL ASSO.
SOCIOLOGICAL INSTITUTE
UNIVERSITY OF AMSTERDAM
P.O. BOX 1X1
AMSTERDAM, NETHERLANDS

INTERN. UNION FOR THE
SCIENTIFIC STUDY OF
POPULATION (IUSSP)
RUE DES AUGUSTINS 34,
B-4000 LIEGE, BELGIUM

INTERN. WOMEN'S HEALTH
COALITION
P.O. BOX 8500
NEW YORK 10150

INTERN. WOMEN'S TRIBUNAL
CTR.
THIRD FLOOR
777 UNITED NATIONS PLAZA
NEW YORK 10017

ISIS INTERN./AFSC/
GABRIELLA/CDA
INTERN. COALITION OF
DEVELOPMENT ACTION
22 RUE DES BOLLANDISTES
1040 BRUSSELS, BELGIUM

KENYA MEDICAL WOMEN'S
ASSO.
P.O. BOX 49877
NAIROBI, KENYA

LEAGUE OF MALAWI WOMEN
MINISTRY OF COMMUNITY
SERVICES
PRIVATE BAG 330
LILONGWE, MALAWI

LESOTHO NATIONAL COUNCIL
OF WOMEN
P.O. BOX 686
MASERU, LESOTHO

LESOTHO WOMEN'S BUREAU
MINISTRY OF RURAL
DEVELOPMENT, COOPERATIVES
AND WOMEN'S AFFAIRS
P.O. BOX 686
MASERU, LESOTHO

MAURITIUS WOMEN'S
COMMITTEE
14 EMPEREURS STREET
ELIZABETH, TOMBEAUBAY
MAURITIUS

MICHIGAN STATE UNIV.
OFFICE OF WOMEN IN
INTERN. DEVELOPMENT
(WID)
202 CENTER FOR INTERN.
PROGRAMS
EAST LANSING, MICHIGAN
48824

APPENDIX A

MINISTRY OF AGRICULTURE
OFFICE OF COMMUNITY DEVELOPMENT
BP 2729
YAOUNDE, CAMEROON

NAIROBI BUSINESS AND PROFESSIONAL WOMEN'S CLUB
P.O. BOX 42542
NAIROBI, KENYA

NATIONAL BLACK UNITED FRONT
P.O. BOX 470665
BROOKLYN, NEW YORK 11247

NATIONAL COUNCIL OF CATHOLIC WOMEN
BOX 31965
LUSAKA, ZAMBIA

NATIONAL UNION OF THE SAHRAOUI WOMEN
B.P. #10
EL MOURAOIA
ALGIERS, ALGERIA

NGO PLANNING COMMITTEE
INTERN. ALLIANCE OF WOMEN
777 UNITED NATIONS PLAZA
8TH FLOOR
NEW YORK 10017

ORGANIZATION PAN AFRICAINE DES FEMMES
23 BOULEVARD COLONEL AMIROUCHE
ALGIERS, ALGERIA

OVERSEAS EDUCATION FUND INTERNATIONAL (OEF)
2101 L STREET N.W.
SUITE 916
WASHINGTON, D.C. 20037

PAN AFRICAN RESEARCH COUNCIL
C/O B. CAMPBELL-BEYAM
175 WEST 87TH STREET #21E
NEW YORK 10019

PAN AFRICANIST CONGRESS OF AZANIA (PAC)
WOMEN'S WING
P.O. BOX 2412
DAR es SALAAM, TANZANIA

POPULATION ASSO. OF AMERICA
P.O. BOX 14182
BENJAMIN FRANKLIN STATION
WASHINGTON, D.C. 20044

POPULATION COUNCIL
ONE DAG HAMMARSKJOLD PLAZA
NEW YORK 10017

POPULATION STUDIES AND RESEARCH INSTITUTE
UNIVERSITY OF NAIROBI
P.O. BOX 30197
NAIROBI, KENYA

SCANDANAVIAN INSTITUTE OF AFRICAN STUDIES
SYSSLOMANSGATAN
P.O. BOX 2126, S-750 02
UPPSALA, SWEDEN

SOUTH AFRICAN COUNCIL OF CHURCHES
P.O. BOX 4921
JOHANNESBURG 2000

SOUTH WEST AFRICAN PEOPLES ORGANIZATION (SWAPO)
P.O. BOX 30577
LUSAKA, ZAMBIA

SWEDISH INTERN. DEVELOPMENT AUTHORITY (SIDA)
BIRGER JARLSGATAN 61
S-10525
STOCKHOLM, SWEDEN

UMBRELLA WOMEN'S ORGANIZATION
MINISTRY OF FOREIGN AFFAIRS
P.O. BOX 518
MBABANE, SWAZILAND

APPENDIX A

UNICEF
EASTERN AFRICA REGIONAL OFFICE
C/O UNEP HQ, GIGIRI
P.O. BOX 44145
NAIROBI, KENYA

UNION OF WOMEN OF TANZANIA (UWT)
P.O. BOX 1473
DAR es SALAAM
TANZANIA

UNITED NATIONS CENTRE AGAINST APARTHEID (UNCAA)
UNITED NATIONS DEPARTMENT OF POLITICAL AND SECURITY CL. AFFAIRS
NEW YORK 10017

UNITED NATIONS DEVELOPMENT FUND FOR WOMEN
777 UNITED NATIONS PLAZA
ROOM DC-1002
NEW YORK 10017

UNITED NATIONS ECONOMIC COMMISSION FOR AFRICA (UNECA)
AFRICAN TRAINING AND RESEARCH CENTRE FOR WOMEN (ATRCW)
P.O. BOX 3001
ADDIS ABABA, ETHIOPIA

UNESCO
7 PLACE DE FONTENOY
F-75700 PARIS

UNITED NATIONS FOOD AND AGRICULTURE ORGANIZATION (FAO)
VIA DELLE TERME DI CARACALLA
1-00100 ROME

UNITED STATES AGENCY FOR INTERNATIONAL DEVELOPMENT (US.AID)
U.S. INTERN. DEVELOPMENT COOPERATION AGENCY
DEPARTMENT OF STATE BLDG.
320 21ST STREET, N.W.
WASHINGTON, D.C. 20523

UNIVERSITY OF DAR es SALAAM
BUREAU OF RESOURCE ASSESSMENT AND LAND USE PLANNING
P.O. BOX 35091
DAR es SALAAM, TANZANIA

UNIVERSITY OF IBADAN
IBADAN, NIGERIA

UNIVERSITY OF KHARTOUM
DEVELOPMENT STUDIES AND RESEARCH INSTITUTE
P.O. BOX 321
KHARTOUM, SUDAN

UNIVERSITY OF LAGOS
LAGOS, NIGERIA

UNIVERSITY OF NORTH CAROLINA
CAROLINA POPULATION CENTER
UNIVERSITY SQUARE
CHAPEL HILL, NORTH CAROLINA 27514

UNIVERSITY OF PENNSYLVANIA
POPULATIONS STUDIES CENTER
3718 LOCUST WALK
BUILDING CR
PHILADELPHIA, PENNSYLVANIA 19104

UNIVERSITY OF ZAMBIA
MANPOWER RESEARCH UNIT
P.O. BOX 32379
LUSAKA, ZAMBIA

VRIJE UNIVERSITEIT BRUSSEL
INTERUNIVERSITY PROGRAMME IN DEMOGRAPHY
CAMPUS OEFENPLEIN
PLEINLAAN 2,
BRUSSELS, BELGIUM

WELLESLEY COLLEGE
WELLESLEY, MASSACHUSETTS 02181

APPENDIX A

WOMEN AND AFRICAN
DEVELOPMENT PROGRAM
AFRICAN-AMERICAN INSTITUTE
833 UNITED NATIONS PLAZA
NEW YORK 10003

WOMEN FOR RACIAL AND
ECONOMIC EQUALITY
130 EAST 16TH STREET
NEW YORK 10003

WOMEN'S AFFAIRS COMMITTEE
P.O. BOX 30302
LUSAKA, ZAMBIA

WOMEN'S LEAGUE
P.O. BOX 30302
LUSAKA, ZAMBIA

WOMEN'S RESEARCH AND
DOCUMENTATION PROJECT
BOX 35185
UNIVERSITY OF DAR es
SALAAM
DAR es SALAAM, TANZANIA

WORLD COUNCIL OF CHURCHES
150 ROUTE DE FERNEY
1211 GENEVA 20

WORLD COUNCIL OF
INDIGENOUS PEOPLES
555 KING EDWARD AVE.
OTTAWA, ONTARIO, CANADA

WORLD FEDERATION OF HEALTH
AGENCIES
WORLD FEDERATION
SECRETARIAT
122 EAST 42ND STREET
18TH FLOOR
NEW YORK 10168

WORLD FEDERATION OF
UNITED NATION ASSO.
C/O PALAIS DES NATIONS
1211 GENEVA 10

WORLD HEALTH ORGANIZATION
EASTERN MEDITERRANEAN
REGIONAL OFFICE (EMRO)
P/O. BOX 1517
ALEXANDRIA, EGYPT

WORLD ORT UNION
1-3 RUE DE VAREMBE
CH-1211
GENEVA

WORLD PEACE COUNCIL
LONNROTINK 25A 6KRS
HELSINKI, FINLAND

YOUNG WOMEN'S CHRISTIAN
ASSO.
P.O. BOX 359
GABOROE, BOTSWANA

ZAMBIA ALLIANCE OF
WOMEN/ZAMBIA ASSO.
FOR RESEARCH
BOX 51068
LUSAKA, ZAMBIA

ZAMBIA ASSO FOR
RESEARCH AND DEVELOPMENT
P.O. BOX 32710
LUSAKA, ZAMBIA

ZIMBABWE MINISTRY OF
COMMUNITY DEVELOPMENT
AND WOMEN'S AFFAIRS
PRIVATE BAG 7735
CAUSEWAY, HARARE
ZIMBABWE

ZIMBABWE WOMEN'S BUREAU
2ND FLOOR MUNNDIX HOUSE
98 CAMERON STREET
HARARE, ZIMBABWE

Appendix B
Official Names and Capitals of African Nations

ALGERIA (DEMOCRATIC AND POPULAR REPUBLIC OF)--ALGIERS
ANGOLA (PEOPLE'S REPUBLIC OF)--LUANDA

BENIN (PEOPLE'S REPUBLIC OF)--PORTO-NOVO, COTONOU
BOTSWANA (REPUBLIC OF)--GABORONE
BURKINA FASO--OUAGADOUGOU
BURUNDI (REPUBLIC OF)--BUJUMBURA

CAMEROON (REPUBLIC OF)--YAOUNDE
CAPE VERDE ISLANDS (REPUBLIC OF)--CIDADE DE PRAIA
CENTRAL AFRICAN REPUBLIC--BANGUI
CHAD (REPUBLIC OF)--N'DJAMENA
COMOROS (FEDERAL ISLAMIC REPUBLIC OF THE)--MORONI
CONGO (PEOPLE'S REPUBLIC OF THE)--BRAZZAVILLE

DJIBOUTI (REPUBLIC OF)--DJIBOUTI

EGYPT (ARAB REPUBLIC OF)--CAIRO
EQUATORIAL GUINEA (REPUBLIC OF)--MALABO
ETHIOPIA (SOCIALIST)--ADDIS ABABA

GABON (GABONESE REPUBLIC)--LIBREVILLE
GAMBIA (REPUBLIC OF)--BANJUL
GHANA (REPUBLIC OF)--ACCRA
GUINEA (REPUBLIC OF)--CONAKRY
GUINEA-BISSAU (REPUBLIC OF)--BISSAU

IVORY COAST (REPUBLIC OF)--ABIDJAN, YAMOUSSOUKRO

KENYA (REPUBLIC OF)--NAIROBI

LESOTHO (KINGDOM OF)--MASERU
LIBERIA (REPUBLIC OF)--MONROVIA

APPENDIX B

LIBYA (GREAT SOCIALIST PEOPLE'S LIBYAN ARAB JAMAHIRIYA)--TRIPOLI

MADAGASCAR (DEMOCRATIC REPUBLIC OF)--ANTANANARIVO
MALAWI (REPUBLIC OF)--LILONGWE
MALI (REPUBLIC OF)--BAMAKO
MAURITANIA (ISLAMIC REPUBLIC OF)--NOUAKCHOTT
MAURITIUS--PORT LOUIS
MOROCCO (KINGDOM OF)--RABAT
MOZAMBIQUE (PEOPLE'S REPUBLIC OF)--MAPUTO

NAMIBIA--WINDHOEK
NIGER (REPUBLIC OF)--NIAMEY
NIGERIA (FEDERAL REPUBLIC OF)--LAGOS, ABUJA

RWANDA (THE RWANDESE REPUBLIC)--KIGALI

SAO TOME AND PRINCIPE (DEMOCRATIC REPUBLIC OF)--SAO TOME
SENEGAL (REPUBLIC OF)--DAKAR
SEYCHELLES (REPUBLIC OF)--VICTORIA
SIERRA LEONE (REPUBLIC OF)--FREETOWN
SOMALIA (DEMOCRATIC REPUBLIC OF)--MOGADISHU
SOUTH AFRICA (REPUBLIC OF)--PRETORIA, CAPE TOWN, BLOEMFONTEIN
SUDAN (REPUBLIC OF)--KHARTOUM
SWAZILAND (KINGDOM OF)--MBABANE, LOBAMBA

TANZANIA (UNITED REPUBLIC OF)--DAR es SALAAM, DODOMA
TOGO (TOGOLESE REPUBLIC)--LOME
TUNISIA (REPUBLIC OF)--TUNIS

UGANDA (REPUBLIC OF)--KAMPALA

WESTERN SAHARA

ZAIRE (REPUBLIC OF)--KINSHASA
ZAMBIA (REPUBLIC OF)--LUSAKA
ZIMBABWE (REPUBLIC OF)--HARARE

Appendix C
Geographical and Historical Name Directory

ABYSSINIA--ETHIOPIA
AFARS AND ISSAS--DJIBOUTI
AL-MAMLAKAH al-MAGHRIBIYAH--MOROCCO
AMATONGALAND--SOUTH AFRICA
ANGLO-EGYPTIAN CONDOMINIUM--SUDAN
ANGLO-EGYPTIAN SUDAN--SUDAN
ANGLOPHONE AFRICA--GAMBIA, SIERRA LEONE, NIGERIA, GHANA
ANNOBAN--EQUATORIAL GUINEA

BANTUSTANS--SEE SOUTH AFRICAN HOMELANDS FOR LIST OF NAMES
BAROTSELAND--ZAMBIA
BASUTOLAND--LESOTHO
BECHUANALAND--BOTSWANA
BECHUANALAND PROTECTORATE--BOTSWANA
BELGIAN CONGO--ZAIRE
BELGISCH CONGO--ZAIRE
BIAFRA--NIGERIA
BIGHT OF BENIN--NIGERIA
BIGHT OF BIAFRA--NIGERIA
BILAD-es-SUDAN--SUDAN
BOPHUTHATSWANA--SOUTH AFRICA
BRITISH BECHUANALAND--SOUTH AFRICA, BOTSWANA
BRITISH CAMEROONS--CAMEROON
BRITISH CENTRAL AFRICA--MALAWI
BRITISH CENTRAL AFRICAN PROTECTORATE--MALAWI
BRITISH KAFFRARIA--SOUTH AFRICA
BRITISH NIGER PROTECTORATE
BRITISH SOMALILAND--SOMALIA
BRITISH SOUTH AFRICA COMPANY--SOUTH AFRICA
BRITISH TOGOLAND--TOGO

CABINDA--ANGOLA
CAMEROUN--CAMEROON
CAPE COAST--GHANA

APPENDIX C

CAPE OF GOOD HOPE--SOUTH AFRICA
CAPE OF THREE POINTS--GHANA
CAPE PROVINCE--SOUTH AFRICA
CAPRIVI STRIP--NAMIBIA
CENTRAL AFRICA--CAMEROON, CENTRAL AFRICAN REPUBLIC, CONGO, EQUATORIAL GUINEA,GABON, RWANDA, BURUNDI, ZAIRE, SAO TOME
CENTRAL AFRICAN EMPIRE--CENTRAL AFRICAN REPUBLIC
CENTRAL AFRICAN FEDERATION--ZIMBABWE, ZAMBIA, MALAWI
CENTRAL SAHARA--NIGER, ALGERIA, CHAD, MALI, LIBYA
CISKEI--SOUTH AFRICA
COLONY AND PROTECTORATE OF LAGOS--NIGERIA
COLONY AND PROTECTORATE OF NIGERIA--NIGERIA
CONGO--ZAIRE
CONGO BELGE--ZAIRE
CONGO (BRAZZAVILLE)--CONGO
CONGO FREE STATE--ZAIRE
CONGO-KINSHASA--ZAIRE
CONGO (LEOPOLDVILLE)--ZAIRE
COTE d' IVOIRE--IVORY COAST
CROWN COLONY OF BECHUANALAND--BOTSWANA
CYRENAICA--LIBYA

DAHOMEY--BENIN
DAMARALAND--NAMIBIA
DEMOCRATIC REPUBLIC OF THE CONGO--ZAIRE
DEUTCH-SUIDWEST AFRIKA--NAMIBIA

EAST AFRICA--UGANDA, KENYA, TANZANIA, MOZAMBIQUE
EAST AFRICA PROTECTORATE--KENYA
EAST AFRICAN COMMUNITY--UGANDA, KENYA, TANZANIA
EAST AFRICAN FEDERATION--KENYA, TANZANIA, ZANZIBAR, UGANDA
EQUATORIAL AFRICA--CAMEROON, CENTRAL AFRICAN REPUBLIC, CHAD, CONGO, GABON, ZAIRE
ERITREA--ETHIOPIA

FEDERATION OF NIGERIA--NIGERIA
FEDERATION OF RHODESIA AND NYASALAND--ZAMBIA, MALAWI AND RHODESIA
FERNANDO POO--EQUATORIAL GUINEA
FEZZAN--LIBYA
FINGOLAND--SOUTH AFRICA
FRANCOPHONE AFRICA--SEE FRENCH WEST AFRICA
FRENCH CAMEROONS--CAMEROON
FRENCH EQUATORIAL AFRICA--CAMEROON, CHAD, CONGO, GABON, CENTRAL AFRICAN REPUBLIC
FRENCH GUINEA--GUINEA
FRENCH MOROCCO--MOROCCO
FRENCH SOMALILAND--SOMALIA
FRNECH SOUDAN--MALI
FRENCH TOGOLAND--TOGO
FRENCH WEST AFRICA--BENIN, BURKINA FASO, ALGERIA, GUINEA, IVORY COAST, MOROCCO, NIGER, SENEGAL, TUNISIA, TOGO, MALI, MAURITANIA

APPENDIX C

GABUN--GABON
GERMAN EAST AFRICA--BURUNDI, RWANDA, TANZANIA
GERMAN EAST AFRICA COMPANY--TANZANIA
GERMAN SOUTH-WEST AFRICA--NAMIBIA
GERMAN TOGOLAND--TOGO
GOLD COAST--GHANA
GOSHEN--SOUTH AFRICA
GRAIN COAST--LIBERIA
GREAT BENIN--BENIN
GREAT NAMAQUALAND--NAMIBIA
GRIQUALAND EAST--SOUTH AFRICA
GRIQUALAND WEST--SOUTH AFRICA
GUINE--GUINEA
GUINEE--GUINEA
GUINEE FRANCAISE--GUINEA

HAUTE-VOLTA--BURKINA FASO
HERREROLAND--NAMIBIA
HIGH COMMISSION TERRITORIES--BOTSWANA, SWAZILAND, LESOTHO
HOMELANDS--SOUTH AFRICA
HORN OF AFRICA--SOMALIA

IDUTYWA--SOUTH AFRICA
IFNI--MOROCCO
ILE DE FRANCE--MAURITIUS
ILES COMORES--COMOROS
ILHAS do CABO VERDE--CAPE VERDE ISLANDS
INTERNATIONAL ASSOCIATION OF THE CONGO--ZAIRE
ITALIAN PROTECTORATE--ETHIOPIA
ITALIAN SOMALILAND--SOMALIA

JIBUTI--DJIBOUTI
JUBALAND--SOMALIA
JUMHURIYAT as-SUDAN ad-DIMUGRATIYAH--SUDAN

KAFFRARIA--SOUTH AFRICA
KAMERUN--CAMEROON
KENYA PROTECTORATE--KENYA
KINGDOM OF ETHIOPIA--ETHIOPIA
KINGDOM OF LIBYA--LIBYA
KONGO--ZAIRE

LESOTO--LESOTHO
LITTLE NAMAQUALAND--NAMIBIA
LOWER CONGO--ZAIRE
LOWER GUINEA--ANGOLA, CAMEROON

MAFIA ISLAND--TANZANIA
MAGHREB--MOROCCO, ALGERIA, LIBYA, TUNISIA
MAGHRIB--MOROCCO, ALGERIA, LIBYA, TUNISIA
MALAGASY REPUBLIC--MADAGASCAR
MALGACHE REPUBLIC--MADAGASCAR
MANICALAND--ZIMBABWE
MAROC--MOROCCO
MARRUECOS--MOROCCO

APPENDIX C

MASCARENES--MAURITIUS, REUNION ISLANDS
MASHONALAND--ZIMBABWE
MATABELELAND--ZIMBABWE
MAURETANIA--MAURITANIA
MAURITANIE--MAURITANIA
MIDDLE CONGO--ZAIRE
MOCAMBIQUE--MOZAMBIQUE
MOYEN-CONGO--CONGO
MOZAMBIQUE COMPANY'S TERRITORY--MOZAMBIQUE

NAMALAND--NAMIBIA
NAMAQUALAND--NAMIBIA
NATAL--SOUTH AFRICA
NGAMILAND--BOTSWANA
NORTH AFRICA--MOROCCO, ALGERIA, TUNISIA, LIBYA, EGYPT, WESTERN SAHARA
NORTHEAST AFRICA--ETHIOPIA, SOMALIA, DJIBOUTI, SUDAN
NORTHERN RHODESIA--ZAMBIA
NYASALAND--MALAWI

OGADEN--ETHIOPIA
OIL RIVERS PROTECTORATE--NIGERIA
ORANGE FREE STATE--SOUTH AFRICA
ORANGE RIVER COLONY--SOUTH AFRICA
OUBANGUI-CHARI--CENTRAL AFRICAN REPUBLIC

PEMBA--TANZANIA
PONDOLAND--SOUTH AFRICA
PORTUGUESE CONGO--ANGOLA
PORTUGUESE EAST AFRICA--MOZAMBIQUE
PORTUGUESE GUINEA--GUINEA-BISSAU
PORTUGUESE WEST AFRICA--ANGOLA
PROTECTORATES OF NORTHERN AND SOUTHERN NIGERIA--NIGERIA

REPUBLIEK VAN SUID-AFRIKA--SOUTH AFRICA
REPUBLIQUE CENTRAFRICAINE--CENTRAL AFRICAN REPUBLIC
REPUBLIQUE GABONAISE--GABON
REPUBLIQUE MALGACHE--MADAGASCAR
RHODESIA--ZIMBABWE
RIFF--MOROCCO
RIO DE ORO--WESTERN SAHARA
RIO MUNI--EQUATORIAL GUINEA
RUANDA--RWANDA
RUANDA-URUNDI--RWANDA, BURUNDI

SAHEL--MAURITANIA, NIGER, MALI, BURKINA FASO, CHAD, SUDAN, ETHIOPIA, PARTS OF ALGERIA AND LIBYA
SEKHUKHUNELAND--SOUTH AFRICA
SENEGAMBIA--SENEGAL, GAMBIA
SIDI IFNI--MOROCCO
SLAVE COAST--TOGO, BENIN, NIGERIA
SOMALILAND PROTECTORATE--SOMALIA
SOUDAN--SUDAN, MALI
SOUDAN FRANCAIS--MALI

APPENDIX C

SOUTH AFRICAN HOMELANDS--SOUTH AFRICA (CISKEI, TRANSKEI, VENDA, BOPHUTHATSWANA)
SOUTH AFRICAN REPUBLIC--SOUTH AFRICA
SOUTH EAST AFRICA--SWAZILAND, LESOTHO
SOUTHERN AFRICA--NAMIBIA, ANGOLA, BOTSWANA, SOUTH AFRICA, LESOTHO, SWAZILAND, ZIMBABWE, ZAMBIA, MALAWI
SOUTHERN RHODESIA--ZIMBABWE
SOUTH-WEST AFRICA--NAMIBIA
SPANISH GUINEA--EQUATORIAL GUINEA
SPANISH MOROCCO--WESTERN SAHARA, MOROCCO
SPANISH NORTH AFRICA--MOROCCO
SPANISH SAHARA--WESTERN SAHARA, MOROCCO
SPANISH WEST AFRICA--WESTERN SAHARA, MOROCCO
STELLALAND--SOUTH AFRICA
SUDANESE REPUBLIC--MALI
SUIDWES AFRIKA--NAMIBIA

TANGANYIKA--TANZANIA
TANGANYIKA TERRITORY--TANZANIA
TCHAD--CHAD
TEMBULAND--SOUTH AFRICA
TERRITORIOS ESPANOLES DEL GOLFO DE GUINEA--EQUATORIAL GUINEA
TOGOLAND--TOGO
TONGALAND--SOUTH AFRICA
TRANSKEI--SOUTH AFRICA
TRANSVAAL--SOUTH AFRICA
TRANS-VOLTA TOGOLAND--TOGO
TRIPOLITANIA--LIBYA
TUNIS--TUNISIA
TUNISIE--TUNISIA

UBANGI-SHARI--CENTRAL AFRICAN REPUBLIC
UBANGUI-SHARI--CENTRAL AFRICAN REPUBLIC
UNIE-VAN SUID-AFRIKA--SOUTH AFRICA
UNION OF SOUTH AFRICA--SOUTH AFRICA
UNITED ARAB REPUBLIC--EGYPT
UNITED REPUBLIC OF TANGANYIKA AND ZANZIBAR--TANZANIA
UPPER GUINEA--BENIN, GAMBIA
UPPER SENEGAL-NIGER--MALI, CAMEROON
UPPER VOLTA--BURKINA FASO
URUNDI--BURUNDI

VENDA--SOUTH AFRICA
VOLTAIC REPUBLIC--BURKINA FASO

WEST AFRICA--SENEGAL, GAMBIA, GUINEA, GUINEA-BISSAU, LIBERIA, SIERRA LEONE, IVORY COAST, GHANA, TOGO, BENIN, NIGERIA, CAPE VERDE ISLANDS, MALI, NIGER, MAURITANIA, CHAD, BURKINA FASO

ZANZIBAR--TANZANIA
ZIMBABWE RHODESIA--ZIMBABWE
ZULULAND--SOUTH AFRICA

Author Index

AUTHOR INDEX

AUTHOR INDEX

AUTHOR INDEX

AUTHOR INDEX

AUTHOR INDEX

About the Compiler

DAVIS BULLWINKLE, a native of California, was raised in the San Francisco Bay Area. Early interest in Black history and African Studies led to undergraduate degrees in history and Anthropology from California State University-Chico. Under the guidance of professors in History and Anthropology, Mr. Bullwinkle specialized in African Studies. He received a Masters of Library Science degree from Emporia State University in Kansas.

Mr. Bullwinkle has published bibliographic articles on Drought and Desertification in Africa, Nomadism and Pastoralism in Africa, and Women in Africa during the 1970's. All were published in the former Washington, D.C., African Bibliographic Center's "Current Bibliography on African Affairs."

Davis Bullwinkle is presently employed by the Arkansas State Library in Little Rock, Arkansas, where he is the Senior Reference Librarian. He recently married and has three stepchildren.